POLITICAL EXCLUSION AND DOMINATION

NOMOS
XLVI

NOMOS

Harvard University Press

I   *Authority* 1958, reissued in 1982 by Greenwood Press

The Liberal Arts Press

II   *Community* 1959
III   *Responsibility* 1960

Atherton Press

IV   *Liberty* 1962
V   *The Public Interest* 1962
VI   *Justice* 1963, reissued in 1974
VII   *Rational Decision* 1964
VIII   *Revolution* 1966
IX   *Equality* 1967
X   *Representation* 1968
XI   *Voluntary Associations* 1969
XII   *Political and Legal Obligation* 1970
XIII   *Privacy* 1971

Aldine-Atherton Press

XIV   *Coercion* 1972

Lieber-Atherton Press

XV   *The Limits of Law* 1974
XVI   *Participation in Politics* 1975

New York University Press

XVII   *Human Nature in Politics* 1977
XVIII   *Due Process* 1977
XIX   *Anarchism* 1978
XX   *Constitutionalism* 1979
XXI   *Compromise in Ethics, Law, and Politics* 1979
XXII   *Property* 1980
XXIII   *Human Rights* 1981
XXIV   *Ethics, Economics, and the Law* 1982
XXVI   *Marxism* 1983
XXVII   *Criminal Justice* 1985

NOMOS XLVI

Yearbook of the American Society for Political and Legal Philosophy

POLITICAL EXCLUSION AND DOMINATION

Edited by

Melissa S. Williams
and
Stephen Macedo

NEW YORK UNIVERSITY PRESS • *New York and London*

NEW YORK UNIVERSITY PRESS
New York and London
www.nyupress.org

Library of Congress Cataloging-in-Publication Data
American Society for Political and Legal Philosophy. Meeting
(2001 : Atlanta, Ga.)
Political exclusion and domination / edited by Melissa S. Williams
and Stephen Macedo.
p. cm. — (Nomos ; 46)
Includes bibliographical references and index.
Papers and commentaries presented at the annual meeting of the
American Society for Political and Legal Philosophy in 2001, in
conjunction with a meeting of the American Philosophical
Association's Eastern Division in Atlanta, Georgia.
ISBN 0-8147-5695-6 (cloth : alk. paper)
1. Political rights. 2. Political participation. 3. Democracy.
4. Marginality, Social. I. Williams, Melissa S., 1960 – II. Macedo,
Stephen, 1957 – III. American Philosophical Association. Eastern
Division. IV. Title. V. Series.
JF799.A46 2001
320'.01 — dc22   2004015013

New York University Press books are printed on acid-free paper,
and their binding materials are chosen for strength and durability.

Manufactured in the United States of America
10 9 8 7 6 5 4 3 2 1

CONTENTS

DEDICATION TO JOHN RAWLS

The philosopher John Rawls, a former president of the American Society for Political and Legal Philosophy (ASPLP) and the greatest political philosopher of the twentieth century, died in November 2002. *A Theory of Justice,* which revived the social contract tradition of Locke, Rousseau, and Kant, was so transformative that even his critics acknowledge that their theories of social justice would not have occurred without his.

Rawls devoted much of his life to an urgent ethical question that is also at the heart of the ASPLP: What does justice require of individuals and institutions, and how can we realize it? "Justice is the first virtue of social institutions, as truth is of systems of thought," he wrote. "A theory however elegant and economical must be rejected or revised if it is untrue; likewise laws and institutions no matter how efficient and well-arranged must be reformed or abolished if they are unjust. Being first virtues of human activities, truth and justice are uncompromising." To be uncompromising, justice must take seriously both the freedom and the equality of individuals.

I first met John Rawls when he kindly welcomed me as an undergraduate into his graduate seminar on justice, and like many of his students who pursued political, legal, and moral philosophy, I later became his friend. He welcomed our criticisms even as he taught us. As hard as it is to imagine Rawls's theory of justice being surpassed in our lifetime, it is far harder to imagine anyone matching his combination of intellectual genius and moral goodness.

John Rawls's devotion to truth and dedication to justice were truly inspiring. In 1999, he was awarded the National Humanities Medal by President Clinton. His work, the citation said, "stimulated a national revival of attention to moral philosophy." If human beings matter, he taught, then justice must matter. The urgent need for our world to attend to Rawls's philosophy shows no sign of fading.

AMY GUTMANN
President, ASPLP

PREFACE

The contributions to this forty-sixth volume of NOMOS center around a group of papers and commentaries first presented at the annual meeting of the American Society for Political and Legal Philosophy, which took place on December 27 and 28, 2001, in conjunction with a meeting of the American Philosophical Association's Eastern Division, in Atlanta, Georgia. As in past years, the topic, "Political Exclusion and Domination," was selected by ballot by the members of the ASPLP.

Danielle Allen, Martha Nussbaum, and James Tully presented the three principal papers at those sessions in Atlanta, and the commentators were Clifford Orwin and Catharine MacKinnon (on Allen), Dan Kahan and Sanford Levinson (on Nussbaum), and Michael Blake and Leif Wenar (on Tully). These were exceptionally lively and provocative sessions. Melissa Williams and I wish to extend our sincere thanks to all those who contributed to the success of the meetings in Atlanta and to the present volume. The original paper givers and commentators have been patient and attentive throughout, as have those who contributed to the volume after the Atlanta meetings. We are delighted with the collection and believe that it illumines a wide range of important issues.

This volume marks a set of transitions: a transfer of responsibilities that has been not only peaceful but amicable and pleasant. Judith Wagner DeCew was secretary-treasurer when we met in Atlanta and she has now been succeeded by Jacob Levy. Thanks to both for their conscientiousness and energy. John Holzwarth, who is now completing his Ph.D. in political theory in the Politics Department at Princeton University, served as managing editor for four years. I am deeply indebted to him for moving these volumes along and assuming more than his share of the burdens at every stage. His good judgment and keen intelligence have improved each of the volumes with which he has been involved. Genevieve Johnson, who is completing her Ph.D. in political theory at the University of Toronto, assumed the position of managing editor with this volume, and she has done an excellent job of helping to get the chapters into final form. Thanks to Catherine Connors for preparing the index. Finally, even though Stephen Magro, our editor at New York University Press, has recently moved on to another position, these volumes have benefited from his support and care over a number of years. Thanks also to Jennifer Yoon and Despina Papazoglou Gimbel at NYU Press who continue to provide timely and very capable production support.

It is my pleasure now to hand over the editorship to Melissa Williams, who can be counted on to guide these volumes with the great discernment, consideration, and fair-mindedness for which she is widely known. It has been a genuine pleasure to work with her on this volume: I recommend the experience to others!

STEPHEN MACEDO
Princeton, N.J., August 2003

CONTRIBUTORS

DANIELLE ALLEN
Classical Languages and Literatures, Politics, and Committee on Social Thought, University of Chicago

VEIT BADER
Philosophy and Sociology, University of Amsterdam

MICHAEL BLAKE
Kennedy School of Government, Harvard University

SANFORD V. LEVINSON
Law, University of Texas

CLIFFORD ORWIN
Political Science, University of Toronto

STEPHEN MACEDO
Politics and University Center for Human Values, Princeton University

CATHARINE A. MACKINNON
Law, University of Michigan, Long-Term Visitor, University of Chicago

MARTHA NUSSBAUM
Philosophy, Law, and Divinity, University of Chicago

PHILIP PETTIT
Politics and Philosophy, Princeton University

JAMES TULLY
Political Science, University of Victoria

MIGUEL VATTER
Political Science, Northwestern University

LEIF WENAR
Philosophy, University of Sheffield

MELISSA S. WILLIAMS
Political Science, University of Toronto

INTRODUCTION

STEPHEN MACEDO AND
MELISSA S. WILLIAMS

NOMOS volumes have tended to explore the meaning of concepts we take to be constitutive of good and just legal and political orders. Even *Coercion* (NOMOS XIV, 1972) addresses a concept that most regard as a necessary, if regrettable, feature of such orders. The current volume marks an apparent departure. Political exclusion and domination are usually understood as paradigmatic forms of injustice in democratic societies. They are not always avoidable, even in a relatively just society. Nevertheless, it would seem that only a Nietzschean of the sternest variety would hold them up as desirable practices.

This "negative" approach to political philosophy, focusing on evils we should seek to avoid rather than ideals we should aspire to realize, puts us in mind of Judith Shklar. Surely exclusion and domination are among the forms of cruelty that her distinctive liberalism teaches us to fear. The varieties of injustice should be studied in their own right, she argued, and not only as the absence of justice positively defined, or what Shklar called the "normal model" of justice.[1] When we fix our gaze on injustice, we find that its sources are deeply inscribed in the frailties of the human psyche. The impulses to injustice do not vanish in the face of persuasive positive theories of justice or the legal prescriptions that flow from them. Positive accounts of justice matter, but they do not tell the whole story, and, studied alone, they may impart an unwarranted confidence that we can fully comprehend and attain what justice requires. Resisting the self-sufficiency of the "normal model" of justice keeps us alive to the remainders of injustice that are an ever-present feature of social and political life. It counsels humility and should lead us to beware of every form of moralizing zeal and self-righteousness.

It is fair to say that the "normal model" of justice is prominent, and some would say prevalent, in contemporary political philosophy. And certainly it has been central to the NOMOS tradition. Nevertheless, theorists besides Shklar analyze injustice and related but more specific negative phenomena, including exclusion, domination, and oppression. Domination, especially as incipient in claims to knowledge and the organization of modern society, is a key feature of Michel Foucault's work, on which several authors in this volume draw. It is also a central category in Philip Pettit's account of republican freedom, upon which he builds in his contribution to this volume. Iris Young has offered a helpful taxonomy of varieties of oppression, each with its own distinct mechanisms and systems of reproduction.[2] Veit Bader, in this volume and elsewhere, offers a taxonomy of unjust power asymmetries. The negative approach to thinking about justice might still be a minority approach, but it may be gaining ground in recent political philosophy.

While both exclusion and domination are relational concepts, they describe broadly different relationships among human beings. As Danielle Allen points out in her essay in this volume, exclusion implies a horizontal relationship, defining who is in and who is out of the political community. Domination, in contrast, has more often been used to describe vertical relationships such as class, defining who has power over whom. Both exclusion and domination can take political, economic, social, and cultural forms, each of which may interact with the others.

Domination, its analysts agree, consists in living under the arbitrary power of another, having to conform one's actions to a will external to one's own. If we view domination from the standpoint of positive justice, it is an opposite of freedom, but it is not only that. Domination is often for the sake of the material benefit of the dominator, as in the exploitation of labor. This is not a necessary feature of domination, however: sometimes people dominate others simply for the sake of demonstrating and glorying in their superior power. Sometimes, as so often in the case of the abusive spouse or parent, the act of domination compensates for the absence of a sense of meaningful agency in other relationships or spheres of life. Domination often operates on two levels, as a personal relationship between its immediate agent and object, or as a systemic phenomenon that structures relations of power between groups. If we seek to understand domination and the practices that sustain it, we need to attend to both of these levels. The individual level of analysis leads us to explore the motivations of the dominator and the subjective experience of being dominated. System-level analysis discloses the legal, cultural, and economic conditions under which some individuals or groups can dominate others. The essays that follow adopt both approaches.

Exclusion, it is almost needless to say, consists in being shut out of the rights and privileges of membership in a community or association. More specifically, political exclusion entails being denied some or all of the formal rights of citizenship, or having no effective access to participation in political decision making, or both. As with domination, we have a clearer understanding of exclusive behavior—especially when targeted at specific social, religious, or racial groups—when we see that it serves to bolster the confidence of insiders in their own worthiness as equal members of a community. Exclusion typically marks off the excluded group as an inferior "other," the "they" in contrast to which "we citizens" claim recognition from each other. The figure of the slave is the epitome of both unjust exclusion and domination, and makes clear that they are not mutually exclusive phenomena.

Chattel slavery constitutes the extreme form of exclusion, marking slaves off as enemies living within the community, as (perceived) inferiors unfit by nature for full membership, or as people who have fallen from membership because of their degraded economic or moral condition. The slave lives in a condition of "social death," bearing no social existence apart from her master and no recognized ties to past or future generations, as Orlando Patterson demonstrated in his magisterial cross-cultural study of the history of human slavery.[3] The slave is excluded not only from the community in which he or she dwells, but from all human community as such, according to Patterson. Slavery is also a thoroughgoing form of domination, maintaining the absolute power of the master and the absolute powerlessness of the slave by coercive, psychological, and symbolic means. In both classical and modern thought, the status of free citizen can scarcely be understood without the counter-image of the slave, and modern struggles for inclusion in the rights of citizenship habitually portray the injustice of exclusion as analogous to slavery.[4]

However intertwined they are in the life of the slave, exclusion and domination do not necessarily entail one another. It is clearly possible to be dominated without being excluded, especially where unequal social ranks are mutually dependent and entwined. The domination of the worker by the employer, or of the wife by the husband, provide ready examples of such relationships. It is also possible to be excluded without being dominated. Limiting immigration and therefore excluding some aliens is not self-evidently a form of domination, at least in the case of wealthy immigrants. (Excluding poor immigrants may be a vehicle of domination, insofar as it keeps them trapped in an economic system where they provide cheap labor without protections for their rights.)

We may understand exclusion sometimes as a response to the fear of domination, perhaps a well-justified one. The Callicles of Plato's *Gorgias* bristles at the fact that his democratic fellow-citizens presumed to govern someone so clearly superior to themselves. Even if Callicles was right about his extraordinary talents, it would have been imprudent for his fellow citizens to bow to his wishes, for he would surely have used the power he sought to dominate them.[5] As Aristotle suggested more generally, if there is one person in the city who is far better than the rest, that person must either rule or be exiled or executed.[6] In contemporary circumstances, it may be more helpful to read the strategy of *self*-exclusion as a way of avoiding domination. Some communities, such as separatist religious minorities, studiously opt out of mainstream social and political processes in order to preserve their ways of life. Otherwise, they would be subject to what they experience as the dominating interference of others in their affairs. In turn, some will then fear that some such groups are seeking to put themselves in a position in which—in the name of avoiding domination of the group—male members may be able to dominate female members, or parents may be able to dominate their children. Claims of domination may conflict with one another, and the concept itself will not allow us to sort out the relative strength of the competing claims. Avoiding domination by more powerful cultural or linguistic groups is often the motive for secessionist movements, as was addressed in the preceding NOMOS volume, *Secession and Self-Determination*.[7] The Boy Scouts exclude gays in the name of freedom of association, and undoubtedly would feel dominated if they lost the right to exclude. Here, however, it is possible to wonder whether this exclusion is arbitrary and invidious and itself complicit in broader social injustice toward gays and lesbians.

In fact, society is pervaded by manifold forms of exclusion, some of which are acceptable or even necessary as conditions of the realization of positive goods. To label institutions, associations, or practices as "exclusive" is not necessarily to condemn them. "Exclusion" can be used to describe practices that are acceptable or invidious, just or unjust. Exclusion may be a concomitant of justifiable selectivity. We expect the New York Yankees, Harvard University, and the American College of Nurse-Midwives to be selective (and so exclusive) in appropriate ways. We can see that justified forms of exclusion are prerequisites of athletic team prowess, of educational excellence, and of high standards of professional performance. Moreover, the principle of freedom of association encompasses the right *not* to associate with others, that is, the right to exclude. Churches have the right to be communities united around a certain conception of God's nature and ultimate human purposes, and in support of that they may define heresy and exclude heretics. The relevant point is that important public institutions should not exclude (or select among) qualified persons on the basis of morally arbitrary characteristics (to borrow John Rawls's phrase). There may be arguments as to whether particular considerations count as a legitimate ground for selection, as ongoing debates around race consciousness in college admissions and legislative districting attest. But exclusion is not always morally objectionable per se.

Even "political exclusion" may sometimes be warranted, insofar as there are appropriate limitations on the right to vote (a residency requirement, for example). Democratic societies need some powers to define the terms of membership in political community, including powers to regulate immigration.[8] With respect to political exclusion, then, we should be clear that it constitutes a paradigmatic form of injustice only when its principles of selectivity are indefensible and harmful to basic human interests, rather than defensible elements of valuable social practices.

"Domination" is more clearly in general a normative idea ("oppression" always is normative, and invidious): we tend to regard it as necessarily including an element of arbitrariness or oppression. Philip Pettit's definition of domination makes this explicit by including the ideas that treatment so designated is arbitrary and at odds with the interests of the dominated party. Of course, the lawbreaker who does not regard a law as justifiable will subjectively experience the law's enforcement as a form of domination. The question is whether a lawbreaker justifiably experiences the law as a form of domination, while those who enforce the law also act justifiably.

Some might argue, as does Miguel Vatter in his chapter, that the rule of law entails domination even where its subjects regard the law as legitimate: general rules of law may be indeterminate in ways that require interpretation and that permit discretion in application and enforcement. In human circumstances, an element of arbitrariness may be likely or even inevitable, but the very idea of legal interpretation and enforcement does not imply arbitrariness.[9] The claim may become more compelling if we bring in the idea that governance requires general rules of law, which necessarily apply to somewhat dissimilar particulars, introducing an inevitable element of "arbitrariness." On some readings, in any event, domination can be legitimate even while it contains elements of arbitrariness. Although we would not want to go this far, some might even say that a liberal society justly seeks to "dominate" racists, sexists, and homophobes by actively marginalizing their views in order to sustain a culture of equality and toleration.

It is arguable that both exclusion and domination may sometimes, in some forms, be both necessary and justifiable for the sake of freedom, equality, and order. Yet their practice always contains the possibility of fostering the uglier tendencies of the human spirit: the desire for power for power's sake, the sense of insecurity in our own status as equals worthy of recognition, which we salve through the exclusion or subordination of "inferior" others. The notion that injustice harms its perpetrator and not only its victim has been a persistent theme in moral and political philosophy since Plato, and it appears in these essays as well. Danielle Allen argues convincingly that the domination of African Americans has done damage to the quality of citizenship for both Blacks and whites in the United States. Acts of exclusion and domination that are arguably defensible, such as the shaming penalties that Martha Nussbaum addresses in her essay, may be worrisome for the damage they do not only to those subject to them but also to us as citizens: by feeding our darker sentiments.

The essays in this volume cover a vast territory in exploring the meaning of political exclusion and domination. They address topics ranging from racial segregation to criminal sanctions, from the role of the political philosopher to the instruments of genocide. They do not yield a univocal or conclusive analytical account of exclusion and domination. In any case, it is doubtful that such a systematic account could ever do justice to the complexity of these concepts or to the myriad relationships we use to describe them. Our essayists disagree, sometimes mildly and sometimes profoundly, over how we should construe the forms of exclusion and domination that most command our attention and condemnation. What our authors share is an unflinching determination to look injustice squarely in the eye (readers may decide who blinks first).

Part I: The Injustice of Domination

In the opening essay, Danielle Allen explores the relative usefulness of exclusion and domination as ways of conceptualizing injustice in a democratic society. What are the stakes involved in using one term rather than the other?

Allen seeks to illuminate this question by comparing the approaches of Hannah Arendt and Ralph Ellison to the question of how to assess efforts to reverse the injustice of racial segregation in the United States. Her starting point is the debate between Arendt and Ellison over the 1957 desegregation battles in Little Rock, Arkansas. These debates reveal, Allen argues, that the two thinkers had surprisingly similar positive accounts of justice and democratic citizenship. Both understood political life as an intricate struggle for recognition among plural and diverse individuals. Both perceived a continuity between the mundane injustices that

flow from daily failures of recognition in ordinary life and the ex-
tremities of injustice of the twentieth century. Both understood
civic friendship as the condition for healthy struggles for recognition, in which all remain visible to one another even as some win a
particular struggle and others lose. Strikingly, both employed the
metaphor of invisibility to articulate the failure of recognition and
to represent injustice toward African Americans.

Despite these important similarities, Allen draws out a key distinction between Arendt and Ellison in the content they give to
the injustice of invisibility. In her reading of Arendt's *Men in Dark
Times*, invisibility is a metaphor for exclusion, being shut out of the
political space in which human equals see and hear one another.
Here again the slave is the icon of such obscurity. Invisibility arises
from politics but functions to remove people from politics. This
exclusion, however, need not taint political action nor corrupt citizenship for those who abide within a political community's circle
of light. For the excluded, however, being rendered worldless and
invisible saps the capacity to act politically. Their history of obscurity rendered the Little Rock parents ill-educated to act as citizens,
and mistakenly led them to introduce their social, apolitical racial
identity into the public sphere.

In Ellison's *Invisible Man*, people are "unsee-able, even in times
of full light," so that invisibility represents a relationship of domination that erases the dominated entirely from the view of the
dominators in whose midst they live. Americans are divided between first-class and second-class citizenship, dominance and acquiescence, each of which developed its own rites and practices,
and each of which is a perverted form of citizenship. Second-class
citizens are invisible *within* the political realm, not outside it as for
Arendt; invisibility is itself a political phenomenon.

Viewing invisibility as exclusion means that the quality of citizenship is not itself flawed; it is just a matter of bringing the outsiders into the fold of healthy citizenship. Viewing invisibility as
domination, as Ellison does, means confronting the distortions of
citizenship that arise from relationships of unequal power. Second-
class citizens must live as "spies in the enemy country" in order to
protect themselves, using their invisibility as a cloak behind which
to get what they can. First-class citizens must blind themselves to

the fact of their dominance in order to live comfortably with their self-congratulatory affirmation of freedom and equality.

Yet while subordination yields this unhealthy practice of subversion and dissimulation, for Ellison it also contains lessons for healthy democratic citizenship: that it teaches us "what it [takes] to live in the world with others." African Americans can take what is healthy from their habits of subordination and use it as a tool for exemplifying healthy citizenship by resisting domination and accepting sacrifices that go with that resistance. By acting as free citizens, African Americans can "agree to death and destruction" with the ideals of freedom and equality, killing off those unjust practices of domination through the practice of freedom itself. People must learn new techniques of citizenship that, in Ellison's words, enable the dominated "to free themselves by becoming their idea of what a free people should be" (Allen, pp. 60 and 61).

For Allen, Ellison's reading of injustice as domination is more powerful than Arendt's reading of invisibility as exclusion, as it opens to view the centrality of *transformative* techniques of democratic citizenship that reshape first- and second-class citizens into members of a shared political community. This transformation cannot be sustained by imagining the "oneness" of the people of which the individual is a part, for this would erase the inescapable —and vital—plurality of the people. But it is sustained by a vision of the "wholeness" of the people: that democratic decisions, however they aim at a common good, always impose sacrifices on some. Healthy democratic citizenship requires of us that we both accept those sacrifices for ourselves and honor the sacrifices of others, taking care that they are, over time, reciprocated.

Clifford Orwin agrees that Ellison's account of domination is superior to Arendt's treatment of invisibility as a form of exclusion. "Exclusion so-called," he notes, "is never . . . actual exclusion from the society in question, but rather domination within it" (p. 77). Ellison and Allen are surely right that the experience of African Americans is deeply relevant for all Americans. But they go too far in making the challenges of African American citizenship paradigmatic for citizenship as such; the tragic vision of citizenship-as-sacrifice is not an appropriate model for everyday citizenship. Any analogy between the experience of African Americans and the everyday losses of politics, Orwin argues, trivializes the former.

Orwin allows that winners in democratic contests should avoid leaving behind disagreements incompatible with ongoing cooperation, but we should not mistake this economy of disagreement for friendship. Friendship, Orwin argues, is more than we can or should ask of politics. Rather than succumbing to the temptations of communitarianism, we would do much better to pin our hopes on rational self-interest on the model of *The Federalist*. Democracy depends upon a civic wholeness that makes room for multiplicity; thus far Allen is correct. But such wholeness is a product of political artifice, as Hobbes teaches us. In a liberal order wholeness subsists in a mutual toleration of our differences coupled with an insistence on our more primary sameness, in the form of the equal protection of the law for all. African Americans' struggle for that equal protection did exemplify a heroic form of citizenship, but we should not hope for a politics that calls for such heroism.

Granted that domination and exclusion are vividly interwoven in the experience of African Americans, are the concepts themselves connected intrinsically? Is exclusion a harm distinguishable from the domination it sometimes obscures?

Philip Pettit has written extensively in defense of republicanism as a political ideal, arguing that what distinguishes republicanism from alternative political ideals is its core conception of freedom as nondomination.[10] Pettit defines dominating power as the capacity to interfere arbitrarily in the choices of another.[11] Interference is *arbitrary*, on Pettit's view, when the interferer is not constrained to track the interests of the person affected. Further, in a relation of domination the dominating agent need not *actually* interfere arbitrarily in another's choices, but merely have the *power* to do so. Not all interference is domination, Pettit emphasizes: it is possible for agents, notably the state, to interfere *nonarbitrarily* in individuals' actions. The rule of law secures the nonarbitrariness of state interference and frees it from the charge of domination. Whereas liberalism, on Pettit's account, construes any interference as an infringement on freedom so that the actions of the state are always in tension with the ideal of perfect freedom, Pettit's republicanism envisions an emancipatory role for the state as an agent capable of overturning social relations of domination. This is the crux of the distinction between Pettit's account of liberal freedom-as-noninterference and republican freedom-as-nondomination.

Pettit's discussion of the good of inclusion suggests that the harm of exclusion is derivative from that of domination: by being denied a meaningful or effective voice in the political process, the excluded have no assurance that decision making will track their interests to a degree that meets the standard of nonarbitrariness. Interference by the state or other agents in the affairs of those who have had no opportunity to contest decisions, then, runs a high risk of domination.

In his contribution to this volume, Pettit extends his defense of republicanism. Every political ideal, he argues, can be cast as an account of the kinds of complaints a political order should especially strive to address, the ills it should especially seek to avoid. We recognize a sound political order by the fact that it gives its members little ground for complaint on the issues that really matter. The differences among political ideals boil down to different accounts of the ills that ought most to be avoided. Some political ideals privilege unhappiness; others privilege injustice; others privilege inequality. We also want political ideals to be feasible: it must be possible for a political order to avoid the ills privileged by a particular ideal. Pettit also reminds us that it must be desirable that the state, rather than some other entity, is the agent with responsibility for combating the specified ill. Having set out these general desiderata, Pettit argues that the political ideal of nondomination is superior to its rivals. Drawing from his past work on republicanism as nondomination, Pettit argues that the ideal of nondomination meets both the feasibility and desirability constraints. States possess the coercive and redistributive powers necessary to remedy relations of domination, and states are more likely to be able to prevent domination than other agents. The domination complaint is, moreover, a complaint of the utmost importance, as it concerns one's very standing as a person who commands the respect of others and is recognized as a full member of the community who does not live at the mercy of others.

But do complaints about domination take precedence over other possible complaints, which are given priority by competing political ideals? Pettit considers five alternatives: liberty, equality, community, relief from poverty (read through the capability theory of Sen and Nussbaum), and a contractualist conception of justice. Each of these can be subsumed within an interpretation of non-domination, Pettit argues, and the principle of nondomination affords specific interpretations of these ideals that are appealing in themselves and reconcilable with one another. Nondomination, then, provides a master concept that encompasses all the rest and guides the resolution of their indeterminacy and possible incompatibility.

Miguel Vatter addresses Pettit in an extended reflection on modern republicanism's efforts to reconcile republican freedom and order. As we have seen, Pettit argues that freedom-as-nondomination is consistent with the rule of law because the latter represents "nonarbitrary interference." Vatter doubts that law and freedom can ever be so fully reconciled. The law is never self-interpreting or self-applying. The institution of law depends upon and does not eliminate the activity of ruling. Someone must decide which particular actions and persons fall under this law or that, and we will often disagree about how the law should be interpreted and applied. Law never rules by itself. The citizen who runs afoul of the law or who is constrained by it is a *subject* of law's ordering force, and of those who interpret and apply it. Governance by the rule of law involves the legal subject in an unequal and asymmetrical relationship of power, and as such constitutes domination even on Pettit's own terms. This domination has a legal, impersonal dimension, and is therefore distinguishable from the illegitimate domination of arbitrary rule—but it is domination nonetheless. Freedom-as-nondomination and the need for order cannot be fully reconciled via the rule of law. Pettit's effort is, Vatter contends, an unsuccessful departure from the modern republican tradition.

What, then, is modern republicanism's alternative? Drawing upon Arendt, Vatter argues that modern republican freedom is better captured by the ideal of "no-rule." The power of the people cherished by republicanism should be understood as a "sovereign indifference to rule itself." We should leave behind Pettit's excessive state-focused view, and regard popular contestation and resistance as revolutionary potentials that should be kept alive as a counterbalance to the order secured by the state, which always entails an element of domination. For Machiavelli, argues Vatter, the possibility of reconciling freedom and order rests in the "necessary conflict not over who should rule, but of whether and how there should be rule at all" (p. 135).

Thus, modern republican thought preserves the difference between the power of the people—*constituent* power—and the *constituted* powers of the state. Incipient within the idea of the constituent power of the people is the possibility of revolution, which is why the themes of revolution and founding are so strong a presence within the modern republican tradition, though not in Pettit's republicanism. The challenge of the modern republican state is to politically institute the standpoint of the people, who wish for "no-rule" (nondomination), without reducing that wish to a desire for negative liberty. Machiavelli saw the solution in the creation of counterinstitutions that give the people an internal check against the state's administration of rule, as in the Roman tribunes.

The antiauthoritarian voice of the people need not be bound by the discipline of reason-giving in order to serve its purpose, argues Vatter: its activity is resistance, saying "no" to power, and not the activity of seeking rational agreement between dominators and dominated. Republicanism holds out the possibility that, through resistance and revolution, the people will assert the political equality of all as *prior to* any particular political order and the social inequalities that every political order inevitably abets.

Thus, the power of the people is *extra*-legal, Vatter argues; it asserts their equality *before* the law not as equal subjects *under* the law but as *prior* to law itself. It is in this sense that revolutionary action is a "return to beginnings," since revolution unsettles the order of law once it has come to be experienced by the people as a source of domination, expressing their "sovereign experience of not being obligated to order and to rule" (p. 149). As constituent power, the people accept the need for order, of which law is a necessary condition. As revolutionary power, the people may throw off an order of law that is no longer authoritative in their eyes. Thus, according to Vatter, the authority of law (the precondition of order) and the power of the people (the condition of freedom) are *jointly necessary* for the legitimacy of the constituted power of a modern republic. The revolutionary potential of the power of the people underscores the *contingency* of law's authority and safeguards law from its tendencies to both arbitrary and legitimate domination.

Veit Bader returns us to the question of what is at stake in our selection among alternative conceptions of injustice. Against Allen and Pettit he argues that we ought to *resist* selecting one conception of injustice—exclusion versus domination, for example—from among the rest. The temptation to a monistic understanding of injustice is understandable as it holds out the promise of an elegant theoretical parsimony, argues Bader, but to succumb to this temptation, as do both Allen and Pettit, is to sacrifice theoretical precision and insight. Allen and Pettit obscure the empirical and the conceptual complexity of injustice. Bader argues that monistic strategies in the social sciences and in political theory often press falsely dichotomous choices upon us. We should instead adopt a pluralist approach to injustice that preserves our intuitions about the varieties of both injustice and the range of possible responses.

Bader offers a taxonomy of five analytically distinct forms of unjust inequality: exploitation, domination/oppression, discrimination, exclusion, and marginalization. Each of these forms of injustice may exist as independent empirical phenomena, but it is also possible—indeed, it is fairly common—that a group of persons may find themselves subject to a number of overlapping and mutually reinforcing power asymmetries at once. Because different institutional remedies are often appropriate for different structures of unjust inequality, our capacity to ameliorate overlapping injustices depends upon a clear analytic understanding of which forms of injustice are in play in a given case.

In a brief reply to Bader and Orwin, Danielle Allen stresses that hers is not a project in conceptual analysis. Nor is it a defense of either communitarianism or neorepublicanism, as her critics suggest. Rather, her purpose is to explore the function of rhetoric—including the rhetorics of exclusion and domination—in establishing the trust among citizens upon which democracy depends.

Philip Pettit's reply to Bader anticipates a theme that is central to the following section of the volume as well: What is the task of political philosophy? Against Bader's critique of monism, Pettit argues that the philosophical enterprise per se involves seeking ordering principles among conflicting values. Without such principles, we are buffeted about by the contingent moral claims that arise in one circumstance or another, and reach for whatever value has most appeal at the moment. The quest for philosophical understanding pulls us to discover the unifying (if multidimensional) principle that enables us to order the phenomena of conflicting value claims. Failing the discovery of such a principle, we should not settle for less than an account of how we can prioritize conflicting claims, something that Bader's multiple definitions of injustice do not enable us to do.

To Vatter, Pettit responds that there appears to be a disagreement between them on the core meaning of the concept of domination, but this is uncertain because it remains unclear what Vatter's definition of domination is. Perhaps, he suggests, the disagreement is only an apparent one, arising from ambiguity as to whether we are considering the rule of law within the realm of ideal rather than nonideal theory. Vatter is correct that under any actually existing order of the rule of law, there will always be a residue of domination; the challenge is to reduce it as far as possible. Within Pettit's ideal account of the rule of law, however, his stipulative definition of domination renders "nonarbitrary domination" an oxymoron.

PART II: EXCLUSION, ASSIMILATION, AND THE ROLE OF POLITICAL PHILOSOPHY

Like Pettit and Vatter, James Tully portrays domination as the absence of democratic freedom. Like Bader, however, he disaggregates the concept of domination, focusing on the two analytically distinct practices of exclusion and assimilation.

Tully situates his analysis of exclusion and assimilation within a broader account of democratic legitimacy and of the distinctive obstacles to legitimacy in our time. In a spirit similar to that of Pettit, Tully argues that legitimacy depends upon the two "equiprimordial" principles: constitutionalism or the rule of law, on the one hand, and, on the other, democratic freedom or popular sovereignty. Constitutionalism requires that the system of social, political, and economic cooperation be regulated by a coherent system of principles, rules, and procedures. Democratic freedom depends upon the *self*-imposition of law by the people through their participation in the exchange of reasons that generates law. The principle of democratic freedom contains within it the expectation that there will always be contestation and "reasonable disagreement" over both the content of laws and the processes by which they are formed. Legitimate democracy therefore contains a necessary and salutary agonistic element; struggle is endemic to democracy. To reconcile this element of contestation with the principle of the rule of law, then, means accepting that the constitutional order will be continuously negotiated or "conciliated," never fixed in stone. Thus, "[d]emocratic constitutionalism is an activity rather than an end state" (p. 196).

Three interrelated contemporary trends pose challenges to the project of democratic legitimacy, according to Tully: the economic globalization of capital, with its new international regulatory regimes and the accompanying "democratic deficit"; the dispersion of political decision-making power to levels both above and below the constitutional nation-state; and the decline of democratic participation and deliberation within the traditional institutions of national representative government. Together, these trends have the effect of diminishing democratic access to decision making and of sapping citizens' ability to contest growing inequalities, domestic and global.

Contemporary "neoliberalism," with its acceptance of economic globalization, is one response to these trends. A more critical response comes from theorists such as Rawls and Habermas and the theories of deliberative democracy that have been inspired by their work. Although these approaches have been salutary in important respects, Tully argues, they misconstrue the task of political philosophy as the development of a comprehensive theory of justice or of procedures for public reasoning. In doing so, they invest theoretical reason with a privileged status in judgments about justice and seek to prescribe the procedures and limits of public reason.

Tully proposes a third alternative, which is also critical of contemporary trends but construes the aim of political philosophy as a kind of citizen activity, seeking to keep prevailing laws, institutions, and principles of justice under constant questioning. Political philosophers do not stand above the fray and should not seek to guide others toward final agreements on universal principles. The only universal principle that democrats should espouse is *audi alteram partem,* "always listen to the other side." In contrast to the Rawlsian and Habermasian approaches, according to Tully, this third alternative embraces the agonistic dimension of democracy as a positive good, not something to be overcome. It also seeks to engage with actual political struggles in contemporary politics on their own terms, and to understand them as the practice of democratic freedom itself.

Tully's account of trends toward globalization and the weakening of structures of democratic accountability draws attention to new and worrying forms of exclusion and domination. *Exclusion* expresses the manifold ways in which individuals are prevented from initiating and participating in democratic negotiation. Exclusion can be formal, as with slavery, or it may be subtle, as when individuals who possess formal democratic rights do not speak out because of their economic circumstances, social biases against them, fear of reprisal, or lack of opportunity, as when people directly affected by the actions of transnational corporations simply have no role in corporate decision making. *Assimilation* occurs in deliberative institutions that are formally open, but which demand that participants conform to preestablished rules of engagement that often shut out the discursive habits and practices of formerly excluded groups.

What is a political philosopher to do in confronting these obstacles to democratic justice? Michael Blake and Leif Wenar argue that, rather than leaving every principle fully open to contestation, as Tully recommends, liberal political philosophy should continue to strive to identify those norms that should be nonnegotiable in democratic societies committed to freedom and equality. The liberal philosopher's project of ordering determinate principles of justice and fixed constitutional norms in a coherent system of thought is not antidemocratic, Wenar argues. Philosophers do not impose or legislate their theories of justice; they propose them to fellow citizens who will either be persuaded by their arguments or not. Philosophers will never produce a theory of justice capable of generating perfect consensus, Blake stresses, but it does not follow that philosophers should stop aiming for arguments whose coherence and completeness could (and should) motivate consensus. The task of philosophy is to seek the truth and state it, and this includes making prescriptive normative claims. The frailties of human reason and the manifold sources of human disagreement counsel philosophical humility, not the abandonment of our search for principles of justice that "all agents ought to accept."

For Blake and Wenar, some normative propositions—that women should not vote, for example, or that gays should be executed, or that that Blacks should be segregated—are so clearly at odds with democratic principles of freedom and equality that they have no proper place in the public sphere. Against Tully's agonistic conception of democracy, Blake argues that philosophers need not wait for democratic deliberation to condemn as beyond the pale any assertions (such as those mentioned above) that are baldly at odds with the moral equality that democratic practice assumes. Indeed, Blake asserts that democrats who seriously treat as unproven the fundamental moral equality of gays or African Americans can hardly claim to be constructing an inclusive public order: gays and African Americans will not welcome Tully's purported "inclusiveness." Tully's own insistence that we must always listen to the other side and practice norms of democratic reciprocity are themselves reasoned substantive prescriptions about how democracy should proceed. On the liberal view that Blake and Wenar appear to share, basic constitutional norms do not confront the citizenry with an alien or imposed order of political justice because they too typically accept that, as Wenar puts it, "democratic action can only legitimate policies within the framework of basic rights that are established by principles of justice."

Wenar also challenges Tully's diagnosis of the contemporary trends that threaten democratic legitimacy, namely, globalization, corporate power, and declining political participation. Corporate power is objectionable, Wenar asserts, not because people do not accept it—the "overwhelming majority" appear to do so, at least in the United States—it is objectionable rather because it leads to injustices that can be specified "independently of any procedures of democratic validation." With respect to political participation, similarly, Wenar argues that over the last fifty years people's resources, education, and access to information have increased, while their participation has declined, and this suggests people want to participate less. Wenar's point is not to endorse this trend any more than he endorses what he terms Americans "dozy acquiescence" to corporate power. His point is that Tully is not really following his own modest injunction to "listen to the people." He seems to suspect that Tully discounts Americans' actual preferences as insufficiently reflective, or as weighted down by consumerism and apathy. Insofar as Tully seeks to transform the political and economic environment so as to enhance democratic energy, reflectiveness, and deliberation does he not join liberal political philosophers in imposing rules "from the outside?"

Tully responds to Blake and Wenar by arguing that the agonistic element of democracy does not mean that "anything goes." Tully's understanding of democratic dialogue does rule out hate speech, but he asserts that this flows from the condition of dialogic reciprocity as distinct from an appeal to a foundational principle of liberal equality. In the wake of what Tully describes as a "dialogical turn in political philosophy," the role of the philosopher is indeed to present careful arguments to fellow citizens, but to do so in a spirit that expects and accepts that these arguments are subject to contestation and will not likely resolve all reasonable disagreement. In fact, Tully allows, Rawls and Habermas, and Blake and Wenar, all agree that philosophers are on a par with other citizens in that they put their foundational principles to the test of public reasons, and he asserts that this constitutes an important transformation in liberalism.

While consensus may stand as a "critical ideal" of democratic dialogue—an ideal that is itself open to challenge—we now understand that treating it as a "regulative ideal" is dangerous because the demand for consensus has so often been the vehicle for exclusion and assimilation. Even agreed-upon and obviously well-justified moral convictions (the injustice of slavery, for example) cannot be removed "once and for all" from democratic discussion without encouraging moral hubris and risking injustice. A fallibilist spirit is the precondition for discovering how our interpretations of foundational principles may function to marginalize or exclude, as they have so often in the past.

Readers will have to decide for themselves whether the argument between Tully and his critics is somewhat at cross-purposes. It may be that certain basic moral guarantees are properly regarded as settled—in at least certain respects—but also open to criticism and revision in other respects. So, Tully has a point when he asserts that, in the spirit of fallibilism (made familiar by Mill,

Popper, and others), any and all accounts of the meaning of
general abstract norms, no matter how foundational, can be challenged and contested. As Tully asserts, there is no basic general
principle of justice whose meaning, extension, and reference we
should ever take to be settled definitively. Nevertheless, Wenar and
Blake may have a point when they assert that it is hard to imagine
some basic guarantees of justice reasonably being called into question. Candidates include the basic humanity of persons of all races
and religions. But we must be careful about the way in which we
regard any such claims as settled. Blake and Wenar may be suggesting that certain aspects of the general principles seem well settled:
that, for example, the most basic forms of respect for persons
cannot be denied based on skin color, as was once thought to be
the case (and as some people still contend, unreasonably, as Blake
points out). This is not to say that we fully understand the principle of racial equality, nor is it to deny that a world of controversies
and reasonable disagreements will continue to surround issues of
racial justice, for the foreseeable future and perhaps for all time.
Specific issues do get settled, and are no longer subject to reasonable contestation, as Mill acknowledged.[12] The basic humanity of
people with black skin is settled as a backstop, not as a fully adequate realization of perfect justice. Similarly, it is well settled that
chattel slavery is wrong. Tully's counterexample, against the proposition that the wrongness of slavery is settled, is the observation
that perhaps certain forms of wage labor may be sufficiently like
chattel slavery to be also decried as among the forms of slavery.
Fair enough. But this in no way contradicts or calls into question
the wrongness of chattel slavery: the settled quality of that specific
conviction serves as a backstop for the further reflection and progress that Tully urges with respect to our understanding of the more
general conception of "slavery." If this is right, then the gap between Tully and his critics may be less than it appears.

PART III: BOUNDARIES DRAWN BY SHAME

Exclusion and domination may be the consequence not only of
law and public policy but also of social norms and attitudes. La-
beling certain categories of actions, or categories of people, as
shameful or disgusting can both exclude these persons from full

participation in social and political life, and reinforce the dominance of the "normal" (normal persons and normal behavior). Without explicitly invoking the categories of exclusion and domination, Martha Nussbaum reveals ways in which shame, disgust, and stigma are used to create and reinforce conceptions of the "normal," conceptions that may be grounded in a narcissistic longing for perfection and completeness. Her account suggests ways in which social patterns of domination may encourage and depend upon self-domination: as when we internalize the disgust and loathing of others.

Nussbaum's essay focuses on the ubiquity of shame in social life and also on its specific employment as a means for punishing violations of criminal law, including sex offenses and drunk driving. We all have characteristics or yearnings that would appear as weaknesses if exposed to the world and judged from the point of view of what is considered normal. Drawing on sources from Aristophanes and Lucretius to Irving Goffman and Donald Winnicott, Nussbaum argues that primitive shame flows from the maturing child's lost sense of "blissful totality": the painful recognition that he or she is not omnipotent and whole, but rather needy and dependent. Without the right nurturing relationships, children may not accept the inevitable imperfections of their own humanity, and grow into adulthood demanding perfection from themselves and others. Shame is to be distinguished from guilt, which is a proper response to the harm or wrongful damage one has done. Shame attaches to the self more deeply and irredeemably: it is a matter of who one is rather than what one has done. In social life we are too ready to ascribe shame to those who deviate from the normal—to the handicapped, to sexual minorities, criminals, and the unemployed—partly as a defense mechanism to hide from our own imperfections. Driven by primitive shame at our own imperfections, we stigmatize others as "cripples," "homos," or "mongoloid idiots," and thereby reaffirm our own normality. A healthy acceptance of one's own imperfections and needfulness is not easy to achieve.

Nussbaum argues against proposals by Daniel Kahan, John Braithewaite, and others that shaming penalties may be appropriate alternatives to incarceration. Shaming penalties violate liberal norms of equal basic dignity by dividing human beings into two groups: the shamefully frail and those who are normal and above it all. In the end, Nussbaum also calls for affirmative measures to overcome the inequalities, shame, and stigma suffered by those regarded as physically and mentally handicapped. Liberal societies should more fully realize their own aspirations to equal dignity by resisting impulses that flow from primitive shame.

Sanford Levinson, in a comment on Nussbaum's essay, argues that the general regime of criminal punishment that is supposedly guilt based rather than shame based nevertheless partakes of many of the objectionable features that Nussbaum decries. Guilt-based punishments may in practice also brand persons deeply and indelibly. Many American states deny convicted felons the right to vote for life. Those who are incarcerated rather than subjected to shaming penalties may still be regarded always as "released felons" rather than "former felons." Many Americans, Levinson argues, shrink at the idea of convicted felons ever being employed as teachers, and many lawyers would permanently exclude convicted murderers from the bar. More moderately, Levinson wonders whether some period of probation is permissible before a person convicted of a heinous crime is allowed to assume positions of trust. Enduring taint is not, Levinson argues, confined to category of shaming penalties. He also points out that Nussbaum's argument against shame is strongest when shame is attached to acts that liberal academics believe not to be shameful: acts that should be decriminalized and accepted, such as homosexual relations. Levinson ends by doubting that taking sides on the abstract question of the permissibility of shaming penalties really settles much when it comes to constructing policies in actual complex circumstances.

PART IV: SEXUAL DOMINANCE

The formal structure of relations of domination is everywhere the same—the subjection of some to the arbitrary power of others—but the devices that create and maintain these relationships are manifold. Domination has many instruments, ranging from legal discrimination and cultural stigmatization to control over life-sustaining material resources to the most extreme forms of violence and terror. Further, we can understand relations of domination in both personal and systemic terms. From the standpoint of the victim of domination, it is often the personal dimension of domination that comes into sharp focus: public humiliation at the hands of an official or employer, beating at the hands of the slave foreman or the abusive spouse. Viewing domination from the standpoint of its victims discloses its devastating psychological impact. But personal relationships of domination are seldom the whole story, since domination generally requires enabling social and legal conditions, and individual-level relationships of domination are often, if not always, part of broader structures of power. The individual-level agent of domination may not invoke, intend, or even be conscious of system-level structures of power, but this is irrelevant to the effectiveness of his or her actions in maintaining those structures.

In the volume's final chapter, Catharine MacKinnon examines rape as an instrument of domination, focusing especially on rape in the context of genocide. MacKinnon begins from the Bosnian case, the first genocide in which the role of rape was widely recognized by the media and—in no small part because of legal cases in which MacKinnon played a leading role—in international law.[13] MacKinnon documents how widespread were sexual violations of non-Serbian women and men by the Serbs during the war, and how ethnic domination was eroticized by Serb military through the filming of sexual atrocities, organizing mass rapes, forced pregnancies, and the dehumanization of Muslims and Croats through public sexual abuses. Through the lens of the Bosnian experience, we can see more clearly the role of sexuality in the Holocaust, MacKinnon shows. And the genocidal functions of sexual violence were all too apparent in the 1994 Rwanda genocide.

What work is sexual violence doing in these genocides? Rape is also a characteristic feature of systems of slavery, where it is a tool for demonstrating the dominance and maintaining the supremacy of that master race or class. Rape functions as an instrument of war —to demoralize the enemy, to desensitize combatants to violence, to demonstrate the dominating power of the aggressor. It functions in these ways in genocidal contexts as well, MacKinnon argues, but with the further purpose and consequence of destroying a people by destroying its individual members and the social fabric that holds the group together as a group. Although genocidal rape often ends in the victim's death, this is not its only contribution to genocide. By targeting women on the dual basis of sex and their ethnic, racial, national, or religious identity, genocidal rape, with other genocidal sexual atrocities, destroys groups by destroying the women in them.

For MacKinnon, the relevant question is not the individual intent of the rapist, but what the sexual assaults do. In genocidal contexts, when women are raped based on their sex and ethnic group combined, rape functions to destroy the group as a group, "as such" in terms of the international Genocide Convention. Rape targets the group systematically, MacKinnon holds, by selecting group members for atrocities on the basis of their group membership. One consequence is terror, a tool for domination, each group member knowing that she or he could be the next target. Systematized sexual atrocity, including rape organized as prostitution on an ethnic basis, also serves to stigmatize not only its immediate victims but the group as a whole, as people to whom these things can be done. In these respects, MacKinnon argues, "What rape does in genocide is what it does the rest of the time: ruins identity, marks who you are as less, hence devastates community, the glue of group. It destroys the willingness to identify with the group designation on the basis of which the rape took place, hence destroys the group as such" (pp. 336–37). In everyday contexts of sex-based inequality outside wars and genocides, where rape's frequency subjects women as such to its systematicity and randomness, it is women as a group who are destroyed. Thus, MacKinnon's boldest thesis here is that genocidal rape enables us to see more clearly the function of sexual domination in the inequality of the sexes, specifically the group-structured consequences of rape's pervasiveness in contemporary societies, including liberal egalitarian ones. In her view, rape is as strikingly effective a tool in maintaining the systematic domination of women as such, destroying them as a group, as it is in establishing the systematic domination of one ethnic, national, religious, or racial group by another.

NOTES

1. Judith Shklar, *The Faces of Injustice* (New Haven: Yale University Press, 1990), 15–28.

2. See Iris Marion Young, "Five Faces of Oppression," *Philosophical Forum* 19(4): 270–99 (1988), and *Justice and the Politics of Difference* (Princeton: Princeton University Press, 1990), chap. 2.

3. See Orlando Patterson, *Slavery and Social Death: A Comparative Study* (Cambridge, MA: Harvard University Press, 1982).

4. For discussion, see, e.g., Philip Pettit, *Republicanism: A Theory of Freedom and Government* (Oxford: Oxford University Press, 1997), 31–35, and Judith Shklar, *American Citizenship: The Quest for Inclusion* (Cambridge, MA: Harvard University Press, 1991).

5. Plato, *Gorgias*, trans. Walter Hamilton (Harmondsworth, UK: Penguin, 1960), esp. 482–83 and 489–90.

6. Aristotle, *Politics*, trans. Carnes Lord (Chicago: University of Chicago Press, 1984), 1288a17–32.

7. *NOMOS XLV: Secession and Self-Determination*, ed. Stephen Ma-cedo and Allen Buchanan (New York: New York University Press, 2003).

8. See, however, Joseph Carens, "Aliens and Citizens: The Case for Open Borders," *Review of Politics* 49(2): 251–73.

9. See Ronald Dworkin's account of strong and weak forms of discretion in the interpretation of law, *Taking Rights Seriously* (Cambridge, MA: Harvard University Press, 1977).

10. See especially Pettit, *Republicanism* and *A Theory of Freedom: From the Psychology to the Politics of Agency* (Cambridge, MA, and New York: Polity and Oxford University Press, 2001).

11. See Pettit, *Republicanism,* 52.

12. "As mankind improve, the number of doctrines which are no longer disputed or doubted will be constantly on the increase: and the well-being of mankind may almost be measured by the number and gravity of the truths which have reached the point of being uncontested" (*On Liberty,* ed. David Spitz [New York: Norton, 1975], 42).

13. MacKinnon's work as counsel for Muslim and Croat Bosnian women survivors of Serbian genocidal sexual atrocities led to the recognition by a U.S. court of rape as an act of genocide under international law. See *Kadic v. Karadzic,* 70 F.3d 232 (2d Cir. 1996), cert. denied 518 U.S. 1005 (1996). In August 2000, a New York jury awarded $745 million in damages to a group of these survivors.

PART I

THE INJUSTICE OF DOMINATION

ABOVE: *Elizabeth Eckford being cursed by Hazel Bryan in front of Central High School. Little Rock, Arkansas, September 4, 1957. (Photo by Will Counts)*

RIGHT: *Elizabeth Eckford at bus stop after having been refused entry to Central High. (Photo by Will Counts)*

1

INVISIBLE CITIZENS: POLITICAL EXCLUSION AND DOMINATION IN ARENDT AND ELLISON

DANIELLE ALLEN

This society is not likely to become free of racism, thus it is necessary for Negroes to free themselves by becoming their idea of what a free people should be.
  —Ralph Ellison, "Working Notes for Second Novel"[1]

1. DOMINATION VERSUS EXCLUSION

In the last fifteen years in the literature of political theory, domination has become a near synonym for injustice. Marxist notions of domination and exploitation as "institutionalized arrangement[s] for appropriating labor, goods, and services from a subordinate population"[2] have been generalized to address, broadly, social structures that prevent human flourishing. Thus, for Axel Honneth domination consists of "social relation[s] of damaged recognition" and for Iris Young of "institutional conditions which inhibit or prevent people from participating in determining their actions or the conditions of their actions."[3] For Young domination is a contributory factor in oppression, which in turn involves "systematic institutional processes which prevent some people from learning and using satisfying and expansive skills in socially recognized settings."[4] Honneth is explicit about the recent broadening of the term and that his own efforts are effected in part through readings of Marx: "Marx does not, therefore, view the unequal distribution of goods and burdens *as such* to be the underlying cause that triggers off the class struggle; rather, unequal distribution

29

only provides such a cause insofar as it results in *a one-sided destruction of the conditions for social identity.*"[5] Lurking in the idea of domination is, thanks to Marx, Hegel's treatment of the master-slave relationship. The idea involves metaphors of up and down and suggests that some people are "on top" and others are "under." In its Freudian variant, the term "domination" is taken to designate a necessary though lamentable aspect of the human condition.[6] All well and good, but where does exclusion fit in? How does it relate to domination? And what are contemporary political theorists to do with these terms?

More often than not, in the literature of political theory the two terms, domination and exclusion, blur into each other and are used indiscriminately. Nonetheless a pattern does emerge. At first blush, "exclusion" seems to be the simpler, and more limited, of the two terms. It regularly denotes formal disbarment from political institutions and rights, the effects of antidemocratic political practices and procedures (like a poll tax), and the development of hegemonies of opinion, and to all of these *qua* instruments of domination. Thus, for Honneth, the instruments of class domination include "methods of cultural exclusion and processes of institutional individualizing";[7] for Young, "exclusion of dependent persons from equal citizenship rights" is a form of marginalization, which is itself one of the faces of oppression;[8] and for Scott, "[a]s a formal matter, subordinate groups in these forms of domination have no political or civil rights."[9] In other words, for these theorists domination is the master term. Exclusion is one of the methods used to effect domination and typically pinpoints the role of legal structures in that process. Yet two more significant differences between domination and exclusion reveal the complexity even of the latter.

As I've already noted, the term "domination," like "exploitation," has gained currency thanks to class analysis. The term "exclusion" has gained its currency because of race, racism, and laws about citizenship.[10] As David Goldberg has argued, racist discourse is founded on exclusionary grammatical constructions such as: "white, not black"; "fair and beautiful, not ugly"; and "virtuous, not vicious."[11] These exclusionary terms have, in practice, been grafted onto institutions of domination like slavery and segregation, but their semantic force has abetted description of those institutions as forms not of domination but of exclusion. Slaves were "people excluded from citizenship"; segregation produced citizens who, despite their citizenship, were "excluded from assorted public places including the front of buses and polling booths"; and the history of the expansion of civil rights in the United States is regularly described as a movement from exclusion to inclusion. This is true regardless of whether the history is told by prominent academics from diverse disciplines (e.g., Rogers Smith, Kenneth Warren) or by public intellectuals who speak for one or another of the major political parties (e.g., Arthur Schlesinger, Abigail and Stephan Thernstrom).[12] Here is just one example of the contemporary truism about the move from exclusion to inclusion, this one from Schlesinger: "As for nonwhite peoples—those long in America whom the European newcomers overran and massacred, or those others hauled in against their will from Africa and Asia— deeply bred racism put them all, red Americans, black Americans, yellow Americans, brown Americans, *well outside the pale. . . .* In practice, America has been more open to some than others. But it is more open to all today than it was yesterday and is likely to be even more open tomorrow than today. *The steady movement of American life has been from exclusion to inclusion.*"[13] In contrast to domination and its vertical metaphors, exclusion involves metaphors of "lines" that can be crossed and horizontal notions of "inside and outside."

"Inclusion," rather than, say, "an end to domination," was in the late twentieth century the "norm often invoked by those seeking to widen and deepen democratic practices."[14] Here we arrive at the second point of contrast to "domination": "exclusion" circulates in policy circles far more widely than does "domination." The library catalog at my university lists papers from recent international policy conferences on "Exclusion, equality before the law, and non-discrimination" (a seminar organized by the Secretariat of the General of the Council of Europe in 1994) and on "Social Exclusion: a Major Challenge for Public Welfare Services" (a European Conference Report issued in 1996), but lists nothing similar for domination.[15] Indeed, in Iris Young's view, "inclusion," in contrast to "an end to domination," is now seen by activists as the strategically wiser term to use. This is because "in existing democracies there is more agreement on the norms of inclusive democracy than there is agreement on whether social and economic arrangements are just. . . . Accusations of exclusion or marginalization often send political leaders and movements scrambling to become more inclusive, or at least to appear to be."[16] Young suggests, in other words, that movements for inclusion will succeed where those aiming to end domination will not. Pragmatism would then dictate that political theorists who are interested in problems of injustice should focus on this term. But is this right? Is "exclusion" finally a more useful term than "domination" for thinking about problems of injustice within democracy and for reversing them?

We should look more closely at the stakes involved in the use of either term before we draw conclusions about relative conceptual merit or pragmatic value. In order to do this, I take a historical case study: the deployment of concepts of exclusion and domination by philosopher cum democratic theorist Hannah Arendt and novelist cum democratic theorist Ralph Ellison in arguments about how to reverse the injustice of segregation in the United States.[17] Hannah Arendt wrote a controversial article against school desegregation in the wake of the September 1957 struggles in Little Rock, Arkansas.[18] It is less well known that Ralph Ellison twice responded publicly to her argument, and she to his response in a private letter. Moreover, throughout the body of their political work, and also in respect to Little Rock, each thinker used the metaphor of "invisibility" to think through issues of injustice. Interestingly, each gave the idea of invisibility a different valence. For Arendt, it symbolized exclusion and established this as the relevant term for understanding and reversing injustice. For Ellison, invisibility set domination front and center. Thus, although the two theorists in fact had relatively similar *positive* accounts of political justice, they developed substantially different accounts of *injustice.* These in turn led to opposed proposals for how any citizenry can move from a today of injustice to a better tomorrow. An examination of their debate will usefully clarify the stakes of prioritizing either exclusion or domination. Such an examination follows in the body of the essay.

It is my hope that close study of the debate between Arendt and Ellison will do three things: (1) Such analysis should underscore that, paradoxically enough, a positive account of justice does not lead inexorably to some one and only account of injustice that is its necessary inverse; rather, to a degree, accounts of injustice and justice stand independent of one another and theorizing justice is never the whole of the matter. (2) Analysis of the debate should turn the attention of contemporary political theorists, in the United States in particular, back to the 1950s and the conceptual formation of that period; current practical political discourse is still working out terms and concepts constructed in that period. (3) My analysis makes a case for viewing the historical period in the United States prior to 1964 in terms of domination and not simply exclusion; such a shift of perspective should help deepen and widen contemporary democratic practice. This third strand of the argument lies at the forefront of the essay; the other two strands provide a contrapuntal background.

2. ARENDT AND ELLISON ON THE EFFORTS OF THEIR CONTEMPORARIES TO REVERSE SEGREGATION

In this section, I outline the conceptual core of the argument between Arendt and Ellison on how to describe and respond to their turbulent political world.

In September 1957, Little Rock, Arkansas, exploded over whether nine African American students who had been admitted to the previously whites-only Central High would in fact attend. Arendt wrote an article that fall, published two years later in *Dissent,* entitled "Reflections on Little Rock," in which she criticized the NAACP and the parents of the children for using political institutions like the courts and the public sphere generally to effect what she considered not a political program but self-interested social advancement.[19] Much affected by the news photographs of fifteen-year-old Elizabeth Eckford being menaced by Hazel Bryan Massery and a nasty mob as she, unaccompanied, tried to enter the school, Arendt argued further that the parents, in pursuing social advancement, were exploiting their children. "The girl obviously was asked to be a hero," Arendt wrote, "[which] is, something neither her absent father nor the equally absent representatives of the NAACP felt called upon to be."[20]

Arendt objected to any strategy that drew children, white or

black, into a political fray, but, when she accused the parents of a
lack of heroism, she also more specifically charged the desegregation movement with a failure to rise to the level of political action.[21] Her position depends heavily on her argument published
almost simultaneously in the *Human Condition* of 1958 that politics, properly understood, is a heroic activity; Achilles, the Greek
hero of the Trojan War, is her paradigmatic political actor.[22] In her
analysis, the parents mistook a "social issue" for a legitimate political battleground. This contention that school desegregation was
not an appropriate object of political action thus rested on her
strong distinctions among private, social, and political spheres. To
the private realm she assigned intimacy and activities like marriage, love, and parenting; in the social world we secure our economic livelihood and also, importantly, discriminate against others
by choosing friends who are like ourselves for ourselves and our
children. Finally, in the political realm, in her account, we secure
political rights, like the rights to vote and hold office and also private rights like the right to marry whom we please. The public
sphere is also the arena for conversations with strangers and for
epic action that brings glory to the actors.

Arendt's central concern in *The Human Condition* was to translate an epic approach to politics into a democratic context. Democratic political actors must construct a common world out of
difference and speak to one another *qua* men and not *qua* members of society (I replicate Arendt's gendered language here for
historiographic purposes).[23] And in a democracy, the ability to
"fight a full-fledged political battle"[24] consists of articulating "one's
own ideas about the possibilities of democratic government under
modern conditions," and of "propos[ing] a transformation of political institutions."[25] Most importantly, political action in a democracy is the opposite of what we do as members of society, which is
merely to "defend economic interests," ask for "due consideration
of vital interests,"[26] and function as "interest parties."[27] In Arendt's
view, only nonheroic economic and "vital" interests were at stake
in Little Rock.

In short, Arendt criticizes the actions of the African Americans
involved in Little Rock as failures of citizenship. Their "nonpolitical" actions in Little Rock caused a crisis that could be solved, she
argued, only by converting the public to new citizenly practices of

tact and restraint. If the democracy of the United States were to succeed in its post-1957 political world, developing enough trust and stability to preserve democracy, citizens would heroically have to surrender their concern with social issues. Only this genteel mode of citizenship, she believed, could convert long-standing divisions into the stuff of public debate and also preserve the public sphere.

Ellison disagreed with Arendt's account of Little Rock and democratic citizenship, and twice responded publicly to her article, offering a positive account of the citizenship in evidence in those tumultuous events. He also presented a different argument about how democratic citizenship needed to evolve given the facts of 1957 and prior history. Thus, in an interview with Robert Penn Warren he remarked: "I believe that one of the important clues to the meaning of [American Negro] experience lies in the idea, the *ideal* of sacrifice. Hannah Arendt's failure to grasp the importance of this ideal among Southern Negroes caused her to fly way off into left field in her 'Reflections on Little Rock.'" He continues:

> [S]he has absolutely no conception of what goes on in the minds of Negro parents when they send their kids through those lines of hostile people. Yet they are aware of the overtones of a rite of initiation which such events actually constitute for the child, a confrontation of the terrors of social life with all the mysteries stripped away. And in the outlook of many of these parents (who wish the problem didn't exist), the child is expected to face the terror and contain his fear and anger *precisely* because he is a Negro American. Thus he's required to master the inner tensions created by his racial situation, and if he gets hurt—then his is one more sacrifice.[28]

Ellison had developed the concepts of ritual and sacrifice at length in his 1952 novel *Invisible Man* and amplified his accounts of both terms throughout his life in his many essays; these concepts were the foundation for a provocative account of democracy.[29] But just how are ritual and sacrifice relevant to an analysis of Little Rock, or of democratic citizenship?

As a novelist, Ellison was obsessed with achieving the "imaginative integration of the total American [read: democratic] experience."[30] He desired to invent forms of narrative that could connect an individual life and its psychic struggles to the larger structures

of American democracy, and also reveal the meanings of that connection. He recognized that democracy puts its citizens under a
strange form of psychological pressure by building them up as sovereigns, and then regularly undermining any individual citizen's
experience of sovereignty.[31] Ellison explicated what it is like to be
an individual in a democratic world of strangers, where large-scale
events are supposed to arise somehow out of one's own consent
and yet never really do.[32] He recognized that every human life is
full of rituals that initiate people into the symbol world, ideals, and
political structure of her community.[33] These are the link between
any particular life and the larger political structure. The rituals
may be as overt as the requirement that students say the Pledge of
Allegiance in school every day or as little noticed as the adult habit
of asking a child upon a first meeting, "What's your name and how
old are you?"[34] (For Ellison that particular ritual at least partially
explains the modern concern with identity.) Similarly, the rituals
may be as obviously political as one's first trip to the polls, or they
may (wrongly) seem to be merely social, for instance getting
drunk legally at the age of twenty-one. But since the purpose of
rituals, Ellison argues, is to create, justify, and maintain particular
social arrangements, they are the foundation also of political structures, and an individual comes to know intimately central aspects
of the overall structure of his or her community by living through
them. Significantly, since every ritual is for Ellison also a form of
initiation, or reinitiation, children are not exempt.[35]

In the moment that Hazel and Elizabeth, two teenagers, met in
the public square, neither was inventing her form of behavior.
Each had already been frequently initiated into the requirements
of adult life in the South. In the Battle of Little Rock, they were
simply tested once more to see how well the lessons from the earlier rituals had stuck. Elizabeth knew the drill and was probably
lucky that she did. This is the force of Ellison's argument to Robert
Penn Warren that the parents of the Little Rock Nine understood
how integral to childhood are rituals initiating the child into the
symbol world and ideals of adults, and so also into adult politics.
Whereas Arendt tried to develop a political theory that could
protect children from politics, by transforming politics into an
epic arena that only full-grown warriors can enter, Ellison had a
more tragic vision: rituals to solidify social order inevitably involve

children in politics, however much one might wish the case were otherwise.

Of all the rituals to which Ellison attends in his novels and essays, sacrifice is preeminent. No democratic citizen, adult or child, escapes the necessity of losing out at some point from a public decision. Ellison writes thus about sacrifice in general: "It is our fate as human beings always to give up some good things for other good things, to throw off certain bad circumstances only to create others."[36] But he also realized that sacrifice is a special sort of problem in a democracy. Democracies are supposed to rest on consent and open up access to happiness for their citizens. In the dreamscape of democracy, for instance à la Rousseau, every citizen consents to every policy with glad enthusiasm. No one ever leaves the public arena at odds with the communal choice; no one would have to accept political loss nor live with the imposition of laws to which she has not consented. But that is a dream.

Ellison's ruminations on the problem of sacrifice ultimately yield the conclusion that a legitimate account of collective democratic action must begin by acknowledging that communal decisions inevitably benefit some members of a community at the expense of others, even in cases where the whole community generally benefits.[37] Since democracy claims to secure the good of all citizens, those people who benefit less than others from particular political decisions, but nonetheless accede to those decisions, preserve the stability of political institutions. Their sacrifice makes collective democratic action possible. Democracy is not a static end state that achieves the common good by assuring the same benefits or the same level of benefits to everyone, but rather a political practice by which the diverse negative effects of collective political action, and even of just decisions, can be distributed equally, and constantly redistributed over time, on the basis of consensual interactions.[38] As far as Ellison was concerned, only sufficiently robust forms of citizenship can give a polity the resources it needs to deal with the problem of sacrifice.

One of the great conceptual achievements of the protagonist of *Invisible Man* is to develop criteria for distinguishing legitimate from illegitimate forms of sacrifice, and also to outline a form of citizenship that helps citizens generate trust enough among themselves to manage sacrifice.[39] Sadly, I do not have space here to give a full account of those citizenly practices. For the present, I can say only that in Ellison's view, sacrifices must be voluntary, seen, honored, and reciprocated. When they are otherwise, sacrificing heroes have been replaced with dominated scapegoats. Here it is necessary, rather, to outline the conceptual bases of such a citizenship. Most importantly, recognition of the necessary fact of loss and disappointment in democratic politics vitiates any effort, such as Arendt's, to hold the social firmly separate from the political.[40] As citizens struggle over political questions, they will necessarily come to understand how political choices affect social experience. The site of sacrifice is between the social world—of custom and of mental, physical, and economic harm from other citizens—and the political world of institutions and practices for the sake of which one wants to master that harm. Thus, Ellison says to Warren of the African American parents behind the events at Little Rock: "We learned about forbearance and forgiveness in that same school, and about hope too. So today we sacrifice, as we sacrificed yesterday, *the pleasure of personal retaliation in the interest of the common good.*"[41] The initiation of citizens into public life entails pain and disappointments that, though generated in the public sphere, are experienced in the social and personal realms. No wonder, then, that Ellison, in powerful contrast to Arendt, so frequently uses the term "sociopolitical."

Because African American parents had, prior to 1957, long recognized the centrality of sacrifice to their experience of life in America, they found it necessary to cultivate in their children habits for dealing with the sacrifices that would come their way. They felt obliged, according to Ellison, to teach their children that the political and legal worlds are imbricated in a social context (sometimes of terror) that constrains the possibilities for action supposedly protected by law.[42] These parents simultaneously also taught their children that they would have to pay a social price for exercising the democratic political instrument provided to them by legal institutions, and that the use of the democratic political instrument and its preservation were worth that price. The ability to make such a sacrifice constituted, for Ellison, "the basic, implicit *heroism* of people who must live within a society without recognition, real status, *but who are involved in the ideals of that society* and who are trying to make their way, trying to determine their true position and their rightful position within it."[43] The sacrifices of African Americans living in a segregated polity were sufficiently extreme to constitute scapegoating in Ellison's terms rather than legitimate sacrifice, and yet, he argued, they nonetheless revealed a truth that applies to all democratic citizens: the political world cannot be entirely separated from our social world, and learning how to negotiate the losses one experiences at the hands of the public is fundamental to becoming a political actor, not only for minorities or those suffering political abuses, but for all citizens. The thrust of his argument is that the Black experience of living under Jim Crow is a metaphor for a basic democratic experience of having the majority make decisions with which one does not concur, and may even actively resent. The Jim Crow period, in this analysis, is not an aberration but fundamentally revealing of some of the most difficult problems to be faced by democratic peoples. In other words, Ellison is willing to treat dramatic events of injustice as something ordinary for the sake of reforming our vision of what ordinary politics is itself like. Citizenship is a tragic, not an epic, business.

For Ellison, then, in contrast to Arendt, the parents of the Little Rock Nine were (tragic) heroes. They were acting politically and even on Arendt's own terms, for as Ellison describes them they were illustrating ideas about how a democratic community might organize itself. They were providing rich lessons in citizenship by revealing the sacrifices citizens make for each other and the necessary connections between the social and the political.

On Ellison's reading of the events of September 1957, the figure of Elizabeth Eckford brought a new mode of citizenship before the public eye.[44] Her parents and those of the other children were enduring social abuse—the taunts and threats addressed to their children—and asking their children, many of whom had wanted to attend Central High over their objections, to endure too, in order to render functional a legal system that had recently banned the legal imposition of segregation on schools. They suffered the abuse of their children, a problem "they wish[ed] didn't exist," to help assure that the law worked. Elizabeth's solitary walk was one more sacrifice. In the face of disagreement, she sought forms of political action that might generate political friendship enough to secure a democratic legal system and convert the distrust arising from political disappointment into trust.

Which account of democracy and citizenship, Arendt's or Ellison's, is the more accurate analysis of the events at Central High and their political significance?

The story of Little Rock, briefly, is this. In the spring of 1957 the Little Rock school board formulated, and was required by courts to abide by, a plan for integrating Central High School the following September. Over the summer, many African American students applied for admission to Central, very often against their parents' wishes, and nine students were finally selected by school authorities. As the NAACP was readying the students, with extra academic training, to enter Central, Governor Faubus worked to pass new legislation reinstating segregation in the state's schools, and citizen groups organized against the projected opening of an integrated Central High. (Strangely, several other schools in Arkansas had been integrated in preceding years without incident.) On September 2, the day before school was to start, 250 National Guardsmen, under the supervision of the state of Arkansas, surrounded Central High on Faubus's orders. He announced on television that this was his response to warnings that car-loads of white supremacists were headed to Little Rock; he also announced that on the next day Central High School would be off-limits to black students and Horace Mann, the black school, would be off-limits to white students.

Central High sat empty on September 3, but the Little Rock school superintendent reasserted his local authority and, rescheduling the opening for the fourth, authorized proceeding with the integration plan. When the morning of the fourth arrived, so did large crowds, watching and waiting as the Guardsmen began to let a few white students through their ranks to the school. Then Elizabeth Eckford, the first black student, arrived. As the crowd surged around her with curses and cries that she be lynched—and radios reported "A Negro girl is being mobbed at Central High"—she walked the length of the mob to reach the school entrance.[45] She had seen the white students enter between the ranks of Guardsmen, but, when she also tried to pass through, the soldiers thrust their bayonets at her chest. She tried twice before turning and returning, passing again along the whole length of the crowd, to the bus stop, where she sat down. There, Benjamin Fine, a white reporter for the *New York Times,* sat down with her, putting his arm around her. With a white woman he tried to help Elizabeth escape, first by cab (the mob prevented this) and then at last by bus. This was the first event in what has come to be called "The Battle of Little Rock," where victory was determined, though the fighting not ended, by the arrival of Federal troops (as distinct from the Guardsmen) on September 24. "Sure, we're in Central. But how did we get in?" one of the students said on the twenty-fifth. "We got in, finally, because we were protected by paratroops. Some victory!"[46] This student regretted that the law had needed military enforcement and could not be enforced simply through the ordinary interaction of citizens.

Daisy Bates, president of the Arkansas State Conference of NAACP branches, gives an account of the events at Little Rock— and some of the negotiations of legal authority involved in them— that confirms Ellison's analysis of both the centrality of sacrifice to democratic politics and the close relationship between sacrifice and democratic legal authority.[47] On the afternoon of the third, the school superintendent called a meeting of leading African American citizens in Little Rock along with the children's parents and "instructed the parents *not* to accompany their children the next morning when they were scheduled to enter Central. 'If violence breaks out,' the Superintendent told them, 'it will be easier to protect the children if the adults aren't there.' "[48] The parents were extremely troubled by this declaration—Superintendent Blossom had not explained *how* the children would be protected —but they agreed. Bates was also worried by the instructions and, doing what she could to provide protection for the children while also following the superintendent's orders, she spent the night making phone calls: first, to a white minister to ask if he could round up colleagues to accompany the children in place of the parents; second, to the police to ask that they accompany the children as close to the school as Faubus's National Guardsmen would permit; third, to the parents to tell them not to send their children straight to school but rather to the ministers and police. Inadvertently, she overlooked contacting the Eckfords because they had no phone. In the morning, not knowing of the new arrangements,

the Eckfords simply followed the superintendent's instructions
and sent Elizabeth directly to school alone.

After being mobbed, Elizabeth slipped inside herself, remaining there wordless during all of the news reports in the following
days, and screaming at night in her dreams.[49] When she began to
talk again, she described the morning of September 4. Her focus is
on her parents:

> While I was pressing my black and white dress—I had made it to
> wear on the first day of school—my little brother turned on the TV
> set. They started telling about a large crowd gathered at the school.
> The man on TV said he wondered if we were going to show up that
> morning. Mother called from the kitchen, where she was fixing
> breakfast, "Turn that TV off!" She was so upset and worried. I
> wanted to comfort her, so I said, "Mother, don't worry."
>
> Dad was walking back and forth, from room to room, with a sad
> expression. He was chewing on his pipe and he had a cigar in his
> hand, but he didn't light either one. It would have been funny, only
> he was so nervous.
>
> Before I left home Mother called us into the living room. She said
> we should have a word of prayer. . . . Then I caught the bus and got
> off a block from the school. . . .
>
> Someone shouted, "Here she comes, get ready." I moved away
> from the crowd on the sidewalk and into the street. If the mob came
> at me, I could then cross back over so the guards could protect me.
> The crowd moved in closer and then began to follow me. . . . They
> moved closer and closer. Somebody started yelling, "Lynch her!
> Lynch her!" . . . Someone hollered, "Drag her over to this tree! Let's
> take care of the nigger."
>
> [Then Elizabeth walked to the school, could not get in, and re-
> turned to the bus stop where she was helped onto a bus.]
>
> I can't remember much about the bus ride, but the next thing I
> remember I was standing in front of the School for the Blind where
> Mother works. . . . Mother was standing at the window with her head
> bowed, but she must have sensed I was there because she turned
> around. She looked as if she had been crying, and I wanted to tell
> her I was all right. But I couldn't speak. She put her arms around
> me and I cried.[50]

Elizabeth's parents obeyed Superintendent Blossom's instructions not to accompany their daughter in order to support the rule of law and the institutions that were purportedly available to all citizens to obtain their democratic rights, and which claimed to offer all citizens equal protection. The result was psychological terror for them and for their daughter, which was endured for a future good that would benefit not only themselves but also the country as a whole. This constitutes sacrifice.

Those involved in events on the ground knew they were negotiating the sacrifices demanded by the rule of law, as their own words reveal. Indeed, an interesting exchange between Daisy Bates and the father of one of the children indicates the degree to which the superintendent's orders were being equated with the law of the land. On September 24, the night before the students were to reenter the school with the protection of the 101st Airborne Division, Daisy Bates went to the home of one of the students. She found an angry father, unwilling to let his daughter face the mobs again. When Bates, "in [her] most pleasant, friendliest voice, and trying to look at him instead of the gun, . . . said that the children were to be at my house by eight thirty the next morning, and that those were the instructions of Superintendent Blossom," the father answered, "I don't care if the President of the United States gave you those instructions! . . . I won't let Gloria go. She's faced two mobs and that's enough." Here was a father who explicitly viewed the sacrifices demanded of him and his daughter as originating from the demands of legal authority.[51]

These are the sacrifices Arendt did not see—one father pacing with pipe in mouth and cigar in hand, another ready to throw the legal system to the winds—when she chastised Elizabeth Eckford's parents and the "absent representatives of the NAACP" for allowing Elizabeth to go to Central High alone, and when she insisted that they were not acting politically. The invisibility of their sacrifice made the NAACP representatives seem "absent" when they were not. Their invisibility in turn ensured the invisibility of those whom they represented. Rushing around at midnight to find white ministers to accompany the children to school instead of their parents, they were unable to shed public light on their situation or on that of the children and parents. Indeed, in *Invisible Man,* invisibility regularly surrounds the experience of sacrifice without recognition or honor. Ellison, by invoking the idea of sacrifice in a discussion of Little Rock in his Robert Penn Warren interview, suggests that the source of this invisibility was not merely the failure of one theorist to see individual sacrifice, but, more broadly, the general absence from democratic practice of a language to comprehend sacrifice, or the losses and disappointments people accept for the sake of maintaining the communal agreements that constitute legality.

Both Arendt and Ellison, then, treat the Battle of Little Rock as an occasion to inquire how to develop habits of democratic citizenship for a passage beyond exclusion, domination, and acquiescence. But each theorist offers different suggestions for how to develop new habits for the interactions among strangers. For Arendt, citizens should focus on reforming political institutions, aiming to ensure their inclusiveness and maintaining public peace by defining some questions, which she calls social questions, as outside of politics. For Ellison, in contrast, the evolution of a new citizenship required addressing those aspects of democratic decision making that domination had hidden in order to shore itself up: the fact that public decisions inevitably distribute burdens unevenly, and the resentment, disappointment, and distrust that follow. Could diverse citizens, he asks throughout his writing, find ways to talk and act that could convert loss into a freely given gift to be reciprocated, and that could transform distrust into trust?

3. POLITICAL JUSTICE: PLURALITY, INTRICACY, AND FRIENDSHIP

Now I turn toward the precise roles played by the idea of exclusion and domination in Arendt's and Ellison's assessments of Little Rock and prescriptions for the future. Surprisingly, their starkly contrasting analyses arise from remarkably similar positive accounts of justice; as we shall see, Ellison and Arendt diverge only in how each decides to describe, analyze, and make metaphors for injustice.

Both Arendt and Ellison argued for a politics that accepts the perpetual existence of difference and disagreement. Moreover, each thematized the attempt to ignore or eradicate plurality, and related abuses, in terms of invisibility and darkness. Ellison's *Invisible Man* of 1952 and Arendt's *Men in Dark Times*, written between

1956 and 1968, both take up the question of how radical disagreement affects politics; invisibility is key to both analyses, as though they were thinking together, in the same figure.

It seems jarring at first to claim that *Men in Dark Times,* which is about anti-Semitism and the approach of the Holocaust, and *Invisible Man,* which is about racism, segregation, and the reign of violence in the South in the first half of the twentieth century, are mainly about disagreement, but the texts support my claim. Arendt's conviction that "human plurality" is "the basic condition of both action and speech,"[52] and therefore of politics, reappears in the final paragraph of the opening essay of *Men in Dark Times* when she warns against modernity's fascination with the possibility of finding "one will" or perfect agreement for a people:

> It might have the result that all men would suddenly unite in a single opinion, so that out of many opinions one would emerge, as though not men in their infinite plurality but man in the singular, one species and its exemplars, were to inhabit the earth. Should that happen, the world, which can form only in the interspaces between men in all their variety, would vanish altogether.[53]

Similarly, Ellison's most explicit conclusion[54] in *Invisible Man* is as follows:

> Whence all this passion toward conformity anyway? Diversity is the word. Let man keep his many parts and you'll have no tyrant states. America is woven of many strands; I would recognize them and let it so remain. It's "winner take nothing"; that is the great truth of our country or of any country. Life is to be lived, not controlled; and humanity is won by continuing to play in the face of certain defeat. Our fate is to become one, and yet many—this is not prophecy, but description.[55]

But, Ellison often points out, as different perspectives fill the public sphere we always choose among them by making laws and installing politicians who enact before us representations of who we are as a citizenry. Our speech and action in the public sphere thus return to us as policies that make us feel the force of our disagreements.

But how can either Arendt or Ellison move so easily from considering the stark injustices of twentieth-century political life to casual comments about prosaic disagreements? As we saw in the preceding section, Ellison argued for a structural similarity between the world's singularly dramatic acts of injustice and the ordinary forcefulness of the law in our daily political lives.[56] He uses Jim Crow and, in *Invisible Man*, events like riots to explain how existentially and politically bracing are ordinary citizens' everyday experiences of loss and sacrifice. Segregation and riots (on the order of those that followed the beating of Rodney King) allegorically capture an ordinary part of democratic life. Arendt, too, in the above passage argues for a homology between extreme injustice and prosaic abuses of plurality. But how can a fair and legal majority decision, with which one disagrees, be justly compared to Jim Crow or Nazism? Neither writer means to challenge the extremity of the twentieth century's great injustices; each merely insists that politics is always a struggle of wills and that, sadly, one will usually wins over another. In the psychological literature, domination is similarly understood as a fact of ordinary life, an unfortunate outcome of a fundamental struggle for recognition. As Jessica Benjamin puts it:

> [D]omination originates in a transformation of the relationship between self and other. Briefly stated, domination and submission result from a breakdown of the necessary tension between self-assertion and mutual recognition that allows self and other to meet as sovereign equals.[57]

The struggle for recognition sometimes results in a staggering injustice; sometimes it is stabilized through the justice of majority vote. Too rarely does it resolve into consensus.

The question for both Arendt and Ellison, then, is how a politics of plurality and diversity or, I would prefer, of intricacy, can ensure that the winner of an argument "takes nothing," to quote Ellison, especially when some people remain unconvinced by the outcome of debate. Why add the term "intricacy" to "plurality" and "diversity"? All members of a citizenry are tied to one another in a complicated web of benefits and losses gained from and suffered for others.[58] Cigarette smokers who keep their smoke outdoors have lost something from which many others gain. Bourgeois casual drug users are not without responsibility for the massive drug economy that affects so much of our public life—through crime and systems of penalty. The Federal Reserve's policy of maneuvering interest rates to control the level of unemployment (including sometimes with the goal of increasing it) ties those who profit from interest rate speculation to those who suffer the experience of marginal employment, and both groups are tied to those citizens who benefit from an economy that seems to them by and large stable. Iris Young argues that "the scope of the polity . . . ought to include all those who dwell together within structural relations generated by processes of interaction, exchange, and movement that creates unavoidable conditions of action for all of them."[59] The idea of intricacy expands on her analysis by suggesting that the structural relations that connect citizens generate an economy of benefits and burdens that regularly make citizens one another's benefactors and beneficiaries. The practical effects on a democratic polity of the inevitable fact of plurality is that all citizens are, by definition, philanthropists to one another.[60] The question to be faced, then, in a politics of intricacy is how an economy of benefits and burdens can function such that winners "take nothing." The problem is not how to be a good loser in the political process, but how to be a good winner. Or, to put the problem in the terms of recognition theory, it is how to achieve "the reciprocity of self and other, the balance of assertion and recognition. While this may seem obvious, it has not been easy to conceptualize psychological development in terms of mutuality. Most theories of development have emphasized the goal of autonomy more than relatedness to others."[61] In my account of political intricacy, however, our relatedness to others is not a goal but a fact. The challenge is to see and describe those relations and to respond justly to them.

How can disagreements be handled such that winners take nothing? Arendt and Ellison both believe that ordinary human experience already provides some guidance. We are not always "locked" in the struggle for recognition with the others in our lives and succeed best of all in dealing with it in good friendships. Arendt, again in *Men in Dark Times*, admires Lessing because "any doctrine that in principle barred the possibility of friendship between two human beings would have been rejected by his untrammeled and unerring conscience."[62] And in *The Human Condition* she writes: "What love is in its own, narrowly circumscribed sphere, respect is in the larger domain of human affairs. Respect . . . is a *kind of 'friendship'* without intimacy and without closeness."[63] In good friendships friends learn to avoid the master-slave relationship not because of their emotional attachments but because they develop highly refined forms of reciprocity, habits, that allow them to circulate the benefits and burdens of their relationships equitably. These habits of friendship, as distinct from its emotions, should be both a guide and an aspiration in political interaction.[64] Ellison never settled on a single term to describe the analogy he wished to draw between justice and friendship. Whereas his protagonist seeks an "unnamed something" like brotherhood[65] and "*that something* for which the theory of Brotherhood had given me no name,"[66] Ellison in his own voice argued: "The way home we seek is that condition of man's being at home in the world, which is called love, and which we term democracy."[67] But he was very specific about the practice by which this condition might be achieved. Democratic citizens needed habits of "antagonistic cooperation."[68] Clearly, this phrase would be equally at home in an Arendtian, as in the Ellisonian, context.[69]

I discuss at length the content of this political friendship in my forthcoming book, *Talking to Strangers: On Little Rock and Political Friendship*.[70] Here it suffices that I have pointed to the remarkable parallel in Arendt and Ellison's positive accounts of political justice. To understand the differences in their diagnoses and prescriptions for Little Rock, we must turn to their characterizations of injustice. Here, at last, exclusion and domination are the central terms.

4. POLITICAL INJUSTICE: INVISIBILITY

For both Arendt and Ellison, unjust collective decisions that undo the possibility of political friendship hurtle the world into "dark times" and cast some of its inhabitants into invisibility, the central metaphor each uses for figuring injustice.

What, then, is this invisibility? Here I want to examine two long sets of excerpts to establish the similarities in Arendt's and Ellison's answers. In *Men in Dark Times*, Arendt writes:

1. "Everywhere . . . the public realm has lost the power of illumination which was originally part of its very nature" (p. 4).
2. "For what was wrong and what no dialogue and no independent thinking ever could right, was the world— namely, the thing that arises between people and in which everything that individuals carry with them innately can become visible and audible" (p. 10).
3. "History knows many periods of dark times in which the public realm has been obscured and the world become so dubious that people have ceased to ask any more of politics than that it show due consideration for their vital interests and personal liberty" (p. 11).
4. "[Then] a brotherly attachment to other human beings . . . springs from hatred of the world in which men are treated 'inhumanly.' For our purposes, . . . it is important that humanity manifests itself in such brotherhood most frequently in 'dark times.' This kind of humanity actually becomes inevitable when the times become so extremely dark for certain groups of people that it is no longer up to them, their insight or choice, to withdraw from the world" (p. 13).
5. "But it is true that in 'dark times' the warmth which is the pariahs' substitute for light exerts a great fascination upon all those who are so ashamed of the world as it is that they would like to take refuge in invisibility. And in invisibility, in that obscurity in which man who is himself hidden need no longer see the visible world either, only the warmth and fraternity of closely packed human beings can compensate for the weird irreality that human relationships assume wherever they develop in absolute worldlessness, unrelated to a world common to all people" (p. 16).
6. " . . . wherever a friendship succeeded at that time . . . a bit of humanness in the world become inhuman [was] achieved" (p. 23).

When people are expelled from or withdraw from politics, they settle into conditions of weird unreality. Without a place to be seen and heard and therefore be able to act, pariahs and also those who are attracted to escaping from a polity they abhor turn to fraternity, says Arendt, and forsake politics.

Ellison too engages the themes of the loss of reality and of the world, the turn to fraternity, the need for action, and the absurdity of invisibility. The protagonist of *Invisible Man* says this:

1. "I am an invisible man. . . . I learned in time though that it is possible to carry on a fight against them without their realizing it. . . . My hole is warm and full of light. Yes, *full* of light. . . . And I love light. Perhaps you'll think it strange that an invisible man should need light, desire light, love light. But maybe it is exactly because I *am* invisible. Light confirms my reality, gives birth to my form . . . To be unaware of one's form is to live a death." (*Prologue.*)

2. "I could feel the words forming themselves, slowly falling into place. . . . [I said to the crowd:]'I feel your eyes upon me. I hear the pulse of your breathing. And now, at this moment, with your black and white eyes upon me, I feel . . . I feel . . . I feel suddenly that I have become *more human.* . . . Not that I have become a man, for I was born a man. But that I am more human. I feel strong, I feel able to get things done! My true family! My true people! My true country! I am a new citizen in the country of your vision, a native of your fraternal land. I feel that here tonight, in this old arena, the new is being born and the vital old revived.'" (*From the scene of the protagonist's first official speech on behalf of the Brotherhood party.*)

3. "Now I was painfully aware of other men dressed like the boys, and of girls in dark exotic-colored stockings, their costumes surreal variations of downtown styles." (*His reaction after the death of Tod Clifton.*)

4. "All life seen from the hole of invisibility is absurd." (*Epilogue.*)

Despite the similarity of the material on invisibility that I have just quoted, one already ought to have begun to sense a critical difference in the two approaches to invisibility. The very titles of their books suggest a mirror inversion of perspective: *Invisible Man/Men in Dark Times.* In one case, people are unseeable, even in times of full light; in the other case, seeable men have retreated or been pushed into the dark. Nothing less is at stake in this inversion than a diagnosis of the past. For Arendt, invisibility is primarily a trope for exclusion; for Ellison, it represents mainly domination. Their two contradictory visions of the future of citizenship grow out of the orientation of the one toward remedying exclusion, and of the other toward undoing domination. Let us look, then, where Arendt and Ellison part company on invisibility.

Both Arendt and Ellison describe invisibility and darkness as phenomena that arise within the political sphere. Arendt argues that "the presence of others who see what we see and hear what we hear assures us of the reality of the world and ourselves."[71] Collective decisions thus have the power to establish "reality," and Arendt insists that the expulsion of Jews from the German political arena in the first half of the twentieth century, as well as the retreat of some non-Jewish, non-Communist Germans from it, be seen as the result of the communicative power to establish reality. "Flight from the world in dark times of impotence can always be justified as long as reality is not ignored, but is constantly acknowledged as the thing that must be escaped. . . . [People who flee] must remember that they are constantly on the run, and that the world's reality is actually expressed by their escape."[72] Ellison likewise makes the argument that the political exclusion of African Americans in the post-Reconstruction period involved brutalization and sacrifice "in the name of a plan";[73] the Invisible Man rebels against what he calls "a swindle, an obscene swindle!" perpetrated by men who "had set themselves up to describe the world."[74] Such men were, he says, "lost in a dream world." And he continues: "But didn't [*they*] control that dream world—which, alas, is only too real! —and didn't [*they*] rule me out of it?"[75] "Realities" rule out and expel. Collective agreements entail loss; in their most extreme form, they bring dark times and invisibility by hiding from view, in more or less violent forms, that which threatens the collectively chosen "reality" or "the plan."

Arendt, however, treats invisibility as a condition that, although it arises *within* politics, nonetheless then sets invisible people *outside* of politics, or the common world that produced their invisibility, whether or not they have ended up outside politics because they were pushed out or because they left. "Inner emigration" signified that "on the one hand that there were persons inside Germany who behaved as if they no longer belonged to the country, who felt like emigrants; and on the other hand . . . that they had not in reality emigrated, but had withdrawn to an interior realm, into the invisibility of thinking and feeling."[76] The text of "Men in Dark Times" was originally a speech given at Arendt's acceptance, in Germany, of the Lessing prize. And here, in accepting "inner emigration" as a real form of invisibility, she holds out an offer of reconciliation to those non-Jewish Germans who had retreated from politics and claimed not to be involved in their country's doings. She is taking their withdrawal seriously and with it their claim to have been outside politics. As a result, the "inner emigration" can be treated analogously to the invisibility of the enslaved and disfranchised, the latter being the groups she most regularly describes as invisible.[77]

In *On Revolution*, Arendt explicitly sets "invisible people" outside of politics when she deals with John Adams's discussion of the political experience of the poor. She quotes Adams as writing:

> The poor man's conscience is clear; yet he is ashamed. . . . He feels himself out of the sight of others, groping in the dark. Mankind takes no notice of him. He rambles and wanders unheeded. In the midst of a crowd, at church, in the market . . . he is in as much obscurity as he would be in a garret or a cellar. He is not disapproved, censured, or reproached; *he is only not seen*. To be wholly overlooked, and to know it, are intolerable.[78]

Arendt uses the opportunity provided by Adams's remarks to argue for a very different formulation of invisibility's significance to the democratic founding. She writes:

> [T]he fact that John Adams was so deeply moved by [obscurity], more deeply than he or anyone else of the Founding Fathers was ever moved by sheer misery, must strike us as very strange indeed when we remind ourselves that the absence of the social question from the American scene was, after all, quite deceptive and that abject and degrading misery was present everywhere in the form of slavery and Negro labor. . . . From this, we can only conclude that the institution of slavery carries an obscurity even blacker than the obscurity of poverty; the slave, not the poor man, was "wholly overlooked."[79]

For Adams, citizens became invisible *within* the body politic; rights to vote and hold office did not ensure political influence or agency. In responding to his argument, Arendt shifts the condition of obscurity and political poverty from the citizen to the slave and, in so doing, moves the analysis of invisibility beyond the political realm. Mundane, everyday disagreements and legal structures are no longer at issue, only those that explicitly disfranchise.

Arendt is surely correct to argue that slavery and disfranchisement constitute an extreme violation of the recognition due to members of a polity from one another, but her transfer of the language of invisibility from poverty to slavery deprives democrats of an important tool to assess the degree to which democracies are fulfilling their promise. There is an implicit argument built into her approach to invisibility that only laws of constitutional stature —laws that secure citizenship, voting rights, and rights to hold office—are capable of producing invisibility. Indeed, in the *Human Condition,* she was boldly unconcerned for everyday law, or statutory law, as distinct from constitutional law, and adopted what she wrongly considered the position of the Greeks. They, she says, "did not count legislating among the political activities."[80] Instead, it was a form of *poiesis,* or making, and thus alien to the sphere of action proper to politics as she described it. By ignoring the question of statutory law, Arendt avoids facing the truly difficult question of democratic diversity: How should we deal with law's necessary forcefulness? She quite tellingly argued that public space "is constituted by [men's] acting together and [public space] then fills of its own accord with the events and stories that develop into history."[81] In her account, differences of perspective somehow, on their own, develop and resolve themselves into a single history. But even her dispute with Ellison had policy implications. Political action reaches its conclusion not only when narratives of how we should organize our common world suggest our need for new laws, but also when those new laws are tested to see what sort of new common world they in fact bring into being. This working through of law's forcefulness is the central project of democratic citizenship.[82]

Once Arendt has argued that a condition, invisibility, which arises from politics, actually removes people from the political arena, it is no surprise that she argues that invisible people lose

not only the context but also the ability for political action. Although "the world's reality is actually expressed by [people's] escape [into invisibility]," she argues, "we cannot fail to see the
limited political relevance of such an existence, even if it is sustained in purity. Its limits are inherent in the fact that strength and
power are not the same; that power arises only where people act
together, but not where people grow stronger as individuals."[83]
This alone, she argues, are they able to do in conditions of invisibility, and political skills atrophy in conditions of invisibility:

> Humanity in the form of fraternity invariably appears historically
> among persecuted peoples and enslaved groups. . . . This kind of
> humanity is the great privilege of the pariah peoples; it is the advan-
> tage that the pariahs of this world always and in all circumstances
> can have over others. The privilege is dearly bought; it is often ac-
> companied by so radical a loss of the world, so fearful an atrophy of
> all the organs with which we respond to it—starting with the com-
> mon sense with which we orient ourselves in a world common to
> ourselves and others and going on to the sense of beauty, or taste,
> with which we love the world—that in extreme cases, in which pari-
> ahdom has persisted for centuries, we can speak of real worldless-
> ness. And worldlessness, alas, is always a form of barbarism.[84]

Worldlessness is a condition in which citizens have forgotten
how to act politically and "men have become entirely private, that
is, they have been deprived of seeing and hearing others, of being
seen and being heard by them. They are all imprisoned in the subjectivity of their own singular experience, which does not cease to
be singular if the same experience is multiplied innumerable
times."[85] People trapped in worldlessness, she argues, are unable
to move from articulations of subjective social desires to visions of
the future relevant to a whole society. Nor can they muster an
"openness" to worldy discussions as is necessary for political action. Arendt here converts her account of invisibility into a theoretical justification for distinguishing people who know well how
to act politically from those who know only, because of political exclusion, how to act socially. This theoretical substructure underlies
her argument in "Reflections on Little Rock" that "[o]ppressed
minorities were never the best judges on the order of priorities in
such matters and there are many instances when they preferred to

fight for social opportunity rather than for basic human or political rights."[86]

In using invisibility to signify exclusion, Arendt develops an account of political injustice in which those who perpetrate injustice can nonetheless have, among themselves, relatively healthy and just forms of political practice. On this exclusion-based analysis, under segregation, some people lived inside an essentially healthy political sphere although others lived outside it; to understand the nature of the public realm, one had only to look at the activities of those who are "within the pale" of the people; the habits of the invisible were not part of citizenship. Undoing injustice thus understood means bringing the invisible into the public sphere, and this was and still is taken to mean into practices of citizenship that are already up and running and presumed to be reasonably decent. Those who have been outside must be educated into the habits of citizenship developed by those inside. An inclusive democratic citizenship thus involves two projects, in Arendt's view: first, an effort to make political institutions fully inclusive; and second, an attempt to educate minorities to convert their fraternity within the group into the stuff of a broader citizenship already developed by those within the political realm. Arendt's essay, "Reflections on Little Rock," itself offers minorities this education (hence its admonitory tone), and so serves as an example of the democratic citizenship she advocated. In particular, such an education would teach citizens about what does and does not count as political, and minorities would learn how not to take their group identities into the public sphere, reserving the experience of identity, and so of fraternity, for the social realm. Arendt's use of the metaphor of invisibility is in these ways connected to what she prescribed for Little Rock and the rest of the segregated United States (more than just the South) in 1957.

What about Ellison, and his use of invisibility? Ellison had, in fact, developed the metaphor in an entirely different direction. Whereas Arendt's invisible people are excluded from politics, Ellison's contribute to it. Whereas her invisible citizens are outside of the political realm, his are dominated within it. Moreover, the habits of citizenship within this polity are not healthy; and, since the actions of the invisible as well as the visible constitute a crucial part of citizenship, the political order in fact rests on the basis of two complementary, equally perverted, forms of citizenship. The citizenship of the dominators is workable only because those whom they dominate have practices and habits, a citizenship if you will, of acquiescence.[87] Nor does the story end here.

James Scott has analyzed patterns of domination and resistance and developed terminology that will be useful. He uses the phrase "public transcript" to refer to the behavioral norms that establish the publicly acknowledged habits that hold together an oppressive social structure. But, as he shows, in contexts of domination, there are also always two hidden transcripts, one for the dominant and one for the subordinate group.

> Virtually all ordinarily observed relations between dominant and subordinate represent the encounter of the *public* transcript of the dominant with the *public* transcript of the subordinate. . . . Eventually we will want to know how the *hidden* transcripts of various actors are formed, the conditions under which they do or do not find public expression, and what relation they bear to the public transcript. . . . A second and vital aspect of the hidden transcript that has not been sufficiently emphasized is that it does not contain only speech acts but a whole range of practices. Thus, for many peasants, activities such as poaching, pilfering, clandestine tax evasion, and intentionally sloppy work for landlords are part and parcel of the hidden transcript. For dominant elites, hidden-transcript practices might include clandestine luxury and privilege, surreptitious use of hired thugs, bribery, and tampering with land titles.[88]

In Ellison's analysis, then, the stability of the U.S. political world prior to 1957 depended on two complementary types of citizenship: habits of domination for first-class citizens, and of acquiescence for second-class citizens. Each type of citizenship involved practices and habits that were recorded in the "public transcript," but each also entailed practices belonging to a "private transcript." The two types of citizenship so constituted were both highly malformed in being distant from those ideal practices of citizenship that can sustain true democracy. In Ellison's view, the project of undoing the domination of the invisible would require not educating them into the citizenly habits of the dominators, which were themselves malformed, but rather reforming everyone's habits of citizenship. Out of the two distorted forms of citizenship, a new citizenship would emerge open to and shared by all.

Ellison's analysis is conveyed in narrative. His protagonist's life story begins when he overhears his grandfather's last words: "Son, after I'm gone I want you to keep up the good fight. I never told you, but our life is a war and I have been a traitor all my born days, a spy in the enemy's country ever since I give up my gun back in the Reconstruction. Live with your head in the lion's mouth. I want you to overcome 'em with yeses, undermine 'em with grins, agree 'em to death and destruction, let 'em swoller you till they vomit or bust wide open. . . . Learn it to the young 'uns."[89] Even the invisible never leave, and the position of invisibility is not, for Ellison, one of "inner emigration" but one of "being a spy in the enemy's country," always actively engaged with its politics even if no one is noticing. But what does it mean to "agree 'em to death and destruction"? Or to be swallowed in such a way that the swallowers "bust wide open"? These words torment the Invisible Man throughout the whole of his odyssey and return in the epilogue, when he thinks he is finally beginning to understand them:

> I'm still plagued by his deathbed advice. . . . Could he have meant—
> hell, he *must* have meant the principle, that we were to affirm the
> principle on which the country was built and not the men, or at
> least not the men who did the violence. Did he mean say "yes" be-
> cause he knew the principle was greater than the men? . . . Or did
> he mean that we had to take responsibility for all of it, for the men
> as well as the principle, because we were the heirs who must use the
> principle because no other fitted our needs? . . . Or was it, did he
> mean that we should affirm the principle because we, through no
> fault of our own, were linked to all the others in the loud, clamor-
> ing, semi-visible world? . . . "Agree 'em to death and destruction,"
> grandfather had advised. Hell, weren't they their own death and
> their own destruction except as the principle lived in them and in
> us? And here's the cream of the joke: Weren't we *part of them* as well
> as apart from them and subject to die when they died?[90]

The Invisible Man deliberates (democratically arguing with himself) on how best to fulfill his commitment to democracy. Can he affirm democratic principles while harboring hate in his heart for

particular people? Or does citizenship inevitably implicate our attitudes toward strangers? Do we fail as citizens if we hate other citizens? What is required of our interactions with strangers, given
that "through no fault of our own, [we are] linked to all the others
in the loud, clamoring, semi-visible world"? In weighing his democratic responsibilities, he comes to a breakthrough:

> Was it that we of all, we, most of all, had to affirm the principle, *the
> plan in whose name we had been brutalized and sacrificed*—not because
> we would always be weak nor because we were afraid or opportunist,
> but *because we were older than they in the sense of what it took to live in the
> world with others* and because they had exhausted in us, some—not
> much, but some—of the human greed and smallness, yes, and the
> fear and superstition that had kept them running?[91]

Something in the African American experience of sacrifice, he argues, has brought extra knowledge about the nature of democracy
—"we were older than they in the sense of what it took to live in
the world with others." This knowledge could be the basis of a new
approach to citizenship. Back, then, to the grandfather's riddle.

"Agree 'em to death and destruction," the old man had said. Be
"spies in the enemy's country." The Invisible Man's commitment
to brotherhood seems to militate against espionage or duplicity,
but this depends on how one plots the geography of the enemy's
country and describes the nature of the injustice that characterizes
it. Take the segregated South as an example. If exclusion is the
basic injustice perpetrated by segregation, the segregating regime
is a fundamentally sound political order but for the unfortunate exclusion of black people. Then the charge that one should
"agree 'em [those who are included in the public sphere] to death
and destruction" seems an injunction to destroy a fundamentally
healthy public sphere, and a refusal of brotherhood. If, however,
one sees that segregationist regime in terms of domination, as Ellison did, the matter is otherwise. The dominated are inside the political sphere already ("Weren't we *part of them* as well as apart from
them?"), with its two complementary forms of citizenship: one for
the dominators and one for the dominated. The political cultures
and forms of citizenship belonging to both groups are diseased.
The target of the covert action is, therefore, not a fundamentally
healthy order but rather a corruption within a failing polity. To

"agree 'em [segregationists] to death and destruction" is to kill off the segregationist within any given citizen, in order to allow that citizen to be reborn as a full democrat.

But how on earth is "agreeing" supposed to bring about the sort of destruction that is really a transformation? The grandfather's sense of the subversive power of apparent agreement is traditional in African American culture: the paradox of agreeing to death invokes a characteristic trickster strategy. How does it work? First, the grandfather knows that his riddling counsel suits the U.S. enlightenment political system, threatened as it is by its paradoxical racist sophistry. The way to engage the issue of racism in the United States is to begin by agreeing to the rights of humanity; this way leads to cultural self-contradictions and so, in the ideal, to political transformation. But the grandfather's second insight is more subtle. He realizes that those who agree, in the face of violence and domination, cast aggressive acts into the starkest relief by allowing them to expend their full force. Those who are agreeable in this way show up violent citizens for what they are, and force witnesses to the spectacle to make a choice about whether to embrace or disavow the violence. This was the effect of the Elizabeth Eckford photograph, and Ellison saw the techniques of activists like Martin Luther King, Jr., who "became overtly political through the agency of passive resistance" as serving precisely this purpose.[92]

Here it is crucial to understand, as Ellison did, that the modes of citizenship of the dominators and the dominated are not comprehensively diseased; each also retains some healthy elements.[93] For instance, something in the African American experience of sacrifice, the Invisible Man argues, has brought extra knowledge about the nature of democracy. The "agree" in the phrase "agree 'em to death and destruction" stands in for an instruction to the Invisible Man to overemphasize the fundamentally healthy elements of the citizenship of subordination—the ability to agree, to sacrifice, to bear burdens in order to force contradictions in the citizenship of the dominated, until this citizenship caves in upon the rottenness of its inherent ills. From Ellison's perspective, the central question for an effort to craft new citizenly techniques, then, is how to integrate into one citizenship the healthy political habits of both the dominators and the dominated. Such an integration—and, importantly, it is integration or blending, not assimilation—is the response to injustice that he advocates. It heals by destroying and destroys by healing. The effort to "agree 'em to death and destruction" should heal those who suffer from deeply embedded habits of injustice—both the dominators and the dominated—by letting their diseased habits kill themselves off.

Ellison's belief in the possibility of killing off malformed practices of citizenship by overemphasizing their healthy components rests on complicated ideas about the relationship between psychology and politics, which I cannot explore here. For the time being, the best way to explain Ellison's suggestion that the healthy elements of malformed modes of citizenship can be used as political weapons is to consider again the epigraph to this essay: "This society is not likely to become free of racism, thus it is necessary for Negroes to free themselves by becoming their idea of what a free people should be." The remark underscores the fact that even the dominated have forms of citizenship that contribute to the stability of the polity; if they change their own habits, the structure of the polity will be obliged to shift around them as a functional necessity. Second, the remark admonishes (all of us) that only citizens who recognize that domination breeds forms of citizenship suitable to it can undo its legacy and develop alternative habits for interacting with strangers that befit freedom and mutuality. As Elizabeth Eckford knew, citizens must have new habits to slip into if they are not to revert to yesterday's patterns. The invisible can exercise their own political agency precisely by converting the wisdom derived from their experience into the material from which to refashion the meaning of citizenship for everyone. All democratic citizens possess the agency of inventiveness.

The time has come for some conclusions about the conceptual and pragmatic consequences of prioritizing exclusion, on the one hand, or domination, on the other, at least as those consequences are visible in the Arendt-Ellison debate about desegregation. As the terms are cashed out in their debate, each has the following consequences:

The term "exclusion" (1) works against attending to the agency of the dominated; if anything, it reduces their agency; (2) implies that the citizenly habits of people who are inside the public sphere are fundamentally healthy; and (3) encourages, as the best way to deal with a past of injustice, prescription of a policy of education, wherein those who have been excluded must be educated in the healthy habits that have been developed within the political sphere and must assimilate those habits.

In contrast, the term "domination" (1) insists, paradoxically, on the agency of the dominated both in their own submission and in resistance to that domination; (2) insists that both the dominators and the dominated have citizenly habits that are crucial to maintaining the stability of the polity; that both of these sets of habits are fundamentally corrupted and unsatisfactory; and that each of these forms of citizenship does have healthy elements that could be instructive for developing a more fully democratic form of citizenship that would be open to and shared by all; and (3) encourages, as the best way to deal with a past of injustice, prescription of a policy of imagination, wherein both those who have dominated and those who have been dominated must begin to envisage and act out a new idea of "a free people" that in no way relies on domination to stabilize itself. The hope is that the result of such an approach would undo and bury as far as possible the terms of domination, rather than reversing them.

In my view, in regard to Little Rock, Ellison, and not Arendt, was right about how to move from a today of injustice to a tomorrow of freedom, mutuality, and broadened democracy. It takes not assimilation and mere inclusion of the dominated in political systems but, indeed, the development of truly democratic techniques of citizenship for both the former dominators and the formerly dominated.[94]

I would like, in closing, to initiate discussion of what these new techniques might be if we were to follow Ellison's suggestions.

5. Epilogue: Democratic Techniques of Citizenship

"This society is not likely to become free of racism, thus it is necessary for Negroes to free themselves by becoming their idea of what a *free people* should be."[95] For Ellison, new techniques of citizenship would require revisiting, in particular, ideas of "freedom" and of "peoplehood." The project of his novel, *Invisible Man*, is arguably to rethink the meaning of freedom, and he takes up the same task frequently in his essays. For the present, however, I leave this term aside and turn to a subject less frequently discussed: How *should* democratic citizens imagine "the people" of which they are a part?[96]

Out of many, a democratic people should become one, or so many citizens of the United States firmly believe. I quote Schlesinger's *Disuniting of America* again as a recent example of an important commentator who has taken the metaphor of "oneness" as a proper description of the central aspirations of a democratic people. In 1992, Schlesinger argued that the turn toward ethnicity of the 1970s and 1980s was gutting the old American ideal of the melting pot, wherein all citizens believed themselves to be a part of "one people." He tells a simple fable of historical decline: before World War II, we were "one people"; now no longer one, we are in danger of losing our remaining unity to balkanization. To fix this, he argues, we must restore our commitment to being "one people" and to oneness, understood as "assimilation." But he is hopeful: "The vigorous sense of national identity accounts for our relative success in converting Crèvecoeur's 'promiscuous breed' into one people and thereby making a multiethnic society work . . . the historic forces driving toward 'one people' have not lost their power."

The briefest glance at the photograph that provoked both Arendt and Ellison to reflect on how the citizens of the United States could move beyond their past of injustice instantly reveals the limits of the metaphor of "oneness" as a description; it could not in 1957 and cannot now capture Elizabeth and Hazel's experiences of citizenship, for they lived radically different versions of democratic life. Though they were members of the same democracy, each was expert in a different etiquette of citizenship: dominance on the one hand and acquiescence on the other. The picture records the "twoness" of citizenship in the United States. in 1957.

More significantly, the metaphor of oneness is also inadequate to describe the proper aspirations of a democratic people to solidarity and community. When Elizabeth and her antagonists met in the streets in 1957, thanks to Congress all of them had for the three previous years been daily pledging their devotion to being "one nation under God," the one in her black school, the others in their white schools. Had Elizabeth made it to school on that September morning, she would have recited the same phrase in a room full of black and white students, for the first time in the lives of all those students. What a mockery, then, the photo of the battle in the Little Rock streets made of those students' daily ritual, their daily devotion of themselves to the cause of "one people." Division, not unity, had marked the lives of these students; they knew that "oneness" could capture their experience only through hypocritical idealizations.

But the photo does more than simply undermine the idea of the people as "one" as either description or aspiration. It also suggests an alternate metaphor that might be more useful for cultivating solidarity within a diverse citizenry. Schlesinger's desire to restore "oneness" despite its transparent flaws as a metaphor derives from his awareness that democratic peoples *need* metaphors to make "the people," the body of which they are a part, conceivable to themselves. Citizens who hold the conviction that politics is by, for, and of the people can assume a place in politics only by imagining *the people* and a place for themselves in, or in relationship to, that body. But where, what, and who is this "the people"? And how does it act? The term produces a quandary of the imagination. If modern democratic citizenship seems mostly to be about voting, this derives from the beliefs that *the people* exists only when a "will" has been expressed and that this occurs only through a mass compilation of votes. Voting does not merely legitimate democratic politics but also provides a practical solution to the imaginative dilemma. Metaphors are vehicles for the imagination no less than institutions and, indeed, are central to securing "the people" for democratic life. In short, citizens can explain their role in democracy only by expending significant conceptual and imaginative labor to make themselves part of an invisible whole.[97]

Now, with the phrase "invisible whole," we have hit upon the central term. Citizens must imagine themselves part of a "whole" they cannot see. "The people" is the name for that "whole," and, in fact, wholeness, not oneness, is the master term in the history of the production of democratic peoples. As populist rumblings surged in England in the late sixteenth and early seventeenth centuries, politicians and jurists repeatedly invoked the idea of "the whole people," not the "one people." We owe the idea that out of many the people must arise as "one" to Thomas Hobbes, who

made the idea of "the people" useful to himself precisely by sup-
planting the image of wholeness with the metaphor of oneness.[98]
He rejects the idea of "the people" as a key political term in his
early writings, but after he has established "oneness" as the defining feature of the term, it becomes central to the argument of
Leviathan.[99] The key to establishing the oneness of the people was
the argument that "the people" exists only when represented by
sovereign institutions capable of acting in a unitary fashion, such
that their wills exist "virtually in the sovereign."[100]

Hobbes achieved this redefinition of the people primarily in *Elements of Law* and *De Cive.*[101] But after he had completed the theoretical restructuring, one more task remained: his version of the
people had to be not only conceptually coherent but also capable
of capturing the imagination. In order for the will of the citizens to
be represented by the sovereign institutions of the people, the people had to become a virtual reality. It would become a virtual reality
primarily when citizens had cultivated the psychological attitudes
toward their sovereign that Hobbes recommended. Now he had to
determine what types of imaginative forms might cultivate the appropriate psychological orientations within the citizenry.

Hobbes's disgust with rhetoric, metaphor, and images reveals
how crucial they are not only to his own argument, but also to any
populist politics. His definition of the people, like anyone else's,
can be stabilized only with figurative language. In *Leviathan* he
employs both metaphor and image to convert his lengthy arguments about politics and the people into a neat symbol that citizens might assimilate easily, and with it a whole set of propositions
about political life. As early as 1640, he had defined "the people"
as a collective body "virtually contained in the body of the commonwealth or sovereignty." The organizing metaphor of *Leviathan*
illustrates this idea. Leviathan, the sea monster in Job, is a symbol
for the authoritative sovereign who has swallowed up all the citizens in a single, massive (and monstrous) body. But Hobbes was
not content to engage his readers' imagination with arguments
alone, nor merely with arguments plus metaphors; he also designed *Leviathan*'s famous frontispiece.

That frontispiece image illustrates the idea of the people as "virtually contained in the body of the sovereignty." Now at last, because it is imaginable even at the level of the image, the people

existed. An early seventeenth-century political buzzword had coalesced finally into a dense and exceptionally stable concept. Hobbes had first used description to stabilize the idea of "the people," writing: "When the multitude is united into a body politic, [they] are a people in the other signification, and their wills virtually in the sovereign."[102] Then in *De Cive* he had turned to definition: "*The people is somewhat that is one, having one will, and to whom one action may be attributed.*"[103] In the definition, the important metaphor of oneness is already beginning to surface. Then, in *Leviathan*, definition evolves fully into metaphor. "The people" becomes one in the body of the sea-monster sovereign Leviathan. And finally metaphor evolves into image: a single figure, the sovereign, faces the reader; his body is composed of a multitude of individual figures who, backs turned toward the reader, direct their gaze at the sovereign's face. Before the inhabitants of the state of nature developed institutions to speak on their behalf, "they [were] as many and (as yet) not one."[104] *E pluribus unum* is virtually a quotation by Hobbes. Here at last was "the people."

What is the conceptual content of the image Hobbes relies on to make his political argument effective? It lays bare the citizenly habits that remain fundamental today. In an earlier draft of the image, all the members of *the people* faced outward, toward the reader. By turning the citizens' gaze inward from equal toward a superior, Hobbes transformed them into the people, as he defined it. The citizens all look alike but are isolated from one another by their attention to the sovereign's face. Contained within the body of Leviathan, they can act only through him. The image illustrates our habit of focusing on institutional duties and of studiously ignoring one another. In 1589, George Buchanan wrote about Scottish politics that the whole people (*universo populo*) must be imagined as coming together to overthrow tyrants.[105] More than fifty years later, Hobbes responded that a multitude can come together as "the people" only if pictured in and through sovereign institutions. His frontispiece implies that as long as citizens trust their institutions they need not trust one another. And as long as sovereigns cultivate allegiance to institutions, they can ignore the subjective experiences of citizens. They could stabilize political life by shoring up citizens' commitment to their institutional obligations and encouraging passivity in respect to personally or factionally held opinions. Citizens suppress disagreements, disappointments, and discontent, he realized, in order to preserve institutions that make them feel safe. They ignore the diverse effects on citizens of public policies. They do not try to see what citizens sacrifice for others, or where a public decision about the common good has produced resentment. They contentedly accept the institutional production of "oneness" as adequately representing their investment in the polity. Hobbes encourages his sovereigns to shore up this attentiveness toward institutions and blindness to fellow citizens by beating the drum of security.

What if history had followed a different route and the idea of "the whole people" had remained more influential than the "one people"?[106] The word "whole," derives from Old English and Germanic forms meaning "uninjured, sound, healthy, and complete." Now it means rather "full," "total," "complete," and "all." Neither the *Oxford English Dictionary* (2nd ed.) nor *Merriam Webster's Collegiate Dictionary* (10th ed.) treats "one" as its synonym. The reason for this is simple. A speaker cannot use the word "one" to mean multiplicity, but the word "whole" entails just that. The effort to make the people "one" cultivates in the citizenry a desire for homogeneity, for that is the aspiration taught to citizens by the meaning of the word "one" itself. In contrast, an effort to make the people "whole" might cultivate an aspiration to the coherence and integrity of a consolidated but complex, intricate, and differentiated body ("I pledge allegiance to the United States of America, the whole nation . . .").

What image might we draw of "the people as a whole"? The positive forms of citizenship involved in trust building require that citizens turn their attention toward one another, and not merely to the sovereign. The body of the polity must be constituted by a multitude of citizens exchanging glances while holding firmly to legitimate institutions of collective decision making. The suggestion that citizens must turn their glances toward one another and not merely toward the sovereign does not lead to an exhortation to citizens to spend more time in the public sphere. Instead, citizens are asked to see what is political in the interactions they already have with other citizens. They are asked to see the citizens they already encounter with the eyes not merely of a customer, employer, employee, or attendant, but of a citizen.[107] They are asked to act toward them in accord with their idea of what a free people should be, aspiring to develop habits for treating strangers as though they are friends.

What, more specifically, would be the habits of citizenship for members of a polity that rested on the idea of "the whole people"? What practices would help citizens generate the networks of trust and mutuality necessary to sustain democratic practices for distributing and constantly redistributing benefits and burdens? Here, for lack of additional space, I can do no more than repeat an earlier gesture. Citizens should know that collective decisions, even those that are for the common good, always impose loss on someone; they should never try to pretend otherwise. And they should ask whether those sacrifices are being borne voluntarily, whether they are being acknowledged and honored, and whether they are being reciprocated. Asking these questions, at least, would be a start. Where the answers to these questions are unsatisfactory, they should be ready to respond as political friends.[108]

NOTES

1. Ralph Ellison, *Juneteenth,* ed. John Callahan (New York: Vintage, 1999), Appendix, 356.

2. James C. Scott, *Domination and the Arts of Resistance: Hidden Transcripts* (New Haven: Yale University Press, 1990), x.

3. Axel Honneth, *The Fragmented World of the Social: Essays in Social and Political Philosophy,* ed. C. W. Wright (Albany: SUNY Press, 1995), 14, and Iris Marion Young, *Justice and the Politics of Difference* (Princeton: Princeton University Press, 1990), 38.

4. Young, *Justice and the Politics of Difference,* 38.

5. Honneth, *The Fragmented World of the Social,* 13.

6. Jessica Benjamin, *The Bonds of Love: Psychoanalysis, Feminism, and the Problem of Domination* (New York: Pantheon, 1988), 8–10.

7. Honneth, *The Fragmented World of the Social,* 213.

8. Young, *Justice and the Politics of Difference,* 54, and idem, *Inclusion and Democracy* (Oxford: Oxford University Press, 2000), 6, 34, and 53–56.

9. Scott, *Domination and the Arts of Resistance,* x.

10. Abebe Zegeye, Leonard Harris, and Julia Maxted, eds., *Exploitation and Exclusion: Race and Class in Contemporary U.S. Society* (London: Hans Zell Publishers, 1991), x, and David Goldberg, "Racist Discourse," in ibid., 95.

11. Goldberg, "Racist Discourse," 89–95.

12. See Rogers Smith, *Civic Ideals: Conflicting Visions of Citizenship in U.S. History* (New Haven: Yale University Press, 1997); Kenneth Warren, "Ralph Ellison and the Reconfiguration of Black Cultural Politics," *Yearbook of Research in English and American Literature* 11 (1995): 139–157; Arthur Schlesinger, Jr., *The Disuniting of America: Reflections on a Multicultural Society* (New York: Norton, 1992); and Stephan Thernstrom and Abigail Thernstrom, *America in Black and White: One Nation Indivisible* (New York: Simon and Schuster, 1997).

13. Schlesinger, *The Disuniting of America*, 14 and 134.

14. Young, *Inclusion and Democracy*, 5; Rogers Smith, *Civic Ideals*, 5; and Anthony Marx, *Making Race and Nation* (Cambridge: Cambridge University Press, 1998).

15. The United Kingdom even presently has a "Social Exclusion Unit." Although "domination" does not appear in the catalog in contemporary policy conference reports and proceedings, there are a few items from the 1970s on colonial domination and the struggle for independence of, in particular, African states. Also, there was a U.S. government item from the 1950s on "communist domination of labor movements."

16. Young, *Inclusion and Democracy*, 36.

17. It is important to remember that segregation extended beyond the states of the Confederacy, which are typically thought of as the "South." For instance, California segregated Mexican Americans; Michigan segregated African Americans.

18. Arendt, "Reflections on Little Rock," *Dissent* 6 (1959): 45–56.

19. On this issue of social advancement in regard to Arendt's understanding of racial and racist politics, see Elisabeth Young-Bruehl, *Hannah Arendt: For Love of the World* (New Haven: Yale University Press, 1982), 308–318; Seyla Benhabib, *The Reluctant Modernism of Hannah Arendt* (Thousand Oaks, CA: Sage Publications, 1996), 146–155.

20. Arendt, "Reflections on Little Rock," 50. On September 5, 1957, the *New York Times* ran two photos of young women facing mobs as they tried to enter school. One was Elizabeth Eckford in Little Rock, Arkansas; the other was Dorothy Counts in Charlotte, North Carolina. As it happens, Arendt reversed the photos and the one she describes in the essay as representing Little Rock in fact represents Charlotte. That is, only the Charlotte photo includes the "white friend of her father" to whom Arendt refers.

21. The literature on Arendt's essay divides between the pieces that focus on her desire to protect children (e.g., Young-Bruehl, *Hannah Arendt*) and those pieces that focus on the failures of her distinction between the social and the political (e.g., Benhabib, *The Reluctant Modernism of Hannah Arendt*; James Bohman, "The Moral Costs of Political Pluralism:

The Dilemmas of Difference and Equality in Arendt's 'Reflections on Little Rock'," in L. May and J. Kohn, eds., *Hannah Arendt: Twenty Years Later* (Cambridge, MA: MIT Press, 1997), 63. Part of what comes out in Arendt's essay, though, is the degree to which the point of her distinction between the social and political was to protect children. For a recent comprehensive analysis of Arendt's use of the distinction between social and political, please see Hanna Pitkin, *The Attack of the Blob: Hannah Arendt's Concept of the Social* (Chicago: University of Chicago Press, 1998).

22. Arendt, *The Human Condition* (Chicago: University of Chicago Press, 1989 [originally 1958]), 25, 193, and 194.

23. Ibid., 219.

24. Ibid.

25. Ibid., 216.

26. Arendt, *Men in Dark Times* (New York: Harcourt, Brace, and World, 1968), 11.

27. Arendt, *The Human Condition*, 218.

28. Robert Penn Warren, *Who Speaks for the Negro* (New York: Random House, 1965), 343–344.

29. See Danielle Allen, "Law's Necessary Forcefulness: Ellison vs. Arendt on the Battle of Little Rock," *Oklahoma City Law Review* (2001), and Allen, "Ralph Ellison on the Tragi-Comedy of Citizenship," in Lucas Morel, ed., *Raft of Hope* (Lexington: University Press of Kentucky, 2004). See also Meili Steele, "Metatheory and the Subject of Democracy," *New Literary History* 27 (1996): 473–502, "Democratic Interpretation and the Politics of Difference," in *Comparative Literature* 48 (1996): 326–342, and "Arendt versus Ellison on Little Rock: The Role of Language in Political Judgment," *Constellations* 9 (2002): 184–206.

30. "On Initiation Rites and Power," in John Callahan, ed., *The Collected Essays of Ralph Ellison* (New York: Modern Library, 1995), 525.

31. See, for instance, "An Extravagance of Laughter," in *The Collected Essays of Ralph Ellison,* 613–658. For more on this line of argument, see Allen, "Ralph Ellison on the Tragi-Comedy of Citizenship."

32. Ellison regularly makes the argument that, whereas white Americans have been able to live with illusions about how democracy works, blacks in contrast "are an American people who are geared to what *is,* and who yet are driven by a sense of what it is possible for human life to be in this society" ("What America Would Be Like without Blacks," in *The Collected Essays of Ralph Ellison,* 584; see also "An Extravagance of Laughter," in *The Collected Essays of Ralph Ellison*).

African Americans, in his argument understand how the collective decisions of a democracy impose on some citizens. White Americans have

been able to avoid that knowledge because one minority group was assigned to bear the bulk of these burdens. "When we look objectively at
how the dry bones of the nation were hung together, it seems obvious that
some one of the many groups that compose the United States had to suffer the fate of being allowed no easy escape from experiencing the harsh
realities of the human condition as they were to exist under even so fortunate a democracy as ours" ("What America Would Be Like without
Blacks," 583).

33. From T. S. Eliot's, *The Wasteland* and Lord Raglan's *The Hero,* Ellison took a conviction that myth and ritual are fundamental to both
human life and literature, and he invokes the idea of ritual throughout
his essays. For instance, in "The Myth of the Flawed White Southerner"
(*The Collected Essays of Ralph Ellison,* 553), he refers to himself as "a novelist
interested in that area of national life where political power is institutionalized and translated into democratic ritual and national style." To piece
together Ellison's account of ritual, see particularly "Twentieth-Century
Fiction and the Mask of Humanity," "Art of Fiction: An Interview," "Hidden Name and Complex Fate," "Initiation Rites and Power," and "An Extravagance of Laughter," in *The Collected Essays of Ralph Ellison.*

34. "Hidden Name and Complex Fate," in *The Collected Essays of Ralph
Ellison,* 195.

35. Importantly, the rituals Ellison identifies regularly concern gen-
der; indeed, the events in Little Rock on which Arendt and Ellison com-
mented depend heavily for their significance on the function of gender in
U.S. politics. I examine this issue in my forthcoming book, *Talking to
Strangers: On Little Rock and Political Friendship* (Chicago: University of
Chicago Press, 2004), and so leave it aside here.

36. "Hidden Name and Complex Fate," in *The Collected Essays of Ralph
Ellison,* 208. Almost everyone with whom I have discussed these materials
has objected that the term "sacrifice" does not properly belong to politics
and is too dangerous to introduce into political discussion. And yet, despite general disavowals of the topic, the word comes up frequently in political theory and political discussions. A casual survey turns up the word
in two out of every three works published in political theory.

37. The arguments I make here about Ellison's "conclusions" are
based on reading his two novels for the arguments constructed out of the
interplay of characters and then setting these arguments against those developed in his essays. This method of reading concords with Ellison's own.
He and his letter writing companion, Albert Murray, discussed how to give
the reader "an adventure" by "presenting process" not "statements." Thus,
Ellison writes to Murray: "I would like more Emdee . . . or Jaygee because
with them Jack could arrive at his theories through conflict. . . . His ideas

are not the usual ones (sic.) and I think much *unrevealed* revelation lies in the story of how he attained this kind of transcendence" (Ralph Ellison and Albert Murray, *Trading Twelves*, ed. John Callahan and Albert Murray [New York: Modern Library, 2000], 28). Thus, I read Ellison's novels in order to work out what the sets of conflicts of ideas are; from there I try to assess what concerns on the part of the author led to the focus on these particular conflicts. I never take the words of any particular character as examples of Ellison's opinions, unless they are the words that have won some particular argument that his books are having with themselves.

38. Here is another section of the interview with Robert Penn Warren that is relevant to this notion of redistribution:

> WARREN: Here in the midst of what has been an expanding econ-
> omy you have a contracting economy for the unprepared, for
> the Negro.
>
> ELLISON: That's the paradox. And this particularly explains some-
> thing new which has come into the picture; that is, a determina-
> tion by the Negro no longer to be the scapegoat, no longer to
> pay, to be sacrificed to—the inadequacies of other Americans.
> We want to socialize the cost. A cost has been exacted in terms of
> character, in terms of courage, and determination, and in terms
> of self-knowledge and self-discovery. Worse, it has led to social,
> economic, political, and intellectual disadvantages and to a con-
> tempt even for our lives. And one motive for our rejection of the
> old traditional role of national scapegoat is an intensified aware-
> ness that not only are we being destroyed by the sacrifice, but
> that the nation has been rotting at its moral core." (Warren, *Who
> Speaks for the Negro*, 339)

My thanks to Melissa Williams for pointing out that "this is a twist on Robert Dahl's argument in *A Preface to Democratic Theory* that in a just democracy 'major*it*ies rule', i.e., there is no permanent majority and no permanent minority, but wins and losses cycle through the population from issue to issue because of cross-cutting cleavages." I make two points here: (1) democratic theory needs to accommodate the possibility of en-during cleavages that do make for permanent majorities and minorities (interestingly, these ideas entered the U.S. political vocabulary only in the 1950s when legal segregation was being taken apart); Lani Guinier is an example of a theorist who does try to understand what the fact of perma-nent minorities and majorities requires of democratic justice; and (2) the presence of a permanent minority should lead to an analysis of *why* losses are not circulating throughout the citizenry as well as to efforts to rectify institutional and social barriers to unencumbered circulation.

39. This is the project of my manuscript in progress, "Talking to Strangers: On Rhetoric, Distrust, and other Democratic Difficulties."

40. Benhabib, *The Reluctant Modernism of Hannah Arendt*, 146–155; See also Allen, "Law's Necessary Forcefulness."

41. Warren, *Who Speaks for the Negro*, 342. Emphasis added.

42. On the role of terror in domination, see Scott, *Domination and the Arts of Resistance*, xi.

43. Warren, *Who Speaks for the Negro*, 342. Emphasis added.

44. See note 38.

45. Daisy Bates, *The Long Shadow of Little Rock* (New York: David McKay Company, 1962), 66.

46. Ibid., 106.

47. Ibid.

48. Ibid., 63.

49. Ibid., 72.

50. Ibid., 76.

51. Bates concludes the story thus: "[The next morning, however,] Mr. Ray, shy and smiling, led Gloria into the house. He looked down at his daughter with pride. 'Here, Daisy, she's yours. She's determined to go'" (ibid., 102–103).

52. Arendt, *The Human Condition*, 175.

53. *Men in Dark Times* (New York: Harcourt, Brace, and World, 1968), 31.

54. See note 37.

55. Ellison, *Invisible Man* (New York: Vintage Books, 1995 [originally 1952]), 577.

56. For a theorist who does this, see Jane Mansbridge, "Using Power/Fighting Power: The Polity," in Seyla Benhabib, ed., *Democracy and Difference: Contesting the Boundaries of the Politica* (Princeton: Princeton University Press, 1996), 60.

57. Benjamin, *The Bonds of Love*, 12.

58. On June 17, 2000, citizens of the United States woke to news of the first large rise in unemployment in eight years. This growth in joblessness had a history. Between January and April 2000 the Federal Reserve (the central U.S. bank) had, for the good of the country, raised interest rates several times in hopes of slowing the economy. Joblessness was increased by design and justified by the idea of the common good, which shows that political decisions can impose loss not by accident, but intentionally, even when the intentions behind them are generally benign. Indeed, the phrase "the common good" obscures that the good of a whole polity is always constructed out of a differential distribution of benefits and harms throughout the citizenry. How are democratic citizens to think and talk

about the fact that a regime constructed for the good of all (liberal democracy) must live day-to-day on decisions that are almost always better for some? Notably, the front page of the *New York Times* business section, which reported the June 2000 rise in unemployment, separated the stories of loss and gain. The left-hand, or less significant column, reported: "The nation's private sector employers shed 116,000 jobs in May. It was the largest drop in more than eight years and the first decline since the economy began to soar in the mid-1990's. The unemployment rate edged up to 4.1 percent from 3.9 percent, with blacks and Hispanics *absorbing most of the loss*" (B1) (emphasis added). On the right-hand side of the same page, the lead article spun the story thus: "The Nasdaq composite index soared 6.44 percent yesterday, ending its best week ever, as *investors cheered data suggesting that the nation's economy is slowing* and the Federal Reserve may be almost done raising interest rates" (B1)(emphasis added). This headlined article was illustrated with a photograph of traders cheering on the market floor.

59. Young, *Inclusion and Democracy*, 197.

60. This might be called a comic view of politics, which stresses the necessity of having citizens recognize that their fellows act in blindness. This view overlooks the problematic motivations of fellow citizens, chalking infelicitous actions up to foolishness. On this, see J. Albrecht, "Saying Yes and Saying No: Individualist Ethics in Ellison, Burke, and Emerson," in *PMLA* 114 (1999): 46–63.

61. Benjamin, *The Bonds of Love*, 25.

62. Arendt, *Men in Dark Times*, 29.

63. Arendt, *The Human Condition*, 243 (emphasis added).

64. Here they both take a position within an Aristotelian tradition. Aristotle, too, thought the practices of friendship could be separated from its emotions (*Nicomachean Ethics* 4.6).

65. *Invisible Man*, 420 (emphasis added).

66. Ibid., 453 (emphasis added).

67. "Brave Words for a Startling Occasion," in *The Collected Essays of Ralph Ellison*, 154.

68. See *The Collected Essays of Ralph Ellison* (e.g., in "The Little Man at Chehaw Station," 509). See also Ellison and Murray, *Trading Twelves*.

69. See Jürgen Habermas, "Hannah Arendt's Communications Concept of Power," in L. P. Hinchman and S. K. Hinchman, eds., *Hannah Arendt: Critical Essays* (Albany: SUNY Press, 1994), 211–230, and Bonnie Honig, *Feminist Interpretations of Hannah Arendt* (University Park: Pennsylvania State University Press, 1995).

70. Allen, *Talking to Strangers*, chap. 9.

71. Arendt, *The Human Condition*, 50.

72. Arendt, *Men in Dark Times,* 22.

73. Arendt, *Invisible Man,* 547.

74. Ibid., 507.

75. Ibid., 14.

76. Arendt, *Men in Dark Times,* 19

77. See Arendt, *Men in Dark Times* and *The Human Condition,* 50 and 55.

78. Quoted by Arendt in *Men in Dark Times,* 69 (emphasis in the original).

79. Ibid., 70–71.

80. Arendt, *The Human Condition,* 194.

81. Arendt, *Men in Dark Times,* 9.

82. See Mansbridge, "Using Power/Fighting Power," and Allen, "Law's Necessary Forcefulness."

83. Arendt, *Men in Dark Times,* 23.

84. Ibid., 13.

85. Arendt, *The Human Condition,* 58.

86. Arendt, "Reflections on Little Rock," *Dissent* 6: 46.

87. "A major tendency in feminism has constructed the problem of domination as a drama of female vulnerability victimized by male aggression. Even the more sophisticated feminist thinkers frequently shy away from the analysis of submission, for fear that in admitting woman's participation in the relationship of domination, the onus of responsibility will appear to shift from men to women, and the moral victory from women to men. More generally, this has been a weakness of radical politics; to idealize the oppressed, as if their politics and culture were untouched by the system of domination" (Benjamin, *The Bonds of Love,* 9). "Coercive powers have been used to define citizenship according to race—states bind the nation they claim to represent by institutionalizing identities of racial inclusion and exclusion. The extension of citizenship rights has been blocked by constructing racial boundaries. . . . States . . . play a central role in imposing the terms of official domination, with unintended consequences. Official exclusion, as by race, legitimates these categories as a form of social identity, building upon and reshaping historical and cultural solidarities" (Marx, *Making Race and Nation,* 5–6).

88. Scott, *Domination and the Arts of Resistance,* 13–15.

89. *Invisible Man,* 16.

90. Ibid., 574–575.

91. *Invisible Man,* 547, emphasis added.

92. Working Notes to *Juneteenth.*

93. On one level, this simply reiterates the famous Augustinian point that there is justice even among thieves.

94. On Ellison's idea of technique, see "Hidden Name and Complex Fate," in *Collected Essays of Ralph Ellison.*

95. Emphasis added.

96. Rogers Smith is rare in discussing the subject. In *Civic Ideals,* he has recently argued both that ideas of "the people" are central to the histories of exclusion (his term) and domination (my term) in the United States and that if liberal political approaches are to withstand illiberal movements in the future, they must find ways to talk about why "the people they aspire to govern . . . are a people . . . without ultimately sacrificing key liberal values." Smith, *Civic Ideals: Conflicting Visions of Citizenship in U.S. History,* 9–10.

97. The suggestion that modern democratic politics requires the active engagement of the imagination is not original. Benedict Anderson argued in 1993 in *Imagined Communities* that modernity has required citizens of large nation-states to develop methods of imagining themselves into relationships with their fellow citizens. The development of national languages and newspapers that circulate throughout a whole community allow people to see themselves (read: imagine themselves) as part of a larger group despite the literal impossibility of ever seeing the whole nation-state or citizenry at once. It is the impossibility of seeing the group to which one belongs that requires the engagement of the imagination if politics based on such groups is to succeed.

I suggest here, in a move away from Anderson, that it is not the size of the modern nation-state that requires the engagement of the imagination. It is instead the attempt to base politics on *the people* that has fueled the role of the imagination in modern politics. For where is "the people"? And what is it? And how does it act? No citizen can explain her role in modern democratic practice without fairly significant conceptual and imaginative labor by which she makes herself part of an invisible whole.

98. A chapter of my *Talking to Strangers* is devoted to this issue and quotes both the pre-Hobbesian texts that emphasize wholeness and the Hobbesian texts that effect the transition. The relevant passages in Hobbes are *Elements of Law* 2.2.1; *De Cive* 12.8 and 13.3.

99. Ibid.

100. *Elements of Law* 2.2.11.

101. For a full account, please see *Talking to Strangers,* chap. 6.

102. *Elements of Law* 2.2.11.

103. *De Cive* 12.8.

104. *Elements of Law* 2.1.2.

105. *De jure regni apud Scotos* (1579), 97.

106. One can find examples from the sixteenth to the twentieth centuries of the importance of "wholeness." Thus in Schlesinger: "The old

American homogeneity disappeared well over a century ago, never to return. Ever since, we have been preoccupied in one way or another with the problem, as Herbert Croly phrases i[t] 80 years back in *The Promise of American Life*, 'of preventing such divisions from dissolving the society into which they enter—of keeping such a highly differentiated society fundamentally sound and whole.' This required, Croly believed, an 'ultimate bond of union.'" (Schlesinger, *The Disuniting of America*, 134).

107. This is to reject the argument made by Constant in "On the Liberty of the Ancients and Moderns," and also the argument of George W. Bush, Jr., after the events of September 11, 2001, that we should focus on being consumers.

108. Please see *Talking to Strangers* for a full answer.

2

TRAGIC VISIONS, MUNDANE REALITIES: A COMMENT ON DANIELLE ALLEN'S "INVISIBLE CITIZENS"

CLIFFORD ORWIN

Professor Allen has offered us an extended meditation on Ralph Ellison's vision of the dilemma facing American Blacks in the 1950s and of its implications for our conception of American politics today. At the heart of her chapter is her discussion of the emergence of Black Americans from the invisibility so long visited upon them. She makes a strong and (to my mind) entirely persuasive case for viewing that invisibility with Ellison in terms of "domination" rather than with Hannah Arendt in terms of "exclusion." She reminds us in Ellison's name that exclusion so-called is never and was not in this case actual exclusion from the society in question, but rather domination within it. It was crucial for Ellison that African Americans see themselves (and that the whites come to see them) not as excluded from the society or in any sense apart from it but as in it up to their necks, even or precisely in their "invisibility." It was their unique burden to be called to practice citizenship precisely by being denied it.

I welcome Professor Allen's project of reviving *Invisible Man* as a work of unique insight into the Black experience. The question is whether that experience was, as Ellison thought and Allen would have us think, paradigmatic of the experience of democratic citizenship generally. She opposes Ellison's "tragic" to Arendt's "epic" view of democratic citizenship.

> For Ellison, in contrast, the evolution of a new citizenship required addressing those aspects of democratic decision making that domination had hidden in order to shore itself up: the fact that public decisions inevitably distribute burdens unevenly, and the resentment, disappointment, and distrust that follow from this. (This volume, p. 44)

So, to address these submerged aspects of political life precludes too dogmatic a distinction between the political and the social.

> The political world cannot be entirely separated from our social world, and learning how to negotiate the losses one experiences at the hands of the public is fundamental to becoming a political actor, not only for minorities or those suffering political abuses, but for all citizens. . . . Citizenship is a tragic, not an epic, business. (P. 39)

I will leave it to the proponents of the tragic view of citizenship to fight it out with those of the epic view. My question concerns the applicability of Ellison's model to everyday problems of current democracy. Understandably, he wished to show that the experience of Black Americans was relevant not to them alone but to all Americans. So he sought to present it as paradigmatic for democratic citizenship simply, in which Professor Allen follows him. But don't they go too far in this? Yes, now as always every political decision gratifies some and disappoints others, and "resentment, disappointment, and distrust" follow in its wake. In a stable liberal democracy, however, a setback on this or that policy issue typically falls so far short of the tragic that to couch it this way verges on the comic. In our temples of deliberation, no log lies unrolled and no one loses his shirt. No one is pushed to the wall, and no one reverts to invisibility. Take tort law reform, for example. Sure, it would be a blow to personal-injury lawyers, and they would squawk tragically about it. This is America, however, and at the end of the day they would still somehow make their payments on their Hummers.

All right, so I've loaded the dice by using this example of trial lawyers, the wealthiest identifiable group of contributors to the Democratic party. But if I had used schoolteachers or the Teamsters or softwood lumber producers, the basic point would still be the same. In disputes that never approach a zero-sum game, to invoke the past sufferings of African Americans would inevitably be to trivialize them.

Now you might argue that other specified groups have succeeded Blacks as invisible, say illegal immigrants laboring in sweatshops to work off extortionate debts to snakeheads. If you did, however, it would not be to make the point that our mainstream burdens are like unto theirs. While a few marginal groups may toil in (relative) invisibility, they are the exceptions that underline the rule. Their cases will not yield a paradigm for liberal democratic politics as usual.

Professor Allen anticipates this objection:

> But how can either Arendt or Ellison move so easily from considering the stark injustices of twentieth-century political life to casual comments about prosaic disagreements? As we saw in the preceding section, Ellison argued for a structural similarity between the world's singularly dramatic acts of injustice and the ordinary acts of violence of our daily political lives. (Pp. 45–46)

The question is whether this "structural similarity" will bear the load she assigns it. To face lynching is one thing; to settle for your second choice among federally funded drug plans is another. "The ordinary acts of violence of our daily political lives"? This seems overheated as a description of even the rowdiest day in Congress.[1]

So that's my first reservation. Here's a second. Professor Allen assimilates not only Ellison but Arendt to the politics of difference of which we've heard so much of late:

> Both Arendt and Ellison argued for a politics that accepts the perpetual existence of difference and disagreement. Moreover, each thematized the attempt to ignore or eradicate plurality, and related abuses, in terms of invisibility and darkness. (P. 49)

This proves to be Professor Allen's leitmotiv, but I find myself perplexed by its ultimate implications. She sees and raises her models by promoting a "politics of intricacy."

> The question for both Arendt and Ellison, then, is how a politics of plurality and diversity or, I would prefer, of intricacy, can ensure

> that the winner of an argument "takes nothing," to quote Ellison,
> especially when some people remain unconvinced by the outcome
> of debate. (P. 46)

> We are not always "locked" in the struggle for recognition with the
> others in our lives and succeed best of all in dealing with it in good
> friendships. (P. 47)

Winners in a debate "take nothing" when they leave behind no
more disagreement than is compatible with friendship.

I hate it when people talk like that. They sound like communitarians, for Pete's sake. In fact, politics can never be free of more
disagreement than is compatible with friendship. Friendship is too
much to ask for in the political realm; to do so conflates the public
and the private. Madness lies that way, or illiberalism (or, more
commonly, in societies that remain fundamentally liberal, just
empty rhetoric). The wholeness of a liberal regime can never be,
and was never meant to be, the wholeness of friendship. If, on the
other hand, Professor Allen were to recommend malice toward
none, charity toward all, I could go for that, since the duty of charity transcends friendship and enmity.

My reservations about friendship-talk aside, I readily agree that
winners in democratic debate ought to leave behind no more disagreement than is compatible with agreeing to disagree on some
issues while remaining open to agreement on others. But of this,
the principal guarantor must be a political system that makes them
pay a prohibitive price for behaving otherwise, and that requires
them (and the interests they champion) to get along with yesterday's opponent because you may need him as tomorrow's ally. In
short, I much prefer the wisdom of *The Federalist* to the social psy-
chologists and civic habit-formers invoked by Professor Allen.

Professor Allen concludes her essay with a criticism of the reign-
ing view of oneness as the proper model of peoplehood. In its
place she proposes wholeness. Here her stalking horse is Arthur
Schlesinger, Jr., whom she admits speaks on this matter for just
about every respectable authority, whether liberal or conservative.
Wholeness, she observes, is not synonymous with unity, for "a
speaker cannot use the word 'one' to mean multiplicity, but the
word 'whole' entails just that." I take it that she means that while
wholeness implies unity it is unity of a certain kind, for the exis-

tence of a whole implies that of parts and so of multiplicity. Yet it
also implies unity, as that which qualifies the parts as a whole.
Wholeness may imply multiplicity, but multiplicity doesn't imply
wholeness. After all, most societies celebrated for their wholeness
have enjoyed the advantage of a great deal of sameness, and most
of those marked by persistent difference—ethnic, linguistic, religious, ideological, or even geographic—have struggled to achieve
or maintain wholeness.

Professor Allen rejects Schlesinger's vision of Americans as "one
people" on the grounds that it implies "habits of citizenship" and
"citizenly practices" that in fact excluded many, notably black
Americans. Yet, as she must admit, Schlesinger too laments this
past exclusiveness. It's not simply true that "he tells a simple fable
of historical decline," for by the very same token that he regrets
the current vogue for "difference," he celebrates the progress in
racial and other kinds of integration whereby those once denied
full membership in the one people have come to enjoy it. Con-
ceding Professor Allen's claim that the metaphor of oneness was
inadequate to the reality of the segregated America of 1957, he
continues to promote it as the bar at which that sordid reality
proved wanting. Professor Allen fails to explain why invidious discrimination necessarily follows from Schlesinger's vision rather
than comprising a departure from it. She fails to expound to my
satisfaction "[the] transparent flaws [of oneness] as a metaphor"
(p. 63).

Professor Allen claims that "the metaphor of oneness is . . . inadequate to describe the proper aspirations of a democratic people to solidarity and community" (p. 62). Going after bigger game
than Schlesinger, she proceeds to Hobbes and his conception of a
people in terms of oneness rather than wholeness. She claims that
"as populist rumblings surged in England in the late sixteenth and
early seventeenth centuries, politicians and jurists repeatedly in-
voiced the idea of 'the whole people,' and not the 'one people'"
(p. 63). Call it an incipient wholesome tradition of wholeness.
Hobbes himself took rather a different view. Yes, wherever you
turned in his day you saw this or that pretension to wholeness
(here the people were the least of the offenders)—each more di-
visive than the last.

Hobbes too was concerned with wholeness; it's just that he took the hardheaded view that there was no effective wholeness except that of oneness. Because human beings were naturally many and not (*pace* Aristotle) parts of a whole, because they were individuals who participated in no whole beyond themselves, the wholeness of the political community was radically conventional and fictive. Because the only politically significant wholeness was that of subjection to a fictive will that mimicked the sole natural will (which was that of the individual), there was no wholeness but that of the oneness of a multitude become a people through its self-subjection to a sovereign. If "in Hobbes' view *the people* can be pictured only in the figure of the sovereign," that's because the sovereign is the sole means through which a people so much as comes into being, the fictive unity by means of which it surmounts its natural diversity.

Professor Allen offers harsh words for the frontispiece of *Leviathan*.

> By turning the citizens' gaze inward from equal toward a superior, Hobbes transformed them into the people, as he defined it. The citizens all look alike but are isolated from one another by their attention to the sovereign's face. Contained within the body of Leviathan, they can act only through him. The image illustrates our habit of focusing on institutional duties and of studiously ignoring one another. (P. 65)

As regards the isolation of the citizens, Hobbes's answer is clear: that isolation is by nature; their union, such as it is and can be, is only by convention. More precisely, it is only by means of their creation of and submission to the will of the sovereign, that artificial man, that they become citizens at all. Hobbes does not "call the mass of citizens the multitude," for so long as men remain a multitude they are not citizens, and once they have become citizens they are no longer a multitude. (They remain naturally a multitude, of course, but a citizen is something fictive.) Lurking in Professor Allen's argument is the presumption that citizens form a whole apart from their subjection to a common sovereignty. But it is precisely this presumption that Hobbes is at such pains to rebut.

Because all civic identity is by and through submission to the sovereign, Hobbes commonly speaks not of citizens but of subjects. In a human world generated by sovereignty, there is no room for citizenship; when Hobbes speaks of the citizen (as even in the title of *De Cive*), it is only to redefine him as the subject. This may be a damning defect in Hobbes, but we should not slight the power of his case for it. Subjects must look to the sovereign rather than at each other because it is only in and through him that they enjoy a civic identity. Hobbes is only too aware of the "centrality of trust-building to citizenship," but precisely because such trust must be built from the ground up, that is, because "nature dissociates man" (*Leviathan,* chapter 13). Since all trust is conventional, there can be none except by virtue of the sovereign.

Even so, it is wrong on at least two counts to suggest that Hobbes envisions or counsels that the "citizens studiously ignore one another." For one thing, it is precisely because of our ravaging awareness of one another that we look to the sovereign whence comes our help. Each of us hears, over our shoulders, the menacing footsteps of every other. Admittedly this is no communitarian's notion of the tie that should bind, but that is no refutation of it. The sovereign is wholly the creation of our horizontal glances, elected by each of us to relieve the anxiety evoked by those glances. My eyes are fixed on the sovereign because far from studiously ignoring you, I am more than studiously mindful of you.

Nor does this exhaust the horizontality of the civic association as Hobbes conceives it. As he himself so emphatically reminds us, metaphors are misleading, capturing one aspect of a relation but abstracting from the others. There is more to the argument of *Leviathan* than the frontispiece expresses. In Chapter Fifteen of *Leviathan,* Hobbes calls us not only to equal fear of one another but to consequent equal treatment. His notion of the commonwealth is nothing if not inclusive: all who are in it are equally so, and equally entitled to the respect of the others. The consignment of Black Americans to a limbo of second-class citizenship thus violated every principle of Hobbes's politics, for it is precisely the presumption of the natural superiority of some human beings to others—of any human beings to any others—against which his whole system takes resolute aim. Hobbes's liberalism of fear has a lot to recommend it, not least on this issue of inclusiveness.[2]

The civil rights struggle of the late 1950s, the focus of Professor Allen's analysis, was a struggle for the integration of African Americans into American society, a term that indeed implies a goal of wholeness as assimilation would imply one of sameness. Wholeness

resembles sameness, however, in implying that any persisting relation of difference between the parties will not be one of exclusion.
To that very significant extent, progress in wholeness must also be
progress in sameness.

To the founders of liberalism it was precisely this aspect of
sameness—equality of basic rights under a law equitably applied
to all—that constituted the wholeness of the liberal polity. True,
in today's rhetorical climate "difference-within-wholeness" draws
cheers and "sameness" boos. But it remains the case if our wholeness is to prevail over our differences, there must be a ground of
sameness more fundamental than the ground of difference. First-
order sameness, second-order difference: such has always been the
liberal principle. And the liberal principle has grounded the only
viable forms of democracy, the only viable habits of democratic citizenship.

If wholeness is identical with imagined community, then wholeness depends on whatever sameness affords the basis for that imagination. Successful politics depends on centripetal tendencies
prevailing over centrifugal ones, and the centripetal principle is
sameness while the centrifugal one is difference. Here there was
no difference in principle between the great liberal thinkers on
the one hand and Hobbes and Rousseau on the other. The liberal
claim was that the toleration of difference could in fact strengthen
the bonds of sameness by enabling differences to find relatively
harmless expression. (Hence Locke's project of fomenting secondary differences in religion through the promotion of toleration—only secondary ones because the requirement of mutual
toleration assured sameness in the decisive respect.) In such circumstances the toleration of difference could itself contribute to
stability as a crucial component of sameness, outweighing the differences expressed.

So it remains unclear to me on the basis of Professor Allen's
paper why the older liberal notion of inclusiveness needs to be replaced rather than realized. So too does it remain unclear just
what she offers in its place. *E pluribus unum* must go, to be replaced
by *plures in uno*. But how exactly does she conceive the relation between the many and the one? "What," in her own words, "would be
the habits of citizenship for members of a polity that rested on the
idea of 'the whole people'?"

What practices would help citizens generate the networks of trust and mutuality necessary to sustain democratic practices for distributing and constantly redistributing benefits and burdens? Here, for lack of additional space, I can do no more than repeat an earlier gesture. Citizens should know that collective decisions, even those that are for the common good, always impose loss on someone; they should never try to pretend otherwise. And they should ask whether those sacrifices are being borne voluntarily, whether they are being acknowledged and honored, and whether they are being reciprocated. Where the answers to these questions are unsatisfactory, they should be ready to respond. . . . (P. 67)

To respond how? While I admire Professor Allen's civic spirit, I don't see where she proposes to take us. The answers to the questions she would have us pose will always be unsatisfactory, not because our political system is defective but because this defect is inherent in politics. As a competitive activity, it cannot be purged of either the sting of defeat or the smug or vindictive relishing of victory. Yes, people will accept their losses because in our system these are not catastrophic, because they know they have no choice in the matter, and because the ties binding them to their fellow citizens transcend this or that particular issue. And as for the sacrifices so imposed and borne being fully acknowledged, honored, and reciprocated? In the words of Ethan Edwards, that'll be the day. Politics is not and never will be an exercise in mutual self-esteem building.

Ellison offers a magnificent account of the manner in which Black Americans conceived the grievous sacrifices to which they submitted for the sake of a better future for their children and for all Americans. That future has now arrived, unsatisfactory as futures always are, but prosaically so. Blacks and their leaders have been integrated into the mainstream of American politics; they have not and will not transform it. While society is not yet free of racism—Ellison was right about that—neither is racism any longer the dominant factor in the lives of Blacks. All honor is due to Ellison's vision of the civic achievement of oppressed African Americans, and to Professor Allen's powerful account of it. But if she wants those of us who are around today to meet the standard that the best of them did, she will have to find us obstacles, dilemmas, sacrifices and comparable to theirs. That is a task at which no one should wish her luck.

NOTES

1. Of course, not even liberal democracy can be wholly free of the threat of great politics, if only because not everybody out there is liberal. As I write this, America is at war in Iraq. Missing from the American picture, however, here as elsewhere, is the invisibility required for the applicability of the Ellisonian paradigm. If anyone went unheard in the debate preceding the war, it was only because of the din.

2. The with-it reader will catch a distant whiff of Jacob T. Levy's *The Multiculturalism of Fear* (Chicago: University of Chicago Press, 2000). As the only current theorist cited in this comment, may Professor Levy bask in his iconic status.

3

THE DOMINATION COMPLAINT

PHILIP PETTIT

It is possible to conceptualize political freedom as the absence of domination, arguing that a person is free to the extent that others do not stand over him or her, able to interfere at will and with relative impunity in his or her affairs. And this, furthermore, is how political freedom appears to have been conceptualized in the long and broad republican tradition: the tradition that stretches from republican Rome to revolutionary America and France, encompassing figures as diverse as Cicero, Machiavelli, Harrington, Montesquieu, Rousseau, and Madison. I have defended those two claims, respectively philosophical and historical, in earlier writings, as indeed have a number of other authors.[1]

In addition to defending those two claims, however, I have also argued that there is a good case for resuscitating the republican viewpoint as a political philosophy, on the grounds that it has many advantages in comparison with contemporary alternatives. I concentrate in the present essay on this third claim, approaching it from a new angle. The essay is in three sections. In the first, I consider the main constraints that we should expect any candidate for a central or supreme political ideal to satisfy, distinguishing between constraints of feasibility and constraints of desirability. And then in the second and third sections, I argue that the ideal of nondomination does remarkably well in satisfying those feasibility and desirability constraints. The argument in these sections is inevitably somewhat sketchy, since it often recapitulates points that I have elaborated elsewhere.

1. Constraints on a Political Ideal

Ideals and Complaints

Any political ideal that aspires to be a central or supreme political role has to provide a basis for assessing the way the polity is constituted and the way it behaves within the limits set by that constitution. The assessment of a polity turns in the last analysis on how well it serves its citizens or members, answering to interests they avow or are disposed to avow; I abstract from the assessment of the polity for its effects on nonmembers. And this being so, we must therefore expect any would-be political ideal to try and articulate the importance of something in which people clearly have an avowed or readily avowable interest: something whose absence in their lives will spontaneously lead them to make complaint.

This condition is satisfied by every half-plausible political ideal. Take ideals such as those provided by the elimination of poverty, the achievement of equality, the approximation of justice, and the minimization of interference in people's lives or the maximization of happiness. In every case we may expect people to be ready to complain about the absence of the condition recommended under the ideal: that is, to complain about poverty or inequality, injustice, interference, or unhappiness. And that is as it should be. For were people not ready to complain in this way, then the ideal could hardly claim to reflect an interest that they were readily disposed to avow.

So much for what I describe as the basic condition on any would-be candidate for the role of political ideal. With that condition spelled out, we can explore the further constraints that we might want a political ideal to satisfy. These are all well cast as constraints on the sort of complaint that an attractive ideal ought to articulate and I distinguish them into two bunches. So far as the first bunch is satisfied by the complaint, the corresponding ideal will be a feasible ideal for the state to track; so far as the second bunch is satisfied, it will be an ideal that it is also desirable that it should track.

Constraints of Feasibility

The constraints of feasibility are, first, that the state or polity should be able to do something about relieving or remedying the complaint in question; second, that it should be able to provide an effective remedy that does not introduce new problems in place of old; and third, that it should be able to provide an efficient as well as an effective remedy: that is, a remedy that involves lower costs overall than any alternative strategy. In a phrase, the complaint must be politically remediable and remediable in an effective and efficient manner.

That the complaint must be remediable means that it must amount to something more politically interesting than a complaint about the constraints of social life, or a complaint about the *anomie* or *ennui* of human existence, or a complaint about the inequalities of status that emerge among almost all groups of human beings. There is little or nothing that governments can do about such matters, however sharply they may impinge on people's consciousness, and so there is no point in using them as a basis out of which to construct a political ideal.

But a complaint might be remediable without the state or polity being able to provide an effective remedy. It might be that state intervention would be counterproductive, for example, engendering on novel fronts precisely the sort of complaint that it is designed to relieve. Thus, it might do more harm than good in its attempt to reduce the net level of a certain evil—say, interference or domination—in the society: it might perpetrate more interference or domination than it prevents.

Finally, to turn to the third constraint, the fact that the state is able to remedy a complaint, and do so effectively, does not mean that it represents the most efficient way of dealing with it. There may be nonpolitical ways of relieving the complaint that achieve better results for the same or for lower costs. If the complaint is to underpin a feasible political ideal, then the state should be able to remedy the complaint efficiently as well as effectively.

These three constraints are hard to resist, yet many proposed ideals seem to fail them. The first constraint would rule out trying to construct a political ideal out of wholesale antipathy to power, for example, as sometimes appears to happen in the work of Michel Foucault.[2] In railing against the capillary power that runs through the smallest veins of the system, Foucault does sometimes direct attention to phenomena that we might hope to be able to rectify. But often he seems to be castigating a sort of influence that is as inescapable in the social world as gravity is in the natural.

The second, effectiveness constraint, raises serious questions about the libertarian ideal of ensuring that certain allegedly natural rights are respected in social life, in particular the right that people are assumed to have against the coercive restriction of choice. For there is no way in which the state can act so as to achieve that ideal without itself offending against it by coercively restricting the choices of individuals. This is the problem that Robert Nozick acknowledges as a challenge for rights-based libertarianism, going on to make an attempt to resolve it that is ingenious, if not successful.[3] He argues that even if people were entirely respectful of one another's rights, rational self-interest would lead them—without violating those rights—to institute a state: specifically, an "ultraminimal" state of the kind close to that which he himself favors.

The third, efficiency constraint, explains why most of us agree that we should not require the state to concern itself with saving people's souls or elevating their minds—with their fidelity to any particular religion or their achievement of any personal ideal. Seventeenth- and eighteenth-century defenders of tolerance like John Locke made the relevant point when they argued that the way to win people's souls to the practice of any worthwhile religion is by free consent, not state coercion.[4] There are better ways—certainly more efficient ways—to tackle a supposed problem of unbelief than to have recourse to the power of the polity.

Constraints of Desirability

The second bunch of constraints on the sort of complaint that a plausible political ideal should reflect relate to the desirability of the state's relieving the complaint, as distinct from the feasibility of its doing so. There are three constraints that I distinguish in this category. The first is that the complaint be discursively admissible: that is, admissible as a relevant consideration in any open discursive discussion of how things are and should be organized in a society. The other two constraints bear on the substantive character of the complaint itself rather than on such a structural aspect. The second is that it be a significant complaint, that it is hard to dismiss or downplay. And the third is that it be a complaint that subsumes a variety of other significant complaints within it.

The first constraint would rule out of consideration any complaint that is irreducibly relativized to a particular group within the society. Take a complaint of the form, "this is bad for us," where the plural refers to a particular group, not to the society as a whole. This might be just a way of drawing attention to a more general, nonsectional complaint, of course. The background assumption might be that the arrangement leaves others no better off, so that rejecting it would be a Pareto improvement: good for some—the complaining group—bad for none. Or the assumption might be that the respect in which the arrangement is bad for the group is a respect—say, that of access to one's own culture—on which all can agree that no group ought to be disadvantaged.[5] But suppose that the complaint, "this is bad for us," does not reduce to a more neutral form of complaint. In that case, it would not be discursively admissible, though it might be admissible in the context of mutual bargaining. The ordinary practice of discourse or conversation would rule it out as an irrelevant consideration to raise in an unforced, cooperative discussion about how things ought to be politically organized; it would represent a sort of special pleading and would be inconsistent with the assumptions built into such a discussion.[6] The response that the complaint would invite is: "That's not germane; the point is to discover what's best for all of us in the society, not just what's best for your group in particular."

But a complaint can be discursively admissible without being particularly significant, and so without satisfying the second constraint of desirability. It may be that while almost any of us can understand why a certain complaint should be made, none of us thinks that the complaint is of the greatest moment. While believing that someone has a just complaint in some matter, for example, we may feel that the complainant is lucky to have nothing more pressing to complain about. Clearly, any complaint out of which a plausible political ideal is to be constructed had better not be a complaint of this kind. It should be what I shall describe as a significant complaint.

The third constraint I mentioned is that any complaint out of which a political ideal is to be constructed should subsume a variety of other presumptively significant complaints within it. This constraint bears in particular on any ideal that aspires to a central or supreme place in politics. What it is designed to rule out is the sort of ideal whose satisfaction would still leave a variety of other presumptively significant complaints unsatisfied. The ideal of maximal noninterference fails rather dramatically on this front, for example, since a society might realize such an ideal and yet be one where inequality, domination, and poverty prevail. If a complaint is to provide the stuff out of which a central or supreme political ideal is to be fashioned, then the measures taken for satisfying it should serve as far as possible to satisfy such other complaints as well. This constraint may be hard to meet but it clearly represents a plausible *desideratum*. To the extent that a complaint satisfies it, the corresponding ideal will have a claim to a central and perhaps even supreme place among political ideals.

There are other *desiderata* that we might want a political ideal to satisfy, but I shall stick with those just rehearsed. In the next section I look at how far the republican ideal of nondomination satisfies the feasibility constraints, and then in the final section I look at how far it answers to the constraints of desirability. While I shall have to make my points briskly and without much elaboration, I hope that the overview I provide will help to show just how attractive the ideal is.

2. Nondomination and the Feasibility Constraints

The three questions to be asked about the complaint that republican theory privileges—the complaint, as I take it, about being dominated—are whether this is something that the state can take steps to remedy; if so, whether the remedy it can offer is effective, not counterproductive; and if it is effective, whether the remedy provided is efficient, comparing well with alternative strategies.

Defining Domination

Before tackling those questions, however, we must first consider what domination involves. Here I must be brief, drawing on work done elsewhere.[7] I say that individual or group agents dominate an individual to the extent that they are in a position to interfere arbitrarily in the affairs of that person: to the extent, that is to say, that such arbitrary interference is accessible and uncostly.

My understanding of interference is narrow, so far as I take it to require intentionality or at least negligence—quasi-intentionality —on the part of the agent; it does not materialize just by way of brute accident but is something for which the agent can be reasonably held responsible.[8] My understanding of interference is broad, on the other hand, so far as I take it to include, not just removing an option from the range of options otherwise available in some choice to the person interfered with, but raising the costs of taking an option or even denying the person knowledge of the options available or of the costs in prospect.[9] The intuition driving the account is that interference should be equated with any initiative that intentionally worsens an individual's choice situation—and this, even if it is for the person's overall good—where contextual conventions and expectations may be involved in determining whether a certain act counts as a way of worsening that situation. Thus, to illustrate the approach taken, an agent may interfere with someone's choice, not just by forcibly or manipulatively rigging the options available, but also by threatening her sincerely with a penalty if she takes a certain option or by actually penalizing her for taking it. And an agent may interfere in the person's affairs by misleading her, as in the insincere but credible threat of penalty or in the deliberate withholding of information.[10]

An agent is dominated, I said, to the extent that a group or individual is in a position to interfere arbitrarily in his or her affairs. What makes an act of interference arbitrary? Not the effect of that interference itself: not, for example, the fact that it is to the detriment of the victim involved. Rather, the fact that in choosing to interfere, the dominating agent is not forced to track the avowed interests of the individual interfered with—or the interests the victim is readily disposed to avow—but can interfere more or less as his or her own will or judgment dictates. An act of interference will be arbitrary to the extent that it is not controlled by the avowable interests of the victim but, as arbitrary interference usually will be, is controlled by the *arbitrium* of the interferer, where *arbitrium* may refer to will or judgment. Thus, an act of interference may be done for the good of the victim, and may be successful in achieving that good, and yet be arbitrary. That it is arbitrary is fixed by the controls to which it is subject, not the ends that it happens to effect.

There are three respects in which domination, by this account, comes in degrees. An agent may have a greater or lesser capacity to interfere arbitrarily in someone's affairs, for the option may be more or less accessible or uncostly. An agent may have a capacity to interfere more or less arbitrarily, for he may be more or less unburdened by constraints designed to force him to track the avowable interests of the victim. And an agent may have a capacity to interfere arbitrarily in a larger or smaller class of choices by the agent, or in choices that are intuitively of greater or lesser significance to the agent.[11] Domination, then, is not an on-or-off condition but one to which a person may be subject at a higher or lower degree of intensity. This should always be kept in mind, even when convenience of presentation requires us to describe it as if it were an on-or-off matter.

First Feasibility Constraint

Is the complaint about being dominated by others one that the state is in a position, at least in principle, to do something about? Clearly, I think, yes. In the nature of things, the state claims a monopoly of legitimate force in its community—if other agencies exercise legitimate force that is through being allowed to do so by the state—and that claim must be more or less effectively implemented within any well-ordered polity. But if the state has access to the use of force, and to the threat of force—to coercion—then it is in a position to reduce the degree to which people suffer at least certain forms of domination.

One way in which it might do this is by redistributing resources and powers of interference across the population in a society. Where X was previously able with impunity to interfere arbitrarily in Y's affairs, a redistribution might ensure that Y is able to retaliate, so that the expected cost of X's interference goes up and the domination X enjoys diminishes or disappears. Call this the strategy of armament. Another way in which the state might reduce domination is by disarmament: that is, by removing the extra resources and powers that enable some to dominate others. And yet another is by protection—by putting defenses in place for those who might otherwise be dominated.

The armament, disarmament, and protection strategies might in turn be pursued by the state in a more or less direct or more or less indirect way. Those who are dominated may be armed or protected by virtue of explicit legal and political measures. Or they may be armed or protected so far as the state facilitates and sponsors developments in civil society that serve suitable purposes. They may be armed or protected, for example, so far as the state is able to encourage a civic culture of condemnation for various forms of arbitrary interference and a culture of coming to the aid of those who suffer such interference. Again those who dominate might be disarmed by explicit state action or by recourse to less formal methods. Take the case where a monopoly firm in a company town dominates those who depend on the firm for employment. This firm may be effectively disarmed if the state explicitly limits its power of dismissal, or ensures relatively generous unemployment benefits, or provides incentives or facilities that attract other employers into the labor market. The possibilities are legion.

Second Feasibility Constraint

Let it be granted that the state can do something by way of remedying the complaint many people will have—whether or not they phrase it that way—of being dominated by others: the complaint is not one of those irremediable complaints that no one, or at least not the state, is able to do anything about. The next question is whether in seeking to provide a remedy for the complaint of domination, the state is likely to do more harm than good. In particular, is it likely to represent a new force of domination at the very moment that it seeks to relieve people of domination? Is it likely to be counterproductive?

Consider, first, not the ideal of nondomination, but rather that of noninterference. It is commonly acknowledged among those who invoke this ideal—this conception of freedom—that as the state tries to reduce the interference that some agents practice in the lives of others, it will itself have to interfere in people's lives. In order to prevent violence and coercion, it will itself have to coerce people into paying taxes and obeying the laws, and it will have to practice penal violence against convicted offenders, whether in levying fines, imprisoning them, or even resorting to capital punishment. "As against the coercion applicable by individual to individual, no liberty can be given to one man but in proportion as it is taken away from another. All coercive laws, therefore, and in particular all laws creative of liberty, are as far as they go abrogative of liberty."[12] This means that there is a risk of the state being an ineffective agency for promoting noninterference—it may do more harm than good—though it does not mean that the state will necessarily be ineffective: there may be good grounds for hoping that the level of interference it perpetrates is less than the level of interference it prevents.

How do things stand with the state as an agency for promoting nondomination, as distinct from noninterference? They stand even better. For not only is there bound to be a hope, if the state dominates people in some measure, that it will perpetrate less domination than it prevents. There is also a hope that while it interferes in people's lives, it will still not dominate them, or will dominate them only in a relatively insignificant degree.

The reason for this higher hope is that while the state has to interfere with people, if only by way of coercing them to pay taxes and obey the law, it need not interfere with them arbitrarily. It will not interfere arbitrarily, according to the account given earlier, if it is in the ready-to-be-avowed, overall interest of each to have a state that interferes in their lives, and controls their affairs, according to a certain brief. And it is plausible that this will be in the ready-to-be-avowed interest of each, provided that the interference allowed to the state is subject to a controlling brief that helps to ensure that on every issue it has to track the common, readily avowable interests of citizens, and only such interests. I conceive of common interests as those interests whose collective promotion is supported by considerations that people admit as discursively relevant, but others may wish to introduce a different conception at this point.[13] Whatever conception of common, readily avowable interests is adopted, however, the really telling question is whether there is any prospect of constraining the state, once established, so that it acts only for the furtherance of such interests: in the traditional phrase, only for the promotion of the common good.[14]

The republican tradition has given enormous, sometimes almost exclusive attention to this question in the long history that involves Cicero and Machiavelli, Montesquieu and Rousseau, Harrington and Madison. The notion of the blended or mixed constitution—the sort of constitution that Polybius celebrated in Rome —was developed, for example, in the attempt to work out the sorts of arrangements that would constrain the state suitably and effectively, forcing it to serve the common good. And many other notions, some of them implicated in this master idea, were elaborated and varied with a view to finding the best institutional design. They include proposals for dividing up sovereignty both between the legislature, the executive, and the judiciary and—as in bicameral arrangements—within the legislature; for requiring public decisions to be matters of proper legislation, and for legislation to conform to the rule of law; for ensuring that decisions are made according to agreed-upon reasons and for establishing associated possibilities of appeal, review, and consultation; for devising methods of election and appointment to public office that further the prospect of common avowable interests—the common good —being tracked; and for constitutionally limiting the range of matters over which government can have influence as well as for limiting the sorts of decisions it can make.

The most interesting challenge for republican thought today— that is, for the sort of thinking that is oriented around the ideal of nondomination—bears on how to design political arrangements so that, as far as possible, the state really is forced to track all and only the common, ready-to-be-avowed interests of the citizenry. The challenge is to see how far government may operate, so that while it can have the reduction of nondomination as a central or even principal aim, it need not itself represent an arbitrary and therefore dominating influence.[15] I do not say that any institutional design is going to remove domination fully and meet the challenge with complete success. But there is at least a hope that state domination may be reduced to a tolerable minimum: a level that is clearly compensated for by the domination that the state prevents.

That this hope is rational is enough for our purposes here; we do not have to do any more by way of vindicating it. For the fact that it is rational to hope for an institutional design that will curb the dominating potential of the state means that we cannot dismiss the complaint about domination as one that no state could remedy effectively. To dismiss it in such a way would be to surrender preemptively to despair at ever finding the sort of institutional design required.

The position adopted here is not one of utopian idealism. We may concede, for example, that even if the state does not interfere in an arbitrary and dominating way in people's lives, it is still bound to do some harm to their enjoyment of nondominated choice. It is bound to limit the range over which people may enjoy nondominated choice, just as natural obstacles limit that range. Like the nonintentional obstruction that the natural world or the social system may impose, nonarbitrary but intentional interference will condition people's enjoyment of nondomination, even if it does not compromise it: even if it does not itself represent a form of domination.[16] It will restrict the number of choices in which people may take advantage of their not being dominated.

The fact that the state is bound to condition people's enjoyment of nondominated choice in this way does not mean that it will be an ineffective agency for promoting nondomination. We may disagree about how exactly to weight the two, but the compromising of nondomination that the state can prevent is intuitively more important than the conditioning of nondomination that it is bound to impose. Still, there is an important lesson that follows from the fact that even the nondominating state conditions people's enjoyment of nondomination. This is that, as between two forms of state that do equally well in reducing domination, where one involves deeper-running legislation and coercion than the other, we ought to prefer to have the one that interferes less.

Finally, we have an objection. If the state espouses nondomination as a goal, won't it find itself shackled to a project that will demand more and more in the way of resources and interference? Won't it be at the mercy of an essentially insatiable goal? The range of matters that the state is allowed to take under its purview will increase dramatically, one may say, as the baseline of nondomination rises. And so it is bound to give rise over time to counterproductive, dominating effects that will leave people worse off in terms of nondomination than they would have been under a more modest regime.

This challenge articulates a danger, however, not an inevitability. And the danger teaches us that if we are to devise a set of policies for the state to espouse in the attempt to remedy complaints of domination, then we should be on our guard against the sort of power creep envisaged. There is undoubtedly a lot of room, starting from the sort of society most of us live in today, for the state to explore new policies. Imagine, then, that we introduce those initiatives incrementally, with a view to seeing how well they do overall in coping with domination. As we increase the initiatives explored, thereby enlarging the reach of the state, we should be alert to the likelihood of there being a point where there is no net gain in evidence or in prospect. At that point, the state itself will begin to condition people's enjoyment of undominated choice in such a measure, or will threaten to compromise people's undominated status in such a degree that the lesson is: Stop! From that point on the certain damage done by state activity, even as it is assessed in the ledger books of nondomination, will be too great to compensate for any likely benefit it may achieve.[17]

There will undoubtedly be differences among people on the question of whether at any point the state has done all that it can do without becoming counterproductive; espousing the ideal of nondomination does not mean having an automatic resolution of those differences. The point to note here, however, is that no matter how great those differences are, it can be agreed on all sides that there is an end at some point to what the state can productively do. There will be agreement that the cause of remedying complaints of domination does not threaten to legitimate rampant, uncritical recourse to the state. And that there is bound to be agreement on that point means that the complaint about being dominated does not hold out the specter of an insatiable political ideal.

Third Feasibility Constraint

We turn finally to the third question of feasibility. This is the issue of whether relying on the state promises to do better than any

other likely strategy for reducing domination in a society; in particular, whether relying on a state that is designed to track all and
only the readily avowable, common interests of citizens promises
to beat alternatives. If it does not promise to do better than other
instrumentalities, then this is going to mean that it does not represent an efficient agency on this front.

The salient alternative to introducing a state, and authorizing it
to act against the domination of some by others, is to rely on the
spontaneous measures of economic and civil society to give rise to
high levels of nondomination all around. But there is little or no
prospect of spontaneous interactions and formations supporting a
regime of nondomination. The problem is that resources generally attract more resources, power more power: to them that have
it shall be given. Thus, if social life is left to evolve without any political shaping, it will tend to allow the emergence of relatively few
positions of influence and to open the way for the domination of
the many by the few who command those positions. This is a
melancholy observation but one that is supported by common
sense, historical experience, and the testimony of many literary
traditions.

As the state promises to be an effective agency in acting against
domination, then, it looks likely to represent the most efficient instrumentality available. The state will be able to achieve only very
little, as the long republican tradition emphasizes, if it cannot rely
on a fund of civic virtue and commitment for ensuring a regime
of nondomination: "Just as good morals, if they are to be maintained, have need of the laws, so the laws, if they are to be observed, have need of good morals."[18] But without the state as a
guiding presence, as indeed Machiavelli takes for granted, there is
no hope of such virtue and commitment—such good morals—
achieving anything.

3. Nondomination and the
Desirability Constraints

First Desirability Constraint

The first constraint of desirability on a political ideal is that the
complaint it articulates be one that can be raised as a relevant con-

sideration in discourse among people as to how their social and political affairs can be best organized. Does the complaint about domination come across as a consideration admissible in presumptively cooperative discussion, and not just as a complaint of the self-seeking kind that will be deemed irrelevant—an instance of special pleading—in such exchange? Does it present itself as a complaint that all must countenance and take into account? I believe that it does present itself as a complaint of that kind, and for the deepest of reasons.

When a number of people engage in discourse, their aim being to determine what is so in some domain or how it is best for them to act as a whole, then they give exclusive privilege to a particular form of influence that they may have on one another: that which occurs by virtue of producing reasons relevant to the outcome that is to be resolved. Thus they eschew the ways in which people influence one another when they exercise violence, or coercion, or intimidation, or anything of that kind. They authorize one another as voices that are generally capable of providing reasons relevant by discursive criteria and as ears that are generally capable of recognizing such reasons when they are once produced. From the point of view of the discourse that they essay, only properly reason-mediated influence is legitimate.[19]

This being so, any party to discourse is certainly going to be able to complain admissibly about the existence of a form of influence that reduces their capacity to exercise or undergo discursive influence proper. It will be absolutely reasonable for anyone to complain, for example, about being pressured or coerced by others to go along with a certain line; those who attempt such pressure or coercion do not honor the constitutive requirements of discourse: they are playing another game. But the existence of a relation of domination between one party and some other or others means that that party is subject to a form of influence that reduces their capacity to interact discursively—it reduces their capacity to influence and be influenced in a purely reason-mediated way—and so it is going to be perfectly admissible for someone to complain about domination of that kind.

Why is domination going to reduce a person's capacity to interact discursively with others? Because, as a long tradition of thought insists, the fact of being exposed to the possibility of arbitrary

interference from another impacts in a serious way on the likelihood that a person will speak his mind.[20] It will put in place a powerful incentive to keep the dominating parties on side, however
beneficent they may be: to keep them sweet both by positive measures of ingratiation and by negative measures of avoidance and
self-censorship. There is an old ideal, celebrated for example in
the Quaker tradition, of speaking truth to power. But speaking
truth to power is an ideal, precisely because it is recognized on all
sides to be difficult. The person who speaks truth to power, never
flinching from the most unpalatable forms of advice or rebuke, or
the most unwelcome expressions of opinion, is a saint or a hero,
not someone of merely regular nerve.

Not only is domination likely to lead someone to warp his or
her voice, tuning it to the expectations and tastes of potentially
dangerous potentates. This being a matter of common recognition—as it always has been—domination will also lead others not
to take seriously the words uttered by anyone in a position of subordination and dependency. How can people trust the remarks of
the vulnerable person, especially when they are tailored to fit with
the opinions of someone in relation to whom they suffer vulnerability? They may seek out their opinions, particularly when it is
they who are in the position of power—it is always pleasing, after
all, to have some reinforcement of one's own views—but they will
have no reason to take the dominated person really seriously; they
will have no reason to grant that person a real voice or give him or
her a genuine hearing.

I hope that these remarks will make it plausible that the complaint of being dominated is well suited in respect of discursive
admissibility to underpin a central political ideal. But is the complaint a truly significant one, in particular a complaint fit to engage the attentions of the polity? That is the next question to be
considered.

Second Desirability Constraint

The feature that marks human beings off from other species is our
capacity to enter discourse with each other, relying on a common
language in which we authorize one another as generally competent speakers and listeners: as speakers who warrant and deserve a

hearing, and as listeners who can acknowledge our claim to a similar hearing in turn. Let someone be denied full access to discourse with her fellows, or a full presence there, and she is denied full enjoyment of the treatment—the authorization or respect—that marks her off as a person among persons.

The primary reason why the complaint about being dominated is of the first significance is that domination almost invariably undermines a person's capacity to enjoy respect in this sense. Where one person dominates another, it is almost bound to be a matter of common awareness among the people involved, and among other relevant parties, that this domination exists. The question as to whether someone is dominated by another is one that will interest all those involved, after all, and the answer to that question will be obvious in most cases from the sorts of resources they control relative to that other. Thus we may expect most people to recognize domination when they see it, and this in turn being obvious, to recognize that others will recognize it too, thereby giving rise to the usual hierarchy of common awareness; each will believe that the person is dominated, each will believe that each believes this, and so on.[21] Once it is recognized as a matter of common awareness that someone is dominated, however, then that person will no longer be able to enjoy the basic respect that we think personhood entitles him to. He will no longer have the sort of voice that can be reliably forthright, or can be expected to be forthright. He will always be under suspicion of playing to the audience of the powerful and never having anything worthwhile to say in his own right.

Dominated subjects of this kind may not be ignored or dismissed outright: they may be treated magnanimously to the trappings of respect. But they will not command respect; they will receive it only in the manner of supplicants. They may be treated as if they had the status of persons, so we might put it, but they will not really have that status. Being a person is inseparable from earning and receiving respect as of right—as of effective, not just formal right—and in their case there will be no question of earning or receiving as of right. What they receive, they will receive only as a gift—only by grace of the powerful.

This line of thought is a familiar and recurrent one in republican thought. It is worth mentioning in connection with it that Kant, the great philosopher of respect and personhood, seems to have shaped many of his ideas on that subject in his reflections on Rousseau's *Social Contract,* itself a book that belongs at least among the apocrypha of the republican tradition. The point is emphasized by J. B. Schneewind, who quotes Kant as saying: "It is not all one under what title I get something. What properly belongs to me must not be accorded to me merely as something I ask for."[22] Schneewind comments: "If nothing is properly mine except what someone graciously gives me, I am forever dependent on how the donor feels toward me. My independence as an autonomous being is threatened. Only if I can claim the others *have to* give me what is mine by right can this be avoided."[23]

Given the connection between enjoying respect as a person and not being subject to domination, there is every reason to treat the complaint of being dominated as extremely significant. What more serious complaint could there be than one that draws attention to a relationship in virtue of which one's very standing as a person who can command the attention and respect of others is put in jeopardy? This is no mere trifle to do with having one's nose put out of joint, or one's feathers ruffled. It is a complaint of the first moment. Let some people be dominated and to that extent they will be put out of any community that involves those who dominate. They may aspire to community with such others and their presence may even be tolerated among those others. But they will always cut somewhat sorry or comic figures, and will always invite only condescension or contempt. They will have no more standing, in a somewhat archaic image, than dogs that cower at their masters' feet or that snuggle up to their mistresses' skirts.

One word more on the significance of the complaint about being dominated. People don't reveal their minds only in the words they explicitly stand over in discursive settings. They also express their discursive minds in the actions they choose to perform, because they routinely acknowledge that they may be held answerable for their actions in discourse: they don't deny the relevance of discursive challenge as to the legitimacy of what they do. But if someone is dominated by another—and even if that other does not exercise the domination in attempts at pressure or coercion—then we may expect the relationship to warp the things they do as well as the things they say. We may expect people to take positive measures of self-ingratiation and negative measures of self-censorship that would not appeal to them in the absence of the domination. And that being so, the deleterious impact of domination will be obvious, even short of actual interference by the dominating person, in the deeds as well as in the words of the victim.

This observation is worth adding, because it shows that just as the dominated person cannot be taken to enjoy the freedom of thought that is necessary if someone is to be worth hearing, they also cannot be taken to enjoy freedom of choice, either. Operating within the gravitational field that relationships of domination establish, people are deprived of a measure of discursive control that would otherwise be available. When they purport to speak their minds or to display their minds in action, therefore, there is a robust possibility, marked in everyday expectation, that they are not fully their own masters; they are not reflecting their own best opinion of what circumstances require but rather the opinion that materializes most comfortably at their particular place in the field of dominating force.

The significance of the complaint about being dominated is borne out in the rich idioms associated with the complaint and with the many changes that have been rung, and that continue to be rung, on them. This is cast in melancholy tones as a condition of servitude or subordination, subjection or subjugation—at the limit, a condition of slavery—in which one can do nothing but by the leave or permission of others, one lives under their thumb as those in the Roman circus lived under the thumb of the emperor, one has to fawn and toady and kowtow in their direction, one has to ingratiate oneself with them or at least placate and humor them, and one has to tug the forelock or tip the cap, acknowledging them as one's superiors and betters. The condition in which the complaint has no ground is cast, by contrast, as an ideal of being able to stand on one's own two feet, and to walk tall, having a standing on a par with others; an ideal of being able to look others in the eye, not showing fear or deference, and not seeking grace or favor; and an ideal of being one's own man or woman or master: an ideal in Roman terms of being *sui juris*.

These phrases have often been formed in relation to contexts that no longer obtain very commonly. But there are contexts aplenty in contemporary society where the message they convey—ultimately, the complaint they carry—still clearly applies. Think of

the child of the emotionally volatile parent; the wife of the occasionally violent husband; or the pupil of the teacher who forms arbitrary likes and dislikes. Think of the employee whose security
requires keeping the boss or manager sweet; the debtor whose fortunes depend on the caprice of moneylender or bank manager; or
the small business owner whose viability depends on the attitude
taken by a bigger competitor or a union boss. Think of the welfare
recipient whose fortunes turn on the mood of the counter clerk;
the immigrant or indigenous person whose standing is vulnerable
to the whims that rule politics and talk-back radio; or the public
employee whose future depends, not on performance, but on the
political profile that an ambitious minister happens to find elec-
torally most useful. Think of the older person who is vulnerable to
the culturally and institutionally unrestrained gang of youths in his
or her area. Or think indeed of the young offender whose level of
punishment depends on how far politicians or newspapers choose
to whip up a culture of vengeance.

In all of these cases, someone lives at the mercy of others. That
person is dominated by those others in the sense that even if they
don't interfere in his or her life, they have a more or less arbitrary
power of doing so on a greater or larger front and in a more or
less substantive measure: there are few restraints or costs to inhibit
them. If the dominated person escapes ill treatment in such a situation, that is by the grace or favor of the powerful, or perhaps by
dint of a native cunning and deception. The price of liberty in
such a world is not eternal vigilance but rather, in a phrase once
used by Gore Vidal, eternal discretion. The person lives in the
power or under the mastery of others: they occupy the position of
a *dominus* in his or her life.

Third Desirability Constraint

That the complaint about being dominated not only passes the
feasibility constraints but is admissible and significant already goes
a long way to establishing that it ought to have a serious place in
politics—in effect, that the ideal of nondomination ought to be
targeted by the state. But the complaint might be all of these
things and not connect in any substantial manner with other complaints that have traditionally been placed within the province of

the polity's responsibility. We turn now to the question as to whether that is how things stand with the complaint about being dominated. Is it a more or less stand-alone complaint such that rectifying it leaves many other putatively relevant political complaints unaddressed? Or is it a complaint such that if the state takes serious steps to put it right then it will at the same time take steps that put many other complaints right? Is it a complaint that subsumes a range of other complaints in that sense? I argue that it is a characteristically subsumptive complaint, not one of the stand-alone variety.

The best way to support this point, at least in the short compass available, is to consider how far the rectification of complaints about domination in a society would go to establishing a sample of other ideals. I shall include in my sample liberty, equality, and community—the three ideals of the French Revolution—as well as functioning capability, in Amartya Sen's phrase,[24] and a contractualist conception of justice.

Liberty

I have argued elsewhere that liberty or freedom was long conceptualized precisely as the absence of domination: not being under the thumb of a master.[25] If that construal is accepted, then it follows that someone may be unfree in doing something, even though there is no natural obstacle that constrains them to do it and no one forces or coerces them to do it. This will happen so far as the person is inhibited or intimidated by the presence of a power that has to be kept sweet. But if the construal is accepted, then another perhaps more surprising result also follows: this is that someone is not necessarily rendered unfree by the fact of a natural obstacle removing an option or raising the costs of taking it, or by the fact of an intentional agency interfering in her affairs to a similar effect. The natural obstacle won't dominate the person so it can't make her unfree. And the interfering agency may not dominate the person—the agency may be forced to track the person's avowed interests—in which case it won't make her unfree, either. How easy is it to live with this implication, while claiming that the relief of domination will advance the ideal of liberty?

It is quite easy, I suggest, to live with this conclusion so long as we recognize that without compromising the enjoyment of non-domination—without itself being dominating—a natural obstacle or an intentional agency may still have a negative effect on that enjoyment; it may condition it, as we saw earlier, by restricting the range over which—or indeed the ease with which—the person exercises undominated choice. Even if liberty is taken to require the absence of natural limitation or the absence of intentional interference, then, we can see that the systematic remedying of the complaint about domination is going to involve, so far as possible, the reduction of nonintentional obstacles, and of intentional but nondominating obstacles, to people's choices; we already mentioned this point in the second section.

If nondomination is used to conceptualize liberty, therefore, it leads us to distinguish between primary and secondary restrictions on liberty. The primary form of restriction is domination by another person or group: in this case the person or group has more or less ready access to more or less arbitrary interference across a more or less substantial range of choices. The secondary form of restriction is the limitation imposed by nonintentional forces and the interference practiced by intentional but nonarbitrary agencies. It seems right and intuitive to me that this distinction is made between these two different grades of restriction, since only the primary form is inimical to an agent's status as a person; one is not de-authorized or disrespected by nonintentional or nonarbitrary influences in one's life. But it is important that even if people worry about the secondary form of restriction, they will see that a state committed to advancing the enjoyment of nondomination will go a long way toward satisfying their concern.[26]

Equality

What now of the ideal of equality? There are many interpretations of that ideal, as there are notoriously many ways in which people may or may not be equal with one another. But from our point of view a very significant aspect of the ideal is going to be equality of nondomination: in effect, equality of the kind that is provided when people equally command the attention and the respect of others. An obvious question, then, is whether the attempt by a state to redress the complaint that individuals may have about

being dominated is likely to push toward equality of nondomination or whether it is likely to create or support large inequalities,
with nondomination being maximized at a point where there are
such inequalities between people. It is often said that the maximization of people's subjective utility or happiness may require
that some are very unhappy, and in particular much less happy
than others; that is how the sums may come out. Is the same sort of
thing likely with the maximization of nondomination? Or is there
a closer tie between promoting this ideal overall and ensuring that
the distribution across people tends toward equality?

As it turns out, there is indeed a close tie between maximizing
and equalizing the enjoyment of nondomination.[27] Whether a person is to enjoy a good measure of nondomination in relation to
others depends not on their absolute level of power—their power
of interfering, retaliating, defending themselves, and so on—but
on their level of power relative to the power of others. A level of
power that would give me absolute supremacy in one society may
leave me relatively badly off in another; in the land of the blind,
the one-eyed man is king. This means that if the power of some
people is increased with a view to increasing the nondomination
they enjoy, then by that very token the degree of nondomination
enjoyed by others falls; any positive move on one front is at the
same time a negative move on another.

But not only is there going to be interaction between different
fronts in this way. A second equally plausible observation suggests
that it will always be better from the point of view of maximizing
the enjoyment of nondomination in a society to act on fronts that
make for its equalization among members of that society. As we increase the relative powers of people with a view to increasing their
nondomination, there will tend to be a better result available so
far as we focus on relatively powerless rather than on relatively
powerful individuals. The more powerful people are, the smaller
will be the gain in making them more impregnable to others—the
extra resources may be redundant—and the larger the loss in
making others more vulnerable to them: the extra resources will
impact ever more significantly on the prospects of the weak.

If the level of people's nondomination is sensitive to their
relative degrees of power, and if this sensitivity is greater for
the weaker than for the stronger, then any attempt to maximize

nondomination overall is bound to focus at every stage on improving the lot of the weaker, and it is bound thereby to push toward more and more equality. This represents a fundamental tie between the ideal of nondomination and the ideal of equality, and one indeed that was well recognized even in Roman times.[28] Any society where people's nondomination is at a maximum will be a society in which people enjoy a corresponding equality of status, with each doing as well as can be expected in commanding the respect of their fellows. This sort of equality does not entail equality in every other dimension; it is consistent, for example, with inequality in the subjective well-being that people enjoy and with at least a certain degree of inequality in the objective resources at their command: in their wealth. But it still represents a substantial kind of equality and it should encourage egalitarians who might otherwise have balked at making nondomination into a central, even supreme, political ideal.

Community

As there is a tie between valuing nondomination and valuing equality, in particular equality of status, so there is also a tie between valuing nondomination and valuing community. There are three points to make about this connection. The first is that nondomination has been understood in the long republican tradition —and is understood here—in such a way that it cannot be enjoyed by the solitary individual. To enjoy nondomination it is necessary, first, to have other people around with whom one interacts; and second, that one not be dominated by those people: that one enjoy standing in relation to them, being able to look them in the eye, commanding their attention and respect. It is not sufficient that there be no one in one's vicinity and so, *a fortiori*, that one not be dominated. One must enjoy the absence of domination in a context where it is a real possibility, not enjoy it as a mere by-product of total isolation. This condition already ensures a connection between nondomination and community, for it means that the ideal of nondomination is an inherently social value, not an atomistic one.

The second point to make in underscoring the tie to community is that if people are secured against domination by the operation of the institutional instrumentalities available for the state to deploy—the institutions of armament, disarmament, and protection—then the connection between being nondominated and those institutions is constitutive and not merely causal. To be nondominated is to be more or less immune to the possibility of arbitrary interference, and this immunity will come into being simultaneously with the introduction of measures that realize it, not as a causal consequence of those measures being in place: a consequence that might take time to realize. The connection between immunity to arbitrary interference and the presence of those measures will be like the connection between immunity to a certain disease and the presence of suitable antibodies in the blood. The physical immunity will not materialize as a contingent consequence of the antibodies that take a certain time to eventuate; it is present as soon as the antibodies are there, being realized by the antibodies. And similarly a person's immunity to arbitrary interference—a person's nondomination—will not materialize as a causal result of the institutional measures taken to realize it; rather, it will be constituted by those measures, being present just as soon as they are present.[29]

The fact that nondomination requires a community of individuals, and that a person's nondomination will be constituted by the institutional measures that make him or her more or less secure against arbitrary interference by other members of the community, means that for the state to work at promoting nondomination is just for the state to work at ensuring that people enjoy a certain sort of community: a sort of community that is bound to have the aspect of an ideal. The third point I want to add further emphasizes this connection between promoting the two ideals.

The value of nondomination is tied up with its being a matter of common awareness that one is not dominated, as we saw earlier. That means that if we are to enjoy nondomination properly, we have to be more or less secure against arbitrary interference, being personally protected, or having access to personal resources of retaliation. But it also means, we should notice, that others in any salient class to which we belong have got to be secure in the same way. Suppose that you are a black or a woman or an indigenous person in a society where people in those classes are generally dominated in certain ways. The fact that you have purely personal resources against domination, say because of being very wealthy, will not ensure that you enjoy nondomination properly. For membership in that vulnerability class will convey the message to many that you are dominated and will constantly put pressure on the discursive status that you can enjoy; you will have to vindicate your standing, case by case, time after time. Thus, if you are to achieve the proper enjoyment of your nondomination, it had better be the case that all others in your vulnerability class escape domination too. You cannot enjoy freedom as nondomination without others in every salient class to which you belong—including, in the last analysis, others in the society as a whole—enjoying that sort of freedom as well.

Functioning Capability

I said that there are two other ideals, apart from those associated with freedom, equality, and community, that are subsumed in the ideal of nondomination. The first is functioning capability in Amartya Sen's sense, and the second is justice in the contractualist sense associated with John Rawls[30] and T. M. Scanlon.[31]

To enjoy functioning capability is to be in a position where the things one can do and be in one's society mean that by local criteria one functions perfectly well: intuitively speaking, one is not poor or deprived, even if one is not particularly rich. Capability in this sense will require access to conditions such as being fed, being healthy, being housed, being linked with family or friends, communicating with others, following what happens in public life, and tracking the opportunities for work and related activities.[32] There are two grounds for thinking that the ideal of nondomination subsumes this ideal of functioning capability.[33] The first is that to the extent that a person lacks such capability, to that extent he or she will be vulnerable to all sorts of arbitrary interference on the part of others. And the second is that even if someone's poverty or lack of capability does not expose him or her to further domination, it will still limit the range or ease with which he or she can enjoy nondomination, so that there is reason why a state that wants to advance such enjoyment should want, costs allowing, to put such lack of capability right, too.

Contractualist Justice

Roughly speaking, an arrangement will be just in a contractualist sense so far as people cannot reject it on the grounds that it violates an unobjectionable principle for regulating relations between mutually respectful individuals, in particular for regulating them politically; that the principle is unobjectionable means that it would attract no reasonable objection: no objection, as we may understand it here, that would survive discursive interrogation. Will a regime in which nondomination is maximized be likely to count as just in this sense? I think so. The sort of person who may be expected to complain about its injustice is one who suffers some redistribution of resources toward the poorer or some diminution of native advantages of power. But it is hard to see how the complaint made by such a person could stand up in the contractualist court.

The person envisaged acquiesces in the need for a regulation of the relations between mutually respectful people; specifically, in the need for a political regulation of those relations; and more specifically still, in the need for their regulation by a state that is designed as well as possible to advance all and only the readily avowable, common interests of citizens. There would be no issue to be considered, were this not so. The question, then, is whether this person could identify an unobjectionable principle on the basis of which to protest against the loss he or she suffers as a result of a redistribution of relative powers, even when the redistribution is necessary for increasing the nondomination enjoyed by people under the polity: that is, is necessary for meeting the complaints of various others about being dominated.

The person cannot dismiss the complaints about being dominated as being unnecessary to heed in discourse about how the state should be organized; after all, it is an admissible and significant sort of complaint, by the argument provided above. The only grounds on which the person can protest the redistribution, therefore, must be that the pattern of benefits and burdens it imposes is deemed unfair. But those grounds are bound to look hollow. In seeking to remedy complaints of domination, the state is trying to advance a common interest that all are ready, so we may presume, to avow. The benefits to be gained for the interest of the weaker are great and the costs to the person complaining are not comparable; the person does not lose out substantially in terms of nondomination, after all, even if he or she suffers some financial loss or some loss of privilege. And so it is hard to see how the person envisaged can identify any unobjectionable principle on the basis of which to protest the redistribution. Any redistribution that advances the cause of nondomination is also likely to advance the cause of justice in the contractualist sense.

Conclusion

I hope that these brisk remarks will help to establish the powerful case that can be made for putting the complaint of domination right at the center of political concerns and for making the ideal of nondomination one of the central ideals in politics, if not the supreme political ideal. The state can do something about this complaint, something that provides both an effective and efficient remedy. The complaint is admissible in any open discourse on the best form of the state and directs us to a significant and subsumptive ideal. The performance of the complaint on these fronts gives it a serious claim on our attention in normative political thought and, presumptively, as my passing comments have tried to indicate, a more serious claim than any of its rivals.

I said earlier that there are other *desiderata* or constraints that we might expect a political ideal to satisfy, apart from those we have considered. In conclusion, I might mention that one of these is the *desideratum* of being a measurable ideal, on which many recent writers have focused.[34] The measurable ideal will enable us to determine how well individuals within a polity are doing in relation to that ideal and how well the polity does in comparisons across time or with other regimes. The ideal of nondomination does not count as a highly measurable ideal. First of all, domination and nondomination come in degrees along at least three separate dimensions that are not easily weighted against one another: it may involve more or less easy access to more or less arbitrary interference across a more or less substantive range. Second, there are two respects, also not easily weighted against each other, in which we will want the state to do well by the ideal: one, by reducing domination itself—by reducing the influence of factors that compromise undominated choice; and two, by reducing the presence of nondominating factors that condition such choice without compromising it.

In view of these complexities, the ideal of nondomination is not going to lend itself to ready measurement; there will always be issues of weighting that need discussion in any instance where it is to be applied. We might try to resolve those weighting issues at the abstract level, but I see little prospect of doing so in a way that is going to win general support. Still, however, I don't think we should lose heart. The important thing with any political ideal is that it be amenable to disciplined arbitration in the course of a conversation that involves all relevant sides; it is not a vague and nebulous notion that allows everyone to think what they will. And in this respect nondomination promises to do quite well. While people may not easily come to agreement on weightings to be assigned in the abstract to the different elements it involves, it will usually be clear how these elements should be weighted in the context of concrete issues. The ideal may not make the algorithmic adjudication of political arrangements possible, but it does represent a yardstick that will not easily bend to the grain of individual interest or bias.[35]

NOTES

1. See Philip Pettit, "Freedom and Antipower," *Ethics* 106 (1996): 576–604; idem, *Republicanism: A Theory of Freedom and Government* (Oxford: Oxford University Press, 1997); idem, *A Theory of Freedom: From the Psychology to the Politics of Agency* (Cambridge and New York: Polity and Oxford University Press, 2001); idem, "Keeping Republican Freedom Simple: On a Difference with Quentin Skinner," *Political Theory* 30 (2002); Quentin Skinner, *Liberty before Liberalism* (Cambridge: Cambridge University Press, 1998); and Maurizio Viroli, *Machiavelli* (Oxford: Oxford University Press, 1998).

2. See Michel Foucault, *Power/Knowledge: Selected Interviews and Other Writings, 1872–1977,* ed. and trans. Colin Gordon (New York: Pantheon Books, 1980).

3. See Robert Nozick, *Anarchy, State, and Utopia* (New York: Basic Books, 1974).

4. See John Locke, *A Letter Concerning Toleration*, ed. James Tully (Indianapolis: Hackett, 1983).

5. Will Kymlicka, *Multicultural* Citizenship II (Oxford: Oxford University Press, 1995).

6. See Jürgen Habermas, *A Theory of Communicative Action*, Vols. 1 and 2 (Cambridge: Polity Press, 1984, 1989); Jon Elster, "The Market and the Forum: Three Varieties of Political Theory," in *Foundations of Social Choice Theory*, ed. Jon Elster and Aanund Hylland (Cambridge: Cambridge University Press, 1986); and Pettit, "Democracy, Electoral and Contestatory," *Nomos* 42 (2000): 105–44.

7. See Pettit, *Republicanism*, and idem, "Capability and Freedom: A Defense of Sen," *Economics and Philosophy* 17 (2001): 1–20.

8. See David Miller, "Constraints on Freedom," *Ethics* 94 (1984): 66–86, and idem, ed., *Liberty* (Oxford: Oxford University Press, 1993).

9. *Pace* Hillel Steiner, *An Essay on Rights* (Oxford: Blackwell, 1994), and Ian Carter, *A Measure of Freedom* (Oxford: Oxford University Press, 1999).

10. See Philip Pettit, "Agency-freedom and Option-freedom," *Journal of Theoretical Politics* 15 (2003): 387–403.

11. Charles Taylor, *Philosophy and the Human Sciences: Philosophical Papers 2* (Cambridge: Cambridge University Press, 1985).

12. Jeremy Bentham, "Anarchical Fallacies," in *The Works of Jeremy Bentham*, ed. John Bowring (New York: Russell and Russell, 1962).

13. See Pettit, "Democracy, Electoral and Contestatory."

14. See Philip Pettit, "The Common Good," in *Justice and Democracy: Essays for Brian Barry*, ed. Keith Dowding, Robert Goodin, and Carole Pateman (Cambridge: Cambridge University Press, forthcoming 2004).

15. See Pettit, "Democracy, Electoral and Contestatory," and idem, *A Theory of Freedom*, chap. 7.

16. See Pettit, *Republicanism*, chap. 2.

17. John Braithwaite and Philip Pettit, *Not Just Deserts: A Republican Theory of Criminal Justice* (New York: Oxford University Press, 1990).

18. Niccolo Machiavelli, *The Complete Work and Others*, trans. Alan Gilbert (Durham, NC: Duke University Press, 1965), 241.

19. See Philip Pettit and Michael Smith, "Freedom in Belief and Desire," *Journal of Philosophy* 93 (1996), and Pettit, "Capability and Freedom."

20. See Quentin Skinner, *Liberty before Liberalism*.

21. See Pettit, *Republicanism*, chap. 2.

22. J. B. Schneewind, "Autonomy, Obligation, and Virtue: An Overview of Kant's Moral Philosophy," in *The Cambridge Companion to Kant,* ed. Paul Guyer (Cambridge: Cambridge University Press, 1992), 311.

23. Ibid.

24. See Amartya Sen, "Capability and Well-Being," in *The Quality of*

Life, ed. Martha Nussbaum and Amartya Sen (Oxford: Oxford University Press, 1993).

25. See Pettit, *Republicanism.*

26. See Pettit, "Agency-freedom and Option-freedom."

27. See Pettit, *Republicanism,* chap. 4, and Francis N. Lovett, "Domination: A Preliminary Analysis," *Monist* 84 (2001): 98–112.

28. See Chaim Wirszubski, *Libertas as a Political Ideal at Rome* (Oxford: Oxford University Press, 1968).

29. See Pettit, *Republicanism,* chap. 4.

30. See John Rawls, *A Theory of Justice* (Oxford: Oxford University Press, 1971).

31. See T. M. Scanlon, *What We Owe to Each Other* (Cambridge, MA: Harvard University Press, 1998).

32. See Martha Nussbaum, "Human Functioning and Social Justice." *Political Theory* 20 (1992): 202–46, and Sen, "Capability and Well-Being."

33. See also Pettit, *A Theory of Freedom,* chap. 7.

34. See Steiner, *An Essay on Rights,* and Carter, *A Measure of Freedom.*

35. This paper was presented at the University of Valencia in July 2001, the European University Institute in October 2001, and Chiba University March 2003. I am most grateful for the very helpful comments that I received during those discussions. I am also most grateful for the final editing assistance of Genevieve Johnson.

4

PETTIT AND MODERN REPUBLICAN POLITICAL THOUGHT

MIGUEL VATTER

1. Introduction: The Character of Modern Republican Political Thought

The recovery of the modern republican tradition of political thought in the last decades, spurred by the reconstruction of its history carried out by Skinner and Pocock, has proven to be a productive resource for those wishing to offer an internal critique of liberalism, as the employment of republican themes in the work of Habermas, Taylor, or Michelman shows.[1] With Pettit's attempt to resuscitate "the republican viewpoint as a political philosophy," another possible employment of this tradition has come to the fore: that of refashioning republicanism as a viable alternative political ideal or model to both liberalism and socialism.[2] To do so, republicanism must respond on its own terms to the fundamental needs that called these two political models into existence: safeguarding the freedom of the individual, and abolishing relations of domination in society. Pettit believes that republicanism meets this challenge through a theory of ideal government, making the state central to the achievement of individual freedom from domination.

Pettit's reconstruction of republicanism entails a significant departure from the legacy of its tradition. For the tradition of modern republican political thinking reveals the state to be a form of legal domination. In this tradition one finds not only arguments in favor of a conception of freedom as nondomination, as Pettit shows, but also arguments as to why, in order to establish and maintain this ideal of freedom, it becomes necessary to criticize the belief that a suitable state is both a necessary and sufficient condition of a free political life. As I show below, none other than Machiavelli, whom Pettit acknowledges as one of the fathers of modern republicanism, provides the paradigmatic modern critique of political rule and gives the conceptual distinctions that are needed in order not to identify subreptitiously political freedom with the practice of legitimate state domination. Modern republican political thinking offers a rather inhospitable space of reasons for those wishing to pursue the Platonizing project of imagining an ideal answer to "the question of Who rules Whom,"[3] in order to impose it on a rebellious and recalcitrant people. Instead, it is a rich source of insights for those who understand that the work of freedom calls on the art of "how not to be governed so much,"[4] and therefore need to learn how to practice critique.

The tradition of modern republican political thought distinguishes itself from the liberal and socialist traditions by its profusion of discourses aimed at elucidating the freedom of the political association, that is, the conditions of a republic. One of the most concise formulations of these conditions comes from Arendt: "the rule of law, resting on the power of the people, would put an end to the rule of man over man."[5] According to this formulation, a republic is a political association characterized by freedom from domination, by the absence of "The rule of man over man." One component of a republic is the power of the people,[6] on which the state or form of government has to rest, in order to put an end to the status of being dominated. If a form of government is what establishes the difference between rulers and ruled, then the power of the people, as the republican tradition employs this term, stands outside of this difference and makes it in principle possible to "live under conditions of no-rule, without a division between ruler and ruled."[7] The modern republican ideal of nondomination identifies the power of the people as the ground from which to question the legitimacy of ruling as such. By way of contrast, the ancient or classical republican ideal aims at a political condition such that "it is just for equal people to rule no more than they are ruled, and, therefore, to do so in turn."[8] The classical ideal provides a model for the best, or just, kind of rule, as opposed to the modern ideal of no-rule. Only the latter accounts for the constant connection between modern republicanism and the phenomenon of revolution.[9] But the modern republican tradition has a realistic, not a utopian, approach to freedom. It does not believe that the dimension of rule can be simply abolished in human association. For that reason, the second component of a modern republic is the "rule of law." The rule of law names a principle of government intended to assure that the people be ruled by laws, before which each is equal, rather than by personal commands, before which everyone is unequal. The rule of law secures a stable political order for an otherwise revolutionary political freedom.

According to the main tradition of modern republican political thought, a free political life requires a balance between the component of freedom, linked to the power of the people, and the component of order, linked to the rule of law, in their inevitable tension.[10] In my opinion, Pettit's republicanism diverges from this tradition to the extent that it subsumes the pole of freedom and power under that of law and order, such that the conditions of nondomination are preponderantly tied to the state-centered maintenance of the rule of law. In so doing, Pettit restricts the scope of the ideal of freedom as nondomination found in the tradition.

By focusing on freedom as the absence of domination, Pettit recovers a new and powerful way to criticize the liberal understanding of individual freedom as the absence of interference. At the same time, because he restricts the definition of domination to mean a capacity of arbitrary interference and understands the rule of law merely as a form of nonarbitrary interference, Pettit obscures from view the fact that the rule of law also entails a dimension of domination. Pettit is then led to make political freedom unduly dependent on the constituted power of the state, rather than on the constituent power of the people to contest and resist it (section 2). The rule of law contains a component of domination that comes from its being a species of rule. This rule is a form of domination and not simply a species of nonarbitrary interference as Pettit holds, because it generates relations of subjection. The subjection coming from the rule of law is unlike the arbitrary domination to which a slave is submitted by its master; it is a nonarbitrary, impersonal kind of domination to which subjects are submitted by their public institutions, and not by private persons. Consequently, the rule of law cannot be identified with the ideal of freedom as nondomination without serious reservations (section 3).

In order to confront this internal criticism, Pettit's republicanism needs to be amended by integrating the elements found in the modern tradition of republicanism that reestablish its characteristic creative tension between freedom and order. Pettit's reconstruction of republicanism makes space for the "democratic contestability" of government. This concept needs to be reconnected to the republican conception of the power of the people and its application widened so that it may express the possibility of contesting every form of domination, including that of the rule of law. In so doing, contestability is placed at the basis of a free political life, thereby recovering the motif of the primacy of social conflict with respect to the achievement of political unity found in the modern republican tradition (section 4). In turn, the state can be understood as a function of its capacity to respond to the demand for nondomination that invests it a priori. One response consists in making the enterprise of ruling secure for both itself and its subjects. The modern state achieves this security of rule in the form of a system of individual rights. This state-centered response to the demand for nondomination founds civil liberty and equality but compromises the achievement of political freedom and equality for the people because securing rule is not the same as countering it. The other response requires the state to adopt institutions that empower the people by allowing them to counteract the administration of rule from within the state itself. Only through the second strategy, when constitutionalism is understood as a way of setting the state against itself, can one speak of a republic (section 5).

But what prohibits the tradition of modern republican political thought from being reduced to a theory of ideal government, to a "political philosophy," is that, having identified the state as a source of legal domination, it defends the possibility that the power of the people, and its contestation of domination, express itself extraconstitutionally, as occurs in revolutionary struggles of recognition of political equality (section 6). Lastly, modern republicanism requires that one distinguish the rule of law from the authority of law. If the revolutionary potential of the power of the people may come to stand in contradiction to the rule of law, the same cannot be said for its relation to the authority of law. On the contrary, it can be shown that the power of the people and the authority of the law call for each other. The balance between freedom and order, power and rule, depends on establishing the internal relation between political revolution and legal authority (section 7).

2. PETTIT'S STATE-CENTERED CONCEPTION OF FREEDOM AS NONDOMINATION

Pettit defines domination as a state of being "subject to the arbitrary power" of an individual or group who can "interfere on an arbitrary basis with the choices of the dominated" without having to track the interests and opinions of the person affected.[11] Conversely, freedom as nondomination means to live in "a world without interference by arbitrary powers . . . by virtue of your being secured against the powerful."[12] The goal of reducing, if not eliminating, domination in society expresses an "ideal of being able to look others in the eye, not showing fear or deference, and not seeking grace or favor."[13] Such a mutual respect and recognition between equal individuals is not a natural endowment or condition of individuals, but rather an achievement of political association. The status of being "immune" or "secure" from domination can only be achieved in virtue of living in a society that is politically free.

The first fundamental feature of Pettit's republican conception of freedom is that the individual cannot be considered to be free unless she lives as a citizen in an association that is politically free.[14] One of the crucial achievements of Pettit is the definitive demonstration that political freedom is not a "causal" but a "constitutive" condition of individual freedom. In other words, republican political freedom is not simply "instrumental" to the preservation of liberal negative liberty, but it makes up a different species of negative freedom: freedom as nondomination, rather than as noninterference.[15] This feature clearly distinguishes republicanism from both the liberal and socialist traditions insofar as these necessarily require that the individual be considered "free" independently of any political association she may enter into (whether this freedom is figured in a "state of nature" or "original position," as in liberalism, or established in a "society without classes," as in Marxism). For the liberal tradition, in particular, it is in principle conceivable that a political association preserve some aspect of the "natural" freedom of the individual by means of political domination, that is, through an association that calls for a contract of political subjection (as Rousseau points out in *The Social Contract*, referring to both Hobbesian and Lockean types of liberalism). For Hobbes, infamously, an individual can in principle be just as free (in the sense of not being interfered with) in a despotic state as in a republican one, because freedom is negatively defined as the liberty that one is left with in virtue of the "silence" of the laws, and this "silence" is the same regardless of the kind of state. Harrington thought this Hobbesian claim patently absurd. He understands the freedom of the individual as a function of the absence of domination, rather than of interference, and the absence of domination has to be positively determined through a legal and political order, provided it was designed in such a way as to restrain the tendency to despotism found in all government.[16]

Pettit's distinction between individual freedom as nondomination and individual freedom as noninterference has the great merit of permitting a clearer demarcation of republicanism from liberalism than has been possible heretofore.[17] Given Pettit's definition of nondomination as a state of security from arbitrary domination, it is clear how one can be dominated without being interfered with, since domination occurs in a relation between individuals in which someone is constitutively open to the sway of the arbitrary rule of someone else, without any arbitrary interference actually having to be exercised.[18] In a state of domination, one may very well find oneself incapacitated, literally powerless, to express one's own thoughts in a free manner and to pursue one's most proper desires, without thereby having come into conflict with the person who dominates, and therefore without this dominating power having to interfere in the life of the dominated individual.[19] Hence it is possible to have a great deal of personal freedom from interference, while being subject to the arbitrary rule of some person or group or government. This convincing insight allows Pettit to formulate a potentially devastating criticism of liberalism: if "political liberty is simply the area within which a man can act unobstructed by others,"[20] then such liberty not only is not contrary to political domination, but actually requires it.

Conversely, Pettit's definition of domination makes it also possible to think that one can be interfered with, without for all that being dominated. This belief forms the basis of the second fundamental feature of Pettit's republicanism. If domination is essentially a matter of arbitrary interference by persons, then nondomination would seem to be in principle constituted by the "immunity" from arbitrary powers provided by an impersonal, nonarbitrary form of interference, by "the restraint of a fair system of law, a nonarbitrary regime,"[21] insofar as it can function as a "nonmastering interferer."[22] The second major criticism that Pettit levels against liberalism is its lack of a proper theory of government. From the republican point of view, liberalism is forced to reduce the rule of law and the state to instruments of coercion, of interference, that are acceptable only to the extent that they can be used to pursue a greater overall noninterference compared to remaining in a state of anarchy. In contrast, Pettit's republicanism views the state as an essential condition for achieving the status of nondomination, provided that the state not be dominating in turn. It offers one of the strongest rationales for bringing the regulatory function of the state back into society with the aim of securing nondomination for its members.[23] In this sense, republicanism strongly rejects the belief, found in socialism and anarchism as well as in libertarian understandings of liberalism, according to which the state needs to be kept as much as possible "out of" the individual's life. The latter belief relies on the assumption that social systems, above all the economic system, have a capacity for self-generation and self-regulation that dispenses, in principle and in the progress of history, with the state and with politics, and as a consequence with the question of political freedom. In my opinion, Pettit's arguments show that keeping a republican state from interfering in society is tantamount to giving a free hand to bullies everywhere, with the resulting increase of domination and exploitation of a majority by a minority (both nationally and internationally).

In sum, Pettit's republicanism argues that "freedom is a status . . . that exists only under a suitable legal regime."[24] A legal regime is "suitable" if the state provides "good law[,] . . . law that reduces the domination to which *dominium* may lead without introducing the domination that can go with *imperium.*"[25] The reliance of the idea of freedom as nondomination on a suitable idea of the state explains why, when it comes to arguing for republicanism as a "political philosophy," Pettit postulates that it is necessary for any "candidate for the role of political ideal" to satisfy two sets of constraints: "The corresponding ideal will be a feasible ideal for the state to track . . . [and] it will be an ideal that it is also desirable that it [the state] should track."[26] According to these criteria, if a political ideal cannot, or ought not, to be realized by the state, then it immediately ceases to be an ideal that can be the basis of a "political philosophy." In so doing, the latter is reduced to the discursive practice of justifying the state-form. Politics, in turn, becomes what this state does to its subjects, or legally permits its subjects to do to it.[27] Given his definition of "political philosophy," it is absolutely essential that Pettit show how nonarbitrary rule, or the "suitable legal regime" of a state, as a matter of principle, is only a form of nonarbitrary interference rather than a form of nonarbitrary domination, otherwise his claim that republicanism and its ideal of nondomination should be the basis of a "political philosophy" is simply self-contradictory.

Generally speaking, although I can conceive how it would be possible not "to reduce public affairs to the business of dominion,"[28] I find it difficult to follow Pettit's attempt to do just the opposite and reduce political life to the business of the state, in order to argue that, if suitably constituted, this business has nothing to do with exercising domination. My difficulty consists in the impossibility of disassociating completely the modern state from Weber's definition of it, according to which "just like the political associations which preceded it historically, the state is a relationship of rule [*Herrschaft*] by human beings over human beings, and one that rests on the legitimate use of violence (that is, violence that is held to be legitimate)."[29] As Weber's definition suggests, every state, insofar as its business is that of ruling, exercises a form of domination. But whereas a state that embodies a "rule of persons" tends to exercise an arbitrary form of domination, a state that embodies a "rule of law" tends to exercise a nonarbitrary, impersonal, or legitimate form of domination. Pettit, instead, thinks that it is possible to design a "suitable legal regime" that would only interfere with, but not dominate, individuals insofar as these are involved in dominating others.[30] I shall try to show that this is, in principle, impossible; that Pettit thinks otherwise is due to his narrow definition of domination, which is designed to exclude the rule of law as a candidate for domination.

3. The Rule of Law and Impersonal Domination

In the last section of this essay, I shall defend the possibility that the practice of subscribing to the abstract considerations expressed by law in our choice of actions needs to be construed without reference to domination (either *dominium* or *imperium*). But irrespective of this possibility, what can hardly be doubted is that by itself law cannot rule. Without some public persons, procedures, institutions, and techniques exercising the functions of rule, there can be no rule of law. Impersonal domination enters into the rule of law through ruling. For "rule of law" (just as "constitutional state" or *Verfassungsstaat*) is a composite expression containing two terms, each of which is employed in distinct grammars, and refers to distinct realities, that Dworkin usefully groups under the expressions "grounds of law" and "force of law," respectively.[31] The former gives an answer to the question of what is modern law, and it does so through a discussion as to whether this question is most appropriately answered through a theory of authority (as one finds in Hobbes, for instance) or through a theory of justice (as one finds in Kant, for instance). Discussions of the "force of law" refer to the kind of rule, and the kind of subjection, required by law. Not to take into account the distinction between law and rule, and therefore to ignore the whole problem of their internal relation, hides from view the possibility of impersonal or legal domination that is exercised in the rule of law.

One of the fundamental questions that can be posed about the rule of law is simply this: Why does law require rule? Despite their distinct formulations of the rule of law, Machiavelli, Hobbes, Spinoza, Locke, and Rousseau all agree that it is not possible to determine the validity of the law (its "ground") independently from its facticity (its "force"), while at the same time neither is reducible to the other.[32] The short answer that can be garnered from all of these thinkers is that order is necessary to law, and that it is ruling, rather than the authority or the justice of the law, that establishes order. Oakeshott, whose presentation of the formal features of the rule of law is still to be counted as among the most perspicuous, summarizes the issue very clearly: "The civil condition, then, because it is association in terms of *lex* and because *lex* is unable to interpret, to administer, or to enforce itself, postulates an apparatus of rule."[33] In general, this apparatus of rule is charged with achieving "the assurance, or at least the expectation, that the conditions [i.e., *lex*] will be generally and adequately subscribed to."[34] Ruling is to bring about that order without which the subscription to the impersonal conditions spelled out as law would not be safe, and thus without which there would be no generalized subscription, and so no "rule" of law properly speaking.[35] Without order, law would have no force (although it could keep its grounds).

Even if one assumes, for the sake of argument, that the enterprise of ruling, properly understood, has as its substantive goal only the maintenance of law,[36] so that no rulers are possible without prior laws that constitute their office, it is still the case that the practice of ruling itself is not rule-bound to the extent that ruling is not an activity that consists exclusively in subscribing to rules.[37] Applying, changing, or enforcing rules are not actions that can be described simply as subscriptions to these or other rules; they are not actions that can be characterized as rule-following. Ruling cannot be carried out in the form of law because, at a minimum, ruling is the practice of ordering the particulars of a situation or event in such a way that these can, in principle, be determined by the law in virtue of falling under it: law by itself cannot achieve this ordering. Therefore, ruling takes place either below or above the law, but never "before the law." Said otherwise, ruling is intrinsically a practice of subjecting something or someone to something or someone else. The only conceivable response to a ruling is that of subjecting oneself to it or not. Which is all to say, as Machiavelli, Hobbes, Spinoza, Locke, and Rousseau already remarked in their different ways, that the state, insofar as its task is the imposition of order, that is, insofar as its business is that of ruling, by definition cannot be comprehensively restrained by law: if it were, it could not be in the position to actually deliver a rule of law.

The main tradition of political philosophy contains a variety of accounts of the difference between order and law. The existence of this difference and its significance is not my topic in this essay, so I shall only mention two recent examples. In Schmitt one finds the idea of ruling as a supralegal condition for the rule of law. For Schmitt, all law is "situational law."[38] All law presupposes an order, a situation, in which it can apply. In a state of chaos, where there are only exceptions to the law, by definition no law can apply, and therefore its validity is suspended. Does the law find itself in a "normal" situation or in a "state of exception"? "He is sovereign who definitely decides whether this normal situation actually exists."[39] The state, insofar as it is sovereign, assures order such that valid law is applicable.[40] The law, by definition, is impotent to establish such an order. Although for Schmitt only a person, and not a law, can make decisions, it is also evident that the sovereign person is characterized by a "monopoly to decide,"[41] and therefore neither its person nor its decisions can be reduced to the kind of arbitrary decisions that characterize individuals in society. Pettit's definition of arbitrary power only refers to the sway that private arbitrary decisions can have over the lives of others; it does not take into account Schmitt's concept of a public decision taken by a public person. Even if the way in which Schmitt draws the distinction between state and law may be flawed, still, in periods of constitutional crisis, when "the state remains, whereas law recedes,"[42] it seems that some such distinction necessarily comes to light and should have some import on thinking about the possibility of legitimate, as opposed to arbitrary, domination.

Foucault offers a way to think of ruling as operating "below" the law, as an infralegal condition for the rule of law. For Foucault, unlike Schmitt, the establishment of order through an apparatus of rule is not associated with the sovereign power of the state. As his book on discipline tries to show, "the general juridical form that guaranteed a system of rights that were egalitarian in principle was supported by these tiny, everyday, physical mechanisms, by all those systems of micro-power that are essentially non-egalitarian and asymmetrical that we call the disciplines."[43] Again, the point is not so much whether Foucault is right as a matter of historical fact that disciplinary power is the actual form in which "a guarantee of the submission of forces and bodies" is elicited for the sake of the functioning of the "formal, juridical liberties." The crucial point is philosophical: some such "guarantee" or "assurance" or "order" is necessary for law to constitute itself as a form of rule, and such a need for order can be satisfied only through infra- or supralegal practices of domination that inscribe an asymmetry and inequality of power responsible for the dependence of those who are subject to laws by virtue of being legal subjects. This kind of domination is therefore impersonal and legal, far removed from the arbitrary domination exercised by a person unbound by laws to which Pettit restricts his definition of domination.

The ruling entailed by the rule of law is a form of nonarbitrary domination, not a form of nonarbitrary interference, because the "subjectivity" of the legal subject is a function of its subjection, that is, a function of the individual coming to stand in a power relation that is nonegalitarian and asymmetrical and therefore constitutes a species of domination in Pettit's own terms. One does not stand before ruling as one stands before a "natural obstacle": by the former I am placed or confirmed in a state of subjection, but not by the latter.[44] That is why it is impossible to think of the rule of law as a form of nonarbitrary interference (indeed, it is even difficult to think of the relation of a law to an action that subscribes to it as being one of "interference": the law is adverbial, it modifies the action without "interfering" with it). Of course, the kind of domination that turns me into a legal subject is not the same as the one that turns me into a slave, but it is still, evidently, a form of domination—a legal, impersonal one. As Spinoza makes clear, to be subject to legal domination as opposed to arbitrary domination needs to be in "my self-interest," but it does not thereby lose its character of domination.[45] Thus, the fact that a suitable legal regime would track "the common, readily avowable interests of citizens, and only such interests" does not change the character of this rule from being dominating to being nondominating.[46] In a situation of arbitrary domination, my subjection is due to my being vulnerable to the arbitrary sway of another person's commands. In a situation of legal, nonarbitrary domination, my subjection is due to my being vulnerable to the control of an impersonal procedure that is intended to "immunize" me from arbitrary domination. If the rule of law, according to Pettit, is a system of rule that constitutes my "immunity" from arbitrary powers, this result is achieved through the domination of a nonarbitrary power before which my objective "insecurity" with respect to an impersonal power increases at the same rate as this power provides for my subjective "security" from arbitrariness. In this sense, the rule of law is open to an "autoimmune" process.[47]

Pettit does not deny that the state, just like another person, can become a source of domination. But for him this kind of domination exercised by the state, *imperium,* remains a species of domination defined as a function of arbitrary interference. It occurs only because private persons, carriers of arbitrariness, are left with discretion to use the instruments of the state for their own private interests. Against this eventuality, his theory of government (contained in Part II of *Republicanism*) offers two recipes: constitutionalism (whose elements are rule of law, division of powers, and antimajoritarianism) and what he calls "democratic contestability."[48] If what I said above concerning the rule of law stands, then constitutionalism, at best, can restrain the state from becoming the instrument of personal domination, but it is in principle ineffectual as a response to the impersonal domination exercised by the state or its apparatuses.

In order to confront impersonal domination it is necessary to widen the scope of the ideal of nondomination such that this ideal may express the tension between political freedom and any form of political rule, not just illegitimate forms, as is obvious, but also legitimate forms of domination. This requires approximating nondomination to the modern republican idea of no-rule, and so retrieving the possibility of a critique of the state-form, including that of the constitutional state, based on a standpoint outside of the state. In thinking about freedom as no-rule, one can still follow Pettit's point that individual freedom is inconceivable apart from a free political life, but one is no longer obligated to identify, fallaciously, a free political life with the "freedom" of the state. No longer does politics have to be reduced to what the state does, whether legally or illegally, or what political groups do, legally or illegally, in order to attain control of the state.

The issues at stake in expanding Pettit's conception of nondomination so as to take into account the idea of no-rule are not merely terminological, but also theoretical and historiographical. Theoretically, it can be shown that it is not possible for the rule of law to "put an end to the rule of man over man," without appealing to the power of the people. But this kind of power, sometimes called "constituent power" after Sieyès, designates an essential dimension of political freedom that is not reducible to the legal, "constituted power" of the state.[49] The tradition of modern republican political thought preserves the difference between the power of the people and the constituted powers of the state. Only on the basis of this irreducible difference does it then proceed to stage a discussion as to whether the power of the people, and therewith the possibility of revolution, is antecedent to, co-originary with, or merely a posited presupposition of the constituted power of the state. With respect to historiography, the power of the people as a component of political freedom is present throughout the entire tradition of modern republicanism, from Machiavelli and Spinoza through Milton, Harrington, and Rousseau, to Jefferson and Sieyès, and into the nineteenth and twentieth centuries. This tradition has an intimate relation to revolutionary events in modernity, both anticipating and reflecting upon them. For Pettit this revolutionary dimension of modern republican thought does not seem to constitute a salient feature of republicanism.[50]

One reason for this peculiar oversight may be due to Pettit's equating the power of the people with "the full populist position of holding that liberty consists in nothing more or less than democratic self-rule."[51] But if Arendt is right to claim that in modern republican political thought the power of the people is a condition of no-rule, then surely equating this power with any form of "populist rule" or "democratic self-rule" is wrongheaded. To mistakenly identify power with rule is to miss a great deal of the novelty of modern republican political thought in relation to classical democratic theory. Arendt's treatise on republicanism, in contrast to Pettit's, is essentially written in order to establish the distinction between the power of the people, which she calls the "republican principle,"[52] and every form of rule, including direct democracy, and for this reason the treatise receives the entirely appropriate title "On Revolution" rather than "On Democracy."[53] For modern republican political thought does not have a bias in favor of the

rule of the people; rather, it has a preference for the empowerment of the people, such that it may be capable of resisting, contesting, and, if necessary, overthrowing all forms of political and
social domination and subjection.[54]

For these reasons, Pettit's emphasis on democratic contestability within his reconstruction of republicanism is extremely significant. For Pettit, "freedom as non-domination supports a conception of democracy under which contestability takes the place
usually given to consent; what is of primary importance is not that
government does what the people tell it but, on pain of arbitrariness, that people can always contest whatever it is that government
does."[55] This formulation corresponds to the spirit of the tradition
of modern republicanism according to which the people are politically active not by virtue of participating in ruling or governing,
but by virtue of generating a power to contest or resist the practices of ruling and domination, both personal and impersonal.
This tradition follows Montesquieu's intuition that only power (of
the people, i.e., constituent power), and not law, can check power
(of the state, i.e., constituted power).[56]

The problem with Pettit's idea of contestation is that it has been
unduly restricted, just as his conception of nondomination is unduly restricted. According to Pettit there are two reasons to contest
rule. First, as a response to the fact that officials in government are
also private persons, and thus their decisions while in office are liable to the kind of arbitrariness befalling personal decisions.[57] Second, because contestability is counterfactual, it is the only feasible
way "to ensure that public decision-making tracks the interests and
the ideas of those citizens whom it affects; after all, non-arbitrari-
ness is guaranteed by nothing more or less than the existence of
such a tracking relationship."[58] The problem with both reasons for
contestation is that neither seems to give a ground for contesting
impersonal "law and order," as opposed to personal "decisions." If,
in accord with my initial assumption, domination is also exercised
by the former, then Pettit's construal of contestability cannot effectively achieve nondomination. Which is only to say that I have not
found in Pettit's republicanism an argument for the internal relation of nondomination and democratic contestability, but only
one for the internal relation of nondomination and constitutionalism. That no such argument exists is perhaps further indicated by

the instrumental character of contestability. Contestation, insofar as it is helpful in keeping the state on the "tracks" of the interests of its subjects, is valued as a means to achieve "good law," that is, law that reduces domination because it "answers systematically to people's general interests and ideas."[59] In which case, presumably, the ideal state (and the ideal of the state) in which the general interests of the subjects are unfailingly "tracked" and then implemented through the rule of law has no need for democratic contestation.

4. POLITICAL UNITY AND THE PRIMACY OF SOCIAL DISCORD

I shall now pass to the constructive part of this essay in which I offer some suggestions about what would need to be added to a theory of republicanism such as Pettit's to make it more adequate for the idea of freedom as nondomination, where domination is also of the impersonal and legal kind. The basic amendment consists in reversing the order of priority that Pettit assigns to the rule of law over democratic contestation. Machiavelli, one of the fathers of modern republicanism, offers the strongest rationale for this reversal.[60]

Machiavelli is singularly aware of the dependence of law on the infra- and supralegal establishment of order.[61] "[The laws and orders made in] a republic at its birth, when men are good, are no longer to the purpose later, when they have become wicked. If laws vary according to the accidents of the city, its orders never vary, or rarely; this makes new laws insufficient because the orders which remain fixed, corrupt them."[62] According to Machiavelli, the corruption of the members of the political association is due to the very stability and perdurance of the legal order under which they live and which makes them "become wicked." Corruption does not simply mean "our natural tendency to ignore the claims of our community as soon as they seem to conflict with the pursuit of our immediate advantage";[63] rather, it signifies the increase and acceptance of inequality between members under the cover and protection of the existing and legitimate orders and laws. As Skinner and Pettit, among others, have rightly pointed out, the phenomenon of corruption poses a stumbling block to liberalism, which it has trouble overcoming through its conception of freedom as non-interference, given that "to insist on rights as trumps . . . is simply to proclaim our corruption as citizens. It is also to embrace a self-destructive form of irrationality."[64] But if Machiavelli's account of corruption is correct, then classical "civic republicanism" fares no better than liberalism in overcoming the problem, since appealing to "civic virtue" and to the unquestioning allegiance ("patriotism") to the "common good" figured by the laws and orders of the state only upholds the forms that generate corruption in the first place. Recognizing the internal relation between the rule of law and nonarbitrary domination, Machiavelli does not fall prey to the illusion that the former (with or without the healthy doses of "civic virtue" and "patriotism" needed to motivate adherence to it) is sufficient to constitute freedom from domination.

Machiavelli offers an entirely different solution to the dependence of law on order, and the deleterious effects to freedom that follow from it: freedom as nondomination requires recognizing the priority of a change of orders over the securing of order. Freedom as nondomination is linked to a practice of resistance to order and to a positive revaluation of political disorder, discord, and contestation. This in turn calls for an idea of political *virtù* that has little use for the pieties of civic virtue.[65]

Since Machiavelli links legal domination to the fixation of political order, he is able to think of nondomination as a function of the critique, and even the revolution, of political order. Disorder, disagreement, and conflict become productive principles for society and politics. "For in every city these two diverse humors are found, which arises from this: that the people desire not to be commanded nor oppressed by the nobles, and the nobles desire to command and oppress the people. From these two distinct appetites one of three effects occurs in cities: principality or freedom or license."[66] The importance of Machiavelli's revaluation of social conflict for the development of political thought in modernity cannot be overemphasized. Its first major innovation is the idea that social division is primary with respect to political unity.[67] For Machiavelli, association (and thus society) exists on the ground of passionate and conflictual relations, and not on the ground of reasonable relations of cooperation: antagonism, not consent, is the essence of the social bond.[68]

The second major innovation lies in the character that Machiavelli ascribes to the social antagonism. For if the antagonism were simply one between agents interested in ruling over one another, it would be possible to show (or, at least, since Plato one has thought so) that such antagonism cannot possibly produce a social bond, but its opposite: the degeneration of society. This kind of objection would not affect Machiavelli's concept of social antagonism. For him, people and nobles do not designate natural kinds: whoever speaks and acts out of a desire to dominate assumes the standpoint of the nobility, and whoever speaks and acts out of a desire for nondomination assumes the standpoint of the people. One and the same individual may therefore occupy these different standpoints at different moments. A minority can act as a people, just as a majority can be ennobled. Furthermore, what counts as desiring nondomination is not predetermined nor does it have to be univocal. People and nobles are entirely differential terms.[69] The primary social conflict is therefore irreducible to the contest over who should rule. The conflict that traverses society is not a hegemonic struggle, that is, a struggle for who is going to rule; it is a conflict between those who want to rule and those who want no-rule. "Without doubt, if one considers the end of the nobles and of the ignobles, one will see great desire to dominate in the former, and in the latter only desire not to be dominated."[70] Machiavelli thinks the possibility of political unity, and thus the possibility of political rule, from the existence of a necessary social division on the matter of rule, of a necessary conflict over the question not of who should rule, but of whether and how there should be rule at all. Insofar as this question remains open, the social bond remains in existence and remains a conflictual bond. In this way, one does not have to appeal to either of the opposite but equally phantasmatic conjectures of a "war of all against all" (Hobbes) and of a "fair system of cooperation" (Rawls) that result from thinking the possibility that everyone wants to rule, or no one does.

Insofar as the question remains open, and society remains in existence, the answer to the question can only be given by politics and as politics. But politics now loses its *focus imaginarius* of the "common good." Since the contradiction between the desire to dominate and the desire for nondomination cannot be dissolved in a third, mediating term, it follows that there is no "general" or "common" interest present in society that could, in principle, give an uncontestable legitimacy to the "suitable legal regime" that would be capable of tracking it.[71] From Machiavelli's viewpoint, every modern state attempts to answer a demand raised by the conflict between domination and nondomination ("the domination complaint") that can only and always be a partial and contingent response. That is why, from this viewpoint, it cannot be left up to the state to determine when, where, and on what terms its rule is to be politically contested.[72] Rather, the state is more durable the more capable it is of responding to a contestation of its rule that has always already invested it, as a condition of its possibility. For this reason, the possibility to effect a revolutionary change of political order conditions the possibility of the institution of political order. Machiavelli's republicanism puts forward a general principle of modern politics, according to which any political order, if it is to be constituted and legitimated, must also be open to its deconstitution and delegitimation. The only legitimate political order is the one that can be made to suffer its own radical contingency. *The Prince*, with its theory of the modern state, and the *Discourses on Livy*, with its theory of the modern republic, give two complementary illustrations of this general principle of modern politics.

5. On the Difference between State and Republic in Modernity

Once this fundamental contingency of political rule is assumed as the horizon of political action, two kinds of politics emerge into view, both of which are necessary, neither being sufficient unto itself. The first kind of politics seeks to minimize the insecurity of rule by founding a state that lasts through time. Machiavelli's theory of the state as a "civil principality" gives a figure to this politics.[73] The durable state is possible only on condition that the prince take the side of the people against the nobles, and that the people, in turn, become the ground of the state and support its rule.[74] Since the people do not want to be oppressed, Machiavelli argues that this result can be achieved only by securing, but not suspending, the activity of ruling. The civil prince is the name for a state that founds itself by making the practice of rule a matter of mutual security between those who govern and those who are governed.

According to Machiavelli, the security of rule, for both the state and its subjects, is achieved in three stages.[75] First, the civil prince must secure itself against its potential rivals. This stage institutes what Max Weber calls the "monopoly of violence" over a fixed territory that is characteristic of the modern state. Second, the civil prince has to secure the people from the extra- and infralegal desire for domination present in those who have power in society, that is, the nobles. In Pettit's terms, this stage provides security from the *dominium* of the "powerful" in society. The third stage is the decisive one: the civil prince has to assure the subjects with respect to itself, so that they will act as the support of the state. In Pettit's terms, this task corresponds to providing security from the *imperium* of the state itself. Only by achieving this last task does the prince or state, properly speaking, become "civil" because it will have brought "civility" to the relation between individuals and groups in society.

I have made the comparison with Pettit's idea of the state as "nonmastering interferer" in order to show that if freedom as non-domination is merely the security from the power of arbitrary interference (both in the form of the *dominium* of the "nobles" or "powerful" in a given society and in the form of the *imperium* of office holders), then it seems that the state which is to achieve such freedom falls squarely within the logic of legitimate state domination, the logic of Machiavelli's civil prince, and still falls short of Machiavelli's requirements for a republic.[76]

Before discussing these requirements, as distinct from those of a legitimate state or civil prince, it may be useful to recall the most significant conclusion to which Machiavelli's analysis of the state leads. The point of the analysis is to demonstrate how the third and last task of the civil prince, that is, the creation of a civil society, is impossible to achieve without systematic deception on the part of the state. The exercise of a monopoly of violence, even when it seeks to favor the people by interfering with those who engage in *dominium,* cannot but project a "bad" image of the state that is anything but reassuring to its subjects. Therefore, Machiavelli argues that the modern state or civil prince is forced to enter the path of "simulation and dissimulation"[77] in order to construct for itself an image of "goodness" that stands a chance of satisfying the subjects. One could say that the modern state has to become what Althusser once called an "ideological apparatus."[78]

The "ideological" component of the modern state refers to its capacity to transform the violence that it exerts into legal power, into rights for its subjects. The modern language of rights, in fact, cannot be separated from the state-centered politics designed to achieve the security of rule.[79] It is through the recognition of rights to equal individual liberties that the state addresses the demand "not to be commanded or oppressed," the demand for nondomination coming from the people as if it were a demand for negative liberty and formal equality before the law. Negative liberty, liberty as noninterference, is the form in which the state negates the negativity of no-rule in order to determine it in a form, that of rights, that the state has no trouble in assuring through its instruments of legal domination, namely, "by making orders and laws in which the universal security is included . . . and the people see that he [the civil prince] does not break such laws because of any accident."[80] The generation of formal equality before the law is the central strategy through which the state secures for itself the support of the people by providing them with a simulacrum of their desire for no-rule. This simulacrum is nothing but civil liberty, the securing of which establishes the state as the civil prince of a civil society.[81] It is probably due to this internal relation between individual civil rights and the modern state as a "civil prince" that the tradition of modern republican political thought is, for the most part, unwilling to reduce its discourse on freedom as nondomination to a discourse on individual rights, while at the same time maintaining that securing these rights is absolutely indispensable to achieve civility.

In contrast to the project of founding a modern state and its civil society, a modern republican politics, according to Machiavelli, does not have the security of rule as its primary concern, but rather that of bringing freedom as no-rule into political life by giving power and voice to the people desiring it. In order to enter political life, the people must stop functioning merely as a passive legal subject, as a foundation of the legal power of the state, and become the active political subject of a resistance to the state that has the power to question the business of ruling, thereby making this business an unsafe, radically contestable affair.

For Machiavelli, "laws that are made in favor of freedom arise from their [the nobles' and the people's] disunion."[82] The rule of law becomes republican only once it rests on the power of the people. Power here refers to those actions, practices, and institutions through which the people as bearers of the desire for nondomination participate in the life of the state, alongside and countering the practices of legitimate domination, of which traditionally the most important elements have been the deliberations of the "senate" (legislative power) and the commands of the "monarch" (executive power). A republican rule of law, then, exists only on condition that the antagonism between instances of rule and demands for no-rule gets inscribed into the framework of legal domination.

How does the standpoint of the people get politically instituted without having to compromise the desire for nondomination and change it into the desire for mere negative liberty? The answer Machiavelli provides is ingenious and has profoundly influenced the development of modern constitutionalism: the people enter political life through special institutions that critique—that is, that offer an internal check to—the proper activity of the state, the administration of rule. The general formula for such an institution of critique is the separation of powers, but only when it is understood and practiced as a true system of checks and balances, whereby "one branch of the government may be authorized to exercise some active influence on another in order to resist and counteract its power" in view of keeping the entire state in check with respect to the people.[83]

These institutions of political contestation, or counterinstitutions, carve up the state so as to clear a space in which to voice the demands of no-rule.[84] Machiavelli offers a striking series of metaphors to illustrate the peculiar "form" in which Rome became a republic. By expelling the kings from Rome, Brutus cut off the "head" of the monarchical political body, and thereby signaled that ruling (*archy*) would no longer be the sole (*mono*) political issue. A place was left open in political life for the people and their discord against rule. The republic begins once this discord is represented by counterinstitutions, such as the tribunate, that bring the people into political life, thereby giving Rome another "heart" (Lat. *cor, cordis*) that beats, always discordantly and never in unison, with the remaining heart of the Senate.[85] These two hearts of an acephalic political body symbolize the two desires, the two voices, that are at play in a republic. Their dissensus accounts for the nonunivocity of its political life, for the fact that a republican political life does not have the good of the state (the "common good") as its inner purpose, but consists in the practice of effective "public freedom."[86]

Machiavelli's reconstruction of the history of the Roman republic, which systematically goes against the grain of the philosenatorial readings of the same at the hands of Livy, Sallust, and Cicero, highlights the role of counterinstitutions that represent the people's desire for nondomination in the state. The paradigmatic exemplar of such a counterinstitution is the tribunate. Before Machiavelli, the creation of the tribunes was traditionally understood from the ideal of mixed government of Aristotelian derivation. Taking into account such an understanding but moving beyond it, Machiavelli argues that "besides giving popular administration its part in ruling, [the tribunes] were constituted as a guard of Roman freedom."[87] Here political freedom is clearly distinguished from the activity of administering the rule of the state. Viewed from the perspective of the state, the tribunate simply expands the form of the state by adding the part of the people to the administration of rule. But seen from the perspective of the people, the tribunate takes apart the state's machinery of legal rule in order to safeguard freedom as no-rule. The tribunate, as every other such counterinstitution, inscribes a resistance to domination into the state apparatus that administers the rule of law. The "force" of the tribunate essentially consists in the power to veto the claim to rule of a law or magistracy, that is, of the *imperium* of the state. As von Fritz has shown in his analysis of this institution in the Roman republic, "the increase in the veto powers of the tribunes . . . left the community with an excess of negative powers the like of which can hardly be found in any other state in history."[88] Pettit is surely right to recall that "the most interesting challenge for republican thought today . . . bears on how to design political arrangements so that, as far as possible, the state really is forced to track all and only the common, ready-to-be-avowed interests of the citizenry."[89] But this means that republican thought should dedicate itself to the design of new counterinstitutions, because if a state institution is to "force" the state itself to pursue nondomination, then this is possible only in the form of an "excess of negative powers."

The peculiar nature and power of counterinstitutions like the tribunate highlights another important feature of republican politics: the antiauthoritarian voice that contests the voice of "law and order" (echoed in the chambers of legislative, executive, and judicial power) need not be a voice of deliberation; it need not provide "good reasons" for its dissent. For Pettit, conversely, if the republican ideal of freedom is a candidate for a self-standing political model, then "the complaint about domination" must "come across as a consideration admissible in presumptively cooperative discussion."[90] Pettit's condition implies that the complaint about domination must be able to be rationally justified: the demand for no-rule ought to submit itself to be judged as to whether, when, and to what extent it can be satisfied.

But can the contestation, dissent, and revolt against domination be justified before the tribunal of reason? There are good grounds to suspect this. If giving reasons is a practice that presupposes an orientation to finding consensus, to reaching an agreement, if a "good reason" is such in virtue of its "unforced" force of persuasion that brings about a "common understanding," then to engage in reason-giving is already to presuppose that one is going to have a common interest with others, or that one is going "to act as a whole" with them.[91] In which case, from the perspective of "rational discourse," there can be no "good reason" for the kind of disagreement that the political empowerment of the people generates in civil society. To engage in "rational discourse" with others is already to stand in agreement with them over the essentials. These presuppositions of "rational discourse" become problematic if what is at stake is the liberation from domination: between a master and a slave no such commonality, no such agreement, can be presupposed if the slave is to emancipate herself, and hence there is no "rational discourse" possible between them. As slave narratives testify, emancipation is never simply the result of the slave demonstrating her rational capacities to the master: violent or nonviolent rebellion appears to be necessary in wresting the recognition of oneself as free from someone who did not want to give "as of right" such a recognition.[92] Only on the basis of this conquest of freedom will both parties be disposed to give and to listen to reasons. But in this case "rational discourse" is not constitutive of the status of being free or nondominated; at most it is a sign that this status exists between the parties of the discourse.

Pettit reasons that as long as rational discourse is possible between individuals, then they stand in a relation that does not entail domination, and therefore the status of being dominated in the one who complains about domination will necessarily be condemned as being wrong by others who listen to the complaint, and that is why the "domination complaint" is "absolutely reasonable."[93] But this says absolutely nothing as to how the one who is dominated is supposed to achieve this communicative situation. The arguments against domination that depend on the claim that the latter cannot be rationally justified, and that as a consequence the situation of nondomination is one in which rational discourse is unimpeded, have the unintended consequence of demonstrating that there is no way to address the fact of domination, to stage the disagreement between domination and nondomination, in a rational discourse. The paradox implicit in demanding that the complaint about domination be rationally justified is that if one is already in a position to complain about domination in a rational discourse, then there is nothing to complain about, since one is already recognized as not dominated by virtue of being recognized as a participant in a rational discourse. Therefore, if one takes seriously the complaint about domination, one is led to question the appropriateness of the demands of rational discourse and of its normativity when applied to the practice of liberation.

6. POLITICAL EQUALITY, CIVIL EQUALITY, AND THE QUESTION OF REVOLUTION

The counterinstitutions of the state internalize the discord with legitimate domination into the political form: their critique of the state consists in turning the state against itself. But insofar as they remain state institutions, counterinstitutions are incapable of contesting the state in its entirety from a standpoint that is external to it. But it lies within the power of the people to contest the state in its entirety and withdraw itself from the participation in the state afforded them by counterinstitutions, thereby taking away the sole stable support the modern state can have. When this happens, the tradition of modern republicanism speaks of a revolution.[94]

In this tradition, the distinction between critique and revolution corresponds to the following problem: no matter how effectively a state maintains equality before the law (understood as fairness in making the law, as equal protection under the law, and as due process), such equality cannot prevent the constant application of orders and laws from generating inequalities and effects of domination. As the work of Christopher Hill shows, it was intuited quite early in the development of modern law that because the equality before the law is defined by rights to individual liberties (e.g., the right to private property), and because these rights sanction practices that can range from competitive to exploitative and discriminatory, an exclusive and strict adherence to formal equality has the consequence of systematically generating winners and losers.[95] Since the spoils of victory are composed of the conditions for the reproduction of life, the substantive inequality protected by the formal equality before the law supports new relations of mastery and slavery, as is made clear by the continued existence within civil society of so-called subaltern populations generated by classism, racism, and sexism.[96]

Additionally, the formal rights that define the equality before the law constitute an inequality between those who are subject to the law and the rule of law itself, that is, these rights call forth a form of subjectivity characterized by habits of obedience and conformity to rules, rather than by an ability to call into question, transgress, and author new rules. The increase in legal litigiousness corresponds to an increase in political conformism to the legal system of rule. As Habermas correctly points out, "Basic rights guarantee what we now call the private autonomy of legal subjects only in the sense that these subjects reciprocally recognize each other in their role of addressees of laws and therewith grant one another a status on the basis of which they can claim rights and bring them to bear against one another."[97] Therefore, the rights that define the equality before the law cannot possibly establish the equality of all as "authors" of the laws that apply to them as "addressees" of law. Yet without the equality in authoring the laws that apply equally to all, it is not possible to "eliminate the paternalism of the 'rule of law' characteristic of political heteronomy. It is only participation in the practice of politically autonomous lawmaking that makes it possible for the addressees of law to have a correct understanding of the legal order as created by themselves."[98] The ideal of freedom as nondomination should not be limited to eliminating master-slave relations between individuals by securing equality before the law for everyone. This ideal also needs to eliminate the possibility that all shall be the equal "slaves" of that legal system of rule, of that legitimate state, which secures each from becoming a slave to another individual.

In order to redress the inequalities that arise under cover of the law, Machiavelli proposes that the formal equality before the law, that is, civil equality, be distinguished from, and made responsive to, the equality of all to author the laws before which citizens are formally equal, that is, political equality. Freedom as nondomination requires not only civil, but also political equality. On this fundamental point, Machiavelli is followed by most subsequent republican political thinkers. So, for instance, Trenchard affirms the internal relation between private and public autonomy when he states that "no man can be imprisoned, unless he has transgressed a law of his own making."[99] Rousseau simply says that "a people, since it is subject to laws, ought to be the author of them."[100]

Once the difference between civil and political equality is established, the question of revolution turns on the question of whether the political equality to author law stands under law or not, whether it is a species of civil equality or not. Can constituted law turn a legal subject into an "author" of the law as opposed to its mere "addressee"? Can the freedom and power that puts one in a position to exercise authorship of the law be given by constituted law in the form of political rights? For a significant strand of modern republicanism, the answer seems to be affirmative. The general assumption behind this answer is that to be the "author" of the law one must be a "legislator," and because legislating, under the requirements of the rule of law, is a legally instituted practice, the law can only be "authored" in and through the medium of law.[101] As Habermas puts the point: "When citizens occupy the role of co-legislators they are no longer free to choose the medium in which alone they can realize their autonomy. They participate in legislation as legal subjects; it is no longer in their power to decide which language they will make use of. The democratic idea of self-legislation must acquire its validity in the medium of law itself."[102] From this perspective, the people are powerful insofar as they exercise their "political civil rights" of participation in the legislative process. Since these political rights are conceived as a species of civil rights, and thus belong to the rule of law, they require the "private civil rights" that define "the status of legal persons who as bearers of individual rights belong to the voluntary association of citizens and when necessary effectively claim their rights. There is no law without the private autonomy of legal persons in general."[103] If the constituent power of the people can only exist in the form of political civil rights guaranteed by the rule of law, then such power can only be a posit of constituted law (in the last instance: of the legal constitution), and cannot contest it from the outside. In the end, "authorship" of law entails the power to modify the constituted law, even to amend the legal constitution, but not to revolutionize the legal system of rule.

From Machiavelli, Spinoza, and Rousseau, among others, one can draw the outlines of a different argument that questions the claim according to which political equality must stand under law. For this claim confuses the "authority" of the law with the question of the "authorship" of the law. The power of the people and its political equality does not "author" law in the same sense as the legislative power, as the office of the legislator, "makes" law. The latter makes law "in the medium of law itself," and presupposes that the law is "authoritative," apart from having to legislate in accordance with the rule of law and with the principle of equality before the law. For this reason the right to legislate is, primarily, a "civil right" that is further qualified as "political." But, properly understood, this point merely spells out a prior intuition according to which the "authority" of the law can only be determined by the law itself. This intuition about the essence of legal authority needs to be kept separate from the other intuition according to which the power of the people expresses a political, not a civil, equality that can "make" or "author" law in a sense that is essentially distinct from the activity of legislating. The revolutionary power of the people can make for law (it is constituent power), but it cannot legislate (it is not a constituted power).

One way to think about the extralegal dimension of political equality follows from the analysis of the conditions of the rule of law. As I argued above, the law never comes to rule over its situation by means of law alone, but through diverse practices of rule that entail relations of domination. The law maintains itself in such a position also because of the inequalities in economic, social, and cultural forces that its regulations permit and support. The political equality to author law, therefore, must be conquered: it requires a reversal of the relations of forces in a struggle for recognition. As Machiavelli says, it is essential that "men who live together in any given order frequently recognize each other" by "reviewing their accounts."[104] The principle of such a struggle for political equality is that what is unequal shall be made equal, and what is equal shall be made unequal.[105] The political equality to author law is never the result of a "civil" process. Indeed, historically such struggles for liberation and independence have always carried a component of violent (and sometimes nonviolent) expropriation.[106]

If one were to follow the classical understanding of political justice, voiced among others by Aristotle, according to which equals are to be treated equally and unequals unequally,[107] then the modern republican struggle for political equality appears unjust. But one needs to recall that the classical understanding presupposes, and can be applied only in the context of a primordial and necessary division between "citizens" (equals that need to be treated equally, i.e., in accordance to law) and "slaves" (unequals that need to be treated unequally, i.e., without reference to law). On the contrary, for Machiavelli and the tradition of modern republicanism, the struggle for political equality is precisely intended to thematize and then to abolish the division between "citizens" and "slaves." The moment of expropriation by the formerly "unequal" (the slaves, the colonized, the excluded) of the formerly "equal" (the citizens, the colonizers, the privileged), that is, the real possibility for the "unequal" to take the place of the "equal" and conversely, aims exclusively at the mutual recognition of the universal equality of all prior to the economic, social, or cultural inequalities that every political order necessarily abets. That is why a revolutionary struggle for political equality cannot become a principle of political order, of legitimate domination, without completely reversing itself. A republican revolution can never be more than a moment: finite and iterable. If it succumbs to the temptation of permanence, if it believes that a "state" of no-rule is possible, then it enters into contradiction with itself and can neither maintain the power of the people nor institute a rule of law.

The universal equality of all that is experienced in momentary struggles for political equality is an equality that modern law presupposes as a condition for being able to treat everyone who stands before it equally. In order for the law to recognize each as "equal before the law," the equality of all needs to be recognized prior to the law, in order that law may come into being. And this is in fact the only way in which law, simply in virtue of its being law and independent of its force, can take hold over everyone: both over those who once expropriated and are now being expropriated, as well as over those who were once expropriated and are now expropriating. It is in this sense that the political equality "before" the law makes for civil equality under law.

For Machiavelli, as well as for those, like Spinoza or Rousseau, who developed his republican insights, the political equality of all to make law cannot itself be legally or constitutionally predetermined: it is an equality that opens the legal order and the political form to an origin that remains outside of it. That is why a revolutionary event is denoted by Machiavelli as a "return to beginnings": the movement of returning a given legal and political order to its beginning is the movement of its revolution. In a revolution, the legal order is brought back to a beginning that is extralegal. As Arendt points out, "Those who get together to constitute a new government are themselves unconstitutional, that is, they have no authority to do what they set out to achieve."[108] What Arendt means is that in a revolution the people have power but lack authority: constituent power is not the ground of legal authority, of constituted power. And yet, as Machiavelli says, "It is a thing clearer than light that these republics do not last if they do not renew themselves" through such return to beginnings or revolutions.[109] If this is the case, then it must be that the extralegality, the absence of authority, found in the power of the people, far from standing in contradiction with the authority of the law, is its most important resource. Safeguarding the difference between power of the people and authority of the law is the central requirement for maintaining the balance between freedom and order characteristic of a republican political life.

7. CONCLUSION: THE POWER OF THE PEOPLE AND THE ORIGINS OF LEGAL AUTHORITY

What kind of connection between power and authority, between revolution and law, does modern republicanism establish? In what sense can the rule of law be said to "rest" on the power of the people? How is one to conceive the unity between the two elements of "neo-roman" political freedom, *potestas in populo* and *auctoritas in senatu*? For the modern republican tradition, it is essential to distinguish the constituent power of the people that is active in a revolutionary moment from the constituted power of the state that rests on the legally constituted and generated support of the people. To each is associated a different kind of authoritativeness: the legitimacy of the state, in fact, is not the same as the authority of the law.

As Machiavelli explains the principle behind the legitimacy of constituted power, "If one individual is capable of ordering, the thing itself is ordered to last long not if it remains on the shoulders of one individual but rather if it remains in the care of many and its maintenance stays with many."[110] The modern legal order can last through time only if the many, the majority, is set on supporting it. But if the people are to fulfill this function of support, they must be deprived, always already, of the constituent power to begin something radically new, of breaking with the foundation, which, on the contrary, they are called upon to carry out, augment, and amend by building on it.[111] That is why, as the Madison-Jefferson exchange on constitutional conventions exemplifies, some sort of constitutional precommitment is necessary to every constituted power and antithetical to the existence of constituent power. Precommitment is essential to the legitimacy of the constituted powers of the state because through it the constituent power that began the legal order is absolutized, that is, is recognized as an unrepeatable foundation to which all subsequent orders and laws must be tied back in a coherent way, if they are to be legitimate.[112] By absolutizing the significance of the revolutionary beginning, the constituted powers of the state assure that the people will only serve as the support, as the political *subjectum*, of the legal order, and thereby grant duration and legitimacy to the state's legal subjection and domination.

Conversely, the power of the people needs to be conceived as revolutionary in the sense that through this power the people translate their standpoint of nondomination back to the position of founding, and thereby achieves a "return to beginnings," literally a revolution. In returning to the site of foundation, the people conquer for themselves the founder's freedom from having to carry out and obey the new order that they are now in a position to recast. In a revolutionary event, the people are free to remake the state, but they remain equally free from the obligation of following its new order: this is the freedom of the "author" of law. A revolution certainly comes to an end with the constitution of a new order and a new rule, but a revolution can never found this order and this rule, evincing a sovereign indifference with respect to the instance of order and rule, in the sense that it creates no legal obligation toward it. From a republican viewpoint, what is fundamental about the experience of revolution is precisely this sovereign experience of not being obligated to order and to rule. This is the only way in which the power of the people (or "popular sovereignty") can be understood within the republican ideal of freedom as no-rule.

Because "the people" is conceived as a political actor characterized by the desire for nondomination or no-rule, it follows that the people cannot participate directly in the process of ruling or governing without going counter to their desire.[113] That is why republican revolutions, based on the idea of the power of the people, far from rejecting the principle of political representation necessarily call for it. But political representation, generally speaking, is not understood as a condition for the pursuit of more effective ways of governing a large population, but as a way to check the powers of the state as agency of legitimate domination, and to ensure that the republic, in the words of Rousseau, "will always be ready to sacrifice the government to the people and not the people to the government."[114] A republican understanding of the principle of political representation identifies its primary function with the separation of the people from the business of government, from the constituted power of the state, for the sake of preserving in the people the sovereign indifference to rule that allows it to contest government from an independent standpoint, to judge the outcomes of its politics on a disinterested basis, and, last but not least, to interrupt its functioning by ceasing to respond to the interpellations of its constituted powers.

As a result, it is impossible for the power of the people to create the obligation to follow the law. But, at the same time, and precisely in virtue of its sovereign indifference to rule, the power of the people safeguards against the temptation to identify the authoritativeness of the state rule, of legitimate domination, with the authority of the law. This opens the possibility that neither the power of the people, nor the rule of the state, but only the law itself generates its own authority.

In order to see this point, it is necessary to distinguish the authority of the law, as opposed to its rule, from all practices of domination and coercion. This is possible as long as the concept of law is rigorously distinguished from that of command. Again, Oakeshott's account of legal obligation is helpful here.[115] According to this account, the laws of a *respublica* are not commands that direct their addressees to do something they would not otherwise have done; law merely prescribes adverbial conditions for self-chosen actions and pursuits. Properly speaking, law never tells one what to want or desire, but only regulates the pursuit in which one is interested and which one chooses to pursue. Interested pursuits are a function of want or desire. Laws prescribe what one is obligated to in pursuing such wants or desires. It follows that by law one can never be obligated to pursue something that one does not want to pursue; one can only be obligated to pursue in some way or another (according to the conditions spelled out in the law) what one wants.

On this conception of law as "noninstrumental adverbial conditions" for the pursuit of self-chosen interests, there is no need to ask for a "ground" of the obligation to follow the law external to the law itself.[116] Since the law does not prescribe anything that goes against what one wants, the obligation to law requires neither the threat of coercion in case of noncompliance nor the conviction of its "truth" or "justice" (whereas both are required in the case of laws understood as commands). On the conception of law as an adverbial condition, there is no "ground" for following the law, other than the recognition of it being law, that is, its "authenticity."[117] The name given to this peculiar groundlessness of legal obligation is authority. Ultimately, it is because the authority of the law leaves behind it all reference to compulsion (whether exerted by the force of violence or by the "unforced" force of the strongest argument), and thus to rule, that the power of the people, characterized by a sovereign indifference to rule and active in achieving the recognition of the political equality of all, serves as an enabling condition of the authority, but not of the rule, of law.

Following rules is not the goal of a possible action or interested pursuit: it is the condition of goal-oriented action. To subscribe to a rule, to follow a law: these are not morally substantive goals of action. If they were, one would subscribe to a law out of some interest (rational, moral, or otherwise), out of some knowledge of what one wants (because it is "good" or "just" for me, others, or everyone to want this). But in that case to follow a rule would be an interested pursuit, and this would prevent the law from regulating interested pursuits, in accordance with its definition. The assumption here is that an interested pursuit cannot regulate an interested pursuit: interested pursuits are not self-regulative.[118] Only rules, not interests (no matter how rational or moral), can determine regulation. That is why, on this view, rules are endowed with authority (they are *lex*), but not with validity (they are not *jus*). The authority of a rule comes from its authenticity as a rule, that is, from its independence or disinterestedness with respect to all interested pursuits. That a rule is disinterested, that a rule is an "authentic" rule, can only be determined by another rule, not by an interest. Indeed, the only thing that a rule can determine for another rule is its authenticity as a rule: and only a rule, not a person or an interest, can possibly determine such authenticity. Only law "makes" law: the authority of the law is essentially "self-authenticating."[119]

From this conception of law, it follows that every attempt to subsume the power of the people under the constituted powers of the state, every attempt to confound the people as "author" of the laws with the legislative power as "legislator" of the laws, every attempt to deny the difference between freedom as nondomination and legitimate domination, threatens in its innermost possibility the self-authenticating character of law, the authoritativeness of law, because it deprives this authority of the only thing that can safeguard it from the prevarications of those who desire to rule (whether in their own interest, or in the "general interest"). Unless legal authority is shielded from rule, the rule of law is itself compromised because the norms that issue from it will have lost their character as law. In this sense, and precisely because they do not stand in a foundational relation to each other, the power of the people and the authority of law, far from being opposed to each other, in fact call for each other.

What the power of the people and the authority of the law, understood together in this republican way, do problematize is the Platonizing ideal of a state or system of rule that is "good" or "just" in virtue of serving the "common interests" of its subjects. If the power of the people, in its capacity to contest rule, is allowed to fall by the wayside, then the authority of the law, the self-authenticating character of law, suffers as well. If the law loses authority, if it can no longer generate an obligation to it from its self-authenticating character, if law needs to appeal for its "authority" to what is not law, that is, to the legitimacy of a state that tracks the "common interest," then law has become ipso facto instrumental. Once law becomes instrumental to the pursuit of interests, it is no longer in a position to regulate these interests, and the very idea of the rule of law is compromised, not from the side of rule, but from the side of the law this time.

The conception of a free political life that Machiavelli bequeaths to modern republicanism is an attempt to overcome the common misunderstanding according to which revolution and tradition, the power of the people and the authority of law, are simply contradictory. This is far from being the case because the law can maintain its authority only to the extent that it is safeguarded from both arbitrary and legitimate domination. In order to be so shielded, the authority of the law needs that the constituent power active in revolutionary struggles for political equality relinquish its "absoluteness," accept its contingency and finitude, so that it may be ready to return again in the course of history. For modern republicanism, the authority of the law goes hand in hand with a tradition of revolution.[120]

NOTES

1. See Quentin Skinner, *Visions of Politics*, vol. 2 (Cambridge: Cambridge University Press, 2002); Jürgen Habermas, *Between Facts and Norms* (Cambridge, MA: MIT Press, 1996); Charles Taylor, "Cross-Purposes: The Liberal-Communitarian Debate," in *Liberalism and the Moral Life*, ed. Nancy L. Rosenblum (Cambridge, MA: Harvard University Press, 1989); and Frank Michelman, "Law's Republic," *Yale Law Journal* 97, no. 8 (July 1988): 1493–1537.

2. Philip Pettit, "The Domination Complaint," this volume, 87.

3. Hannah Arendt, "On Violence," in *Crises of the Republic* (New York: Harcourt Brace, 1972), 142.

4. This is how Michel Foucault defines critique in "What is Critique?" and "What is Revolution?" in Sylvère Lotringer, ed., *The Politics of Truth* (New York: Semiotext(e), 1997).

5. Arendt, "On Violence," 139.

6. As in article 2 of Jefferson's *Virginia Declaration of Rights*, "all power is vested in, and consequently derived from, the People." The power of the people follows directly from the definition of individuals as "equally free and independent" (article 1) (Philip B. Kurland and Ralph Lerner, eds., *The Founders' Constitution*, vol. 1 [Indianapolis: Liberty Fund, 1987], 6).

7. Hannah Arendt, *On Revolution* (New York: Penguin, 1963), 30. Arendt coins the term "no-rule" to translate the Greek ideal of *isonomia*. As she understands it, this term originally meant the desire "neither to rule nor to be ruled" (ibid., 285). Elsewhere she speaks of "a political body in which rulers and ruled would be equal, that is, where actually the whole principle of rulership no longer applied" (ibid., 172).

8. Aristotle, *Politics*, 1287a15.

9. For a good discussion on why modern republicanism is a "revolutionary republicanism," see the contributions to David Wootton, ed., *Republicanism, Liberty, and Commercial Society, 1649–1776* (Stanford, CA: Stanford University Press, 1994).

10. Jürgen Habermas formulates this tension as follows: "Modern natural law theories have answered the legitimation question by referring, on the one hand, to the principle of popular sovereignty and, on the other, to the rule of law as guaranteed by human rights. . . . To be sure, political philosophy has never really been able to strike a balance between popular

sovereignty and human rights. . . . The intuitively plausible co-originality of both ideas falls by the wayside" ("On the Internal Relation between Law and Democracy," in *The Inclusion of the Other* [Cambridge, MA: MIT Press, 2001], 258).

11. Philip Pettit, *Republicanism. A Theory of Freedom and Government* (New York: Oxford University Press, 1997), 31 and 21.

12. Ibid., 24.

13. Pettit, "The Domination Complaint," 105.

14. It shares this feature with Quentin Skinner's understanding of modern republicanism. For Skinner, the characteristic of the "neo-roman" or "republican" ideal of freedom is that "any understanding of what it means for an individual citizen to possess or lose their liberty must be embedded within an account of what it means for a civil association to be free" (Quentin Skinner, *Liberty before Liberalism* [Cambridge: Cambridge University Press, 1998], 23).

15. Pettit, "The Domination Complaint," 110–112.

16. Pettit (*Republicanism*, 37–39) and Skinner (*Liberty before Liberalism*, 84) both analyze at great length Hobbes's disdain for civic republican liberty in the *Leviathan*, II, 21, and Harrington's response "The Preliminaries" in *The Commonwealth of Oceana* (New York: Cambridge University Press, 1992), 20.

17. For a useful discussion of this distinction, see Alan Patten, "The Republican Critique of Liberalism," *British Journal of Political Science* 26, no. 1 (January 1996): 25–44 (who treats Skinner and Rawls, but not Pettit), and Jean-Fabien Spitz, *La liberté politique* (Paris: PUF, 1995), who defends Pettit's idea of republican freedom as a distinct and noninstrumental kind of negative freedom. For the state of the debate, see the clear discussion found in Marco Geuna, "Alla ricerca della libertà repubblicana," in Pettit, *Repubblicanesimo* (Milan: Feltrinelli, 2000), v–xxviii.

18. Pettit, *Republicanism*, 23.

19. Pettit, "The Domination Complaint," 92–94.

20. Isaiah Berlin, *Four Concepts of Freedom* (New York: Oxford University Press, 1975), 122.

21. Pettit, *Republicanism*, 5.

22. Ibid., 31. For another discussion of the thesis that republican freedom depends essentially on the rule of law, see Maurizio Viroli, *Repubblicanesimo* (Bari: Laterza, 1999). Skinner's position is slightly different in that he does not deny the coercive character of the rule of law, but argues that such coercion is required if one is to be free from the state of dependence on someone else's arbitrary will (*Liberty before Liberalism*, 83, fn. 54).

23. Pettit, "The Domination Complaint," 94–95.

24. Pettit, *Republicanism*, 36.

25. Ibid., 182.

26. Pettit, "The Domination Complaint," 88.

27. The state-centered vision of politics in Pettit is apparent from the following passage: "The salient alternative to introducing a state, and authorizing it to act against the domination of some by others, is to rely on the spontaneous measures of economic and civil society to give rise to high levels of non-domination all round" (ibid., 100). I doubt whether political movements like Solidarnosc in Poland would fit under either of the above alternatives.

28. Arendt, "On Violence," 143.

29. Max Weber, *Political Writings* (Cambridge: Cambridge University Press, 2000), 311.

30. If I understand it correctly, this is the thrust of the objection that Skinner makes to Pettit, and that Pettit tries to respond to, unsuccessfully to my mind, in the "Afterword" to the second edition of *Republicanism*.

31. Ronald Dworkin, *Law's Empire* (Cambridge, MA: Harvard University Press, 1986), 110–111. It is interesting to note that nowhere in this book does Dworkin discuss the concept of "empire," that is, the question of the "force of law," of "rule," in relation to the question of "what is law," despite what the title of the book might lead the reader to think. This title is itself a reference to Harrington's "empire of laws and not of men" (Harrington, *Commonwealth of Oceana*, 20).

32. I employ the vocabulary of Habermas who is the latest to insist on the crucial importance of the internal relation between facticity and validity in thinking about the rule of law. Habermas speaks of a "tension between facticity and validity . . . [which] appears in the relation between the coercive force of law, which secures average law acceptance, and the idea of self-legislation . . . which first vindicates the legitimacy claim of the rules themselves" (*Between Facts and Norms*, 39).

33. Michael Oakeshott, *On Human Conduct* (New York: Oxford University Press, 1975), 143.

34. Ibid., 141.

35. As Spinoza says, "The validity of an agreement rests on its utility, without which the agreement automatically becomes null and void. It is therefore folly to demand from another that he should keep his word for ever, if at the same time one does not try to ensure that, if he breaks his word, he will meet with more harm than good. This point is particularly relevant in considering the constitution of a state. . . . Therefore, although men may make promises with every mark of sincerity, and pledge themselves to keep their word, nobody can rely on another's good faith unless the promise is backed by something else" (*Theological-Political Treatise* [Cambridge, UK: Hackett, 2001], chap. 16, 176).

36. An assumption that is of course questionable. Law may very well be construed as itself a means through which violence and war are pursued. For arguments to this effect, see Walter Benjamin, "Critique of Violence," in *Selected Writings*, Vol. 1: *1913–1926* (Cambridge, MA: Harvard University Press, 1996), 236–252; and Michel Foucault, *"Il faut défendre la société"* (Paris: Gallimard, 1998).

37. For instance, to make sure that the rules of soccer are applied during a match, as a referee does, is not the same as playing soccer, that is, as following soccer rules. Is there another set of rules (other than soccer rules) that referees follow in applying soccer rules? If so, then these "rules of the game" for referees of soccer stand in need of their own referees, and these refer to yet another set of rules, and one gets a regress into infinity. Another possibility is that referees appeal not to another set of rules (*lex*) but to a set of conceptions of what is "right" or "just" or "good" (*jus*) in order to do their ruling. To which one can respond that these conceptions modify the quality of the ruling, but do not define the kind of activity that ruling is. It may be that ruling has an internal relation to the question of justice, but that says nothing against the distinction in principle between ruling and following a rule. There is, in addition, the question as to whether the *jus* of ruling is internal or external to the *lex* (the rules of the game) on which it is ruling. But this question can only be decided once it is accepted that ruling and *lex* are heterogeneous.

38. Carl Schmitt, *Political Theology* (Cambridge, MA: MIT Press, 1988), 13.

39. Ibid.

40. "No form of order, no reasonable legitimacy or legality can exist without protection and obedience. The *protego, ergo obligo* is the *cogito, ergo sum* of the state. A political theory which does not systematically become aware of this sentence remains an inadequate fragment. Hobbes designated this . . . as the true purpose of his *Leviathan*" (Carl Schmitt, *The Concept of the Political* [Chicago: University of Chicago Press, 1996], 52).

41. Schmitt, *Political Theology*, 13.

42. Ibid., 12.

43. Michel Foucault, *Discipline and Punish* (New York: Vintage, 1979), 222.

44. Pettit compares the rule of law to a "natural obstacle" that interferes but does not dominate ("The Domination Complaint," 98 and 107–108). He also refers to the rule of law as a "nonintentional obstruction" (ibid., 98).

45. "But in a sovereign state where the welfare of the whole people, not the ruler, is the supreme law, he who obeys the sovereign power in all

things should be called a subject, not a slave who does not serve his own interest" (Spinoza, *Theologico-Political Treatise,* chap. 16, 178).

46. Pettit, "The Domination Complaint," 96.

47. On the logic of immunity and autoimmunity in politics, see Jacques Derrida, *Voyous* (Paris: Galilée, 2003).

48. Pettit, *Republicanism,* 173 and 183.

49. For an acute treatment of the difference between constituent and constituted powers, see Pasquale Pasquino, "The Constitutional Republicanism of Emmanuel Sieyès," in B. Fontana, ed., *The Invention of the Modern Republic* (Cambridge: Cambridge University Press, 1994).

50. As far as I have been able to ascertain, the only reference to revolution in *Republicanism* comes on p. 202 and it refers to Locke's justification of revolution in case the people lose trust in their government. Incidentally, Locke also affirms the state-dissolving power of the people: "The community may be said in this respect to be always the supreme power, but not as considered under any form of government, because this power of the people can never take place till the government be dissolved" (Locke, *Second Treatise of Government* [Cambridge, UK: Hackett, 1980], XIII, 149).

51. Pettit, *Republicanism,* 30.

52. Arendt, *On Revolution,* 171.

53. For Arendt, "The American revolutionary insistence on the distinction between a republic and a democracy or majority rule hinges on the radical separation of law and power, with clearly recognized different origins, different legitimations, and different spheres of application" (ibid., 166).

54. For another discussion of the tension between the power of the people and the form of the state, see Sheldon Wolin, "Norm and Form: The Constitutionalizing of Democracy," in *Athenian Political Thought and the Reconstruction of American Democracy,* ed. J. Peter Euben, John R. Wallach, and Josian Ober (Ithaca, NY: Cornell University Press, 1994).

55. Pettit, *Republicanism,* ix, and see also 185–202.

56. According to Montesquieu, political freedom "is there only when there is no abuse of power. . . . To prevent this abuse, it is necessary from the very nature of things that power should be a check to power" (*The Spirit of the Laws* [Cambridge: Cambridge University Press, 1989], XI, 4).

57. Contestation secures citizens from being "exposed willy-nilly to that pattern of decision-making: they are able to contest decisions at will and, if the contestation establishes a mismatch with their relevant interests or opinions, able to force an amendment" (Pettit, *Republicanism,* 186).

58. Ibid., 184.

59. Ibid., 35.

60. For a more elaborate discussion and defense of the interpretation I offer of Machiavelli's political thought, I take the liberty to refer the
interested reader to my *Between Form and Event: Machiavelli's Theory of Political Freedom* (Dordrecht: Kluwer, 2000).

61. This is the sense one should give to Pocock's assertion that Machiavelli's "great originality is that of a student of delegitimized politics." See
J.G.A. Pocock, *The Machiavellian Moment* (Princeton, NJ: Princeton University Press, 1975), 163.

62. Machiavelli, *Discourses on Livy* (Chicago: University of Chicago
Press, 1996) I, 18.

63. Quentin Skinner, "The Republican Ideal of Political Liberty," in
Machiavelli and Republicanism, ed. Gisela Bock, Quentin Skinner, and Maurizio Viroli (Cambridge: Cambridge University Press, 1990), 304.

64. Ibid., 308. See also Pettit, *Republicanism,* chap. 8.

65. On Machiavelli's distance from the virtues of "civic humanism,"
see Harvey Mansfield, "Bruni, Machiavel et l'humanisme civique," in *L'enjeu Machiavel,* ed. Gérald Sfez and Michel Sennelart (Paris: PUF, 2001),
103–121.

66. Machiavelli, *The Prince* (Chicago: University of Chicago Press,
1998), IX. Emphasis mine.

67. For the genealogy of the idea of society as a "war" or "conflict" between groups or classes, see Foucault, "*Il faut défendre la société.*"

68. As Pierre Bayle, following Machiavelli and Spinoza, puts it, the
"true principle of the actions of man" is to be found in "the dominant pas-
sion of the heart, to the inclination of the temperament, to the force of
adopted habits, and to the taste for or sensitivity to certain objects" (*Various Thoughts on the Occasion of a Comet* [Albany: SUNY Press, 2000], 168–
169).

69. For a similar conception of "people," see Jacques Rancière, "Ten
Theses on Politics," *Theory and Event* 5, no. 3 (2001), thesis 5.

70. Machiavelli, *Discourses on Livy,* I, 5.

71. Claude Lefort's interpretation of Machiavelli, as well as of modern
republicanism, has the great merit of emphasizing that the dissymmetry
between the desires of the people and those of the nobles lies at the basis
of political freedom. See Lefort, *Le Travail de l'oeuvre Machiavel* (Paris: Gallimard, 1972), 472–477, as well as his reconstruction of modern republicanism in terms of the priority assigned to social division over political
unity in *Writing: The Political Test* (Durham, NC: Duke University Press,
2000). On how the heterogeneity of desires stands in contrast to the
"logic of common interest" and its presupposition that, at some basic
level, all citizens share a same desire and a same fear, see Gérald Sfez,

Machiavel, la politique du moindre mal (Paris: PUF, 1999). For another important perspective on the question of citizenship in republicanism seen from the viewpoint of the priority of social conflict, see Christian Lazzeri, "La citoyenneté au détour de la république Machiavélienne," in *L'enjeu Machiavel*, 73–101.

72. For another attempt to define politics in terms of the priority of conflict and disagreement, see Jacques Rancière, *Dis-agreement: Politics and Philosophy* (Minneapolis: University of Minnesota Press, 1999).

73. Machiavelli, *The Prince*, IX.

74. "Whence it must be noted that, in taking a state, he who occupies it must be capable of securing the people and win them over by providing for their welfare [*nel pigliare uno stato, debbe l'occupatore d'esso assicurare gli uomini e guadagnarseli con beneficarli*]" (*The Prince*, VIII).

75. "[Cruelties] can be called well used (if it is permissible to speak well of evil) that are done at a stroke, *out of the necessity to secure oneself* [*la necessità dello assicurarsi*]. . . . In taking hold of a new state, he who occupies it should review all the offenses necessary for him to commit, and do them all at a stroke, so as not to have to renew them every day and, *by not renewing them, to secure the people* [*assicurare gli uomini*] and gain them to himself with benefits. Whoever does otherwise . . . is always required to hold a knife in his hand; nor can one ever *found himself on his subjects* [*fondarsi sopra li sua sudditi*] *if, because of his fresh and continued injuries, they cannot be secure of him* [*assicurare di lui*]" (*The Prince*, VIII).

76. In "The Domination Complaint" Pettit seems to follow Machiavelli's civil prince closely since he argues that in order to impose non-domination in society, the state has three strategies available: "armament," "disarmament," and "protection" ("The Domination Complaint," 111). These match the three stages in the constitution of the civil principality.

77. "There are two ways of fighting, one with laws and the other with force. The first is proper to human beings, the second of animals. But as the first method does not always suffice, you sometimes have to turn to the second. Thus a prince must learn how to use well both the animal and the man. . . . Since a prince must learn how to use well the animal, he should pick for imitation the fox and the lion. . . . It is necessary in playing this part [of the fox/MV] to conceal it well, and be a great simulator and dissimulator [*simulatore e dissimulatore*]" (*The Prince*, XVIII).

78. See Louis Althusser, *Machiavelli and Us* (London: Verso, 1999).

79. See, for instance, Kant's definition of the social contract as grounding "the right of men [to live] under public coercive law, through which each can receive his due and can be made secure from the interference of others" (Kant, "On the Proverb: That May Be True in Theory, But Is of No Practical Use," in Kant, *Perpetual Peace and Other Essays* [Indianapolis:

Hackett, 1983], 72). In this sense, when Karl Marx asserts that "security is the supreme social concept of civil society . . . the concept that the whole of society is there only to guarantee each of its members the conservation of his person, his rights and his property," he is simply voicing the fundamental intuition behind the modern idea of rights, from Hobbes through Kant and Mill ("On the Jewish Question," in *Early Writings* [New York: Vintage Books, 1975], 230). Security is inscribed at the heart of the right to equal individual liberties: "Liberty therefore is the right to do and perform everything which does not harm others" (ibid., 229).

80. Machiavelli, *Discourses on Livy*, I, 16.

81. Here my analysis of Machiavelli's theory of the modern state as civil principality converges with the general claim, made by both Skinner (*Liberty before Liberalism*, chap. 2) and Pettit (*Republicanism*, chap. 1), that the liberal conception of negative liberty emerges as an attempt to neutralize, in favor of the interests of the monarchical state and of *Raison d'État*, the early modern republican conception of freedom as nondomination. My point is that both the republican conception, and its liberal neutralization and cooptation, are necessary moments of a modern political life.

82. *Discourses on Livy*, I, 4.

83. Bernard Manin, "Checks, Balances and Boundaries: The Separation of Powers in the Constitutional Debate of 1787," in *The Invention of the Modern Republic*, ed. B. Fontana (Cambridge: Cambridge University Press, 1994), 31.

84. Analogously, Sheldon Wolin speaks of rotation and lot in Athenian democracy as "institutions that subvert institutionalization" ("Norm and Form," 43).

85. Machiavelli is giving his interpretation of the Roman republican formula: *auctoritas in senatu, potestas in populo*. The reference to the "head" of the monarchical political body is found in *Discourses on Livy*, I, 2; the reference to the people as the "heart" of the republic is found in ibid., II, 30.

86. The unruliness and dissensus that the integration of the people and their desire for nondomination bring into political life makes the latter exceed the strictures of "civil" society imposed and maintained by the state as "civil" prince. To describe this excess of political freedom over civil freedom, Claude Lefort employs the term "savage democracy" and Sheldon Wolin that of "fugitive democracy." For Jacques Rancière "there is politics inasmuch as the people refers to subjects inscribed as a supplement to the count of the parts of society, a specific figure of 'the part of those who have no-part.' Whether this part exists is the political issue and it is the object of political litigation" ("Ten Theses on Politics," thesis 6). For another reading of the people in Machiavelli that intersects with some

of these motifs, see John McCormick, "Machiavellian Democracy: Controlling Elites with Ferocious Populism," *American Political Science Review* 95, no. 2 (June 2001): 297–314.

87. Machiavelli, *Discourses on Livy*, I, 4.

88. Karl von Fritz, *The Theory of the Mixed Constitution in Antiquity* (New York: Columbia University Press, 1954), 209. Von Fritz concludes that "the political order of the Roman Republic . . . [has as] its most distinctive characteristic the superabundance of negative powers to prevent action which it developed in the course of the struggle of the plebeians against the patrician aristocracy" (ibid., 219).

89. Pettit, "The Domination Complaint," 97.

90. Ibid., 101.

91. As Pettit says, "When a number of people engage in discourse, their aim being to determine what is so in some domain or how it is best for them to act as a whole, then they give exclusive privilege to a particular form of influence that they may have on one another: that which occurs by virtue of producing reasons. . . . Thus they eschew the ways in which people influence one another when they exercise violence, or coercion, or intimidation, or anything of that kind" (ibid., 101).

92. For one of the philosophically most sophisticated arguments to this effect, see Frederick Douglass, *Narrative of the Life of Frederick Douglass* (New York: Anchor Books, 1989), especially chap. 10 and the analysis of the "battle with Mr. Covey": "a glorious resurrection, from the tomb of slavery, to the heaven of freedom" (ibid., 74).

93. Pettit, "The Domination Complaint," 101.

94. *The Federalist* speaks of "that fundamental principle of republican government which admits the right of the people to alter or abolish the established Constitution whenever they find it inconsistent with their happiness" (in Alexander Hamilton, John Jay, and James Madison, eds., *The Federalist Papers* [New York: Penguin, 1987], 78).

95. See Christopher Hill, *Liberty against the Law: Some Seventeenth-Century Controversies* (New York: Penguin, 1996).

96. Not even the systematic application of a Rawlsian "difference principle" of justice could redress this situation, since this principle of justice redistributes the opportunity of being a winner to a loser, but neither the capacity to win, nor the victorious outcome, as Amartya Sen, among others, has shown. See Amartya Sen, *Development as Freedom* (New York: Anchor Books, 1999), chap. 3. In any case, the Rawlsian difference principle of justice suffers from an original vice: the redistribution of opportunity that it calls for can lead to a fairer outcome only if discriminatory conditions in the exercise of rights and goods are absent. In other words, the second principle of justice works if and only if there would be no racism,

classism, or sexism in society, but it is incapable of achieving this outcome on its own, given the existence of the latter.

97. Habermas, *Between Facts and Norms*, 123.

98. Ibid., 121.

99. Trenchard, *An Argument, Shewing, that a Standing Army is inconsistent with a Free Government, and absolutely destructive to the English Monarchy* (1697).

100. Rousseau, *The Social Contract*, II, 6. Habermas still echoes these intuitions: "As soon as the legal medium is used to institutionalize the exercise of political autonomy, these [individual liberty] rights become necessary enabling conditions; as such, they cannot restrict the legislator's sovereignty, even though they are not at her disposition. Enabling conditions do not impose any limitations on what they constitute" (Habermas, *Between Facts and Norms*, 128). See also Habermas, "On the Internal Relation Between Law and Democracy," in *The Inclusion of the Other*, 260–261.

101. For the state of the debate on this point, see Jürgen Habermas, "Constitutional Democracy: A Paradoxical Union of Contradictory Principles?" *Political Theory* 29, no. 6 (December 2001), 766–781; and the replies by Alessandro Ferrara and Bonnie Honig in the same volume. On the paradoxes of political equality, see Christoph Menke, *Spiegelungen der Gleichheit* (Berlin: Akademie, 2000).

102. Habermas, "On the Internal Relation," 260.

103. Ibid., 260–261.

104. Machiavelli, *Discourses on Livy*, III, 1.

105. Ibid., I, 26–27; III, 21–22.

106. Machiavelli gives a memorable account of the logic of expropriation in a struggle for political recognition in the famous description of the Ciompi rebellion. See Machiavelli, *Florentine Histories* (Princeton: Princeton University Press, 1988), III, 13: "Do not let their antiquity of blood, with which they will reproach us, dismay you; for all men, having had the same beginning, are equally ancient and have been made by nature in one mode. Strip all of us naked, you will see that we are alike; dress us in their clothes and them in ours, and without a doubt we shall appear noble and they ignoble, for only poverty and riches make us unequal. . . . But if you will take note of the mode of proceeding of men, you will see that all those who come to great riches and great power have obtained them either by fraud or by force; and afterwards, to hide the ugliness of acquisition, they make it decent by applying the false title of earnings to those things they have usurped by deceit or by violence. And those who, out of either little prudence or too much foolishness, shun these modes always suffocate in servitude or poverty."

107. "Justice seems to be equality, and it is, but not for everyone, only

for equals. Justice also seems to be inequality, since indeed it is, but not for everyone, only for unequals" (Aristotle, *Politics,* 1280a10).

108. Arendt, *On Revolution,* 184.

109. Machiavelli, *Discourses on Livy,* III, 1.

110. Ibid., I, 9.

111. The point is made by Stephen Holmes: "It is meaningless to speak about popular government apart from some sort of legal framework which enables the electorate to have a coherent will. For this reason, democratic citizens require cooperation from regime-founding forefathers. Formulated somewhat facetiously: without tying their own hands, the people will have no hands" ("Precommitment and the Paradox of Democracy," in *Constitutionalism and Democracy,* ed. Jon Elster and Rune Slagstad [New York: Cambridge University Press, 1988], 231).

112. On the "religious" attachment to the founding as a source of *auctoritas,* see Arendt, *On Revolution,* chap. 5, passim.

113. For this reason Madison is perfectly consequent when he claims, in the same article of *The Federalist,* that "the people can never willfully betray their own interests," and that the distinguishing feature of "American government lies in the total exclusion of the people in their collective capacity from any share in the latter" (Hamilton, Jay, and Madison, eds., *The Federalist Papers,* 63).

114. Rousseau, *The Social Contract* (New York: Penguin, 1968), III, 1.

115. In what follows I refer to the ideas expressed in Michael Oakeshott, "On the Civil Condition," in *On Human Conduct.*

116. Michael Oakeshott, *On History and Other Essays* (Indianapolis: Liberty Fund, 1999), 142.

117. "A rule . . . is an authoritative prescription of conditions to be subscribed to in acting and its counterpart is an obligation to subscribe to these conditions. . . . It is neither more nor less than an acknowledgment of the authenticity of the rule" (ibid., 141). See also the discussion of this point in Oakeshott, *On Human Conduct,* 148–154.

118. On this view, it is a misunderstanding of the nature of law (*lex*) to think of it as expressing a "generalizable or common interest," as if law were the "form" in which one must "generalize" one's interests (as in Rousseau and Kant). A "general" interest is no more self-regulative than a "particular" interest. At most, the pursuit of a "general interest" can be used to "legitimate" the coercion of the pursuit of "particular interests," but it cannot be the basis of the authority of the law.

119. Oakeshott, *On Human Conduct,* 150.

120. I would like to thank Bonnie Honig, Christian Lazzeri, Vanessa Lemm, Christian Nadeau, Melissa Williams, and Linda Zerilli for their comments on the various drafts of this essay.

5

AGAINST MONISM: PLURALIST CRITICAL COMMENTS ON DANIELLE ALLEN AND PHILIP PETTIT

VEIT BADER

Which master-concept best serves to describe, explain, and combat against unjust inequalities? Since the early 1980s, political theorists have put forward a wide range of contenders for this title, including exploitation, oppression, domination, exclusion, discrimination, misrecognition, and marginalization. Exploitation has been the traditional (neo-) Marxist concept; domination and oppression have been put center stage by Philip Pettit,[1] Iris Young,[2] and others; discrimination and misrecognition by David Miller,[3] Axel Honneth,[4] and others; exclusion by neo-Weberians like Frank Parkin.[5] In the heat of the battle, some are tempted to claim that their favored master-concept would be wholly sufficient to describe and explain objective inequalities or structural power-asymmetries, subjective injustices, and the motivational bases of collective action, and also to serve as unifying concepts of injustice in moral and political philosophy (see table 5.1, which is further explained in Section 1).

Such theorists may be termed "monists" because of their search for the single unifying concept that can make complete sense of all forms of injustice. A pluralist approach to understanding injus-

TABLE 1
PLURALIST VERSUS MONIST STRATEGIES

PLURALIST		MONIST[a]	
Objective Injustices (inequalities, structural power-asymmetries)	*Subjective Injustices, Motivational Bases of Collective Action (experience, feeling, claim to be)*	*Unifying Motivational Bases of Collective Action (if any). Feeling treated:*	*Unifying Concepts of Justice/Injustice (if any)*
Exploitation	exploited	unjust	Fairness
Domination/ Oppression	dominated/ oppressed	unfair	Reciprocity
Discrimination	discriminated	unequal	Equality
Exclusion	excluded	dominated	Nondomination
Marginalization	marginalized	misrecognized	Recognition

[a] I have arranged the subheading here in a perpendicular relationship to the subheading under Pluralist strategies in order to avoid the impression that the unifying motivational bases of collective action within Monist strategies are the same as in the first two columns. Rather, "Fairness," "Reciprocity," "Equality," "Nondomination," and "Recognition" cut across "Exploitation," "Domination/Oppression," and so forth because the claim by monists is that these objective injustices motivate only if experienced as "unjust, unfair, unequal," etc. This cross cutting is best expressed, in my view, by not arranging them horizontally.

tice, in contrast, accepts that the phenomena of injustice are too complex and multifarious to be captured by a single concept. From a pluralist standpoint, therefore, the task of theory is to discriminate carefully among the phenomena of injustice, to tie a particular conceptualization of injustice precisely to its phenomena, and thereby to facilitate the identification of the specific practices or institutions that might be capable of remedying each form of unjust inequality.

Although pluralist descriptive and explanatory strategies may go together with monist moral strategies and vice versa, there seems to be a selective affinity between conceptual, descriptive, and explanatory monism and monism in moral and political philosophy. As a convinced conceptual, theoretical, moral, and institutional pluralist, I want to raise some critical challenges against the more or less explicit monist strategies defended in the articles of Danielle Allen and Philip Pettit in this volume. As a critical sociologist, I question the *conceptual strategy, the descriptive and explanatory power of "domination,"* the master-concept favored by Allen and Pettit (Section 1). In Section 2, I focus on *normative issues.* As a political philosopher and political theorist, I criticize the link of their monist account of injustices in terms of domination with a monist conception of justice in terms of nondomination. Even if this link is not "logical" or necessary, it seems typical for many critical political philosophers. Monist conceptions or *principles* of justice may be compatible with institutional pluralism. Very often, however, and also in the case of Allen and Pettit, they are coupled with monist *institutional designs and policies* as well. I conclude my comments with some critical remarks on monist republicanism.

1. DOMINATION VERSUS EXCLUSION? DESCRIBING AND EXPLAINING INEQUALITIES

Critical political theory depends on critical social sciences. The recent state of the art in the latter, however, is unfortunately characterized by huge conceptual ambiguities, contested master-concepts, drastic reductions of the complexity of inequalities or power-asymmetries, and poor descriptions and explanations. It is even more unfortunate that these failings are often reproduced by critical political theorists. Allen reconstructs the discussion in political philosophy as one between adherents of a domination paradigm and adherents of an exclusion paradigm. One reason for setting up her essay in terms of a choice between these two concepts may be that she is speaking directly to the themes declared in this volume's title: *Political Exclusion and Domination.* In any case, Allen argues that *domination* as a "master term" emerges from a broadly Marxist tradition linked to "class," to "exploitation," to "oppression" or "damaged recognition," focusing on "vertical" relations and on "social and economic arrangements" or institutions (pp. 29–30). *Exclusion,* she writes, has gained currency "because of race, racism, and laws about citizenship" (p. 30) focusing on "horizontal" relations and on "political" injustices such as "disbarment from formal political institutions and rights," and "from equal citizenship rights" (p. 30). The respective normative aims, in her view, are the more radical "end to domination" (p. 31), at least "as far as possible" (p. 61) rather than the more "pragmatic" and moderate aim of "inclusion." While she recognizes that the concepts often "blur into one another and are used indiscriminately" (p. 30) and that the relationship between domination and exclusion is fairly troubled, she still thinks that one has to make a choice (i.e., "either/or," "rather than" [pp. 32, 31]). She chooses the concept of domination. Pettit is much more outspoken and explicit in his choice for domination as the central or overarching roof concept.

In my view, monistic strategies in the social sciences have the following four disadvantages:

1. Rivaling master-concepts seduce us to think of "exploitation," "domination," "exclusion," "misrecognition," etc. as *mutually exclusive concepts* that press *dichotomous choices* upon us. Instead of clearly defining the content of these concepts so they do not overlap, and demarcating them as distinct categories that then can be used to identify, describe, and explain empirically and historically overlapping inequalities, they seduce as to make a choice in all these regards between "either/or."

2. Monistic strategies seduce us to declare one type of inequality to be *more "fundamental"* without much theoretical or empirical scrutiny. The other types then figure as *"epiphenomenal" forms* of exploitation (in neo-Marxism), oppression,[6] misrecognition,[7] or exclusion.

3. Monist strategies *block rich descriptions and adequate explanations of overlapping inequalities.* The empirical circumstances of injustice do not usually fall exclusively within one category or the other. They cannot be captured exclusively in terms of exploitation, domination, exclusion, etc. In order to prevent such theoretical and empirical reductionism, we have, first, to recognize that social inequalities are structured in a highly complex way; second, to keep concepts analytically distinct; and third, to elaborate adequate analyses of the relevant causal mechanisms.

4. Roof-concepts such as "objective injustices," "structural

power asymmetries," and "objective inequalities" (covering all specific forms or types of inequalities (or injustices, or power-asymmetries) have to be sufficiently abstract and general.[8] They are inevitably normatively loaded: not all unequal power is a problem (some distinction between "developmental" and "extractive power"—e.g., the one developed by C. B. Macpherson[9]—is needed); not all inequalities are unjust; not all domination is "arbitrary." If one puts the entire burden of injustice on a single type of injustice ("domination," "exclusion," or "misrecognition"), this abstraction and generalization causes a lot of *strain with the core meaning in everyday language and scientific language*. It also usually results in quite a lot of *ambiguity of the core concepts*.

In Allen's case this strain is evident. She does not precisely define her concepts, but from the way she uses "exclusion" I can see that she has a fairly narrow understanding of it: exclusion from politics (and not also from labor markets, professions, education, social interaction, etc.); exclusion by law (and not also by the full range of practices, intentional or not); exclusion of "races" (and not of all ascriptively categorized people). Her concept of *domination* lacks any clear focus but seems to be much broader than traditional concepts requiring some formal hierarchy and subordination.

Pettit defines domination abstractly and broadly: "individual or group agents dominate an individual to the extent that they are in a position to interfere arbitrarily in the affairs of that person" (p. 92). Compared with similar roof-concepts such as structural power-asymmetries,[10] his agent-centered concept is, if I understand it correctly, too narrow because it explicitly requires intentionality (p. 93), it focuses on individuals as dominated agents only, and it does not spell out the structural societal sources of "domination." In my view, it sits a bit uneasily between a broad sociological analysis of "power relative to the power of others" (p. 109) (domination 1), and a more narrowly conceived concept of domination requiring intentionality and arbitrariness (pp. 93–94) (domination 2), which is meant to cover all relevant positional and allocational inequalities. If "domination 1" were abstract and

general enough, then one would have to introduce another concept of "domination 2" describing what traditionally has been the
focus of *Herrschaft.*

The price of such monistic conceptual strategies is, in my view,
a loss of the distinctive meaning of terms, usually followed by a
reintroduction of complexity and diversity when it comes to the
interpretation and application of the respective master-concepts.
A pluralist conceptual analysis of power-asymmetries is free from
such ambiguities and closer to the meaning of concepts in everyday and scientific language.

In critical discussion with multidimensional approaches in sociology, I have argued for a distinction between the following structural inequalities:[11]

a. *Exploitation* (the core of Marxian theory), in which ex-
   ploiters appropriate surplus labor from exploited.
b. *Domination*/oppression (one core of Weberian analysis),
   indicating democratically illegitimate relationships of for-
   malized or factual subordination.
c. Collective *discrimination*/misrecognition (the core of critical status-sociology),[12] or the structural lack of chances
   for equal recognition based in predominant prestige-
   hierarchies.

Together, the above constitute the three main *positional inequalities.*

d. Illegitimate closure or *exclusion* (in the Weberian tradition), which *allocates* categories of people into structurally
   defined unequal societal positions.
e. More or less full exclusion from all societal chances or a
   more or less full overlap of exploitation, domination, and
   discrimination may lead to complete *marginalization.*[13]

Pluralist concepts and research strategies, in my view, promise
and deliver thicker descriptions and better explanations compared
with old and new "Marxist" and new domination- or misrecogni-
tion-monism. Against such a background, Allen's strategy to describe the historical period in the United States prior to 1964 as
one of domination rather than exclusion seems deeply misguided.
I fully agree with her criticism that Hannah Arendt's approach
"(1) works against attending to the agency of the dominated; if

anything, it reduces their agency; (2) implies that the citizenly habits of those people who are inside the public sphere are fundamentally healthy; and (3) encourages, as the best way to deal with a past of injustice, prescription of a policy of education" (p. 60). It is, however, not "the term 'exclusion'" which does all these ugly things, but Arendt's premodern, heroic republican approach that not only gives, like all republicans, priority to "the political" narrowly understood, but also privatizes and subjectivizes "the social" and incapacitates dominated or excluded agents, making them less powerful and more invisible than they actually are (see Allen's quotations from Arendt on p. 49). And it is also obvious that African Americans—apart from being excluded from crucial civil and political rights and from a broad range of societal chances and relations—have also been exploited, dominated/oppressed, and discriminated against. It is not "the term 'domination'" that does the trick, but a more adequate scientific approach insisting on their agency and making the "publicly" invisible visible. It is not astonishing that good novelists like Ellison are much more sensitive in this regard than bad sociologists—reproducing the status hierarchies of the dominant even methodologically[14]—and predominant political theory. We should urgently learn to listen to the silent or hidden voices of the "dominated" onstage and, particularly, offstage.[15] We should, in my view, also stop overdramatizing the impact of "domination" on agents' capacity to act and "interact discursively" (Pettit, pp. 100–102) or on their psychic health (Allen, pp. 55–61) gaining prominence in recent theories of psychic, moral, and cognitive incapacitation.[16] Otherwise, political philosophers continue to make the "dominated" appear even more powerless than they actually are.

2. NONDOMINATION? EVALUATING AND FIGHTING INJUSTICES

It is true that "a positive account of justice does not lead inexorably to some one and only account of *injustice* that is its necessary mirror inverse; rather, to a degree, accounts of injustice and justice stand independent of one another" (Allen p. 32–33, emphasis added). We may agree on "nondomination" (Pettit) or on "liberty, equality, community, capability, or contractarian justice"

(Pettit's other candidates, see pp. 107–114), or on "inclusion" or "recognition" without commanding good conceptual resources and empirical studies of injustices. More generally speaking, one could combine pluralist accounts of objective inequalities or injustices with monist accounts of subjective experiences of injustice and motivational bases of collective action.[17] And one could combine pluralist accounts of objective and subjective injustices with a monist moral philosophy of unifying concepts such as fairness, reciprocity, equality, nondomination, inclusion, and recognition (see table 5.1).[18] Perhaps one could even—counterintuitively—combine monist accounts of injustice with pluralist accounts of justice, though I think that pluralist conceptual, theoretical, and empirical analyses of injustices—along the lines laid out in Section 1— pave the way toward more historically and empirically informed normative theories of injustices.[19] After all, we have to address the same phenomena in critical social sciences and moral or political philosophy, and we can use the same concepts.

Allen and Pettit seem to defend monist strategies regarding moral concepts and/or political ideals. When it comes to "*political justice*" under conditions of "plurality/difference" and "intricacy/ disagreement" (Allen, pp. 114–48), Allen is attracted by the idea that there is *one* adequate method of overcoming domination. She thinks that one new citizenship based on "friendship/respect without intimacy"; one strategy—"passive resistance" (p. 59); and a policy of imagining "the people" as a whole (versus unity, oneness) are required. It is unclear to me what these remnants of moderate republicanism would mean institutionally and how they are related to concepts and models of plural or multiple citizenship designed to address the conditions of cultural diversity.[20] Pettit clearly and explicitly claims that there should be "*one*," "central," and "supreme political ideal" only (pp. 87, 88, 92, and 114). The desirability constraints proposed by Pettit—complaints have to be discursively admissible, significant, and to subsume a variety of other significant complaints within it (pp. 90–91)—bear on "any ideal that aspires to a central or supreme place in politics" (p. 92). It is not clear to me whether these constraints bear also on moral principles ruling out moral or value pluralism right from the start in favor of a monistic moral philosophy.[21] They clearly bear, however, on political ideals and are meant "to rule out . . .

the possibility of an ideal whose satisfaction would still leave a variety of other presumptively significant complaints unsatisfied" (p. 92). Whether an ideal that is only "central" without being "supreme" would satisfy his constraints remains somewhat ambiguous (e.g., "or" [pp. 87, 88, and 92], "and perhaps even" [p. 92], "if not the supreme" [p. 114]). It is fairly obvious that his preferred political ideal of nondomination responds to significant complaints, but so do rival political ideals such as liberty, equality, community, capability, and contractarian justice.

Monist strategies in moral philosophy seem to be motivated primarily by the assumption that moral pluralism (clearly to be distinguished from "ethical" or "value pluralism," from the "reasonable pluralism" of conceptions of the good life) would inevitably result in moral relativism, a claim that is forcefully rejected by Isaiah Berlin,[22] William Galston,[23] and others. In addition, moral monism seems to provide one unifying language to talk about necessary trade-offs among principles (liberty versus equality, different liberties, different equalities)[24] if tensions and conflicts between moral principles are taken into account or taken seriously at all. On a closer look, however, the unifying language provides little or no guidance in resolving these trade-offs on a moral metalevel (as demonstrated by Roberto Unger and others).[25]

If Pettit is understood to argue not for moral monism but for a monism with regard to "political ideals" only—the link between moral principles and political ideals remains unclear—this still raises at least two questions. First, why is it desirable to have one political ideal only? If the reasons were realist or prudential ones, the argument seems very weak: apart from radical libertarians, all other relevant political theories and political parties combine a specific mix of several political ideals and have been able to respond to legitimate complaints, to mobilize and organize. If the reasons were moral reasons, then the argument would only be convincing if nondomination were the one and only significant or central moral principle. Second, only if domination is such a broad concept that it covers all structural inequalities or injustices could nondomination possibly subsume all legitimate complaints. But is it? And does Pettit make this plausible?

In my view, Pettit's dismissal of at least some of the rival ideals addressed is not convincing: the broad sets of *liberties* are reduced to "absence of domination" focused on an agent's status as a person (pp. 107–108). In line with increasingly fashionable "recognition" talk in political philosophy, Pettit seems thereby to accept serious economic inequalities. The broad meaning of *equality* is— again in line with David Miller and other neorepublicans—reduced to an "equality of status" (pp. 108–110), knowing that "this sort of equality does not entail equality in every other dimension" but too easily accepting serious economic inequalities. To make his claim plausible to other egalitarians, Pettit would not only have to state the obvious—equality of status is an important or "substantial kind of equality" and a central ideal—but claim that it is "the supreme one." The guiding intuition behind the capabilities theory à la Amartya Sen and Martha Nussbaum, like the intuition behind basic needs approaches,[26] has been explicitly pluralist, fully taking into account complex equalities. Pettit's attempt to "subsume" (p. 112) all capabilities under the ideal of nondomination loses all the advantages of such a more specified focus on the *conditions* of "domination" and gains only the illusory simplicity of one ideal. But even if we assume that Pettit could plausibly demonstrate that all reasonable complaints and political ideals can be subsumed under the umbrella of nondomination, still we would have to reintroduce the diversity of inequalities, complaints, principles, and political ideals when it comes to interpretation and application in order to spell out what nondomination means, includes, excludes, and so forth.

Neorepublicans are not only attracted to one supreme principle and/or political ideal of nondomination. They also, quasi-naturally, seem to be *institutional* monists. There seems to exist a selective affinity—again, this is in no way a "logical" or "necessary" link—between conceptual, theoretical, moral, and institutional pluralism, on one hand, and monism, on the other. Pettit's own proposals for "best institutional design" (p. 97) share the traditional republican focus on political institutions (see p. 97: dividing up sovereignty between the legislative, the executive, and the judiciary, bicameral arrangements; appeal, review, and consultation; methods of election and appointment, constitutional courts). In his view, "The most interesting challenge for republican thought today . . . bears on how to design *political* arrangements so that, as far as possible, the state really is forced to track all and only the common, ready-to-be-avowed interests of the citizenry" (p. 97; emphasis added). In our times, when traditional government has lost considerably both in terms of accountability and democratic legitimacy, and in terms of efficiency/effectiveness,[27] Pettit retells the old mythical story of the state as the "effective agency in acting against domination" and "the most efficient instrumentality available" (p. 100)—of course, only if backed by civic virtues and good morals. Where others try to find intelligent mixes of markets, networks, associations, communities, private and public hierarchies and inquire how to make "shifts in government" (multilevel polities) and "shifts from government to governance" more democratic and accountable without losing effectiveness,[28] from Pettit we can learn only what we already know: that we should not "rely on the spontaneous measures of economic and civil society" because they cannot support "a regime of nondomination" if "left alone to evolve without any political shaping" (p. 100). This distracts us from pressing the boundaries of our current understanding by investigating the inherent advantages and disadvantages of different modes of coordination (markets, networks, associations, communities, private hierarchies, and public hierarchies). How can these structures be productively combined? Most importantly, how can they be made more transparent and democratically legitimate without falling back on outdated, state-centered interpretations of the rule of law and democratic legitimacy?

Conclusion

If neorepublicans wished to convince pluralist opponents, they would have to come up with plausible substantive arguments to address these questions rather than trusting that parsimony, elegance, or the reputation of unity or oneness would do the trick. If just one concept (domination) were sufficient to describe and explain injustices, if one moral principle (nondomination) were a sufficient guide and political ideal, and if we eventually understood nondomination narrowly as "political" nondomination, then the old and new republican focus on democratizing the state would make more sense. If all this is not true—as convinced conceptual, theoretical, moral, and institutional pluralists like myself claim—than we should not only democratize the state but economy and society as well, and we should do so in a way compatible with the rule of law, and with efficiency and effectiveness in complex modern societies. This, in my view, is the really "interesting challenge" for political theory today.

NOTES

1. See Philip Pettit, "The Domination Complaint," this volume.

2. See Iris Marion Young, *Justice and the Politics of Difference* (Princeton: Princeton University Press, 1990).

3. See David Miller, *On Nationality* (Oxford: Clarendon Press, 1995).

4. See Axel Honneth, *Anerkennung oder Umverteilung* (Frankfurt: Suhrkamp, 2003).

5. See Frank Parkin, *Marxism and Class Theory* (London: Tavistock, 1979).

6. See Young, *Justice and the Politics of Difference.*

7. See Honneth, *Anerkennung oder Umverteilung.*

8. Roof-concepts are constructed to cover all rivaling master-concepts in the field, whereas master-concepts try to drive competing concepts out of the discursive arena. This game can, obviously, be repeated on the level of roof-concepts that are themselves contested. It seems plain, however, that "injustices," "inequalities," or "power-asymmetries" are more abstract and general than "domination," "exclusion," "misrecognition." They seem more fit to do the job and, it seems to me, that the choice between injustice, inequality, and structural power-asymmetries is much less contested historically and much less consequential compared with the choice of one and just one master-concept.

9. See C. B. Macpherson, *Democratic Theory* (Oxford: Oxford University Press, 1973).

10. See Veit Bader and Albert Benschop, *Ungleichheiten* (Opladen: Leske and Budrich, 1989), 120, and chaps. 6 and 7. Structural power-asymmetries are defined by the unequal power chances of different kinds of actors. These chances are extremely plurifom and heterogeneous, but, contrary to Max Weber, they are not "amorphous." They are based on unequal control of different kinds of resources and the chances to mobilize them. See Veit Bader, *Kollektives Handeln* (Opladen: Leske and Budrich, 1991), chap. 8.

11. Recently, Nancy Fraser has added struggles for "representation" to her two-dimensional frame of struggles against exploitation and for recognition, reinventing Max Weber's three-dimensional analysis of "class,

status, power" together with all its inherent ambiguities. See my criticism: Bader and Benschop, *Ungleichheiten,* 20–23, and notes.

12. See Edward Shils, "Reflections on Deference," in *Center and Periphery* (Chicago: University of Chicago Press, 1975), 275–303; Harold Lasswell, "Class and Stratum," *Science and Society* 42 (1965): 62–81; W. G. Runciman, "Class, Status, and Power?" in *Social Stratification,* ed. J. A. Jackson (London: Cambridge University Pres, 1968); Norbert Elias, *Die höfische Gesellschaft* (Frankfurt: Suhrkamp, 1969); and Pierre Bourdieu, *La Distinction* (Paris: Minuit, 1979). See my critical analysis in Bader and Benschop, *Ungleichheiten,* 20–28, 141–153, and notes.

13. See Veit Bader, "Verfügungsgewalt über direkte und indirekte Ressourcen," in *Soziologie der sozialen Ungleichheit,* ed. Bernhard Giesen and Hans Haferkamp (Opladen: Westdeutscher Verlag, 1987), 255–301; Bader and Benschop, *Ungleichheiten;* and Bader, "Ethnicity and Class" in *Multiculturalism in North America and Europe,* ed. Wsevolod W. Isajiw (Toronto: Canadian Scholars' Press, 1997), 103–128.

14. The objectivity of "collective prestige" of predominant prestige-hierarchies is not easy to understand, because prestige-hierarchies are constituted by subjective evaluative judgments depending on "time t, space s, and perspective p." In societies characterized by deep class and elite cleavages and by deep cultural diversity and inequality, there is no informational, cognitive, and evaluative consensus to be expected regarding specific partial (like occupational, income, living-room) or total prestige-hierarchies: What is when, where (in public, in private, onstage or offstage), ranked by whom? See Bader and Benschop, *Ungleichheiten.*

Methodologically, prestige or status research has to spell out exactly whose evaluations are at stake (and it has to focus on the evaluations of the different classes or groups of actors themselves instead of those of sociologists, panel experts), what is evaluated exactly, and, particularly, distinguish very clearly between actual evaluations and rankings by respondents, their expectations and opinions with regard to evaluations by others, their expectations regarding predominant rankings in society, and their respective attitudes regarding these presumably predominant hierarchies. Only in such a way can we stop using and reproducing fictions or producing sociological artifacts.

15. Compare Allen in this volume with James Scott, *Domination and the Arts of Resistance: Hidden Transcripts* (New Haven: Yale University Press, 1990). See also James Tully's excellent article in this volume and my analysis in my chapter on articulation in *Kollektives Handeln* (Opladen: Leske and Budrich, 1991).

16. See my criticism of Honneth's psychology of recognition (continuing elitist theoretical incapacitation by the traditional mix of "false"

or "ideological consciousness" and psychoanalytical notions of internalization well known from the critical theory of Adorno and others), of structuralist theories of "habitualization," and of the "poverty of culture" paradigm in "Misrecognition, Power, and Democracy," paper presented at Symposium: Recognition and Power, University of Utrecht, March 13–15, 2003.

17. This would be the more modest reading of Honneth's theory of recognition. Feeling misrecognized would be the only or at least the most powerful motivational base of collective action, an intuition shared by E. P. Thompson in *The Making of the English Working Class* (Harmondsworth, U.K.: Pelican, 1968), Barrington Moore Jr. in *Injustice* (London: Macmillan, 1978), and James Scott in *Domination and the Arts of Resistance: Hidden Transcripts*. Still, one would have to make plausible why the feeling of being exploited, oppressed, excluded, or marginalized would have to be translated into the feeling of being misrecognized before gaining motivational force.

18. Fairness, reciprocity, equality, and even nondomination would be better candidates for such unifying strategies than recognition because recognition can be, and has historically overwhelmingly been, inegalitarian, nonreciprocal, ideological, etc.

19. In my view, we have good reasons to focus our attention on more modest theories of *injustice* (fighting against harsh exploitation, oppression, serious misrecognition, exclusion and overall marginalization) instead of elaborating *ideal theories of justice,* equality, recognition, etc. As long as ideal theories are confronted with such serious problems (e.g., complex equalities) and seem to produce ever more moral disagreement instead of minimal agreement among moral and political philosophers, we could economize moral disagreement by focusing on serious injustices informed by low threshold theories of basic needs, basic rights, satisfying rough complex equality, minimally required recognition.

20. See Will Kymlicka, *Multicultural Citizenship* (Oxford: Oxford University Press, 1995); Veit Bader, "Citizenship of the European Union: Human Rights, Rights of Citizens of the Union and of Member States," *Ratio Juris* 12 (1999): 153–181; Veit Bader, "Democratic Institutional Pluralism and Cultural Diversity," in *The Social Construction of Diversity,* ed. Christiane Harzig and Danielle Juteau (New York and Oxford: Berghahn, 2003), 131–167.

21. See William Galston, *Liberal Pluralism* (Cambridge: Cambridge University Press, 2002), and Veit Bader and Ewald Engelen, "Taking Pluralism Seriously," *Philosophy and Social Criticism* 29 (2003): 375–406.

22. See Isaiah Berlin, *Four Essays on Liberty* (Oxford: Oxford University Press, 1969).

23. See Galston, *Liberal Pluralism.*

24. Moral monists have to defend the unity of their unifying concepts (e.g., Madison and Hayek on liberty versus liberties) in order to prevent conflicts among "liberties."

25. See Roberto Mangabeira Unger, *The Critical Legal Studies Movement* (Cambridge: Cambridge University Press, 1983).

26. See Bader and Benschop, *Ungleichheiten*, 90–101, and Veit Bader, "Immigration," in *International Distributive Justice*, ed. Simon Caney and Percy Lehning (New York and London: Routledge, 2003).

27. See Veit Bader, "Introduction," in *Associative Democracy: The Real Third Way*, ed. Paul Hirst and Veit Bader (London and Portland: Frank Cass, 2001), 1–15.

28. See Paul Hirst, *Associative Democracy* (London: Polity Press, 1994); Veit Bader, "Associative Democracy: Problems and Prospects," in *Associative Democracy*, 31–70. See also Fritz Scharpf, *Governing in Europe: Effective and Democratic* (Oxford: Oxford University Press, 1999); Philippe Schmitter, "Interests, Associations and Intermediation in a Reformed, Post-Liberal Democracy," in *Staat und Verbaende: Politische Vierteljahresschrift*, ed. Wolfgan Streek (Sonderheft 2. Opladen: Westdeutscher Verlag, 1994), 160–174; Philippe Schmitter, *How to Democratize the European Union—and Why Bother?* (Oxford: Roman and Littlefield, 2000); and John Braithwaite and Peter Drahos, *Global Business Regulation* (Cambridge: Cambridge University Press, 2001).

6

A REPLY TO BADER AND ORWIN

DANIELLE ALLEN

In response to Professors Bader and Orwin, I must first emphasize that I did not undertake this essay in the spirit of the analytic philosopher whose goal is to clarify the "concepts" of exclusion and domination. My focus is the metaphorical element of language and the play of metaphor in the political imagination. Political theorists too often ignore how ordinary political thought (take that as a parallel to "ordinary language") moves along tracks laid out by metaphors. These, and their conceptual content, are often what make imaginable the multitude of invisible phenomena that populate the political world: "the people," rights, freedom, equality, and so on. While I agree wholeheartedly with Professor Bader's argument that multiple concepts are necessary for defining and responding to injustice, I think that he underestimates the power of the metaphorical element of language to guide language users in building conceptual structures. While exclusion and domination can certainly be used in tandem (and Ellison in fact uses them together, as I do, to talk about formal exclusion from political institutions as an element of domination), the conceptual core of exclusion remains the image of a door closing someone out from some desirable "indoors." The term insistently reaffirms the unimpeachable desirability, or estimability, of "the inside," and so forecloses certain types of criticism or analysis of the political order. Also, the metaphors out of which "exclusion" is built consistently foster among citizens forgetfulness about the many ways citizens—whether they are dominating, dominated, or equal to each other—are related to one another. The term "domination" cannot accommodate such forgetfulness, and in this regard there *is* a fundamental incompatibility between the two terms.

Democratic theorists, I believe, ought to enhance a citizen's ability to see and describe the cultural, social, and economic connections that inevitably exist within a citizenry. This is not exactly a claim that all citizens have something in common. Sometimes you have the tusks, and I the tail, of the elephant. There are the connections of self-conscious cultural appropriation (Elvis and Eminem are the usual examples), of unwitting borrowing, of environmental impacts, of economic habits that produce effects that constrain the choices of others (driving an SUV, for instance). That I wish to point out all the kinds of connections linking citizens makes me neither a communitarian nor a neorepublican, but a theorist who grounds normative arguments in a sociology of democracy. Citizens' assorted relationships may reflect healthy interactions and exchanges, or they may be the living form of structures of injustice. I do not put positive value on the connections among citizens simply because they exist. Rather, I seek to know what the nature of relations among citizens can tell us about the fate of justice among them.

Like Aristotle, I argue that in a democratic society, friendship should provide the guiding aspiration for our interactions with strangers as well as the criteria against which to judge even our attenuated relationships (his argument about the relationship between friendship and democracy in particular appears in the *Rhetoric*). My concern here is to transfer not the affect of friendship but only its core practices (equity and power sharing) to political relationships. I do advocate a citizenship of political friendship, but significantly, one doesn't even have to like one's fellow citizens to treat them as political friends; one needs only to use the core habits of friendship in interacting with them, regardless of how one feels about them.

Does this mean my argument reduces to an exhortation to citizens to employ empty rhetoric, to paraphrase Professor Orwin? Actually, yes, it is an exhortation to citizens to employ rhetoric. Rhetoric, however, is no inconsequential art. Properly understood, it is the art of generating trust, an invaluable *technê* in any democracy. Even Hobbes thought citizens needed this art, though he was unwilling to call it rhetoric. The only polity that he describes which is held together entirely by fear is the polity by conquest. The Leviathan, in contrast, arises out of covenant—a moment of trust among its future inhabitants. Moreover, no sovereign can achieve the basic level of trust that initiates the rescue from the wretched state of nature; nature's inhabitants must rescue themselves before a sovereign can do anything for them. They can reach the modicum of trust needed to support a populist sovereign only if they adhere to the laws of nature. These are essentially rules from the art of rhetoric and boil down to an injunction to display, whenever possible, sociability. Hobbes wrote in *Elements of Law*:

> The sum of virtue is to be sociable with them that will be sociable and formidable to them that will not. And the same is the sum of the law of nature; for in being sociable, the law of nature taketh place of the way of peace and society; and to be formidable is the law of nature in war . . . the former consisteth of actions of equity and justice, the latter consisteth in actions of honour. (1.17.15)

Figuring out how to take the state of nature and covenant allegories is clearly complicated, but the allegory does at least establish that the Leviathan depends not merely on fear but also, to some degree, on mutual citizenly trust. Hobbes's sovereign can do its work only for so long as the multitude, a body within which there is an adequate level of trust, continues to exist; achieving the perdurance of the multitude, as a body, is the responsibility of its members alone.

In the end, I am neither a communitarian nor a neorepublican, but an advocate of the recovery of the art of trust generation (or rhetoric). Because injustice is always a cause of distrust, practitioners of the art of trust generation more often than not find themselves tackling injustice.[1]

NOTES

1. For a full account of my argument on all these points, please see my forthcoming book, *Talking to Strangers: On Little Rock and Political Friendship* (Chicago: University of Chicago Press, 2004).

7

IN REPLY TO BADER AND VATTER

PHILIP PETTIT

BADER

Veit Bader claims that the phenomena of justice—and presumably, by parity of argument, any set of normative phenomena—are "too complex and multifarious to be captured in a single concept." He presents himself as a sociologist, knowledgeable about the diverse folkways of common thought, and takes Danielle Allen and me to task for the "too narrow" simplicities we espouse. He thinks that we are monists about political value who are insensitive to the variety of evaluative perspectives present in the community for which we would speak.

He thinks that we are led by our monism about values into an undefined doctrine that he describes as institutional monism. We at least "seem" to be institutional monists, he says. And this, because "there seems" to be a linkage between the two "isms." Nor do the charges end there. We are said to opt—or at least to "seem" to opt—for the fashionable views that upgrade the need for recognition and downgrade the call for economic equality. And I at least am guilty of retailing "mythical" stories about the state and am even opposed, it appears, to "intelligent mixes" of markets, networks, associations, and the like.

I will not address particular questions to do with how far I downgrade the importance of economic equality, how far I reject mixes of markets and other networks, how far I go for an institutional monism that only recognizes the importance of the state, and so on. I think that what I have written on these matters elsewhere should speak adequately against Bader's suggestions.[1] But what am I to say in response to the more basic charge, that there is something deeply wrong about looking for a single value on which to base sociopolitical assessment?

The first thing to say is that the rhetoric of recognizing and relishing complexity offers no ground in itself for rubbishing the attempt to look for unity in normative thought. Even if we are led to espouse a number of conceptually distinct values, the serious wish to use those values in an assessment of the *status quo* will require us to try to establish some at least partial order and priority among them. Let the values remain unordered and unprioritized and they will march to whatever tune is willed upon them. With a little variation in the weights assigned, they can be invoked in support of just about any line at all. They will offer all the advantages of theft over honest toil, providing critics with grounds to adduce in support of whatever policy or party happens to appeal, but without putting any constraints on what they are in a position to find—or to claim to find—appealing.

Let us assume that serious evaluative thought always requires some ordering, then—that it is inconsistent with just holding by a relaxed, unorganized plurality of values. That assumption immediately raises a question of strategy. Should we start in political philosophy from the supposition that the best basis for institutional evaluation that we can hope to find will involve an ordered set of distinct values? Or should we hold out for ourselves the prospect of finding a single, unifying value—though no doubt a value with many facets—while remaining prepared to settle, if needs be, for an ordered set of distinct values?

I favor this second strategy, because it offers an intuitively more exciting and interesting possibility. Political philosophy is sourced by the motley movements of complaint and protest—the varied inklings of possibilities for institutional improvement—that bubble up in our best societies. It looks for an empirically informed, conceptually satisfying way of drawing those stirrings together, constructing out of them the vision of an ideal that can engage the imagination and sensibility. An ordered set of distinct values may well offer the best that can be achieved in seeking this sort of constructive cohesion but a single, multifaceted value would do intuitively better. The fewer the independent axioms in the formulation of a theory, the intellectually and aesthetically more satisfying the theory will be. The point applies to political philosophy as well as to exercises in mathematics and science.

Rawls endorsed the constructive or reconstructive vision of political philosophy at which I have just gestured, when he looked for a systematic account of justice that would be in "reflective equilibrium" with considered judgments about the justice of particular arrangements.[2] And Rawls's achievement in pursuit of that project was of immense significance, I would say, precisely because he came up with an idea of great unifying potential. He found in the notion of the basic structure that rational agents would choose behind the veil of ignorance an image of justice that arrests and grips the intellect. It is the unifying force of that idea, I believe, that accounts for the spectacular success that his theory of justice has enjoyed.

The cold eye that Bader casts on my enterprise and Allen's is sourced in a very different methodological perspective from that associated with Rawls. Modern and postmodern social science would foster a refusal of feeling and imagination, drilling us in the distinction between fact and value, or arming us against illusions of intersubjective consensus, even consensus on matters of meaning. It might support a detached, third-personal analysis of the various threads in folk judgments of value, then, but it would ridicule any attempt to engage with ordinary folk and to look for a unifying pattern in their responses. What Bader himself looks for, I think, is precisely the sort of detached, social-scientific examination of people's values associated with this approach, not the exploration of how far those values can be unified and made cohesive. To the extent that this is so, he does not just reject the search for normative unity in political philosophy; he rejects political philosophy itself. Instead of an evaluative theory, such as a constructive political philosophy is bound to be, we are offered a sociological account of people's evaluations.

Perhaps I am misled, however. Perhaps what he means to propose is a constructive political philosophy with plural values figuring within it. But in that case, I must complain that we are given no way of ordering and prioritizing those commitments. And equally I complain that we are given no reason to reject in principle the idea that the commitments might prove capable of being reconciled within the perspective of a single overarching value. To shrink from the prospect of identifying an overall source of normative unity, as Bader would have us do, is to give up on the best that political philosophy might hope to offer.

Finally, to a more personal note. I mentioned Rawls as an example of someone who sees political philosophy in the constructive manner I favor and who actually found a unifying idea in which to source his systematization of judgments of justice. But I might also have invoked the work of recent libertarian thinkers like James Buchanan and F. A. Hayek. If Buchanan and Hayek have had an enormous influence in leading political thought toward the right, that is surely because they have been powerful advocates for a particular unifying ideal. They have been able to urge—plausibly but not, in my view, persuasively—that the best construction to put on our varied political intuitions is to unify them in the vision of a society where interference is at a minimum. In their ideal society, as many resources as possible will be privately owned, as many exchanges as possible will be privately negotiated, and the state and the law will function merely as the guarantor of such a minimal order.

If I find the republican image of freedom as nondomination worth exploring for its normative payoff, and if I am interested in the possibility that it will subsume a variety of intuitively distinct concerns, that is due to looking for a rival ideal to serve a unifying function. As it happens, I believe that there is more to what society and the state can and should do for people—and this, by considered judgments that most of us find persuasive—than libertarians offer. The Rawlsian construction of our intuitions offers a good way of articulating a rival to that libertarian vision, but my own view, at least for the moment, is that the republican construction offers a better way still. It starts from ground shared with libertarians—that freedom is the central political value—and it offers a historically respectable, intuitively attractive construction of freedom (as nondomination) under which much more would be required of the polity than under the libertarian vision of freedom as noninterference.

VATTER

Miguel Vatter approves of the move from conceiving of freedom as noninterference to conceiving of it as nondomination. Like me and many others—and like everyone in the broad commonwealth or republican tradition—he thinks of freedom as requiring status and security in relation to others, not just the fact or the probability of escaping interference. And like me he holds that the rule of law, and related republican protections—in particular, contestatory institutions—are necessary for securing the person against domination. They are necessary to empower the person against the dominium or private power of other individuals and groupings of individuals, and against the imperium or public power of those in authority.

He argues, however, that my regimentation of republican thought on these matters falls short in two ways. First, it defines domination too narrowly, failing to recognize that a fair rule of law can be a sort of domination: "nonarbitrary domination," he calls it. Second, and consequently, it fails to see how radical the contestatory possibilities must be if they are to guard people against this further sort of domination. I will address these points in turn.

By my account, A dominates B in the degree to which A is capable of interfering in B's affairs—how to conceptualize interference is another question—without being forced to track B's avowed or at least ready-to-be-avowed interests. Or, equivalently, A dominates B in the degree to which A has an arbitrary power of interference in B's affairs. Thus, A may dominate B without interfering at all, or while interfering only in a way that actually answers to B's interests. And A may interfere with B without dominating B, where the interference practiced is constrained to satisfy the interests B avows or is disposed to avow.

This definition is stipulative, precisifying ordinary usage. It is designed, as I think of it, to be at once broadly faithful to the tradition and fairly sharply formulated. But note that under this definition it makes no sense to think that there might be nonarbitrary domination. *Qua* domination this would have to involve A having a power of interference over B. *Qua* nonarbitrary, this would have to be a power of interference that was constrained so as to track B's avowed or ready-to-be-avowed interests. But if it is nonarbitrary in this sense, then it does not count as domination. Nonarbitrary domination is as impossible, in my terms, as the square circle.

When Vatter speaks of nonarbitrary domination, therefore, he must have a different conception of domination from me, not just a different view of how far my conception extends. But he does little to explain what his alternative conception is, and this leaves me a bit perplexed. He says that being ruled, being subjected to law, is "coming to stand in a power relation that is nonegalitarian and asymmetrical, and therefore constitutes a species of domination in Pettit's own terms" (p. 129). But I don't see this. Suppose that I have an avowed interest in living under a regime where every ruling is forced to track certain interests I avow or am disposed to avow in common with others. And suppose, very unrealistically, that I am fortunate enough to live under such a rule of law. I will suffer a certain asymmetry in this regime, as I will be coerced to pay my taxes and keep the laws, and I will be penalized if I fail to do so. But this won't make for domination in my sense. Vatter says that "the kind of domination that turns me into a legal subject is not the same as the one that turns me into a slave, but it is still, evidently, a form of domination—a legal, impersonal one" (p. 129). He owes us an account of how he thinks of domination here. For by my definition it is not domination at all.

But I should guard against seeming too optimistic or naïve. I hasten to add, then, that no rule of law will ever be as perfect as the regime just imagined. *Imperium* will always involve some domination, and while we should seek to reduce this to a minimum, we cannot expect to be able to eliminate it altogether. I should also add that even in the utopia imagined, the nondominating rule of law will still, by my account, have a certain negative impact. Like the nondominating natural obstacle, it will condition the exercise of undominated choice; it will leave fewer options available to me.

Vatter's second, related complaint is that while I do insist on the importance of institutionalizing contestability, I do not make room for the radical form of contestability that is required to reduce the "nonarbitrary domination" he associates with every rule of law, no matter how perfect. "The problem with Pettit's idea of contestation is that it has been unduly restricted, just as his conception of nondomination is unduly restricted" (p. 132).

The radical contestability envisaged by Vatter is that which the people as a whole can enforce—the people who "constitute" the law and the state—insofar as they are capable of revolting against any rule of law imposed on them. I do not see why people should revolt against a nonarbitrary rule of law, however, except so far as they wish to dissolve themselves into an anarchic multitude. But I absolutely agree with Vatter that in an ideal or even half-ideal republic the people will retain the power of overthrowing any regime that becomes arbitrary. Indeed, I insisted in my book on *Republicanism,* quoting Adam Ferguson, that the final guarantee against government domination cannot be something as frail as a constitution, written or unwritten, but must be grounded in "the recalcitrant zeal of a turbulent people." And that sentiment, I believe, is wholly in the spirit of Machiavelli's *Discourses,* which Vatter invokes in support of his line.

I think that I differ from Vatter here in one point only. He suggests that the contestation that people can bring against the state, the final guarantee against political domination, is not capable of being "justified before the tribunal of reason" (p. 141). But this cannot be right. If the rule of law is held permanently hostage to a possibility of possibly quite unreasonable contestation—contestation that is not justifiable by some at least apparent failure to track common ready-to-be-avowed interests—then it is policed by a force for ill, not a force for good. Perhaps the difference between us is merely verbal, however. Vatter may mean only that public contestation of the kind he envisages will not be conducted before the tribunal of reason—it will have the character of a protest rather than an argument—not that it won't in principle be justifiable there. If so, we are closer than he thinks. The only real difference goes back to how we conceptualize domination.

NOTES

1. See in particular Philip Pettit, *Republicanism: A Theory of Freedom and Government* (Oxford: Oxford University Press, 1997).

2. John Rawls, *A Theory of Justice* (Oxford: Oxford University Press, 1971).

PART II

EXCLUSION, ASSIMILATION, AND THE ROLE OF POLITICAL PHILOSOPHY

8

EXCLUSION AND ASSIMILATION: TWO FORMS OF DOMINATION IN RELATION TO FREEDOM

JAMES TULLY

INTRODUCTION

Over the last decade, political and legal philosophers have re-flected critically on the principles of legitimacy for constitutional democracy in light of global changes in practice. They clarified two equally basic principles: the principle of constitutionalism (or the rule of law), and the principle of democracy (or democratic freedom). A constitutional democracy is said to be legitimate only if both principles inform the basic institutions in an equally funda-mental way so that one principle is not subordinate to the other. If, for example, powerful actors within states and globally are able to impose a constitutional regime that serves their interests while ex-cluding or assimilating the exercise of democratic freedom by those subject to it, then the constitutional system becomes a closed structure of domination, democratic freedom is subordinated to an imposed system of law and the regime is illegitimate. Section 1 sets out these two equiprimordial principles and the six main fea-tures of how they work together in testing the legitimacy of demo-cratic constitutional practice.

The second section sets out three large-scale trends of con-stitutional change in practice from the perspective worked up in

Section 1. These global trends threaten, diminish, or undermine the co-equality of democratic freedom and thus tend toward domination and illegitimacy. The two major ways that philosophers have responded to these trends by employing the principles of Section 1 are examined in Section 3: the defensive response of neoliberalism and the critical response of deliberative democracy. Section 4, the central section, is an examination of a third, more practice-oriented critical response. It starts from deliberative democracy but seeks to apply the two principles in practice, to expose and analyze the concrete, global mechanisms of exclusion and assimilation that subordinate or undermine the practices of democratic freedom. This critical and practical approach is then used to sketch a direction for further research, one tied closely to the reciprocal elucidation of principles of legitimation and the struggles of democratic freedom against exclusion and assimilation. A short conclusion rounds off the discussion by comparing this interpretation of the present situation to Benjamin Constant's picture of the situation of constitutional democracy in Europe in 1819 in his famous speech at the Athénée Royal in Paris, "The Liberty of the Ancients Compared with That of the Moderns."[1]

1. Two Principles and Six Features of Constitutional Democracy

From the exchange between Jürgen Habermas and John Rawls in 1995 to the present, two critical and abstract principles have been singled out as guiding norms for the critical discussion of the conditions of legitimacy of contemporary forms of political association.[2] These are the principle of constitutionalism (or the rule of law) and the principle of democracy (or popular sovereignty). The principle of constitutionalism (or the rule of law) requires that the exercise of political power in the whole and in every part of any *constitutionally* legitimate system of political, social, and economic cooperation should be exercised in accordance with and through a general system of principles, rules, and procedures, including procedures for amending any principle, rule, or procedure. The "constitution" in the narrow sense is the cluster of supreme or "essential" principles, rules, and procedures to which other laws, institutions, and governing authorities within the association are subject. In the broader sense, "constitution" includes "the rule of law"—the system of laws, rules, norms, conventions, and procedures that govern the actions of all those subject to it.

The principle of democracy (or popular sovereignty) requires that, although the people or peoples who comprise a political association are subject to the constitutional system, they, or their entrusted representatives, must also impose the general system on themselves in order to be sovereign and free, and thus for the association to be *democratically* legitimate. The sovereign people or peoples "impose" the constitutional system on themselves by means of having a say over the principles, rules, and procedures through the exchange of public reasons in democratic practices of deliberation, either directly or indirectly through their representatives (insofar as they are trustworthy, accountable, and revocable and the deliberations are public), usually in a piecemeal fashion by taking up some subset of the principles, rules, and procedures of the system. These democratic practices of deliberation are themselves rule governed (to be constitutionally legitimate), but the rules must also be open to democratic amendment (to be democratically legitimate).[3]

Habermas and Rawls follow Constant in calling the democratic principle the "freedom of the ancients." As Habermas puts it, this freedom consists of "the political rights of participation and communication that make possible the citizens' exercise of self-determination." I will call the freedom of popular sovereignty expressed by the principle of democracy "democratic freedom" rather than "ancient freedom," because it is "the rule of the people." If someone else imposes the rules by which the demos are governed, and even if they have a range of freedoms within this other-imposed regime, they are not self-governing, self-determining, or sovereign and are thus unfree. To be free democratically is not only to be able to participate in various ways in accordance with the principles, rules, and procedures of the constitutional system, as important as this is, but also, and crucially, always to be able to take one step back, dissent, and call into question the principles, rules, or procedures by which one is governed and to enter into (rule-governed) deliberations over them, or usually over a subset of them, with those who govern. Habermas and Rawls also agree with Constant in holding that a modern constitutional democracy strives to "combine" this democratic or "political" freedom with the "freedom of the moderns." In Habermas's formulation, the freedom of the moderns is the "liberty of belief and conscience, the protection of life, personal liberty, and property—in sum, the core of subjective private rights." These two types of freedom are often referred to as "public autonomy" and "private autonomy," respectively.[4]

In summary, a political association is legitimate if and only if it is equally constitutional and democratic: that is, the combination of *constitutional* democracy and *democratic* constitutionalism. The two principles are the basic law implicit in modern constitutions.

Critical discussion over the last decade has brought to light six features of these two norms of legitimation. The first feature is their critical and abstract character. They are "critical and abstract" in the sense that they are not agreed to and applied directly in particular cases. Rather, they are background critical principles of judgment that *orient* participants in their critical discussion and contestation of the legitimacy or illegitimacy of a practice of governance. Participants in political struggles bring very different and often conflicting traditions of interpretation, conceptions, and weightings *of* constitutional and democratic considerations to bear on a case at hand. What is shared by neoliberal democrats, social democrats, socialist democrats, feminist democrats, eco-democrats, pluralist democrats, communitarian democrats, agonistic democrats, and cosmopolitan democrats is an abstract and critical democratic-constitutional *orientation* to the systems of cooperation in which they find themselves (see feature three). They share, so to speak, a mode of problematization of their political identity. Although the principles are "abstract" in this sense, they are not idle. They are norms immanent in the practices of political cooperation of late modernity, and thus they are the orientation of critical self-awareness and self-formation that one takes on in virtue of being a participant in these practices (see feature six).[5]

The second feature is that the two principles are "equiprimordial." They are equally basic. If the principle of constitutionalism gains priority over the principle of democracy, so the constitution is the foundation of democratic rights and institutions but is not itself subject to democratic deliberation, then the association is illegitimate. Politics is said to be reduced to "juridification" and to suffer a "democratic deficit," as, for example, in the European Union or in forms of liberalism that place the constitution prior to and independent of the practices of democratic dispute and amendment. If, conversely, the democratic principle gains priority, then the association is said to be illegitimate because it is "a tyranny of the majority," without rules and procedures, or the licentious experience of "empty willing."[6]

The third feature is the irreducible element of reasonable disagreement. There will always be disagreement among judges, representatives, and citizens over the interpretation, procedures, application, institutionalization, and review in accordance with the orienting principles of constitutionalism and democracy in any instance—disagreements for which there will be good but nondecisive reasons on each side. This is obviously true in nonideal circumstances of real-world politics, but it is also true in ideal theory, as Jeremy Waldron among others has argued. Reasonable disagreement and thus dissent are inevitable and go all the way down in theory and practice (including disagreement over the "reasonable"). There thus will be democratic agreement and disagreement not only *within* the rules of law but also *over* the rules of law. This feature also explains why there are many rival conceptions and traditions of interpretation of democracy and constitutionalism (mentioned under feature one).[7]

This third feature is called the "agonistic" dimension of constitutional democracy because it entails that no rule of law, procedure, or agreement is permanently insulated from disputation in practice in a free and open society. The democratic practices of disputation and contestation that were previously assumed to rest on permanent constitutional arrangements, to which the people were supposed to have agreed once and for all, are now seen to apply to those arrangements as well. Thus, "agonism" (the Greek word for contest) is seen to be a defining feature of democratic constitutionalism, one which partly explains and also reinforces the co-equal status of the two principles.[8]

The fourth feature follows from the first three. Any democratic and constitutional political association, from a city to a multi-layered global order, which seeks to legitimate its arrangements under these two co-equal principles will be a continuously "negotiated" or "conciliated" constitutional order. The constitution or the principles justifying it cannot be seen as a permanent foundation or framework that underlies democratic debate and legislation. They must be reciprocally subject to legitimation through practices of the democratic exchange of reasons by those subject to them over time. No sooner is a constitutional principle, rule, or law laid down as the basis of democratic institutions then it is itself open in principle to democratic challenge, deliberation, and amendment. No particular negotiation and resolution will be definitive because there will always be the possibility of reasonable disagreement, and, secondly, particular negotiations will proceed in accord with some principles, rules, and procedures that are not questioned in the course of the negotiations, on pain of infinite regress, to be *constitutionally* legitimate, but which must be open to democratic review in the future, to be *democratically* legitimate.

In the earlier modern period, it was assumed that there was some definitive ordering of legitimate political associations toward which democratization and constitutionalization were tending. Consequently, the role of political philosophy was seen as working toward the definitive theory of justice or the definitive democratic procedures of legitimation in which citizens themselves could reach final agreements on the just ordering of their association. Now, as the result of two hundred years of constitution making and remaking and of discussions of rival and changing theories of democratic-constitutional justice, we have a better understanding of how the two principles of legitimation work together in this open-ended and nondefinitive manner. Democratic constitutionalism is an activity rather than an end state. Its legitimacy does not rest on its approximation to some ideal consensus, but rather on the mutual relationship between the prevailing rules of law and the democratic and judicial practices of ongoing disagreement, negotiation, amendment, implementation, and review.[9]

The Supreme Court of Canada illustrates this feature in the *Reference re: the Secession of Quebec*. While the clear and procedurally valid expression of the will of the majority of a member of a constitutional association for constitutional change cannot of itself effect that constitutional change unilaterally (such as secession of a province), it does constitute the exercise of the right to initiate constitutional change (the democratic principle) and thus does initiate constitutional negotiations over that change. The other members have a reciprocal constitutional duty to negotiate in good faith, but the negotiations must proceed in accord with the protection of individual rights, minority rights, the principle of federalism, and so on (the constitutional principle).[10]

The fifth feature is the way that the principles of constitutionalism and democracy are modified by political globalization. This is the most difficult feature to articulate briefly. In an earlier period it was thought that the sovereign people could act in a uniform and united way in the exercise of their public autonomy (for example, in a constituent assembly or civil society), over the constitution of one central representative government, and in a self-contained nation-state. These three assumptions were shared by both the Lockean and Rousseauian traditions. They are now seen to be untenable. First, the people are diverse and dispersed: they exercise their democratic freedom in a multiplicity of sites. Second, the functions of government are not located in or controlled by a set of traditional representative institutions and their constitutional framework. There are as many "practices of governance" as there are systems of action coordination, across the public, private, and voluntary spheres, and in which individuals and groups have the right to have a say over the way their conduct is governed. This dispersion of practices of governance and of democratic freedom (often distantly related to the traditional institutions of representative government and the rule of law) is commonly called "governance without government" or the spread of "governmentality." Third, the diversification of peoples and governance is not contained within Westphalian, independent nation-states. The institutions and activities of constitutional democracies are increasingly a mixture of constitutional representative governments in nation-states and newer, overlapping, and multilayered networks of governance that stretch from the local and regional through the national and federal to the supranational and global.[11]

This is not to say that every practice of governance is legitimate only if it operates in accordance with the principles of constitutionalism and democracy. Many forms of governance are often nonconstitutional and nondemocratic, coordinating the activity of the participants without their direct say. Markets, property systems, administrative bureaucracies, families, corporations, military complexes, and regulatory regimes are often claimed to be exceptions to this rule. However, it does mean that if a system of cooperation is not organized democratically and constitutionally, then it requires a public justification that can be made good to the people who are subject to it and its effects, to be legitimate. Justifications such as efficiency, competency, utility and a distinction between public and private are standardly claimed to meet this condition. Yet, these purposed justifications, for the reasons discussed under feature three, must always be open to the democratic disagreement, challenge, and force of the better argument of those seeking to democratize these exceptions to the rule (under feature one).[12]

The sixth and final feature is the pragmatic relationship of the principles of constitutionalism and democracy to practices of "citizenization." Members of constitutional democracies become "citizens" not only in virtue of a set (amenable) of constitutionally guaranteed rights and duties enabling them to participate in the institutions of their association. They also acquire their identity *as* citizens—a form of both self-awareness and self-formation—in virtue of exercising these rights: of participating in democratic-constitutional institutions and, more importantly, participating in the array of practices of deliberation over the existing institutions. Participation in these variegated activities (negotiations over the latest health and equity policy in the workplace, engagement in public debate over legal and political change, party politics and enacting legislation, interest groups, social movements, taking a law to court, deliberations over and voting in constitutional referenda, civil disobedience, and, at the extreme, the Lockean activity of overthrowing an unjust government and setting up a new one) create the type of orientation mentioned in feature one. A participant comes to acquire the identity of a citizen of a constitutional democracy—one who is aware that its institutions are legitimate just insofar as they stand the test of the principles of constitutionalism and democracy and who has formed the abilities of putting them to the test through practices of deliberation.

Participation in these practices of reason-exchanging citizenization also confers legitimacy on the two principles and on the political association in which the democratic deliberation takes place, even though disputation is over the legitimacy of the association and disagreement is permanent. Citizens develop a sense of identification with the principles and the association to which they are applied not because a consensus is reached, or is on the horizon, but precisely because they become aware that, despite its current imperfections and injustices, the association is nonetheless not closed but open to this form of democratic freedom. It is a free association. This legitimacy-conferring aspect of citizen participation generates the unique kind of solidarity characteristic of constitutional democracies in the face of disagreement, diversity, and negotiation.[13]

Let this stand as an incomplete and no doubt controversial summary of the recent critical discussion of conditions of legitimacy of contemporary constitutional democracies undergoing rapid change. The next section turns to three general trends in practice that have played a part in stimulating the critical discussion and thus the elaboration of the six features. These are trends that appear illegitimate in the light of the principle of democracy.[14]

2. THREE ILLEGITIMATE TRENDS IN LIGHT OF THE PRINCIPLE OF DEMOCRACY

Three general trends in constitutional-democratic practice can be seen as illegitimate in the light of the basic equality of the principles of constitutionalism and democracy. These trends have become the sites of legal and political struggles in practice and critical reflection in theory.

The first trend is the processes of global juridification that are accompanying the economic processes of the globalization of capital. The proliferation of hundreds of global regulatory regimes, such as the North American Free Trade Agreement and the World Trade Organization, constitutes complex processes of global constitutionalization. These constitutions lay down the basic rights and duties of individuals, peoples, states, and private corporations that provide the conditions for the expansion of global, corporate capitalism. These constitutional regimes have the capacity to override domestic and national constitutions, forcing them to conform, and to free the economy from the democratic control of existing nation-states.

In light of the principle of democracy, this trend is of questionable legitimacy for two reasons. First, the regimes of juridification do not establish new or renewed local and global representative democratic institutions to govern the economic processes for which they provide the constitutional underpinning. Even emerging global human rights regimes tend to favor the rights of private autonomy over public autonomy. This is unlike the historical development of nation-states and national economies, in which the constitutionalization of market relations was confronted with the representative democratization of the basic social and economic structure of these political associations, at least to some extent. Supranational and global regulatory regimes are nondemocratic and often antidemocratic. Second and more fundamentally, the discussion, design, establishment, and monitoring of these constitutional regimes, including human rights regimes, do not pass through and are not subject to the democratic deliberation of the humans who are subject to them. This is a trend, therefore, in which a specific type of constitutionalism has gained priority, and perhaps exclusivity, over the principle of democracy. It is illegitimate because it violates the equality condition (feature two) and, as a domino effect, the four following features.[15]

The second trend is the devolution and dispersion of political power and forms of political association. This refers to the proliferation of nations, states, and city-states since the beginning of political decolonization in the 1960s; the dismantling and devolution of powers within federal states such as India, Canada, and the European Union to subunits under the pressures of the politics of recognition (multinationalism, multiculturalism, and regionalism); the emergence of multilayered functional governance locally and globally; and the contracting-out of dispute resolution to ad hoc nodes with networklike relations to the more traditional institutions of representative democracy. On the one hand, this global trend toward legal and political pluralism, federalism, and subsidiarity can be seen as the expansion of opportunities for the exercise of democratic freedoms. On the other, it is also a trend toward weaker political units. The new states, autonomous units within complex federations, and global political networks tend to be weak relative to the power of transnational corporations and their complementary regulatory regimes, such as the World Bank.[16]

With the exception of states that are both powerful and democratic, if any exist, political units often lack the power to enforce democratic will, procedures, and outcomes that challenge global corporations and their ability to move elsewhere. The result is that the relatively weak polities become trapped in a "race to the bottom." They reduce constitutional democracy to elections and the security and private autonomy required for the expansion of global capitalism in order to attract the economic development they require to remain solvent. In the poorest and weakest states even the basic democratic rights of assembly, association, and free speech are curtailed and sweatshop work conditions imposed. These political associations are unable to enforce the local self-determination, survival of linguistic and cultural diversity, economic self-reliance, self-determination, or environmental safeguards they were set up to protect and promote. The trend to devolution and dispersion thus tends, to a significant degree, to support rather than challenge the trend toward global juridification and so is of questionable legitimacy for the same reason.[17]

The third trend is the decline of democratic deliberation and decision making within the traditional institutions of representative nation-states. The policies and decisions of representative bodies are increasingly the outcome of unaccountable ministries, on the one hand, and a small circle of representatives elected through nondeliberative advertising campaigns and controlled by wealthy lobbying interests and media corporations, on the other. Constitutional reform tends to be crafted by unelected experts and ratified by referenda subject to mass advertising and spectacles rather than democratic deliberation. Political powers are abjured to the market or passed to global regulatory regimes by small groups of unelected and unaccountable negotiators in private meetings whose self-consciousness has been shaped by careers in ministries or large corporations, not in practices of citizenization. Citizen participation decreases and democratic apathy and malaise increase. Once again, this trend violates the principle of democracy, diminishing the capacities and opportunities for democratic freedom.[18]

Finally, these three trends work together to insulate the growing global social and economic inequalities from public democratic discussion and reform. The only way to struggle effectively against these enormous inequalities in wealth and well-being is through the exercise of democratic freedoms in the most effective fora and also, by these means, to fight for formal democratic freedoms for the worst off. Yet, the trends make this difficult in the best circumstances (where democratic freedoms are constitutionalized) and an offense punished by exclusion, disappearance, or death in the worst (where democratic rights cannot even be discussed). As a result, the unchecked inequalities further erode the very basic prerequisites of diet, health, knowledge and organization necessary to exercise democratic freedom for an increasing percentage of the world's population, even though their condition is the direct effect of a global constitutional system of property rights over which they, by the principle of democracy, should have a right to a say.[19]

This is a "negotiated" constitutional order, to be sure, but powerful, nondemocratic actors, not the democratic citizens and representatives, negotiate it, as feature four requires for legitimacy.

3. THE CRITICAL DISCUSSION OF THE TWO PRINCIPLES IN LIGHT OF THE THREE TRENDS

This section and the next aim to answer the question: What can be learned from the experience described in the previous two sections? It is evaluative and constructive: to elucidate the critical discussion summarized in Section 1 in relation to the three trends of Section 2 with the aim of bringing to light guidelines for the future critical understanding and study of constitutionalism and democracy in the changed circumstances of the twenty-first century. The discussion of the two principles of legitimacy is divided into three types of response to the constitutional changes in practice. The first two responses are analyzed in this section. This lays the ground for the discussion of the third response in Section 4: a response that aims to apply these theoretical insights to the study of mechanisms of exclusion and assimilation that crush and domesticate democratic freedom in practice.

The first response has been to accept these trends, either in an attitude of defense and celebration or of resignation and melancholy. The most influential celebratory side of this first response is neoliberalism, but certain reformulations of social democracy, such as the "third way," have also been influential. Here the coordination and governance of human interaction and cooperation by global markets and regulatory regimes, behind the backs of the impotent participants, is said to be inevitable and without alternative. In any case, it is far too complex and fragile for the subjects to have a democratic voice over the processes that govern them without introducing destabilizing incompetence and inefficiency, which, after all, given the levels of apathy, no one wants. Rather, the demands of democratic-constitutional legitimacy are now met in the space of "lifestyle politics" opened up and made possible by globalization and juridification. One may now turn one's individual or collective life into a democratic enterprise; deliberating about, taking on, and revising a wide range of careers, work relationships, consumption patterns, lifestyles, identities, and voluntary associations around gender, cultures, languages, hybridity, and the environment, and being free to change these as one chooses. Citizens, individually and in groups, enjoy the market "freedoms of the moderns," especially of mobility, consumption, and change, and are free to invent themselves as they move from role to role, and thus to live life like an actor, as Nietzsche predicted. Finally, while it is acknowledged that these modern freedoms are not yet available to the majority of the world's population, these "developing" peoples are nevertheless said to be, in virtue of being brought into global markets and regulation, on the trajectory of "democratization."[20]

The other side of this first type of response is one of resignation, rather than celebration, in the face of global processes that are said to be beyond democratic-constitutional control. The reason for this melancholy attitude is that the modern freedom of lifestyle politics is seen as superficial at best. Given the enormous global inequalities, the freedom of consuming lifestyles is available only to the few, and even for this elite the range of options is narrow and shallow. The vast majority of the world are condemned at best to watch and try to imitate the rich and famous minority in a kind of global "synopticon" and, at worst, to work in sweatshops to produce the commodities the minority consume.[21] Moreover, while all those involved in lifestyle politics are free in a restricted sense, the diverse identities, modes of conduct, and choices by which they construct and reconstruct themselves in their private autonomy are subject to new and diffuse forms of nondemocratic modes of "governance without government" or governmentality that lack immanent practices of democratic freedom. In Michel Foucault's famous phrase, they are governed through their modern freedoms. As regimes of governmentality proliferate globally, they tend to bring more areas of life under their governance (the phenomenon of "biopower"), coordinating lifestyles in the North and local participation in the South with the three trends of the previous section. And, on one speculative account, constitutionalism and popular sovereignty are sublimated into modalities of a global empire of governmentality.[22]

Both the second and third types of response are critical of the three trends and of the celebratory and melancholy justifications of them. They reassert the co-equal importance of the principle of democracy and propose ways in which practices of democratic deliberation can be adapted to, and made good in, these circumstances. It is this critical research in North America and Europe that has spearheaded the discussion and elaboration of the two principles and six features summarized in section one. The major difference between these critical responses is that the third response (the second critical response) is less abstract than the second and more closely and reciprocally related to practice.[23]

Both the second and third responses can be characterized by three contrasts with the first response above. (1) To deliberate alone or in a private group rather than in public with fellow citizens; (2) to deliberate about lifestyle politics rather than about matters of common concern and public goods; and (3) to deliberate in order to act within relations of governance over which one has no say rather than in order to act together in exercising political power over those relations—all this is not freedom but only a certain form of "private" freedom. It is the disappearance of democratic freedom, standardly on the presumption that present neoliberal constitutional democracy is the just and definitive end of political history, requiring only global diffusion and internal adjustments. In contrast to this complacent orthodoxy, the proponents of the two critical responses hold that democratic freedom only makes its appearance when subjects take up the task of acting as citizens in the three ways of the second half of the above contrasts, either directly or in some mediated relation with their representatives.

The second response is associated with Habermas and Rawls and the more theoretical elaboration of deliberative democracy and democratic constitutionalism. According to Habermas, the politics of Western societies has "lost its orientation and self-confidence." The triumphant neoliberal parties have no interest in bringing these trends under democratic control, and they have no "sensibility" for the human resource that is most endangered, "the social solidarity preserved in legal structures and in need of continual regeneration." Consequently, "behind the hackneyed rhetoric, timidity reigns." Notwithstanding this dominant discourse, he claims there is an underlying "unrest" for democratic self-determination:

> The unrest has a still deeper source, namely, the sense that . . . the rule of law cannot be had or maintained without radical democracy. In the final analysis, private legal subjects cannot come to enjoy equal individual liberties if they do not *themselves*, in the common exercise of their political autonomy, achieve clarity about justified interests and standards. They themselves must agree on the relevant aspects under which equals should be treated equally and unequals unequally.[24]

His philosophical task, accordingly, is to turn his "hunch" of an unrest for democratic freedom into a theoretical "insight."

Similarly for Rawls, in conditions of injustice, reasonable citizens will strive to exercise their democratic freedom. When Habermas claimed that Rawls accepts the subordination of the principle of democracy to the principle of constitutionalism, Rawls replied:

> [I]t is not clear what is meant by [Habermas] saying that citizens in a just society cannot "reignite the radical democratic embers of the original position in civic life." We are bound to ask: Why not? For we have seen above in considering the four-stage sequence that citizens continually discuss questions of political principles and social policy. Moreover, we may assume that any actual society is more or less unjust—usually gravely so—and such debates are all the more necessary. No (human) theory could possibly anticipate all the requisite considerations bearing on these problems under existing circumstances, nor could the needed reforms have already been foreseen for improving present arrangements. The ideal of a just

constitution is always something to be worked towards. [W]henever
the constitution and laws are in various ways unjust and imperfect,
citizens with reason strive to become more [publicly] autonomous
by doing what, in their historical and social circumstances, can be
reasonably and rationally seen to advance their full autonomy.[25]

The primary focus of the second response has been to clarify
the two principles of legitimacy and their co-equality, the practices
of deliberation and the exchange of public reasons among free,
equal, and diverse citizens, the critical and abstract character of
the two principles, the role of the courts in balancing the principles and exemplifying the exchange of public reasons, and how
practices of citizen deliberation might be engendered in practice.
It has been responsible for getting various approaches of deliberative democracy and cosmopolitan democracy on the research
agenda and clarifying the first two features of the principles.

In its early phase (as was briefly introduced in Section 1), this
response tended to assume that the exercise of public autonomy
within and over the rules of constitutionalism is oriented toward a
definitive consensus or agreement; the exchange of public reasons
applies only or primarily to constitutional essentials and the basic
structure of constitutional democracy; and democratic deliberation takes place within self-contained nation-states. Correspond-
ingly, the role of political philosophy was assumed to be to develop
a comprehensive theory of justice or of procedures of public reasoning within which citizens themselves could reach agreement on
definitive constitutional principles.

These assumptions were called into question and shown to be
untenable by reflection on practice and by the sorts of considerations that led to features three to six. But they were also undermined by reflection on the principle of democracy itself. If citizens
are to be free, then the procedures by which they deliberate, the
reasons they accept as public reasons, and the practices of governance they are permitted to test by these democratic means must
not be imposed from the outside (that is, legislated by theoretical
reason or a constitution beyond amendment), but must themselves be open to deliberation and amendment *en passant* (not all
at once)—in the course of the exchange of reasons—as the principle of democracy requires. The exercise of democratic freedom

in relation to the existing rule of law is an ongoing, intersubjective, and open-ended public dialogue of practical reasoning.

4. The Third Response: The Study of Exclusion and Assimilation as Means of Domination

This transition to the equality of democratic principles and practices relative to the principles, rules, and procedures of constitutionalism marks the entrance of the third response. It can be defined by two changes in the ongoing critical discussion: (1) a transformation in the understanding of political philosophy and, as a result, (2) a turn from the more or less abstract clarification of principles and features of legitimacy to their practical application to expose cases of exclusion and assimilation. Let us take these two changes up in sequence.

The role of philosophy could no longer be to reflect on practices of democratic deliberation from the allegedly higher-order perspective of theoretical reason and legislate the procedures and limits of public reasons from outside the democratic exchange of reasons: that is, it should be "political not metaphysical."[26] When working out the best procedures for democratic deliberation, what counts as a claim of public reason, where these ought to be applied, and offering a conception of justice, philosophers are on par with citizens, representatives, and judges, and in dialogue with them. They start from and exercise the same types of reflective practical reasoning as other participants, aiming to bring critical clarification to existing or possible practices of deliberation by presenting their (contestable) reasons to their fellow citizens, rather than prescribing the bounds of reason to them.[27]

This transition to a critical and practice-oriented philosophy is the first and defining characteristic of the third response. These scholars have built on the earlier work of the second response, exposed its shortcomings, and elaborated features three through six. They have shifted from an abstract and prescriptive stance to a contextual and dialogical approach to the democratic practices in which citizens come to acquire the abilities to exchange public reasons in the complex circumstances of our times. This is, so to speak, a transition from the more metaphysical orientation of the Kantian and neo-Kantian Enlightenment to the practical orientation of the rival Enlightenment—of Rousseau, Constant, Hegel, Marx, Dewey, and Foucault, who insisted that philosophical inquiry be reciprocally related to practice through mutually enlightening dialogues and aimed at enhancing democratic freedom.[28]

The next maxim of this critical and practical approach is feature three: the acceptance of reasonable disagreement all the way down (in theory as well as practice), not only over different conceptions of the good within a framework of fundamental principles of justice, procedures of deliberation, or constitutional essentials but over any such framework as well. If this is true then "dissent is inevitable" among citizens, representatives, lawyers and supreme court justices, as well as theorists.[29] As a consequence, the orientation of practical philosophy should not be to reaching final agreements on universal principles or procedures, but to ensuring that constitutional democracies are always open to the democratic freedom of calling into question and presenting reasons for the renegotiation of the prevailing rules of law, principles of justice, and practices of deliberation. Hence, the first and perhaps only universalizable principle of democratic deliberation is *audi alteram partem*, "always listen to the other side," for there is always something to be learned from the other side.[30]

The contestable character of constitutional democracy should not be seen as a flaw that has to be overcome. The democratic freedom to disagree and enter into agonistic negotiations over the prevailing constitutional arrangements (or some subset of them) and the dominant theory of justice that justifies them (such as the first response) is precisely the practice of thought and action that keeps them from becoming sedimented—either taken for granted or taken as *the* universal, necessary, and obligatory arrangements. At the beginning of Western constitutionalism, Socrates, in the *Apology*, argued that this freedom of constantly questioning in dialogues what we think we already know about democracy, for which he was willing to die, is the very activity that improves it.

Accordingly, the major contribution of agonistic democrats has been to stress the manifest reality of partisanship, dissent, disagreement, contestation, and adversarial reasoning in the history and present of democratic societies and the positive role it plays in exposing and overcoming structures of inequality and injustice, fostering a critical democratic ethos, and, *eo ipso,* creating autonomous citizens with bonds of solidarity across real differences (feature six). They have argued this against the nonadversarial, classless ideology of constitutional democratization of the neoliberal and third-way defenders of the three trends (of the first response), and against the exclusionary and assimilative dangers of the consensus models of deliberation and the overly abstract conception of public reason (of the second response).[31] By exchanging pros and cons in dialogues with partners who see the constitutional arrangement of a shared political association differently and who can give reasons for their views, citizens are empowered to free themselves from their partial and limited views to some extent (often assumed to be universal), reflect critically together on them, and negotiate the modification of the relations of meaning and power that bear them: that is, to think and act differently.[32]

After all is said and done, the democratic-constitutional citizen is not Lenin. She does not aim for the end of politics and the administration of things. She is more akin to the young Olympian athlete who greets the dawn's early light with a smile, rises, dusts herself off, surveys her gains and losses of the previous days, thanks her gods for such a challenging game and such worthy opponents, and engages in the communicative-strategic *agon* anew.

The second change marked by this approach is its commitment to bringing philosophical discussions into the closest possible relationship with practices of democratic struggle on the ground. For otherwise there is at best a tenuous connection between abstract discussion of principles and concrete practice, and this disconnected abstractness tends to promote a kind of idle, talk-show chatter about public reason in some mythical public sphere, overlooking the situated knowledge, local skills, and passionate partisanship of real democratic deliberation.[33] However, when scholars turned to practice, rather than seeing only the traditional, discrete institutions of constitutional representative democracy, which set the framework for critical reflection for the last two hundred years, they discovered the much more complex negotiated political associations of feature five and the three dominant trends. The study of practices of democratic deliberation could not be restricted to constitutional essentials and constitutional referenda or to the genres of adversarial reasoning in the traditional legal and political institutions. To test the constitutional and democratic legitimacy of dispersed, overlapping, and multilayered regimes of constitutional democracy, it is necessary to study the practices of democratic freedom—the modes of dispute conciliation—in any practice of governance in which those subject to, or affected by it, seek to reignite the embers of public autonomy and have an effective say over how their conduct is governed.

The methodological implication of feature five is to shift to the study of the motley of practices of democratic freedom vis-à-vis practices of governance, of which the traditional courts, representative institutions, public spheres, and constituent assemblies are now seen as an important regulative subset rather than the constitutive set. Furthermore, this requires a broader and more fitting language of description of the object domain of legal and political philosophy, namely, the emerging language of "nodes" (of governance and practices of democratic freedom) in negotiated "networks." Again, this redescription does not displace the traditional language of description of constitutional representative democracy, as the hyperglobalizers advocate, but relocates this familiar vocabulary as one important and enduring family in larger and more complex languages of networks of rule and democratic freedom.[34]

From this broadened horizon, the critical study of democratic freedom includes research on the multiple forms of democratic activism and negotiation in practice that the legal scholar Richard Falk calls "globalization from below," in contrast to the "globalization from above" of the first trend and the "race to the bottom" side of the second trend (Section 2).[35] By "globalization from below" Falk does not mean that the exercise of popular sovereignty occurs uniquely in the lowest stratum of some new overarching global hierarchy.[36] This would be to miss what the metaphor of a network is meant to convey, namely, that hierarchies of money, power, discourse, and violence exist within shifting networks of direct and indirect communication, rule, and insubordination. Rather, as Jeremy Brecher, Tim Costello, and Brendan Smith explain (adapting the work of Michael Mann to Falk's insight), globalization from below refers to the irruption of public autonomy in "interstitial locations," nooks and crannies in and around the dominant institutions. Those who were initially marginal then link together in ways that allow them to outflank those institutions and force a reorganization of the status-quo. . . . At certain points, people see existing power institutions as blocking goals that could be obtained by cooperation that transcends existing institutions. So people develop new networks that outrun them. Such movements create subversive "invisible connections" across state boundaries and the established channels between them. These interstitial networks translate human goals into organizational means.[37]

While this form of interstitial democratic freedom is exemplified by nongovernmental organizations, globalization from below can refer as well to the wider range of actors who, through a variety of ways of having a say and renegotiating the rules of game anywhere in the network of regimes of governance, aim to approximate feature four (a democratically negotiated constitutional order), as Falk and Brecher et alia illustrate. For example, one side of the second trend comprises attempts to increase democratic legitimacy and self-determination through subsidiarity, devolution, and federalization of traditional institutions of government, not through bypassing traditional representative institutions. For another, attempts to make representative institutions more representative of the culturally diverse electorate through proportional representation, whether within nation-states or a second chamber at the United Nations, seek to strengthen rather than go beyond traditional institutions of constitutional and democratic association.[38]

In sum, these are struggles *of* and *for* democratic freedom, practices of freedom in which democratic actors seek, by means of traditional and new forms of deliberation and negotiation, to challenge and modify the nondemocratic ways they are governed. By relating the theoretical discussion of the principles of constitutionalism and democracy to research on these concrete practices of democratic freedom and reworking the languages of description and evaluation accordingly, the third response answers the objections of activists to the abstractness and irrelevance of the second response and establishes a new working relationship between philosophers and democratic activists in which they learn from each other.[39]

The results of this kind of critical and practical inquiry suggest that there are two major types of relations of meaning and power that render contemporary citizens unfree and violate the co-equality of the principle of democracy: relations of exclusion and assimilation and their corresponding mechanisms of operation. These are relations of communication and governance that arbitrarily or unnecessarily constrain citizens from exercising their democratic freedom to engage freely in effective practices of deliberation and negotiation of the rules by which they are governed. These two forms of domination are not restricted to a specific type of democratic struggle today. They can operate in any type of struggle that involves the exercise of democratic freedom (struggles over work conditions, human rights, distribution, recognition, the environment and so on).[40] The relations and mechanisms of exclusion and assimilation comprise the major means by which the trends of Section 2 are able to dominate present constitutional change, unchecked and unbalanced by those subject to them.[41] According to the critical and practical approach, one of the best ways to understand exclusion and assimilation is not to start with an abstract definition but, rather, to begin with a critical survey of examples or case studies of each.

Relations of exclusion refer to the various ways citizens are excluded from initiating and entering into practices of democratic negotiation. In many cases, subjects are formally excluded, as in modern slavery, the denial of democratic rights of association and organization, and military intervention to crush movements of popular sovereignty and impose rule from the outside, either directly or mediated through the postcolonial forms of indirect control exercised by transnational corporations and global regulatory agencies.[42] There is also a variety of forms of exclusion where democratic rights are formally guaranteed. As Noam Chomsky has documented many times, powerful states, such as the United States and Canada, profess support for democratic rights and the United Nations Universal Declaration of Human Rights while pursuing foreign policies that ignore, support, or instigate their abuse and subvert international human rights institutions when it suits their economic and geopolitical interests.[43] In more subtle types of cases, subjects with formal democratic rights are unable to exercise them due to lack of money, time, and knowledge, because their voices are not taken seriously due to deep-seated class, racist, and sexist stereotypes, or because their jobs hang on their silence.[44] Another common form of exclusion in the face of democratic rights occurs when the actors responsible for the exclusion are not accountable to the local rights regime (the problem of the second trend).

The most outstanding form of exclusion remains the one John Dewey identified as paramount: the exclusion of those subject to national and transnational corporations from having a democratic say over them. As we have seen in Section 2, many of these corporations are now more powerful than many constitutional democracies and govern the conduct of more subjects. They also exercise nondemocratic control over the decision making of constitutional democracies (as Rawls stressed). For over a century, corporations have excluded employees and those affected by their operations from having a democratic say on the constitutionally entrenched grounds that they are private persons and so possess the right of noninterference—the freedom of the moderns, yet are not subject to democratic control—the freedom of the ancients. Under this mode of legitimation they have grown to surpass and control the representative nation-state, the type of corporation that has been sovereign for the last four hundred years.

Just as the principles of constitutionalism and democracy were originally designed to bring the absolutist form of the modern state under democratic control, by establishing democratic institutions within it, the task today is to apply the same principles to these new sovereign corporations and bring them under democratic control by establishing practices of democratic freedom within them, as well as governing them from the outside by means of new and effective international representative bodies. For, despite the attempts to keep this form of exclusion from public scrutiny in the dominant neoliberal and third-way ideologies (by eliminating the co-equality of the principle of democracy as a condition of legitimacy), there appears to be no unquestionable reason for this exemption from the exercise of the principle of democracy.[45]

Relations of assimilation and their complex mechanisms of peration bring about the second form of domination. Subjects are permitted and often encouraged to participate in democratic practices of deliberation yet are constrained to deliberate in a particular way, in a particular type of institution, and over a particular range of issues so their agreements and disagreements serve to reinforce rather than challenge the status quo. Through participation in these assimilative practices, they gradually come to relinquish their dissonant customs and ways and acquire the consonant forms of subjectivity. Although they are governed through their freedom to some extent, they nevertheless deliberate within the rules rather than over the rules, as the principle of democracy requires.[46]

Different practices of reasoning-with-others are grounded in distinctive customary local knowledges, repertoires of practical skills, genres of argumentation, and tacit ways of relating to one another. These culturally and historically diverse genres of practical know-how or "savoir faire" (*metis* in Greek) are the intersubjective bases of culturally diverse practices of deliberation—of raising questions and listening to others, of presenting a reason, a story, an example, a comparison, a gesture, or a parable for consideration, showing rather than saying, expressing disagreement, deferring or challenging, taking a point, informing another, advising and taking advice, speaking for another and being spoken for, stonewalling, feet dragging and feigning, dissenting through silence, breaking off talks, working toward a compromise, agreeing conditionally or unconditionally, following the agreement reached in toward and untoward ways, reviewing the agreements reached, restarting the deliberations, and countless other discursive and nondiscursive activities that make up deliberative language games. When formerly excluded people are "included" in practices of democratic deliberation, they often find that the practical knowledge of the practice is different from the ones to which they are accustomed. This is often overlooked by the dominant groups, for it is their customary way of reasoning together; or if it is noticed, it is often presented as canonical, as universal or the uniquely reasonable, modern or "free and equal" way of deliberating, as if there were only one way of exercising democratic freedom. If one wishes to be heard, then, it is necessary to act in accordance with the dominant practice of reasoning together and resolving differences, and, as a result, to gradually develop the form of identity and comportment characteristic of participants of this kind of practice. This is the unfreedom of assimilation, for one is not free to challenge the implicit and explicit rules of the dominant practice of deliberation but must conform to them and so be shaped by them.[47] One is subject to, rather than an actor in, what the proponents of the first response euphemistically call "processes of democratization" (Section 2).

There is a remarkably wide range of relations of communication and power that serve to assimilate through inclusion in unfree practices of deliberation, adversarial reasoning, and dispute resolution. Iris Young has shown that the exchange of reasons cannot be abstracted from different modes of speaking and listening, such as greeting, rhetoric, and narrative, without silencing legitimate voices. The attempt to impose certain allegedly abstract and universal rules often just privileges dominant forms of reasoning, often of a simplified and aggressive kind, typical of many Western institutions of dispute resolution, oriented to winning an exchange with opponents rather than promoting the kind of mutual understanding necessary for progress among partners who disagree but nonetheless need to cooperate freely.[48] The exchange of public reasons also cannot be separated from the cultural, linguistic, ethnic, and gendered identities of those participating or from their substantive conceptions of the good, as the earlier theorists of deliberation sometimes assumed.[49] Just as deeply ingrained sexist, racist, and diversity-blind attitudes can operate to exclude oppressed and subordinated people, they can also operate to discount and ignore their modes of argumentation once they are included, both in practice and in theories of deliberation.[50] If deliberation is oriented to a consensus, then, given reasonable disagreement, this will ensure that some minority voices will be silenced along the way. Moreover, deliberation involves a visceral or passionate dimension that was ignored in the more abstract accounts.[51]

The devolution of democratic practices to groups and peoples within multinational associations to solve problems of assimilation in the institutions of the larger society often overlooks assimilation of weak minorities within the devolved institutions. In addition, the recent repatriation of limited self-governing powers by indigenous peoples from the states that have taken their lands, destroyed their customary practices of governance, and reduced their populations to a fraction of precontact levels perpetuates a powerful form of assimilation called "domestication" or "internal colonization" (an example of the second trend).[52] The ways local residents in poor countries are induced to participate in deliberations associated with development projects and employ their local knowledge in these settings often have the effect of gradually creating a Western identity and outlook and commodifying their traditional knowledge.[53]

The most persuasive form of assimilation, as we have seen in Section 2, is assimilation to the dominant identity of a consumer of lifestyles celebrated in the first response. Most members of contemporary societies are subject to these processes of subjectification most of the time, not only in practices of deliberation, but in virtue of participating in the practices of work and leisure.[54] Furthermore, this kind of assimilation in developed countries is often coordinated with complementary forms of exclusion and assimilation for those in developing countries who make the consumer products that define the various lifestyles, as Naomi Klein's research shows.[55] The danger of assimilation to this form of subjectivity, as the proponents of responses two and three argue, is twofold. It tends to eliminate the self-awareness of the possibility of and reason for democratic freedom itself, by reducing freedom to the freedom of the moderns. And, in virtue of performing most of one's activities in practices that disallow or discourage collective reflection and deliberation over the rules of the practice in a diversity of ways, participants do not acquire the self-formation of democratic freedom, and so they have neither the experience of, nor subjective interest in, democratic participation.

Relations of exclusion and assimilation, finally, work together to block processes of citizenization: that is, the processes of identity formation among diverse citizens who deliberate freely together over their shared and contested rules of recognition, distribution, and coordination, and so conciliate their differences over generations (feature six). The unique kind of solidarity that has the capacity to hold together the diverse contemporary political associations is not generated. In Habermas's phrase, it remains an unfilled promise. Subjects are excluded and assimilated from the practical basis of solidarity's "continual regeneration": namely, forms of life that embody the principle of democracy in endlessly different ways. If this analysis is partially correct, then contemporary constitutional democracies will continue to experience a dominant tendency not only to democratic deficits and illegitimacy but, as a result, also toward a lack of overall cohesion.[56] Without the experience of democratic freedom, citizens tend in the extreme to cohere instead around the protection of their capitalist patterns of consumption at one end and the protection of their excluded religious and cultural identities at the other.[57]

CONCLUSION

Despite the great differences between constitutional democracy in 1819 and today, there is one striking similarity. At the end of "The Liberty of the Ancients Compared with That of the Moderns," Constant warned that the "danger of modern liberty is that, absorbed in the enjoyment of our private independence, and in the pursuit of our particular interests, we should surrender our right to share in political power too easily." This, as I have sought to show, is our danger as well. Like the contributors to the critical discussion today, Constant argued that "far from renouncing either of the two sorts of freedom which I have described to you, it is necessary, as I have shown, to learn to combine the two together." This is a difficult lesson to learn because, as Constant reasoned, and as we have seen in our times, the relations of communication and power in the practices in which moderns find themselves tend to exclude them from ancient freedom and to assimilate them to modern freedom alone. The solution Constant proposed was to petition the legislator to create practices of citizenization and encourage citizens to participate, thereby acquiring the identity formation and desire to continue to exercise and uphold their democratic freedom on a par with their private freedoms:

> The work of the legislator is not complete when he has simply brought peace to the people. Institutions must achieve the moral education of the citizens. By respecting their individual rights, securing their independence, refraining from troubling their work, they must nevertheless consecrate their influence over public affairs, call them to contribute by their votes to the exercise of power, grant them a right of control and supervision by expressing their

opinions; and by forming them through practice for these elevated functions, give them both the desire and the right to discharge these.[58]

While Constant's advice to look to practices of freedom is as pertinent now as then, the suggestion that representative governments and their administrative bureaucracies might play the primary or exclusive role in initiating new democratic practices should be viewed with some skepticism for the host of reasons discussed above.[59] Rather, despite the powerful trends to the exclusion and assimilation of democratic freedom and the dominant discourses that legitimate them, practices of and for democratic freedom irrupt in opposition to them in a multiplicity of nodes and networks, and around a multiplicity of issues. Democratic freedom fighters find ways to organize their unrest and reignite the embers of public autonomy through the vast array of traditional and nontraditional avenues and institutions that make up globalization from below. A public philosophy oriented to testing the constitutional and democratic legitimacy of contemporary polities and to exposing the mechanisms of illegitimacy could do worse than to take these practices of freedom as its field of study and investigate them in the manner canvassed in the last section.[60]

NOTES

1. Benjamin Constant, "The Liberty of the Ancients Compared with That of the Moderns," in *Benjamin Constant, Political Writings,* ed. Biancamaria Fontana (Cambridge: Cambridge University Press, 1988), 308–328.

2. The exchange between Habermas and Rawls was first published in the *Journal of Philosophy* 92, no. 3 (March 1995). Both authors republished their contributions with minor changes in collections with other works that help to explain the more technical terms of the debate. I will refer to the page numbers of these editions. Jürgen Habermas, "Reconciliation through the Public Use of Reason," in *The Inclusion of the Other: Studies in Political Theory,* ed. Ciaran Cronin and Pablo De Greiff (Cambridge, MA: MIT Press, 1998), 49–75, and John Rawls, "Reply to Habermas," in *Political Liberalism,* 2d ed. (New York: Columbia University Press, 1996), 372–434. My discussion of these two principles draws on Habermas and Rawls, but also on an important case by the Supreme Court of Canada in which

their understanding of these two principles of legitimacy is explicated and then applied to the hypothetical case of the secession of a province from the Canadian federation, SCC, *Reference re the Secession of Quebec,* 2 SCR 217 (1998), www.droit.umontreal.ca/doc/csc-scc/en/index.html, and republished with commentary in David Schneiderman, ed., *The Quebec Decision: Perspectives on the Supreme Court Ruling on Secession* (Toronto: Lorimer, 1999), 14–72, particularly sections 32–82. For my interpretation of the Reference case as an application of these two principles of legitimacy, subdivided into four principles for the particular context, see *The Unattained yet Attainable Democracy: Canada and Quebec Face the New Century* (Montreal: Programme d'études sur le Québec, McGill University, 2000). My formulation of the principle of constitutionalism in this paragraph follows the Supreme Court closely. The Supreme Court distinguishes between constitutionalism and the rule of law (sections 70–78) but, like Habermas and Rawls, also uses "constitutionalism" in the broad sense to cover both (section 32).

3. In some versions of the democratic principle it is insufficient to have a say, directly or indirectly. It is also necessary to have a hand in the exercise of power over which one has a say: that is, to exercise public power together, rather than delegating it. I set aside this more stringent condition in this article. I will take it as sufficient that the people or peoples of the association exercise public reasons together over public powers in negotiations that are tied to implementation. Although there is widespread agreement on these two principles of legitimation, there is disagreement on their formulation. Habermas formulates the principle of democracy in terms of two principles ("D" and "U") and Rawls in terms of "four stages" of the exchange of public reasons (Habermas, "Discourse Ethics: Notes on a Program of Philosophical Justification," in *Moral Consciousness and Communicative Action,* trans. C. Lenhardt and S. W. Nicholsen (Cambridge, MA: MIT Press, 1995), 43–115, and Rawls, "Reply to Habermas," 396–406). The Supreme Court of Canada prefers to work out case-specific formulations of the two principles.

4. Habermas, "Reconciliation through the Public Use of Reason," 68–69, and compare Rawls, "Reply to Habermas," 396. Constant sometimes includes public autonomy or "political liberty," the rights of democratic participation in representative democracies, within the "freedoms of the moderns" (pp. 310–311) and other times he separates the two in a manner similar to Habermas and Rawls and says they have to be "combined" (pp. 323–328). In addition, Habermas often equates the principle of constitutionalism with the "freedom of the moderns" on the assumption that the role of a modern constitution is to protect subjective rights or private autonomy. Although this is clearly one role of a modern constitution and

it is often interpreted as *the* role, I, like Rawls and the Supreme Court of Canada, see it as one role among several, and so will not equate the protection of the rights of private autonomy with the principle of constitutionalism. This article is devoted solely to the question of the legitimacy of practices of constitutional democracy relative to the principle of democracy. The question of their legitimacy relative to the principle of constitutionalism is another question.

5. The immanence of the two principles in modern political culture, the plurality of rival yet reasonable traditions of interpretation and application of the principles, and the resulting critical orientation of participants are central to the approaches of Rawls and Habermas and to the contemporary theorists of other democratic-constitutional traditions mentioned in the text. Of course, it is possible to call into question this entire orientation from some other perspective. However, it is interesting to note, as Hegel did, how many of the attempts to do so are either caught up in the two principles in one way or another, and so involve a performative contradiction (as Habermas argues), or else border on idle speculation. For Hegel's argument, see Frederick Neuhouser, *Foundations of Hegel's Social Theory: Actualizing Freedom* (Cambridge, MA: Harvard University Press, 2000).

6. See Habermas, "Reconciliation," 67–73, and Rawls, "Reply," 409–421. In "Reconciliation," Habermas objected that Rawls subordinated the principle of popular sovereignty to the principle of the rule of law, as liberal democrats often do. Rawls replied that his "political liberalism," in which the legitimacy of the basic structure of a political association rests on the exchange of public reasons among free and equal citizens, treats the two principles equally (see especially p. 407 and his reference to Frank Michelman: "I take American constitutionalism . . . to rest on two premises regarding political freedom: first, that the American people are politically free insomuch as they are governed by themselves collectively, and second, that the American people are politically free in that they are governed by laws rather than men. . . . I take them to be premises whose problematic relation to each other, and therefore whose meaning, are subject to an endless contestation"). Rawls clarifies this further in "The Idea of Public Reason Revisited," in *The Law of Peoples* (Cambridge, MA: Harvard University Press, 1999), 129–180. Habermas explores the co-equal status of the two principles further in "On the Internal Relation between the Rule of Law and Democracy" in *The Inclusion of the Other*, 253–264. (Sir Isaiah Berlin is an example of a liberal who grants priority, and sometimes exclusivity, to the principle of constitutionalism.)

7. See Jeremy Waldron, *Law and Disagreement* (Cambridge: Cambridge University Press, 1999), 102–106, and *The Dignity of Legislation* (Cam-

bridge: Cambridge University Press, 1999), 153–154. Waldron argues that Rawls is committed to the earlier view that agreement is possible on constitutional essentials, but it is not clear that he is in *Political Liberalism* (pp. 54–58), and "The Idea of Public Reason Revisited," where he suggests that there will always be a family of rival, reasonable political conceptions of justice. Habermas appears to continue to hold that there could be agreement on both the democratic procedures for testing a norm of action coordination (a rule of law) and agreement on a proposed norm within the democratic procedures, in principle at least. However, it is not clear how we are to take these two types of consensus, given their ideal and quasi-transcendental status. If they are simply critical, rather than regulative, ideals (that is, ideals that are themselves open to criticism from another standpoint, and so always subject to the democratic exchange of reasons), then it is not clear that they are incompatible with the view that disagreement goes all the way down, over questions of the right as well as the good. This is, after all, the status of the two legitimacy principles as well, and it is the way his approach has been interpreted by some of his followers, such as Simone Chambers and Seyla Benhabib.

8. For the agonistic dimensions of constitutional democracy, see Bonnie Honig, *Political Theory and the Displacement of Politics* (Ithaca, NY: Cornell University Press, 1993); William Connolly, *The Ethos of Pluralization* (Ithaca, NY: Cornell University Press, 1995); John Gray, *Enlightenment's Wake: Politics and Culture at the Close of the Modern Age* (London: Routledge, 1995); and Chantal Mouffe, "For an Agonistic Model of Democracy," in *The Democratic Paradox* (London: Verso, 2000), 8–107. Mouffe argues that the disagreement and agonism result from the irreconcilability of the logics of the two fundamental principles of constitutionalism and democracy (pp. 1–35).

9. The "negotiated," rather than "foundational" character of democratic constitutionalism is the central theme of the Supreme Court of Canada *Reference*, sections 66–78 (note 2). I have tried to show that reasonable disagreement and negotiation stem in part from the diversity of the members of contemporary constitutional associations and the complex relations among them, in "Introduction," in *Multinational Democracy*, ed. Alain-G. Gagnon and James Tully (Cambridge: Cambridge University Press, 2001), 1–34. Jo Shaw discusses constitutionalism in the European Union in a similar manner in "Constitutionalism in the European Union," *Journal of European Public Policy* 6, no. 4 (1999), 579–597, and "Relating Constitutionalism and Flexibility in the EU," in *Constitutional Change in the European Union*, ed. G. de Burca and J. Scott (London: Hart, 2000), 337–358.

10. Supreme Court of Canada, *Reference*, sections 83–94 (see discussion in Tully, "Introduction," *Multinational Democracies*). We can also see

that the earlier understanding of constitutional democracy rests on the unrealizable assumption that the people could be, *simultaneously*, sovereign over the constitution (the democratic principle) and subject to it (the constitutional principle). Michel Foucault argues that this sovereign and subject "double" was one of the constitutive and irresolvable tensions of modern thought and practice in *The Order of Things* (London: Tavistock, 1970), 312–328. The late modern or postmodern "negotiated" understanding of democracy and constitutionalism simply recognizes that they cannot be resolved in any definitive way, thereby dissolving rather than overcoming the *aporia*, as Foucault suggests.

11. The decentering of public autonomy and loci of governance is a central concern of Habermas in *Between Facts and Norms: Contributions to a Discourse Theory of Law and Democracy*, trans. William Rehg (Cambridge, MA: MIT Press, 1996). For an extension of his approach to global politics, see Andrew Linklater, *The Transformation of Political Community* (Cambridge, UK: Polity Press, 1998). A slightly different view of these three global changes, called cosmopolitan democracy, is presented by David Held and his associates, summarized in David Held, "Democracy and Globalization," in *Re-imagining Political Community: Studies in Cosmopolitan Democracy*, ed. Daniele Archibugi, David Held, and Martin Köhler (Cambridge, UK: Polity Press, 1998), 11–27. The phrase "governance without government" comes from James Roseneau, "Governance and Democracy in a Globalizing World," in *Re-imagining Political Community*, 28–57. The term "governmentality" comes from Michel Foucault and his students: see Nicolas Rose, *The Powers of Freedom* (Cambridge: Cambridge University Press, 1999), and Mitchell Dean, *Governmentality: Power and Rule in Modern Society* (London: Sage, 1999). See the comprehensive synopsis of research in this area prepared by Neil Walker for the Constitutionalism in Transition Workshop, "The Idea of Constitutional Pluralism." I have discussed some of these changes in *Strange Multiplicity: Constitutionalism in an Age of Diversity* (Cambridge: Cambridge University Press, 1999).

12. The differences among the major schools of constitutional democracy (socialist, neoliberal, ecological, etc.) consist in disagreements over the reasonableness of these justifications for shielding certain areas of contemporary societies from the exercise of public autonomy, standardly in the name of private autonomy. On the general requirement of a discursive justification that can be made good to all those affected, see Rainer Forst, "Towards a Critical Theory of Transnational Justice," *Metaphilosophy*, 32, 1 and 2 (January 2001), 160–179.

13. I am indebted to Anthony Laden, who, in a work inspired by Rawls, has rebuilt liberal political philosophy in response to the critical discussions of these six features, especially the last. See Anthony Laden,

Reasonably Radical: Deliberative Liberalism and the Politics of Identity (Ithaca, NY: Cornell University Press, 2000). For a different yet complementary approach to identity formation in contemporary constitutional democracies, see James Tully, "The Challenge of Reimagining Citizenship and Belonging in Multicultural and Multinational Societies," in *The Demands of Citizenship,* ed. Catriona McKinnon and Iain Hampsher-Monk (London: Continuum, 2000), 212–235.

14. These three constitutional trends are not the only trends that have stimulated reflection on constitutional and democratic legitimacy. They are, however, three trends that have been seen to be of questionable legitimacy under the principle of democracy, and so have helped to stimulate discussion of that principle and its relevance today. They may violate the principle of constitutionalism as well, but this important question must be set aside for now.

15. In general, see David Held, Anthony McGrew, David Goldblatt, and Jonathan Perraton, eds., *Global Transformations* (Cambridge, UK: Polity Press, 1999), 32–86, and 149–234. For a detailed legal analysis of one "economic constitution," see Steven Shrybman, *The World Trade Organization* (Toronto: Canadian Centre for Policy Alternatives, 1999). In this regard note also that the emerging rights regimes in the European Union neither pass through democratic deliberation nor establish practices of democratic deliberation over rights. See Richard Bellamy, "The Right to Have Rights: Citizen Practice and the Political Constitution of the European Union," in *Citizenship and Governance in the European Union,* ed. R. Bellamy and A. Warleigh (London: Continuum, 2002).

16. Decentralization in Canada, for example, finds support from those in favor of local democratic control, on the one hand, and by the major lobby groups for large corporations, on the other. For an introduction to the complexities of this second trend in relation to democracy and constitutionalism, see Alain-G. Gagnon and James Tully, eds. *Multinational Democracies* (Cambridge: Cambridge University Press, 2001), and Will Kymlicka and Wayne Norman, eds., *Citizenship in Diverse Societies* (Oxford: Oxford University Press, 2000).

17. See Richard Barnett and John Cavanagh, *Global Dreams: Imperial Corporations and the New World Order* (New York: Simon and Schuster, 1994); William Greider, *One World, Ready or Not: The Manic Logic of Global Capitalism* (New York: Simon and Schuster, 1997); Richard Falk, *Predatory Globalization: A Critique* (Cambridge, UK: Polity Press, 1999); and David Held, *Democracy and the Global Order* (Stanford: Stanford University Press, 1995), 239–266.

18. Rawls, "Reply to Habermas," 407 ("the present system woefully fails in public financing for political elections, leading to a grave imbal-

ance in fair political liberties; it allows a widely disparate distribution of income and wealth that seriously undermines fair opportunities in education and employment, all of which undermine economic and social equality"). See Robert D. Putnam, *Bowling Alone: The Collapse and Revival of American Community* (New York: Touchstone, 2000); Henry Milner, "Civic Literacy in Comparative Context," *Policy Matters* 2, 2 (July 2001), 1–39; and Guy Debord, *Society of the Spectacle,* trans. Donald Nicholson-Smith (New York: Zone Books, 1994).

19. See Thomas Pogge, "Priorities of Global Justice," *Metaphilosophy* 32, 1–2 (January 2001), 6–24; Noam Chomsky, "Socioeconomic Sovereignty," in *Rogue States: The Rule of Force in World Affairs* (Cambridge, MA: South End Press, 2000), 199–214; and Falk, *Predatory Globalization,* 153–166.

20. Among the "celebrators" Anthony Giddens is widely seen as one of the most sophisticated proponents of this response and defender of it against its critics. See *The Third Way and Its Critics* (Cambridge, UK: Polity Press, 2000). For a range of views of celebration and resignation, see David Held and Anthony McGrew, eds., *The Global Transformations Reader: An Introduction to the Globalization Debate* (Cambridge, UK: Polity Press, 2001). For Nietzsche's prediction and the concerns he had regarding the possibility of acting together for a future good, see Paul Patton, "Nietzsche and the problem of the Actor," *Why Nietzsche Still?* ed. Alan Schrift (Berkeley: University of California Press, 1999), 170–184.

21. See Zygmunt Bauman, *Globalization* (Cambridge, UK: Polity Press, 1998), and Alex Callinicos, *Against the Third Way* (Cambridge, UK: Polity Press, 2001). For a range of voices of resignation, see Held and McGrew, *The Global Transformations Reader.*

22. For the roles of governmentality and biopower, see note 11 above, especially the indispensable work by Nicolas Rose. For their global reach, see, in addition to James Roseneau, Michael Hardt and Antonio Negri, *Empire* (Cambridge, MA: Harvard University Press, 2000), 3–42, 219–350. Hardt and Negri are not resigned to these processes but argue that they create the possibility of democratic action (see below). For the cooptation of local participation and local knowledge in developing countries into global governance and Western development, see Peter Traintafillou and Mikkel Risbjerg Nielson, "Policing Empowerment: The Making of Capable Subjects," *History of the Human Sciences* 14, 2 (2001), 63–86.

23. For the differences between these two Enlightenment traditions of legal and political philosophy, see Michel Foucault, "What Is Enlightenment?" in *Ethics, Subjectivity and Truth,* ed. Paul Rabinow (New York: New Press, 1997), 303–321; James Tully, "To Think and Act Differently: Foucault's Four Reciprocal Objections to Habermas," in *Foucault contra Habermas: Recasting the Dialogue between Genealogy and Critical Theory,* ed.

Samantha Ashenden and David Owen (London: Sage, 1999), 90–142; and David Owen, "Orientation and Enlightenment: An Essay on Critique and Genealogy," in ibid., 21–44.

24. Habermas, *Between Facts and Norms*, xlii.

25. Rawls, "Reply to Habermas," 401–402. Even if a constitution were perfect, Rawls stresses (following Rousseau), the exercise of public autonomy would be necessary for legitimacy and the creation of citizens (pp. 402–403).

26. The phrase comes from Rawls, "Justice as Fairness: Political Not Metaphysical," in *Collected Papers* (Cambridge, MA: Harvard University Press, 1999), 388–414. As I mentioned in note 7, it is a matter of debate whether Rawls and Habermas accepted the full force of these arguments, and thus if their later work should be seen as making the transition to the third stage. For a sample of deliberative democracy representative of the second response, see James Bohman and William Rehg, eds., *Deliberative Democracy: Essay on Reason and Politics* (Cambridge, MA: MIT Press, 1997).

27. This transition to seeing political philosophy as a species of "practical philosophy" is often associated with the work of Richard Rorty, especially his article, "The Priority of Democracy to Philosophy," in *Philosophical Papers*, vol. 1 (Cambridge: Cambridge University Press, 1991), 175–199, without accepting the particular inferences he draws from it, and the work of Charles Taylor, *Philosophical Arguments* (Cambridge, MA: Harvard University Press, 1995). For this transition and Rorty's contribution, see James Tully, "The Agonic Freedom of Citizens," *Economy and Society* 28, 2 (May 1999), 161–182, at 161–169; Matthew Festenstein, "Pragmatism, Social Democracy and Politics," in *Richard Rorty: Critical Dialogues*, ed. M. Festenstein and Simon Thompson (Cambridge, UK: Polity Press, 2001), 203–219. For an account of the transition and its implications for liberal political philosophy, see Laden, *Reasonably Radical*, 14–16. For an agonistic account, see Mouffe, *The Democratic Paradox*, 60–107. For a broader historical account of this way of thinking about constitutional democracy, see Tully, *Strange Multiplicity*, 103–116, 209–212.

28. For a more detailed and internal account of this transition, to which I am indebted, see James Bohman, "The Coming of Age of Deliberative Democracy," *Journal of Political Philosophy* 6 (1998), 399–423, and John S. Dryzek, *Deliberative Democracy and Beyond: Liberals, Critics, Contestations* (Oxford: Oxford University Press, 2000). The case for seeing this transition in terms of Rousseau and Hegel can be seen in Laden, *Reasonably Radical*, 1–73. For the relevance of Dewey, see Matthew Festenstein, "Inquiry as Critique: on the Legacy of Deweyan Pragmatism for Political Theory," *Political Studies* 49 (2001), 730–748. Several authors of the third response remain neo-Kantians, but their Kantianism has been tempered

by the practical objections of Hegel, Marx, Dewey, and Rorty; for an example, see Simone Chambers, *Reasonable Democracy: Jürgen Habermas and the Politics of Discourse* (Ithaca, NY: Cornell University Press, 1996). For the formulation of the critical and practical Enlightenment to which my analysis is indebted, see Foucault, "What Is Enlightenment?"

29. Supreme Court of Canada, *Reference re the Secession of Quebec,* section 68.

30. For the reasons supporting this claim, see Tully, "Struggles over Recognition and Distribution." Flexible institutions of adversarial negotiation and the correlative principle of *audi alteram partem* in response to the fact of reasonable disagreement constitute the main proposal of Stuart Hampshire, *Justice Is Conflict* (Princeton, NJ: Princeton University Press, 2000).

31. See the references to this literature at note 8. Disagreement and contestation has been accepted also by neorepublicans such as Philip Pettit, *Republicanism: A Theory of Freedom and Government* (Oxford: Oxford University Press, 1996), and Richard Bellamy, *Liberal and Pluralism: Towards a Politics of Compromise* (London: Routledge, 1999), liberals such as Laden, *Reasonably Radical,* 194–199, and deliberative democrats such as Dryzek, *Deliberative Democracy and Beyond.*

32. For an attempt to reformulate this Socratic insight into critical dialogue in the terms of hermeneutics, critical theory, and genealogy, see Herbert Kogler, *The Power of Dialogue* (Cambridge, MA: MIT Press, 1999).

33. These are standard objections to the second response. For an excellent example from a practice-based perspective of "civic activism," see Charles Spinosa, Fernando Flores, and Herbert Dreyfus, *Disclosing New Worlds: Entrepreneurship, Democratic Action and the Cultivation of Solidarity* (Cambridge, MA: MIT Press, 1997), 69–89.

34. I owe this general way of putting the transformation of the language of description from a "Westphalian" to a "global" perspective without downplaying the continuing importance of the traditional institutions of representative democracies to David Held. See David Held, Anthony McGrew, David Goldblatt, and Jonathan Perraton, eds., *Global Transformations.* This formulation is also close to Manuel Castells, *End of Millennium: The Information Age: Economy, Society and Culture* (Oxford: Blackwell, 1998). For the corresponding transformation in the orientation of deliberative democracy to concrete practices of governance in networks, see Dryzek, *Deliberative Democracy and Beyond,* 115–140, and Iris Marion Young, *Inclusion and Democracy* (Oxford: Oxford University Press, 2000), 236–276.

35. Falk's approach of "globalization from below" is set out in *Predatory Globalization: A Critique.*

36. For example, Hardt and Negri locate democratic activity in the lowest stratum of a traditional, three-tiered global hierarchy in *Empire,* 309–314.

37. Jeremy Brecher, Tim Costello, and Brendan Smith, *Globalization from Below: The Power of Solidarity* (Cambridge, MA: South End Press, 2000).

38. For these examples, see Alain-G. Gagnon and James Tully, eds., *Multinational Democracy.*

39. For these objections and the kind of response I have laid out here, see Iris Young, "Activist Challenges to Deliberative Democracy," *Political Theory* 29, 5 (2001), 670–690. Both Falk, *Predatory Globalization,* 125–185, and Brecher et al., *Globalization from Below,* set out detailed proposals for uniting normative theory and democratic activism. For an important reformulation of feminist philosophy around practices of democratic activity, to which I am indebted, see Cressida Heyes, *Line Drawings: Defining Women through Feminist Practice* (Ithaca, NY: Cornell University Press, 2000).

40. For a more detailed account of "practices of freedom," adapted from Foucault's initial use of this concept, and the points that follow, see James Tully, "Democracy and Globalization: A Defensible Sketch," in *Canadian Political Philosophy: Contemporary Reflections* (Toronto: Oxford University Press, 2001), 36–62. For a similar account of freedom as forms of democratic activity, see Wendy Brown, *States of Injury: Power and Freedom in Late Modernity* (Princeton: Princeton University Press, 1995), 3–29.

41. For an introduction to the analysis of specific types of exclusion and assimilation in practices of deliberation, see Laden, *Reasonably Radical,* 131–185; Young, *Inclusion and Democracy,* 16–153; James Bohman, *Public Deliberation* (Cambridge, MA: MIT Press, 1997); and Brown, *States of Injury.*

42. See references at notes 17 and 19. For modern slavery, see Kevin Bales, *Disposable People: New Slavery in the Global Economy* (Berkeley: University of California Press, 1999).

43. The research by Chomsky on this form of exclusion is voluminous. See, for example, *Rogue States,* 108–173, and references therein.

44. Laden, *Reasonably Radical,* 131–158.

45. For Dewey, democracy, and corporations, see Robert Westbrook, *John Dewey and American Democracy* (Ithaca, NY: Cornell University Press, 1991). This form of exclusion is a central theme of Falk, *Predatory Globalization;* Held, *Democracy and the Global Order;* and Chomsky, *Rogue States,* among others. Despite the formal exemption this is where many struggles of democratic freedom have been ignited over the last 170 years. For the

rise and fall of the nation-state as the dominant corporation of governance, see Martin van Creveld, *The Rise and Decline of the State* (Cambridge: Cambridge University Press, 1999).

46. Rose, *Powers of Freedom*. See also Clarissa Hayward, *Defacing Power* (Cambridge: Cambridge University Press, 2000), for a complementary analysis of this form of unfreedom. These approaches (and mine) are indebted to the work of Foucault on the agonistic interaction between imposed forms of subjectification and practices of freedom. See Michel Foucault, "The Subject and Power," in *Michel Foucault: Power*, ed. James Faubion (New York: New Press, 2000), 326–348, and "The Ethics of the Concern for Self as a Practice of Freedom," *Ethics, Subjectivity and Truth*, 281–303.

47. For this account of practical reasoning, see James Scott, *Seeing Like a State* (New Haven: Yale University Press, 1998), 309–341; Stephen Toulmin, *Return to Reason* (Cambridge, MA: Harvard University Press, 2000); and Spinosa et al., *Disclosing New Worlds*. As this paragraph is meant to convey, there is nothing specifically "Western" about democratic freedom, of having a say over the way one is governed and often struggling not to be governed in such and such a way, nor is it necessarily related to Western institutions of representative government. On the contrary, three leading trends and their discourses of legitimation in Western societies are opposed to it. Democratic freedom in the sense I am using it seems to be a fairly general human activity that takes different forms in different times and cultures.

48. Young, *Inclusion and Democracy*, 52–80, and her *Intersecting Voices* (Princeton, NJ: Princeton University Press, 1997), 38–94.

49. Laden, *Reasonably Radical*, 159–185, and David Owen, "The Avoidance of Cruelty: Joshing Rorty on Liberalism, Scepticism and Ironism," in *Richard Rorty: Critical Dialogues*, 93–110. For some types of argumentation typical of practical deliberation, see Douglas Walton, *The New Dialectic: Conversational Contexts of Argument* (Toronto: University of Toronto Press, 1998).

50. Charles Mills, *The Racial Contract* (Ithaca, NY: Cornell University Press, 1997).

51. William E. Connolly, *Why I Am Not a Secularist* (Ithaca, NY: Cornell University Press, 1999), 19–46.

52. Duncan Ivison, Paul Patton, and Will Sanders, "Introduction," in *Political Theory and the Rights of Indigenous Peoples* (Cambridge: Cambridge University Press, 2000), 1–21.

53. Traintafillou and Nielson, "Policing Empowerment: The Making of Capable Subjects."

54. For an overview of this literature, see Bauman, *Globalization*, and

John Tomlinson, *Globalization and Culture* (Chicago: University of Chicago Press, 1999).

55. Naomi Klein, *No Logo: Taking Aim at the Brand Bullies* (Toronto: Vintage, 2000).

56. Both these trends are widely noted and studied but they are normally not seen to derive from the lack of democratic freedom. Indeed, the standard account is that increased democratic freedom over the rules of recognition and distribution is the cause of disunity. See the overview in McKinnon and Hampsher-Monk, "Introduction," in *The Demands of Citizenship*, 1–9.

57. This is also the diagnosis of Benjamin Barber, *Jihad vs. McWorld: How Globalism and Tribalism are Reshaping the World* (New York: Ballantine Books, 1996), and Tariq Ali, *The Clash of Fundamentalisms* (London: Verso, 2002).

58. Constant, "The Liberty of the Ancients Compared to That of the Moderns," 326, 327, and 328.

59. For an analysis of the dangers of turning to representative governments and their administrative bureaucracies to reignite the embers of public autonomy, see Brown, *States of Injury*.

60. I would like to thank Melissa Williams and Stephen Macedo for kindly setting up an ASPLP panel on an earlier draft of this chapter, and Michael Blake and Leif Wenar for their engaging commentary and discussion. I am also grateful to Nicola Lacey and Melissa Williams for helpful comments during the final stages of rewriting. An earlier version of this paper was published as "The Unfreedom of the Moderns in Comparison to Their Ideals of Constitutional Democracy," *Modern Law Review* 65, 2 (March 2002), 204–228. For a further exploration of the type of public philosophy presented here, see my "The Unfreedom of the Moderns," 226–228, and "Political Philosophy as a Critical Activity," *Political Theory* 30, 4 (August 2002), 533–555. Finally, I would like to thank Genevieve Johnson for her meticulous editing.

9

LIBERAL FOUNDATIONALISM AND AGONISTIC DEMOCRACY

MICHAEL BLAKE

Liberalism begins with the fact of disagreement. As a historical phenomenon, liberalism first arose in response to the horrors of religious warfare.[1] Liberalism sought political institutions and principles not dependent upon religious affiliation, to serve as foundations for a political society whose inhabitants disagreed about religious truth. More recent liberal theorists have widened this original focus. John Rawls's political liberalism, for example, has sought to develop a conception of justice suitable for a society whose members vary widely in their moral, religious, and cultural identities.[2] In this, again, liberalism's hope is that political justice can be established in the face of deep disagreement. Indeed, it might be argued that disagreement is the prerequisite for liberalism's applicability; in a society without disagreement, it is hard to see what room could be found in which liberalism could do any work.

For all this, however, the relationship between liberalism and disagreement is controversial. It is, at least, an open question as to what forms of disagreement liberalism is bound to treat as matters for principled respect. One compelling vision of liberalism, eloquently defended by James Tully in the accompanying article, argues that liberalism must be open to all forms of political disagreement. In practical terms, this means that all aspects of liberal politics must be open to collective political control; all political norms, rules, and institutions are to be included within the purview of democratic deliberation. This approach also implies that the liberal theorist must see her role not as potential arbiter of democratic deliberation, but as participant. She is precluded from using abstract reason to derive rules to be followed by parties in the political discussion; she must see herself, instead, as part *of* that discussion. In this agonistic conception of democracy, political practitioners and political theorists are both part of an ongoing process of discourse, in which no party has the power to rule any norm or practice off the table.

There is much to admire in this conception of democratic practice. In what follows, however, I want to articulate an alternative vision, in which some norms are regarded as foundational for liberal political practice. This alternative conception—which I term liberal foundationalism—will regard certain norms and principles as being legitimately outside the reach of collective deliberation and control. If what I have to say is correct, then this latter conception of democratic practice has much to recommend it as well; by ruling certain things out, and demanding liberal orthodoxy in certain foundational matters, liberal foundationalism can avoid certain risks inherent in agonistic democracy. Liberal foundationalism will, I think, defend against certain forms of political exclusion unavoidable on an agonistic account of democracy. Ironically, it may be the case that only by taking certain liberal values as not themselves the object of disagreement and collective revision—by insisting that certain objections to them are excluded—can we defend against certain objectionable patterns of political exclusion. The only way to defend liberal pluralism, that is, may sometimes be to insist upon certain forms of orthodoxy.

In this, I will have very little to say about Tully's practical political conclusions. I share many of his conclusions about the legitimacy and effects of globalization and economic integration.[3] My questions deal with how these shared conclusions are to be defended. I will present my argument in two parts. The first will look at liberalism and its relationship to disagreement in more detail. I will attempt to establish that a plausible liberalism may regard certain norms as essential to the continued success of the liberal project. Political assertions contrary to such norms may be ruled out from the sphere of deliberative democracy. The second section will examine the implications of such conclusions for liberal constitutionalism and the self-understanding of liberal theorists. In this section, I will attempt to establish two conclusions. The first is that not all norms need be subject to collective control for a liberal society to regard itself as self-governing. The second is that political theorists need not cease to write and talk as if they were setting rules for the processes of political discourse. From the fact that we will never reach consensus, it does not follow that we should not write as if such consensus were the ultimate goal of political theorizing.

1. Liberal Disagreement and Liberal Foundations

The question I want to examine now is the following: Can a liberal system of governance regard all norms and practices as potentially open to collective revision? Agonistic democracy answers this question in the affirmative, and asserts that this is the best way to interpret the project of liberal self-government. I will, in this section, try to argue the contrary. What I want to establish is that there exist some norms that ought to be regarded as foundational to the liberal project. They are foundational, in this context, in that liberals rightly consider their validity to be off the table for purposes of political justice. I will consider, at present, only one such norm—namely, the moral equality of persons. Liberal states are bound, on this norm, to justify their policies and practices in terms demonstrating equal concern and respect for all those within their sphere of authority.[4] Such a norm, I suggest, must serve as the backdrop to practices of liberal discourse if these practices are to maintain their character as morally valuable. Refusal to regard such a norm as the foundation *of* liberal discourse—rather than itself a potential object of disagreement *within* that discourse—is problematic; it is, I believe, both theoretically unmotivated and politically dangerous.

To see this, we may examine the liberal response to cases of sincere disagreements as to political morality. Are there cases of sincere disagreement about political morality in which the liberal state is rightly able to regard one side to the disagreement as simply wrong?

On one version of this question, the answer is quite obvious: liberal states, simply in virtue of making policy, must come to some concrete position or other about the validity of moral claims, and so must inevitably assert that one party to a dispute is in the wrong. This is not the version of the question I pose here. What I want to ask, instead, is whether some cases of disagreement exist in which one side may be justly shown as wrong *because* what they assert flies in the face of the foundational norm asserted above. Taking the norm as foundational means, in this context, that showing a political assertion to be in conflict with the norm precludes any legitimate demand for further deliberation about the assertion's validity. If such cases are possible, then our proper response to political assertions attacking this norm is not to put the norm itself into question; it is, rather, to assert that those who make such assertions are wrong simply by virtue of that norm's continued salience.

Potential examples of such assertions are, sadly, all too easy to come by. I will here introduce only two examples. Examine, first, the assertions of the Reverend Fred Phelps that the murder of gay men and women is biblically commanded. Phelps is the pastor of the Westboro Baptist Church, which exists primarily as an organizational site for the public promulgation of his ideas. He continues to lead a campaign of public demonstrations against both gays and those institutions he sees as insufficiently harsh toward homosexuality; his targets for the current calendar year include targets as diverse as the Harvard Law School, whose graduation ceremonies he has announced his church will disrupt, and the memorial service for Fred Rogers. His demonstrations are targeted at all those who disagree with his assertion that the United States is an illegitimate nation until it executes all gay men and women.[5] Examine further the teachings of Richard Butler, the founder of the Aryan Nations, whose political program includes the exclusion of all non-whites from the American political community—if necessary, by their extermination. Butler recently criticized a lawsuit against a fellow neo-Nazi with the novel interpretive claim that the First Amendment, since it was written by white men, can clearly have application only to white men.[6]

Such political positions as Phelps's and Butler's are extreme, and it is tempting to dismiss their relevance simply in virtue of that fact. There are few individuals willing to endorse ideals so obviously evil as those articulated by Phelps and Butler. Nevertheless, I believe it is instructive to examine how liberal thinkers ought to respond to such hateful suggestions. Any plausible liberalism—agonistic or foundational—will regard the assertions of Phelps and Butler as obviously, and laughably, wrong. The more interesting question, I think, is in how these liberal theories will defend the conclusion that such assertions are to be condemned. These assertions are political statements, and how we reject them will tell us a great deal about how our own political theories are to be understood.

The agonistic response, I take it, is to regard such assertions as not unlike the normal stuff of democratic deliberation. The fact that such assertions violate the fundamental norm articulated above is not relevant. Since no liberal norms are to be taken as beyond the reach of democratic deliberation, the fact that a political assertion violates a given norm is insufficient to establish that such an assertion is incorrect. On an agonistic liberalism, the hatred of Phelps and Butler will be condemned; but its condemnation will emerge only through the process of democratic deliberation.

The foundational approach, in contrast, will condemn such hatred prior to democratic deliberation by examining the relationship of these hateful utterances to democratic practice. It will look, that is, at the content of what is asserted: namely, that not all those subject to political authority have an equal right to be treated as equals by that authority. It will regard such an assertion as beyond the pale for liberal democracy, because it violates the foundational norm giving liberal democracy its moral value. Some forms of political disagreement respect the norm of moral equality and phrase their assertions as interpretations of this norm. Other forms, such as these hateful utterances, can only be understood as attacks on the foundational norm of equality itself. These latter forms of disagreement are not interpretations of equality, but denials of equality; as such, they are best understood not as disagreements within democratic practice, but disagreements with the very notion of democratic practice itself.

I should be clear at this point about what I am not saying. I do not want to say that a liberal theory is forced to recommend the use of state power against those who make statements like those given by Phelps or Butler; there are good reasons, both moral and pragmatic, to hesitate before making such a recommendation. Still less am I saying that an agonistic theory such as Tully's will defend these hateful statements; any liberal theory, foundational or agonistic, will condemn such statements and the exclusionary moral views they represent. What I am saying is that a foundationalist liberalism has resources available by which this condemnation might occur, and that these resources are not available on an agonistic approach. For a foundationalist, democratic deliberation is not a free-standing good; it represents one means by which the moral project of treating people as equals is brought into the political world. As such, statements which attack this moral project directly need not be treated with the same principled respect as other forms of political discourse. A foundationalist can condemn such hateful rhetoric with reference to the egalitarian premise animating democratic deliberation. She does not need to regard such statements as morally equivalent to other forms of political speech; their contrast with the egalitarian foundations of democracy is enough to argue for their condemnation. In the subsequent section, I will argue that this methodology opens up the way for a division of intellectual labor between theorists and other actors within democratic practice. In the present section, I want only to point out that a foundationalist is able to regard at least one aspect of democratic life—namely, the egalitarian premise underlying democratic deliberation—as not itself subject to collective control and discussion. This premise is not the result of democratic deliberation, but the very foundation by which such deliberation gains its moral standing.

All this is simply to identify the foundationalist methodology as a live alternative to the agonistic model. To this point, I do not think anything I have said is sufficient to establish the superiority of the former model to the latter. Nevertheless, I think some considerations might be introduced in favor of a foundationalist approach. The agonistic approach, in refusing to exclude anything from the sphere of political discourse, runs the risk of excluding marginalized citizens simply from this openness to disagreement. Ironically, it is agonism's very reluctance to exclude any perspective that may introduce a hazard of political exclusion.

To see this, we may examine Tully's vision of the agonistic practitioner as akin to an Olympian athlete, who wakes up each morning thanking her gods "for such a challenging game and such worthy opponents," ready once again to engage in the struggle of democratic self-rule. Such an image, I think, fails to describe the experience of marginalized groups facing pervasive hatred; individuals faced with pronouncements denying their moral equality and very right to participate in political self-government are unlikely to thank the gods for the opportunity to run this particular race again. A gay man faced with the vitriol of Fred Phelps is unlikely to be grateful for the challenging nature of the game he faces. Nor, I think, is a Jew likely to be appreciative of the worthy adversary he faces in figures such as Richard Butler. Such marginalized individuals are, more likely, to ask why it is that they must rehearse the old arguments once again; why it is that they must *still* fight for recognition of their moral equality and equal claim to human dignity. Those facing such hatred face exclusion—an exclusion found simply in the fact that agonistic democratic politics will not regard such hatred as ruled out *ab initio* by the demands of liberal equality. Such individuals face a differential burden; they face a hatred placing demands on them not faced by those who can, confidently and without impediment, exercise their political equality. They must continually argue for what others may simply assume. Agonistic democracy insists that abstract reason cannot establish any norm or practice as beyond the reach of collective dispute and discourse. Those who must face political hatred are unlikely to be grateful for this inclusive vision of political life; such inclusion brings exclusion in its wake. After all this time, they might ask, are there not some things liberals can simply accept as proven, and is our moral equality not among them?

2. Self-Government and Liberal Theory

In what follows, I want to apply the above articulation of liberal foundationalism to certain more specific domains arising within Tully's account. Tully's articulation of agonistic democracy suggests two defects within contemporary liberal thought. The first deals with self-government; Tully argues that unless all norms are brought within the range of collective political control, a political society may not rightly regard itself as self-governing. Liberal theory is wrong to think that it can defend both its foundational norms and the idea that liberal states can properly understand themselves as self-governing communities. The second deals with the self-conception of liberal theorists. Tully argues that no distinction should be drawn between those who participate in liberal practices of deliberation and those who attempt to theorize about such practices. The latter should regard themselves as participants in the agonistic process of self-government, rather than detached theorists using abstract reason to articulate constraints on political participants. Liberal foundationalists, on this account, are illegitimately assuming a divide between theory and practice; they are engaged in a search for a definitive liberal theory—one which, by definition, can never exist.

To my mind, liberal foundationalism has replies to both of these purported defects. I will, in what follows, articulate the competing vision of liberal foundationalism, and try to defend it against these objections.

I will begin with the first charge. Tully argues that liberal foundationalism cannot provide the support for self-government. This claim finds its defense in the simple fact that a people facing a norm not within their collective political control is, on Tully's account, no longer a self-governing people. They are subject to a norm of political justice properly understood as alien and imposed; this norm confronts them as something done to that people from without, rather than accepted from within by the continued process of democratic deliberation about that norm.

This charge, I think, is overstated. To see this, we might inquire about what self-government means, understood as a category deserving of moral approbation. What does it mean, that is, for a community to govern itself in such a way that such continued self-government is morally demanded?

When we speak here of self-government, we may mean one of several things. I address only two here. One is the absence of external political domination. Colonial rule and empire clearly violate this notion of self-rule in this sense; they are practices in which one political society is governed in accordance with norms and practices imposed by the political agents of another, foreign political community. This is not, however, the only morally relevant idea of self-government. An alternative notion of self-rule might be understood as implicit in the moral self-understanding of a liberal society. It insists that the self which rules, and the self which is ruled, must be the same; for a political society to be self-governing in this more demanding sense, it must ensure that all those subject to the power of the state are given an equal share in the determination of how that power is to be employed. All members of political society, on this account, have an equal right to question, critique, and orient political power. This latter sense of self-government links the project of liberal legitimacy with the project of self-rule. Liberal politics seeks to justify political power through reasons acceptable to all those affected by such power, so that mere coercion is thereby transformed into something as close as possible to a cooperative process of self-government.

The two senses of self-government may be complementary; colonial power, for example, represents a violation in either sense of the term. But they are distinct notions, and what violates the first norm may not be quite so alien to the latter. To see this, imagine that what has been defended above is correct—that there might be certain foundational norms of democratic practice that are legitimately beyond the scope of democratic deliberation. Imagine a society that accepts this fact, and so places some such norm in a privileged position; it enshrines it in a constitution, or in its practices of political discourse regards this norm as holding in an unquestioned way. Is this a denial of self-government? Tully's analysis insists that any norm not subject to collective political control is imposed from outside, as an alien form of political dominion. This is to invoke the image of a colonial politics; it argues that any norm not subject to collective political control must be akin to a norm imposed by a colonial power upon an unwilling subject nation. This, I think, blurs the distinction between the two notions of self-rule. Not all norms not subject to collective political control have this character of alien imposition. In some cases, it is better to regard the special status of some norms as stemming from a special concern for self-rule in the second sense—the normative idea that all citizens here ought to be listened to in the creation of policy. If this is so, then placing certain norms foundational to this enterprise beyond the reach of collective control is not a violation of self-rule; it is, instead, one possible means by which self-rule is to be preserved and guaranteed. A society that accepted liberal foundationalism, and regarded the norm of equality of persons as essential for the continued success of the liberal project, would not thereby create a norm rightly understood as somehow imposed upon an unwilling colonized state by a foreign political community. Such a society, I think, would regard this norm as placed beyond the pale of political discussion precisely because it is concerned with the preservation of self-rule. To give these norms a distinct political status would not, on this analysis, represent a deviation from self-rule; it would represent, instead, one interpretation—to my mind, the most plausible—of what a continued commitment to such a norm would demand.[7]

The second topic to be dealt with in this section, finally, makes reference to the self-understanding of the liberal theorist. Tully's agonistic approach to democracy mandates an alteration not only in how we think about liberal democracy, but also how those who think about such things ought to understand their role. If Tully is correct that there are no foundational norms constraining discourse—but that it is, in contrast, discourse all the way down—then those who theorize about liberal politics no longer have a status distinct from those who participate in the political discourse. There is no foundational norm, after all, about which abstract and detached reason can be brought to bear. Political philosophers, then, have no right to understand themselves as detached observers of political practice, dictating to others what would and would not count as acceptable forms of political life; they must, instead, abandon their abstract and prescriptive stance for a critical and immanent one, in which the distinction between theorist and practitioner is abandoned.

Much of the defense of this position is contained in what has gone before; Tully's contention that there are no foundational norms is an integral part of his argument that political theory ought to be reoriented. I have already disputed this former contention and will not rehearse these arguments here. I will, however, address a distinct argument introduced by Tully in connection with this potential reorientation of political theory; namely, that philosophers will never be able to develop a theory capable of sustaining consensus, and so ought to stop writing as if that were their aim. The history of disagreement within liberal theory, on this account, suggests that there can never be agreement about any aspect of liberal practice; is it not, therefore, appropriate for liberal theorists to cease developing abstract theories intended to guide all liberal practitioners, and instead enter the game of liberal practice itself?

In what remains of this paper, I want to dispute this contention, while allowing that it contains within it an important truth: namely, that we will never reach any consensus about the ideal form of liberal political community or practice. From this, however, I do not think it follows that liberal thinkers ought to stop thinking and writing as if such consensus were our aim. No human theory will ever suffice as the final answer to all questions of political life; this is true, I think, simply because no human mind is without limits, and no human life contains within itself all experiences. The product of any human mind, therefore, contains within itself certain assumptions derived from the partial and local nature of human experience; it will also, inevitably, contain within itself countless errors derived from the imperfect and partial nature of human mental faculties. All of this, I think, should incline us toward theoretical modesty, and the recognition that our own theoretical postures can be improved by the criticism of other theorists. We are likely to miss sources of injustice until those who experience the injustice bring it to our attention. We are likely to regard our own experiences as universal until we encounter those with whom it is not shared. This would seem to incline the liberal theorist toward the recognition that the final word about liberal practice is unlikely to be his own—for the very simple reason that such finality is not to be found within the theories of partial and limited creatures such as ourselves.

None of this, however, implies that we should not write as if such finality were not the ultimate goal of our project. Tully insists that philosophers have no right to regard themselves as above the fray, writing as if they had the final account of how others ought to play the game of politics. They ought, that is, to shift from the prescriptive goal of using reason to tell others how to play the game, to the more modest project of playing the political game itself. This, I think, is a conclusion quite beyond what the above considerations require; and I am not entirely sure it is possible for us to make out what it would demand. I am not, in the end, even sure that such a position is coherent. For us to give reasons, in the political realm, is for us to make prescriptive claims against others; it is to make claims we think others ought to accept. The fact that no political assertion or theory will gain universal acceptance should incline us toward modesty; but to stop developing such assertions and theories seems to incline us only toward silence. To play the game of deliberative politics, that is, seems to invoke the very prescriptive stance Tully wishes to avoid. It involves giving reasons to others, often about what sort of political institutions and norms those others ought to endorse. The process of deliberative politics thus seems inevitably to involve invoking precisely those postures Tully insists the theorist ought to avoid. We cannot avoid making prescriptive claims, I think, if our claims are to have any content. In the process of justifying our claims to others, moreover, we cannot avoid the process of giving reasons, which ultimately may require appeal to rather abstract notions of rationality. It is, therefore, rather hard to determine what it would mean for philosophers to give up their stance as practitioners of a prescriptive enterprise founded on abstract reason. To give up that stance, it seems to me, may be to give up on the project of democratic deliberation itself.

I think it possible, finally, that Tully himself is prey to this difficulty. He articulates a political norm of listening to the other side —*audi alteram partem*—as perhaps the only norm with universal applicability to the democratic process. To admit this, however, seems to once again introduce the relevance of abstract and prescriptive reason. This norm, after all, is neither universally accepted, nor self-interpreting. In that it is controversial—certainly, the hateful political speakers discussed above would repudiate it— it maintains its character as prescriptive. Although not universally accepted, Tully puts it forward as a principle all agents ought to accept. If a dissenting agent were to ask why he should endorse such a principle, any attempt to answer him would seem to involve reliance upon rather abstract notions of rationality; we might point out how this norm is presupposed by his own stated beliefs, so that he is trapped in inconsistency were he to deny the norm's applicability. All of this, however, brings back with it the usefulness of abstract and prescriptive reason. To figure out what this norm actually demands, moreover, seems to be a project for which this sort of reason is ideally suited. What, after all, does it *mean* to listen to the other side? How much of a hearing counts as enough? Do we have to listen to those who refuse to listen to us? All of this, I suggest, demands a return to the abstract and prescriptive standpoint Tully repudiates. It is, indeed, a standpoint that cannot be avoided once we begin the process of political discourse. To make any claim at all, in the end, is to make a prescriptive statement capable of philosophical defense and elucidation. Abstract and prescriptive philosophy, therefore, will always have some place to play within democratic practice; political philosophers have no need to alter their self-conceptions in the manner suggested by Tully.

CONCLUSION

There is much to admire in Tully's presentation of an agonistic conception of liberalism. There is also, I think, much that is deeply problematic. All I hope to have shown in the present paper is that a foundationalist liberalism represents a live alternative to such an agonistic vision of democratic practice. A liberalism that regards certain norms as constitutive of democratic practice, and so excluded from democratic revision, represents a coherent and attractive vision of political self-rule. In this very exclusion, moreover, a foundationalist conception may protect against problems of political marginalization an agonistic conception cannot avoid. The project of working out a foundationalist liberalism will never be complete; we will never arrive at any final theory of how we ought to respect moral equality in the design of political institutions. The project, however, should not be abandoned. It is, in contrast, an ongoing task all liberal political agents—political practitioners and political theorists alike—should be proud to accept. Liberal foundationalists, in sum, have no reason to be ashamed of what they do—nor of how they understand their role in the shared project of political self-rule.

NOTES

1. See Judith Shklar, "The Liberalism of Fear," in *Liberalism and the Moral Life*, ed. Nancy L. Rosenblum (Cambridge, MA: Harvard University Press, 1989), 21–37.

2. John Rawls, *Political Liberalism* (New York: Columbia University Press, 1989).

3. I would, however, disagree with his understanding that the set of global norms currently in place constitutes a constitutional order. On my analysis, there is a morally relevant difference between a domestic constitutional order sustaining a coercive legal system, and the set of global institutions affecting trade and international relations. The latter are not immune from criticism, but they are relevantly different from the former in a way demanding special moral attention. See my "Distributive Justice, State Coercion, and Autonomy," *Philosophy and Public Affairs* 30(3)(2002): 257–296.

4. In this, I follow Amartya Sen, who, following Ronald Dworkin, articulates a general norm of equal concern and respect as foundational for all plausible visions of liberal political life. See Amartya Sen, *Inequality Re-Examined* (New York: Russell Sage, 1992).

5. All this information is available at the website of Phelps's Westboro Baptist Church, www.godhatesfags.com.

6. See Marisa Taylor, "Racist Groups Are Mobilizing in Wake of Federal Indictment," *San Diego Union Tribune,* Nov. 22, 2000, B1.

7. I would also note, in connection with the project of liberal constitutionalism, that the foundational norm of equal treatment might help justify and explain the supposedly equiprimordial principles of constitutionalism and democracy. On my understanding, both of these principles are ultimately compelling because of their relation with the liberal project of treating people as free and equal; as such, they can each be explained, and conflicts between them can be adjudicated, with reference to the foundational norm of equality. If this is so, then these principles are both necessary—in that no just liberal order could omit reference to them—but they are not "equiprimordial" in the sense demanded by Tully.

10

DEMOCRACY AND LEGITIMACY: A RESPONSE TO JAMES TULLY'S "EXCLUSION AND ASSIMILATION"

LEIF WENAR

First, a few words first about where I disagree with Professor Tully about the task of liberal political philosophy, and then a few more words about the democratic citizen as the man of Constant's sorrows. I'll put three questions on the table with these remarks.

Liberal political philosophers should do exactly what Tully thinks they should not do. Liberal political philosophers should propose determinate principles of justice for the basic institutions of society—principles that can ground a lasting consensus about how citizens should order their common affairs. That is, liberal philosophers should put forward constitutional principles designed to be "a permanent foundation or framework that underlies democratic debate and legislation."[1] I am certain that this is what, for example, Rawls believes, but for the sake of brevity I will make the point in my own voice.[2]

Tully thinks that doing philosophy in this way is insufficiently democratic. He thinks that the philosopher I describe assumes that liberal institutions will not be open to "democratic challenge, deliberation and amendment," and that the rules of our polity can be anything but continually "negotiated" and "conciliated."[3] The philosopher who proposes determinate and permanent principles of justice, Tully says, is trying to insulate our laws from disputation

—attempting to get people to deliberate "within the rules" instead of "over the rules."[4] Such a philosopher is hoping, he says, to impose practices of governance "from outside" of the procedures of democratic self-rule.[5] "The orientation of practical philosophy," Tully claims, "should not be to reaching final agreements on universal principles or procedures, but to ensuring that constitutional democracies are always open to the democratic freedom of calling into question and presenting reasons for the renegotiation of the prevailing rules of law, principles of justice and practices of deliberation."[6]

As a first response to this objection, let me indicate three places where democracy enters into liberal political philosophy as I understand it. First, all liberal principles of justice will require that each citizen be secured an equal right to democratic participation. Second, many issues within even the most just society will not be matters of basic justice, and so may be settled by proper democratic procedures. Third, liberal theorists will propose their principles of justice to their fellow citizens within a democratic society, in the hope that their fellow citizens will enact whatever reforms of the current order these principles require. This third point shows that the liberal philosopher does not aim to impose practices of governance from outside the procedures of democratic self-rule. Liberal philosophers have neither the desire nor the authority to foist their theories on the polity.

Professor Tully will not be satisfied with this response. He will object that in my view of liberal politics, democratic actors must work within a structure of constitutional rights and may not revise this structure of rights. This description of my view is correct: I believe that within a just society, democratic action can only legitimate policies within the framework of the basic rights that are established by the principles of justice. Tully will object that this view privileges the liberties of the moderns over the liberties of the ancients. He will object that my liberal philosopher is trying to get people to deliberate within the rules instead of over the rules, and so in this way is imposing practices of governance from outside.

The liberal philosopher should plead guilty, but only because there are in fact many rules in a liberal society that should never be open to democratic challenge and amendment. Here are three perfectly obvious rules: there should be no chattel slavery, there should be no persecution of religious nonconformity, and women should have the vote. It is a great achievement of our civilization that these rules have been insulated from democratic disputation, and we should resist any attempt at democratic negotiation or conciliation that attempts to change these rules. Our societies are more, not less, legitimate because these rules are permanently off the agenda of democratic deliberation, and we must try to keep them off that agenda. Our resolution of these issues is "definitive," and concerning them there is no "possibility of reasonable disagreement."[7] The task of the liberal political theorist is to propose principles that account for these fixed points of liberal legitimacy and that clarify our understanding of liberal justice on issues about which we are uncertain.

So, my first question for Professor Tully is this: Do you think our current practices of governance would become more and not less legitimate if everything really were on the democratic agenda? For example, would our current practices of governance become more legitimate if serious and vigorous debates began tomorrow over whether to enslave racial minorities, whether to persecute non-Christians, and whether to deny the vote to women?

Turning now to democratic citizens. Tully identifies three specific threats to his ideal of democratic legitimation: globalization, the power of corporations, and the decline of political participation. Leaving globalization aside, I would like to suggest that—in the American context, at least—if corporate power and declining political participation are worrying, then this has little to do with Tully's principle of democracy.

Tully's principle of democracy does not require that institutions must be formally democratic in order to be legitimate. Tully says that practices of governance like families, markets, and corporations, need not be democratic to be legitimate—so long as the effects of these institutions "can be made good" to the people who are subject to them.[8] Yet my strong sense is that the threats Tully identifies can indeed be "made good" to Americans. If this is correct, then these threats would actually be legitimated by Tully's own democratic principle.

The vast majority of Americans, I believe, broadly accept the role and the effects of corporate power in their lives. More pithily: Americans love corporations. Or, to put this as a question: What would the world look like if Americans loved corporations? If Americans loved corporations then we might expect Americans to identify themselves by wearing corporate names on their chests even more frequently than they identify themselves by wearing crosses or crucifixes. If Americans loved corporations, we should expect the political opposition to corporate power to be insignificant and disorganized, noteworthy more because it breaks things and makes a mess than because it pricks the conscience of the wider society. If Americans loved corporations we would expect Americans not to avoid becoming parts of corporations but to be trying desperately hard to find jobs within them. We would expect Americans to be proud of their possessions, such as cars, clothes, and computers because of the corporation that produced them, and even to be more likely to buy their books, newspapers, and coffee from corporations the larger these corporations are. Indeed, if Americans loved corporations we might even expect that the single most popular standard design to have permanently tattooed on one's body would be a corporate logo.[9]

Now I am not a huge fan of corporations. But what is wrong with corporate power is not that the people don't accept it—because the overwhelming majority do. What is wrong with corporate power is that it leads to injustice, which injustice is specifiable independently of any procedures of democratic validation. Corporate power can be made good to the American people. That is part of the problem.

This point applies not only to corporations but also to Tully's other threat: declining political participation. If there is one thing that the data from the past fifty years tell us it is that Americans want to participate less, not more, in the political process. Consider three facts about the past fifty years. We know that people have voted less and engaged in civic action less during a period when their access to information and economic resources have increased greatly.[10] Moreover, we know that people's understanding of politics has at best held steady during the past fifty years, a period that saw by far the greatest expansion of secondary and higher education in American history.[11] Finally, we know that the people have been capable of participating more in politics when they have wanted to, since they have done so during those exceptional times when they have perceived injustices that needed righting (such as during the civil rights movement). Yet in the main there has not been much Habermasian "unrest" for greater democratic self-determination, there has been little "irruption of public autonomy in 'interstitial locations,'" nor have "democratic freedom fighters found ways to . . . reignite the embers" of popular self-rule.[12] A reasonable inference from these facts is that Americans have had the opportunity to participate more in politics during the past fifty years, and simply have wanted to participate less.

To summarize: Tully implores us to listen to our fellow citizens, yet the one voice that Tully does not hear is the deafening voice of the American majority, which wants more corporations and less participation. Perhaps it isn't surprising that the voice of the majority doesn't register: as they say, whoever first discovered water, it wasn't a fish. Yet this does lead to a second question for Professor Tully: if institutions are legitimate so long as their effects "can be made good" to the people subject to them, why within America aren't high corporate power and low political participation legitimate?

I suspect that Tully's response would be that democratic citizens are presently not in sufficiently good conditions for their acceptance of the current order to legitimate it. Americans are so weighted down in their heavy layers of consumerism and apathy that their dozy acquiescence to the current regime is irrelevant to the regime's legitimacy. If only we could transform the political environment, the vigorous democratic Olympian within each of us would burst out to create a new kind of politics where the procedure of participation would truly legitimate its own results.

Now, if Tully does say that the conditions of political life must be transformed before the will of the people legitimates social institutions, I think that we are entitled to ask more about the substance of these conditions. What would our politics have to be like for democracy to be legitimating? Tully suggests at one point that NAFTA is illegitimate because it did not pass through a process of democratic deliberation.[13] Did it not? Anyone who was in America during the 1992 election campaign will recall that the NAFTA treaty was subject to extensive scrutiny in presidential debates, newspaper editorials, and conversations around the dinner table. If *that* process of democratic deliberation didn't legitimate NAFTA, then we are entitled to ask how radically Tully would have us transform our politics so that they would meet his minimal criteria for democratic legitimacy.

Recall that Tully's original complaint about the principled liberal philosopher was that this philosopher was trying to impose rules "from the outside." My third and final question is this: if Professor Tully is now proposing that we must completely transform our political order so that it can meet his minimal standard of democratic legitimacy, is he now not the one trying to impose rules from the outside?

NOTES

1. James Tully, "Exclusion and Assimilation: Two Forms of Domination in Relation to Freedom," this volume, pp. 195–196.

2. I offer a general interpretation of Rawls's work, centered on the idea of legitimacy, in "The Legitimacy of Peoples," *Global Politics and Transnational Justice,* ed. Pablo de Greiff and Ciaran Cronin (Cambridge, MA: MIT Press, 2002): 53–76, and a longer version of the same in "The Unity of Rawls's Work" (forthcoming).

3. Tully, "Exclusion and Assimilation," 196.

4. Ibid., 195.

5. Ibid., 207.

6. Ibid., 208.

7. Ibid., 196.

8. Ibid., 198.

9. Hint: the corporation produces motorcycles.

10. As Tully puts it on p. 201, "Citizen participation decreases and democratic apathy and malaise increase."

11. See, for example, Michael X. Delli Carpini and Scott Keeter, *What Americans Know about Politics and Why It Matters* (New Haven: Yale University Press, 1996).

12. Ibid., pp. 205, 210, and 218.

13. Ibid., p. 199.

11

A REPLY TO MICHAEL BLAKE
AND LEIF WENAR

JAMES TULLY

I would like to thank Michael Blake and Leif Wenar for their thoughtful comments. Each reasserts a type of "liberal foundationalism" in response to my chapter on the recent transformation of liberalism and its implications. In reply I will sketch how their responses are seen from the perspective of this transformed liberalism.

In my chapter I argue that Habermas and Rawls tried to bring a type of liberalism, founded on the priority of the rule of law and certain nonnegotiable principles of justice, into an internal relation of equality with its major competitor over the last two centuries—social democracy—founded on the priority of popular sovereignty and the will of the people. They did this by reconstructing liberalism on the basis of two orienting and contestable equiprimordial principles of legitimacy: constitutionalism or the rule of law (the liberty of the moderns) and democracy or popular sovereignty (the liberty of the ancients).

This transformation implies first that any rule (law, norm, right, principle) would always be open in principle to the challenge and negotiation of the agents (individuals and groups) who are subject to it through the exchange of public reasons. This is the defining freedom of the democratic tradition. Conversely, this democratic freedom could not be seen as the exercise of majority-will democracy over the rule of laws, for that would be to place the principle of democracy (interpreted as the will of the majority) prior to the principle of constitutionalism. Rather, the exercise of freedom with respect to a contested rule would itself have to be exercised through the latest rules of law protecting individual and minority rights, due process, the procedures of public reason, civic disobedience, the liberal right to revolt, and so on (the liberty of the moderns), even though these rules in turn could be challenged on another occasion, in order to respect the equiprimordiality of the two basic principles.

Blake thus appears to misunderstand the reciprocal interrelation of the two primary principles when he writes several times that this type of liberal democracy would entail that "all aspects of liberal politics must be open to collective political control." As I explain in Section 1, this interpretation would be to place the principle of democracy prior to constitutionalism and thus upset the equiprimordiality of the two principles.

The second implication is that liberalism can be said to be reformulated on a dialogical foundation: that is, on the ideal of the exchange of public reasons *within* and *over* the rules to which citizens are subject. The work on deliberative and agonistic democracy that I refer to is a development of this aspect of the new democratic liberalism. The consequence, which Blake and Wenar challenge, is that no rule is treated as foundational and permanently exempt from challenge, for the political association is founded on the ongoing interaction between the prevailing rules and the discursive practices of testing their acceptability through the exchange of public reasons.

The third implication is that the exchange of reasons in ideal and nonideal circumstances will not, except in exceptional circumstances, lead to an uncoerced and permanent consensus on a proposed rule, but to reasonable disagreement. There will be good but nondecisive arguments on more than one side. As a result, again challenged by Blake and Wenar, each rule (law, set of rights, principle) through which we are governed should be open in principle to reason-based dissent (review and possible renegotiation) *en passant,* thereby reinforcing the equiprimordiality of the two principles of legitimacy.

Blake objects that "agonistic democrats," in their "reluctance to exclude any perspective," leave oppressed minorities open to and silenced by the hatred of powerful racist and sexist groups. While this may be a correct interpretation of some agonistic democrats, it is not my argument. To enter into the contestation of a rule is to be able to present public reasons for or against it and to abide by the reciprocity conditions intrinsic to dialogue. While the current theories and civil procedures of public reason and reciprocity must be open to reasonable challenge and amendment in the course of the struggle, this reflexive, bootstrapping and nonfoundational feature of dialogue is nevertheless rule governed and thus not equivalent to "anything goes." As in Blake's type of liberalism, an argument can be shown to be wrong because it violates a foundational norm, but more convincingly because the foundational norm itself can be challenged and tested. And, as I argued in Section 4, the reciprocal conditions of dialogue, rather than his principle of liberal equality, rule out the asymmetrical kind of hate speech he mentions.

It seems to me that liberal philosophers have responded in two complementary ways to this dialogical reformulation of liberalism and democracy. The first is to focus primarily on the conditions for the exchange of public reasons among free and equal citizens. This is the path taken by Rawls and Habermas and is explored further and more radically by the other authors I discuss. As my chapter is primarily designed to show, it leads to a new way of analyzing and criticizing forms of domination: that is, forms of exclusion *from* the free exchange of public reason and the unjust forms of assimilation *within* closed practices of public reason. This stream of liberalism, as Blake notes, is unavoidably committed to a principle of reciprocity intrinsic to dialogue (such as *audi alteram partem*), but as my chapter shows and he emphasizes, this principle, like others, is subject to continual contestation and elucidation in both theory and practice.

The second path of liberalism focuses primarily on the articulation of foundational liberal principles of justice and the best reasons that can be presented for them in public fora. This is the route taken by Blake and Wenar, and also by Rawls when he presented his own proposal for a political conception of justice as one conception among several. However, as both respondents realize, this type of liberal foundationalism is not the same as it was before the dialogical turn in two significant respects.

First, the reasons for the foundational principles now will be seen as reasons presented to fellow citizens who disagree and have reasons for their disagreements and counterproposals. Liberal theorists, like everyone else, will have not only a right to speak but also a duty to listen to the nonliberals and to respond to their arguments, or it will not be an exchange or dialogue. Their principles will not legislate the form or content of the dialogue prior to the dialogue (by, say, some monological test of universality). They will be on par with the others *in this respect,* putting their favored principles to the test of public reasons. Blake and Wenar appear to agree with this crucial change in the relation of philosophers to public affairs, as they both speak of "putting forward" their foundational principles to fellow citizens as equals. Blake is correct to add, as I did not, that political philosophers will continue to have a distinct contribution to make in other respects: of clarification, elucidation, and abstract reasoning.

Second, liberals will be no different from their social-democratic, conservative, Muslim, feminist, multicultural, postcolonial, ecological, and socialist adversaries engaged in the struggle over the contested rule. They will all put forward their foundational principles and claims of justice with the aim of getting their fellow citizens to accept them as foundational for the political association. Here I agree with Blake and Wenar. For example, my arguments against unjust forms of exclusion and assimilation are presented in this manner, against their many defenders in the celebratory, neoliberal response to the trends of globalization (whether they comprise "the vast majority of Americans," as Wenar claims, is another question). However, I think there are two ways this feature of political struggle and argument can be interpreted.

The first way is to argue as if uncoerced and permanent consensus either can be reached or has already been reached on foundational rules that are thereby exempt from further argumentation, as Wenar puts it. Here consensus functions as a regulative ideal of dialogue. If reasonable disagreement is a feature of practical reason, then this is an inappropriate regulative ideal. Moreover, like the opposite extreme of "anything goes," it is dangerous in practice. The regulative ideal of consensus can function as an instrument of domination, to silence or assimilate those who dissent from the dominant position on the ground that they must be unreasonable (as I argue in Section 4). If the possibility of consensus is to be kept open, the better method is to treat it as a critical ideal: that is, a rule of argumentation that is open to challenge. Note also that if finality were attainable, a liberalism founded on public reasons would be a mere passing means to a different, end-state kind of liberalism—the kingdom of ends (this is a problem for Habermas).

The second and preferable mode of argumentation is the pluralist one of expecting reasonable disagreement over fundamental principles and their sense, reference, and application. On this Millian or fallibist attitude, one enters into the dialogue with the expectation that the limitations of one's free-standing principle will be tested and improved by the interaction with others who disagree and have different comprehensive doctrines, conceptions of public reason, principles, and interpretations of the same principles. At best, the rules agreed upon will be reasonable accommodations of the aspects of each side that survive the test of dialogue as far as possible here and now. Here reasonable disagreement functions as a critical ideal of public argument (always open to challenge by the consensualists). It gives a sufficient degree of authority to the rules for liberals while leaving them open to review and improvement in the future, thus giving them authority for democrats.

For example, Wenar asks if a government would be more legitimate if there were serious and vigorous debate over slavery, the persecution of non-Christians, and the denial of the vote to women. Yet, these were once justified by foundational principles that earlier liberals held in an unquestioned way. They were changed only because citizens and noncitizens challenged them by exercising their democratic freedom at great cost. What analogous injustices are hidden in the foundational liberal principles today that Wenar would exempt from debate? Or are we to presume that our generation is somehow more far-seeing than Locke, Kant, Jefferson, Wollstonecraft, and Mill? Like Mill, I can see many benefits in rehearsing the history and reasons for and against the injustices of these three practices. Moreover, limiting public discussion of the evaluative aspect of these practices (their injustice), on the ground that these questions have been settled once and for all, tends to limit at the same time a vigorous public discussion of their contestable sense and reference. In my chapter I mention a new form of global slavery that is rarely discussed in these terms partly because slavery tends to be equated with one particular historical type of slavery. The same applies to a formerly vigorous debate over "wage slavery" under capitalism, which is not taken seriously today partly because slavery is said to be over. Racial profiling, cultural and religious discrimination, and the mistreatment of indigenous peoples today tend in a similar fashion to be disconnected from the earlier persecution of non-Christians, and the current unjust assimilation of enfranchised women to a male norm is disconnected from their earlier exclusion from the vote. I am sure that Wenar is opposed to these consequences that attend the restriction of public discussion of past injustices; but unless he can give an overriding public reason for the restriction, the default position should be that the disputation over their history and relationship to current practices should be public.

Another example is Blake's attractive vision of liberal foundationalism, which shares several features with dialogical liberalism. The main difference is that it is oriented toward placing some norms "beyond the pale of political discussion" because they are "concerned with the preservation of self-rule." His candidate for such a norm is the "moral equality of persons." By placing this norm beyond political discussion, he explicitly violates the democratic principle that those subject to the norm should have a say over it (what he calls the second notion of self-rule). His justification is that it is a constitutive norm of democratic practice that protects against exclusion and discrimination. There will be endless debate over how to "respect moral equality in the design of political institutions," but there will be no debate over the principle itself. While this neo-Kantian liberal foundationalism is attractive, I think (for the reason that follows) it would be a more defensible exemplar of the second path of liberalism if the status of this principle were reformulated in line with what I call the second mode of argumentation, where the free exchange or reasons and reasonable disagreement function as the critical ideal.

The Kantian principle of the moral equality of persons (as I argue in Section 4) has been used to legitimate some of the worst forms of exclusion (of "nonpersons": women, indigenous peoples, nonwhites, foreigners) and assimilation (of culturally different others to an allegedly difference-blind standard of equality). For example, feminists, multiculturalists, postcolonial theorists, and critical race theorists have exposed and criticized its nonuniversality. Social democrats have criticized its priority relative to their principle of substantive equality, and minorities have criticized its priority relative to the equality of minorities and peoples. And it has been criticized in turn by others who advance different foundational principles, such as ecologists, neo-Hegelians, and cultural pluralists. Kantians have listened to these arguments and reformulated the norm of the equality of persons in response. They have not reached a formulation that all would accept but they have made considerable advances. Therefore, if I am not mistaken, the rich tradition of which Professor Blake is a present heir has advanced precisely because the principle he would exempt from the free exchange of reasons and reasonable disagreement has been subject to them.

I am sure this brief reply is far from adequate but I hope it has helped to clarify the agreements and disagreements among us. I look forward to continuing the dialogue.

PART III

BOUNDARIES DRAWN BY SHAME

12

INSCRIBING THE FACE: SHAME, STIGMA, AND PUNISHMENT

MARTHA NUSSBAUM

If someone has been condemned to a gladiatorial school or to the mines for the crimes he has been caught committing, let him not be marked on his face, since the penalty of his condemnation can be expressed both on his hands and on his calves, and so that his face, which has been fashioned in the likeness of the divine beauty, may not be disgraced.

—Edict of the Emperor Constantine, A.D. 316

Before her disfigurement [amputation of the distal half of her nose] Mrs. Dover, who lived with one of her two married daughters, had been an independent, warm and friendly woman who enjoyed traveling, shopping, and visiting her many relatives. The disfigurement of her face, however, resulted in a definite alteration in her way of living. The first two or three years she seldom left her daughter's home, preferring to remain in her room or to sit in the backyard.

—Cited in Erving Goffman, *Stigma*

Thus, by being born we have made the step from an absolutely self-sufficient narcissism to the perception of a changing external world and the beginnings of the discovery of objects. And with this is associated the fact that we cannot endure the new state of things for long, that we periodically revert from it, in our sleep, to our former condition of absence of stimulation and avoidance of objects.

—Sigmund Freud, *Group Psychology and the Analysis of the Ego*

1. THE BLUSHING FACE

Like disgust, shame is a ubiquitous emotion in social life. When I was a child, one of my uncles, fond of advice giving, used to say to all children, "Soar with your strengths and learn to cover your weaknesses." And of course we all do learn to cover our weaknesses as we go through life, whether by compensating for them with other strengths, or by training to overcome them, or by avoiding situations in which they will inevitably manifest themselves. Most of us, most of the time, try to appear "normal," a notion whose strangeness I shall later discuss, but whose allure is undeniably strong in all modern democratic societies. Sometimes, however, our "abnormal" weaknesses are uncovered anyway, and then we blush, we cover ourselves, we turn away our eyes. Shame is the painful emotion that responds to that uncovering. It brands the face with its unmistakable signs.

Because we all have weaknesses that, if known, would mark us off as in some ways "abnormal," shame is a permanent possibility in our lives, our daily companion. As Erving Goffman memorably wrote in his classic book *Stigma*:

> [I]n an important sense there is only one complete unblushing male in America: a young, married, white, urban, northern, heterosexual Protestant father of college education, fully employed, of good complexion, weight and height, and a recent record in sports.[1]

But of course few are ever like that, and nobody is like that for long. Shame, therefore, dogs our footsteps. As Goffman says, "The issue becomes not whether a person has experience with a stigma of his own, because he has, but rather how many varieties he has had his own experience with. . . . The stigmatized and the normal are part of each other."[2]

I shall argue, indeed, that shame is on the scene already even before we are aware of the "normal" perspective of the particular social value system within which we dwell. For it is present for all of us in the infantile demand for omnipotence, for fullness and comfort—accompanied, as it increasingly is as the infant matures, by the awareness of finitude, partiality, and frequent helplessness. Shame therefore cuts beneath any specific social orientation to norms, and serves as a highly volatile way in which human beings negotiate the tensions inherent in their humanness—in, that is, their awareness of themselves as beings both finite and marked with exorbitant demands and expectations.

Some people, however, are more marked out for shame than others. Indeed, with shame as with disgust, societies ubiquitously select certain groups and individuals for shaming, marking them off as "abnormal" and demanding that they blush at what and who they are. People who look different from others—people with visible diseases or so-called deformities, the mentally and physically handicapped—wear their shame on their faces, so to speak: social behavior tells them every day that they ought to blush to show themselves in the company of the "normal." When there is no visible brand, societies have been quick to inflict one, whether by tattooing and branding or by other visible signs of social ostracism and disapproval. The branding of criminals—frequently, as Constantine's edict observes, applied to the face—is a practice that keeps reappearing in one or another form, and thus shame has been a pervasive part of legal practices throughout European history.

Today we find two diametrically opposed views about the role shame should play in the law. On one view, the shaming of those who are different is a pernicious aspect of social custom that should not be sanctified by building it into our legal practices. According to this view, law should protect the equal dignity of all citizens, both by devising ways in which those already stigmatized as different can enjoy lives of greater dignity and by refusing to make law a partner to the social infliction of shame. This view has deep roots in the history of European law, as my passage from Justinian records: even the Romans, who meted out many extreme punishments, were loath to brand the part of the human body in which human dignity is thought primarily to reside. So too today, some prominent legal thinkers hold that, while punishments must be meted out for reasons including both the deterrent and the retributive, a concern with the dignity of the offender should always be solidly built into the system of punishment, and, with it, the idea of eventual reintegration of the offender into society.

On the second view, what is wrong with modern societies is that they don't make a large enough place for shame. We are adrift without a moral compass, in large part because we have lost our sense of shame. For Christopher Lasch, for example, America is in trouble precisely to the extent that we have lost "the shared social and legal boundaries that shame once policed."[3]

The pedigree of this view about shame is conservative, and it does end up defending entrenched social norms as good sources of both behavior and law. But the apparently conservative position has also been endorsed by some thinkers on the left (as perhaps Lasch once was), apparently with an interest in mobilizing opposition to callous behavior on the part of the dominant classes. Dan Kahan of Yale Law School has led the campaign, arguing that shame penalties ought to be favored over other alternatives to imprisonment, such as fines and community service.[4] In a wide range of legal areas, ranging from sex offenses to drunken driving to public urination, Kahan favors bringing back the brand on the face, so to speak: offenders should be forced to wear signs on their property, or car, or to perform some clearly humiliating ritual before the public gaze. Kahan likes shaming because of its expressive power: no other mode of punishment as vividly and surely expresses society's disapproval of the offender. He thinks of the view as a progressive view, and is able to sell it that way to some extent, in part because he dwells on examples in which the humiliated person is a powerful person. (He particularly likes a punishment ordered by the city of Hoboken, New Jersey, in which businessmen who urinate in public have to scrub the street clean with a toothbrush.)

I will be supporting the first position and criticizing the second. But I think that we gain a new understanding of our reasons for so doing if we investigate the natural history of shame and shaming, and the deeper underlying reasons why human societies again and again seek to brand the faces of some of their members with what Erving Goffman perceptively calls a "spoiled identity." Only then will we be in a position to understand what forms of shame might be pernicious in human life and what forms might actually be connected with valuable forms of aspiration. For I shall argue that the normative situations of shame are highly complicated. Some forms of shame indeed have a positive ethical value; thus, if we do criticize many roles shame plays in the law, as I think we should, it must be because those roles make appeal to a primitive or bad form of shame, or are at risk of doing so.

I shall, then, spend a good deal of space developing an account of shame and its roots in infancy that is closely linked to object-relations psychoanalysis, and in particular to the work of Donald Winnicott.[5] I shall then use that account of shame and pathological narcissism to analyze social shaming and its pathologies, using examples from ancient Rome and modern Europe. Finally, I shall apply my general model to two particular issues that face us as we think about the role of shame in the law: legal treatment of the mentally disabled, and the use of shame penalties for criminal offenders. As I confront these issues, I will argue that modern liberal societies can make an adequate response to the phenomena of shame only if they shift away from a very common intuitive idea of the normal citizen that has been bequeathed to us by the social contract tradition so influential in the history of European thought: the image of the citizen as a productive worker, able to pay for the benefits he receives by the contributions he makes.

2. Primitive Shame, Narcissism, and the Golden Age

Human beings are born into a world they have not made and do not control. After a time in the womb, during which needs were automatically met, they enter the world, thus making, as Freud put it in one of my epigraphs, "the step from an absolutely self-sufficient narcissism to the perception of a changing external world and the beginnings of the discovery of objects." Human infants arrive in the world in a condition of needy helplessness more or less unparalleled in any other animal species. What they encounter is both alarming and delightful. In a passage that lies at the origins of European thought about infancy, the Roman poet Lucretius writes that the infant, helpless and weeping from the disturbance of birth,

> like a sailor cast forth from the fierce waves, lies naked on the ground, without speech, in need of every sort of life-sustaining help, when first nature casts it forth with birth contractions from its mother's womb into the shores of light. And it fills the whole place with mournful weeping, as is right for someone to whom such troubles remain in life.[6]

A "gentle nurse" now calms the child with calm talk and caresses, as well as nourishment. The poet bleakly remarks that the rougher, better-equipped wild animals have no need of such soothing.[7] The prolonged helplessness of the human infant marks its history; and the early drama of its infancy is the drama of helplessness before a world of objects—a world that contains both threatening things and the good things, the things it wants and needs. The infant's central perception of itself, Lucretius suggests profoundly, is as an entity very weak and very powerless toward things of the greatest importance. Freud, noting the same facts, comments that "we cannot endure the new state of things for long, [so] that we periodically revert from it, in our sleep, to our former condition of absence of stimulation and avoidance of objects."

But the infant is not altogether helpless. For from the first there are agencies in the environment that minister to its needs, supplying what it cannot supply for itself. These agencies therefore take on an intense importance in the infant's inchoate and as yet undemarcated awareness of the world. Its relationship to them focuses, from the first, on its passionate wish to secure what the world of nature does not supply by itself—comfort, nourishment, protection.

Lucretius presents a picture, not a theoretical account. But we may extrapolate an account from it. Unlike some psychoanalytic accounts, but like those developed in the object-relations tradition, the Lucretian picture makes the drama of infancy focus on what the ancient world called "external goods"—uncontrolled external objects of high importance. From the first the infant feels a need for the removal of painful or invasive stimuli, and for the restoration of a blissful or undisturbed condition. This need gives a central importance in the infant's "object world" to that or those object(s) who are perceived as the agents of this restoration of the world. Whether it is mother, father, nurse, or some other caretaker or caretakers who plays or play the primary role here, this restorative agency will at first be experienced by the infant not so much as a distinct object, but as a process of transformation through which the infant's own state of being is altered. For this reason analyst Christopher Bollas speaks of the caretaker as a "transformational object," and perceptively remarks that much of a human being's subsequent history bears the imprint of early longing for this object, in the form of a desire for a "second coming" of that shift toward bliss, and for an object that can be its vehicle.[8] Still in a state of utter helplessness, the infant can do little to control the arrival of the transformational process, and its sudden arrivals and disappearances mark the infant's world as a chancy and unpredictable one, in which the best things arrive as if by lightning, in sudden penetrations of light and joy.

Consider a myth that plays a central role in ancient accounts of emotion. It is, I think, best seen as an imaginative attempt to recreate this world of infancy. This is the well-known story of the Golden Age—an age in which people do not have to do anything for themselves, to labor, to act, to move here and there. For the earth itself brings forth nourishment exactly where they are. Rivers of milk and honey spring up out of the ground; the mild climate gives no need for shelter. The people of this age, Hesiod remarks, lack prudential rationality—presumably because they have no need of thought. They live in a state of blissful totality. Stoics who repeat the story add that in this age "crime is far off":[9] there is no aggression, because everything is complete. What this myth describes is the omnipotence of the infant, its sense that the world revolves around its needs and is fully arranged to meet its needs.

But of course, as our Lucretian image lets us see, the infant's experiential world is from the very start unlike the world of the Golden Age. Perhaps, as Freud observes in our epigraph, rudimentary prebirth experiences give the infant a true Golden Age: hooked up securely to the sources of nourishment and comfort, the infant is indeed in a state of blissful totality. But birth disrupts all that, as Freud says, bringing the infant into a world of objects, in which it must depend on those external things and persons for its survival. Thus, although at times the infant's world is a Golden Age world, these times alternate with times when the world is hungry, distressed, and in discomfort.[10] The earth does not give everything automatically, and the infant's world of sudden transformations is felt from the start as chancy, porous, full of uncertainty and danger.

A dependent being who sees itself as such will have both love and anger toward the agencies on which it depends. Anger understood this way is not an innate instinct of destruction: it is a reaction to one's life situation. As Fairbairn, Bowlby, and other object relations theorists argue, we have no need to introduce a destructive instinct to explain infant behavior, and much reason, in the infant's primary clinging and comfort-seeking behavior, to refuse to introduce it. On the other hand, the process of development entails many moments of discomfort and frustration. Indeed, some frustration of the infant's wants by the caretaker's separate comings and goings is essential to development—for if everything were always simply given in advance of discomfort, the child would never try out its own projects of control.[11]

On the other hand, the infant can hardly be in a position to comprehend this grand design. Its posture is one of infantile omnipotence—well captured in Freud's famous phrase "his majesty the baby"—in which the entire world revolves around its wants. But, as we have insisted, our world is not and never was that world. The child's evolving recognition that the caretaker sometimes fails to bring it what it wants gives rise to an anger that is closely linked to its emerging love. Indeed, the very recognition that both good things and their absence have an external source guarantees the presence of both of these emotions, and guarantees their close interrelationship.

Where in this history should we locate shame? I can approach this topic by introducing yet one more classical myth, the story of the origins of love told by Aristophanes in Plato's *Symposium*, which builds on the classic Golden Age story. Human beings were one whole and round, says Aristophanes. Our spherical shape was the outward image of our totality and our power. We were "awe-inspiring in force and strength," and "had great ambitions."[12] Humans, in consequence, assailed the gods, with the aim of establishing their control over the universe as a whole.[13] Instead of wiping us out completely, Zeus simply, making us "weaker", made us humans—creating for us the condition of need, insecurity, and incompleteness that sets an unbridgeable gulf between us and the gods. He accomplished the change by cutting the spherical beings in two, so that they walked on two legs—and then he turned their faces around so that they would always have to look at the cut part of themselves. Incompleteness is revealed to us, then, by the very form of our bodies, with their pointy jutting limbs, their oddly naked front parts, their genitalia that betray our need for one another. The navel represents the gods' sewing together of what they have cut, and is thus a "memorial of our former suffering (*mnêmeion tou palaiou pathous*)."[14] Even this small detail suggests that the myth is intended to capture the traumatic character of birth into a world of objects: for of course what the navel really reminds us of is our separation from the sources of nutrition and comfort, and the beginning of a needy life.

Thus, Aristophanes portrays shame as a painful emotion grounded in the recognition of our own nonomnipotence, and he suggests that a memory or vestigial sense of our prebirth omnipotence and completeness underlies the painful emotion as it manifests itself in life. We sense that we ought to be whole, and we know that we are not. We sense that we ought to be round, and we see that we are jagged and pointy, and soft and wrinkled. The way in which the speech connects sex and shame seems deeply perceptive: primitive shame is not about sex per se, but about sexual need as one sign of a more general neediness and vulnerability. It seems plausible that Aristophanes is right: a kind of primitive shame at the very fact of being human and incomplete underlies the more specific types of shame that we later feel about handicaps and inadequacies.

We can already see that this primitive shame is closely connected to aggressive wishes toward those people who fail to minister to the infant's needs; thus we can look down the road to see that some difficulties for social interactions may arise if primitive shame is not adequately dealt with. We can now observe that the behavior of caretakers or parents makes a great difference in setting the trajectory that this primitive shame will take. Let me now focus on Winnicott's modification of object-relations theory, which provides an especially valuable account of these matters. Winnicott draws attention to the way in which holding that is "good enough" permits the child to be at one and the same time omnipotent and utterly dependent, both the center of the world and utterly reliant on another. The parents' (or other caregivers') ability to meet the child's omnipotence with suitably responsive and stable care creates a framework within which trust and interdependence may thus gradually grow: the child will gradually relax its omnipotence, its demand to be attended to constantly, once it understands that others can be relied on and it will not be left in a state of utter helplessness. On the other hand, to the extent that a child does

not receive sufficiently stable holding, or receives holding that is
excessively controlling or intrusive, without space for it to relax
into a relationship of trust, it will cling, in later life, to its own omnipotence, demanding perfection in the self and refusing to tolerate imperfection either in object relations or in the inner world.

These ideas receive a fascinating development in the fragment
of a lengthy analysis by Winnicott posthumously published under
the title *Holding and Interpretation*.[15] The patient B, a young male
medical student, suffered from an inability to be spontaneous or
to express any personal thought. In the presence of others, he
could not initiate either conversation or activity, and he was found
extremely boring. The petrified and lifeless persona he presented
to others was an attempt to maintain omnipotent control over his
inner world, by constant vigilance of language and thought.

During the analysis, it emerged that B had suffered from rigidly
anxious and unresponsive parenting in early life.[16] His mother required perfection of herself, and interpreted any neediness on the
part of the infant as a signal that she had not achieved the desired
perfection (which she saw as commanded by a quasi-paternal ide-
alized husband).[17] (Winnicott notes that the mother's tendency to
idealize her husband implied that she did not love him. "[N]ot
being concerned with a real person, she emphasized the quality of
perfection.") As B makes contact with these memories of a holding that was stifling, the patient gradually becomes aware of his
own demand for perfection in everything—as the corollary of his
inability to permit himself to be a needy child. Because his mother
wanted perfection (which he felt as a demand for immobility and
even death), he could not allow himself to be dependent on, or to
trust, anyone. "Imperfect for me means being rejected," he finally
tells Winnicott. And then: "I feel that you are introducing a big
problem. I never became human. I have missed it."[18] Signs of humanness were rejected by his mother, who, because of her own
anxiety, was pleased only by a quiet, perfect baby.

Already in the first months, then, the character of parental care
and "holding" shapes the child's attitude to its own human neediness—either creating the sense that human neediness is all right
and that its helpless body is a source of pleasure and concern, or,
on the other hand, sending the message that perfection is the only
tolerable state and that anything else will be repudiated.

In our terms, what has happened to the early emotions of this unfortunate man? First, the dynamics of both love/gratitude and anger have been thrown off by his inability to trust that he is being held, that his mother wants to hold and care for a dependent needy baby. A feeling of "infinitely falling" lurks in the background. This feeling gives rise to an especially intense anger, and a possessive love that brooks no human reality. The patient so fears his own anger that he frequently makes himself fall asleep. As Winnicott says to him, "There is very great hostility wrapped up in this sleepiness."[19] Second, for this reason the play of a normal human child's imaginative capacity has been arrested: the creativity that grows in a context of trust and holding has never matured, and the patient's way of presenting himself is stilted, rigid, entirely impersonal. In a personal relationship imperfect things might happen, but the patient's way "makes it all impersonal, and there is no excitement or anger or elation, and I do not want to get up and hit you."[20] This rigid impersonality in turn marks his relations to persons: one constant feature in the analysis is the patient's inability to describe his wife or any other person, and his frequent inability to use people's Christian names.[21] Winnicott tells the patient that in a real personal relationship there is an element of "subtle interchange": this was lacking in his early relationship with his mother, and that his sleepiness expresses hopelessness about finding such a relationship anywhere. The patient responds with real excitement: "I must have been aware of the idea of a subtle interchange because I recognize that I have been looking for just something like that, without really knowing it." Winnicott points out that he has just been achieving it: "We are both engaged in this matter of subtle interplay. I think that the experience of subtle interplay is pleasurable to you because you are so vividly aware of hopelessness in this respect." The patient responds: "I would go so far as to say that it is exciting." Love, concludes Winnicott, means many things, "but it has to include this experience of subtle interplay, and we could say that you are experiencing love and loving in this situation."

Finally, we notice that there is another primitive emotion that dominates this patient's entire existence: it is what we can call primitive shame, connected to the very fact of his own humanness. All infant omnipotence is coupled with helplessness. When an infant realizes that it is dependent on others, we can therefore expect a primitive and rudimentary emotion of shame to ensue. For shame involves the realization that one is weak and inadequate in some way in which one expects oneself to be adequate.[22] Its reflex is to hide from the eyes of those who will see one's deficiency, to cover it.

Note, then, that shame is far from requiring diminished self-regard in any very simple way. In a sense, it requires self-regard as its essential backdrop.[23] It is only because one expects oneself to have worth or even perfection in some respect that one will shrink from or cover the evidence of one's nonworth or imperfection. A good development will allow the gradual relaxing of omnipotence and transcendence in favor of trust, as the infant learns not to be ashamed of neediness and to take a positive delight in the playful and creative "subtle interplay" of two imperfect beings. B's mother, instead, understood that all that was not perfect was worthless, and that her child was worthless just by virtue of being a child and wanting to be held and comforted. "Imperfect for me means being rejected." His crying, his demands to be fed, all these signs of his human nakedness were so many signs of worthlessness in her own eyes. The good feeding, as he understood, would be one that blotted him out completely. (Thus he dreams of being smothered by his mother's hair.) "There is only one way of achieving anything," he concludes, "and that is by perfection."[24]

B therefore becomes obsessed with the way in which others will look at him, wanting them to see him as perfect, and knowing that if they see the real him they will not see perfection.[25] His rigidity, his unwillingness to express himself, are attempts to maintain omnipotent control over his inner reality, so that he need not feel the shame of allowing his needy dependent self to manifest itself. Sleep was a defense against anger—but it was also the reflex chosen by his shame lest some human part of himself be revealed. A baby asleep is a good and perfect baby, and this is what his mother had wanted. Shame, then, causes the real vulnerable self to hide, the robotic and inauthentic "false self" to come to the fore. Recognizing that he had also expected perfection in Winnicott, and prompted by the analyst's gentle reminder that this idea is a defense against anxiety, the patient remarkably states, "The alarming thing about equality is that we are then both children and the question is, where is father?"[26] Here he arrives momentarily at a position of trust and playful holding that many children attain in infancy.[27]

This case shows us the extent to which the infant's ambivalent relation to its own lack of omnipotence can be shaped for better or worse by interactions that either exacerbate primitive shame or reduce it. A primitive shame at one's weakness and impotence is probably a basic and universal feature of the emotional life. But a parent who takes delight in having a child who is a child, and who reveals in interacting with the child that it is all right to be human, eases the ambivalence of later object relations; B's mother so exacerbated primitive shame that the real man was obliged to go underground, his place to be taken by a simulacrum, or by prudent sleep. "A feature of excitement," says B, "is irritation that it is not private. . . . I have always had a difficulty that in sexual relationship with a girl there is no privacy, because there are two people. It is undesirable."[28]

Shame, of course, comes in many forms. Any ideal to which one holds oneself has shame as its permanent possibility. What I have termed "primitive shame"—the demand for perfection and the consequent inability to tolerate any lack of control or imperfection—is a specific type of shame, closely connected with narcissism, or infantile omnipotence. What my account suggests, however, is that the primitive type of shame is very likely to be an ongoing danger in the moral and social life—especially for someone whose development, like B's, has been skewed in the direction of pathological narcissism, but to some extent for us all, since we all retain a certain resentment of our finitude, and, perhaps especially with advancing age, want and fully expect to be what we can never be, complete and immortal. Thus, primitive shame and the aggression that accompanies its narcissism may lurk behind a more acceptable form of shame, and may manifest itself in many forms, among them being the shaming of others.

One more point should now be emphasized, before we turn to social and legal issues. The immediate family is one very powerful agent of shame development, whether healthy or unhealthy. But the surrounding society is another. In B's case, the explanation for his hypertrophy of shame lay primarily in his parents' behavior. But societies vary, too, in the type of developmental pattern they hold up as normal. What Winnicott prescribes is a form of life in which parents understand and present themselves as imperfect, and nourish in the child a sense of delight in the sort of "subtle interplay" that two equally incomplete figures can have. This can be done, for example, by showing delight in the child's playfulness and creative efforts.[29] Such a familial or social culture requires giving up a certain type of safety, namely, that to be found in the type of rigid system in which a perfect and merciless father prescribes all duties from on high.

B's is an extreme case. But we should note that many familial and cultural norms contain elements of the demand made by B's mother, the demand to be without need, the demand not to be a child. Such a demand, Nancy Chodorow argues, is implicit in the developmental history of males in many cultures of the world.[30] Taught that dependence on mother is bad and that maturity requires separation and self-sufficiency, males frequently learn to have shame about their own human capacities for receptivity and play, whereas females are more likely to get the message from their parents that maturity involves a continued relation of interdependence, and that emotions expressing need are appropriate. In the light of our discussion of B, we can now see that the males Chodorow describes will frequently, like B though less extremely, both hide their need for others and avert their own gaze from their inner world, not mapping it with care. This can become a vicious bad cycle, as unscrutinized and undeveloped emotions remain at an infantile level and are therefore felt to be all the more shameful, all the more out of step with the controlling adult self who appears.

3. SHAME AND GUILT

Shame, then, is in many respects a productive and potentially creative emotion. Shame is subtle: for it goads us onwards with regard to many different types of goals and ideals, some of them valuable. In that sense, it is not inherently self-deceptive, nor does it always express a desire to be a sort of being one is not. It often tells us the truth: certain goals are valuable, and we have failed to live up to them. And it often expresses a desire to be a type of being one is, or at least can be: a good human being doing fine things. But because shame has its origins in a desire to be complete and completely in control, it is potentially linked to denigration of others and to a type of aggression that lashes out at any obstacle to the self's narcissistic projects. Narcissism and its associated aggressions are dangers that always lurk around the corner of even a rightly motivated shame, and it will be a wise person and society indeed that can always keep the two distinct.

Because it is standard to contrast shame with guilt, I must now pause to give my own view on this perpetual question. Guilt, like anger, responds to a harm or damage; it aims at the righting of the wrong. So too, I shall now suggest, does guilt, in the particular case where the wrongdoer is oneself. Guilt is a type of self-punishing anger, reacting to the perception that one has done a wrong or a harm. Thus, whereas shame focuses on defect and thus on some aspect of the very being of the person who feels it, guilt focuses on an action (or a wish to act) but need not extend to the entirety of the agent, seeing the agent as utterly defective through and through. In developmental terms—although there is no opportunity to offer a detailed analysis here—guilt originates in the child's perception that her aggressive wishes have harmed, or have projected harm toward, another person who does not deserve to be harmed. It is the manifestation of ambivalence toward parental caretakers, but at a stage at which the child already acknowledges that these parents are separate people who have the right to exist and go their own way. In and of itself, guilt recognizes the rights of others. In that way, its very aggression is more mature, more potentially creative, than the aggression involved in shaming, which aims at a narcissistic restoration of the world of omnipotence. Guilt aims, instead, at a restoration of the wholeness of the separate object or person. As W. R. D. Fairbairn eloquently argued, in his writing on "the moral defense," guilt is thus connected to the acceptance of moral demands and to the limiting of one's own demands in favor of the rights of others. And as Melanie Klein argues, it is also, for that reason, linked to projects of reparation, in which the child tries to atone for the wrong that it has either done or wished.

One way of getting at this difference is to return to B. Because B had to be perfect, he could not see himself as someone whose aggression was a bad *deed* that he had *done*. As yet incapable of guilt, because he had not renounced his narcissism, he saw his own aggression, instead, as an inexorable badness covering his whole self. Shame, not guilt, was thus his primitive response: hiding, and shutting down. He had no way of coping with his own anger, and so he simply refused to go through the struggle most children fight with their anger and envy. "I see now," B concludes, "that there can be value in a struggle later when things have gone well at the beginning. . . . To sum up, my own problem is how to find a struggle that never was."[31] Winnicott says he is "cluttered up with reparation capacity" because he has not yet found the anger "that would indicate the use of the reparation phenomenon."[32] In consequence, he of course became utterly incapable of morality, since morality involves the use of reparation capacities, respect for the humanity of another person, and regard for the other's neediness.

Thus, in my account guilt is potentially creative, connected with reparation and the acceptance of limits to aggression. Shame of the primitive type is a threat to all possibility of morality and community, and indeed to a creative inner life. Guilt can, of course, be excessive and oppressive, and there can be a corresponding excessive focus on reparation, one that is unhealthily self-tormenting. On the other side, shame of a specific and limited sort can be constructive, motivating a pursuit of valuable ideals—within a context in which one already renounces the demands of narcissism. But in their role at a pivotal stage of a child's life, shame, with its connection to narcissism, would appear to be the emotion, of these two, that poses the bigger danger to development. I connect this suggestion with the idea that one of development's central tasks is the renunciation of infantile omnipotence and the willingness to live in a world of objects. Guilt is a great aid in this task, because it contains the great lesson that other people are separate beings with rights who ought not to be harmed; whereas shame threatens to undermine the developmental task entirely, subordinating others to the needs of the self.[33] This account, if correct, suggests that the law would be well advised both to express society's feelings of guilt about crime and to rely on guilt as a social motive; shame will be a more slippery and unreliable tool.

4. Stigma and Brand: Shame in Social Life

All societies mark some people as normal. As Goffman trenchantly observed, all deviations from the normal are marked as occasions for shame. Each person in a society looks out at the world from the perspective of its norm of normalcy. And if what he or she sees when looking in the mirror does not conform to that norm, shame is the likely result. Many occasions for social shame are straightforwardly physical: handicaps and disabilities of various kinds, but also overweight, ugliness, awkwardness, lack of skill in sports, lack of some desirable secondary sexual characteristic. Some are features of the person's form of life: sexual minorities, criminals, and the unemployed are major recipients of stigma.

These latter types of deviation from the normal are not branded on the face. Societies have, in consequence, found it convenient to inflict a visible mark. The word "stigma" is in fact the name for this mark. As the edict of Constantine records, tattooing and branding have therefore been used in many societies to mark criminals. And the evidence shows, time and again, that those singled out for branding include not just those convicted of a particular offense, but various other undesirables: slaves, the poor, members of sexual and religious minorities.

What is going on when societies stigmatize minorities? How might this behavior be connected to the dynamics of human development I sketched out above? At this point any account is bound to be highly conjectural, but we are dealing with phenomena of such ubiquity that we ought at least to try to understand them. At the heart of the matter is the strange notion of the "normal," with its way of linking what might seem to be two altogether distinct ideas.[34] On the one hand, there is the idea of statistical frequency: the normal is the usual, that which most people are or do. The opposite of "normal" in that sense is "unusual." On the other hand, there is the notion of the good or normative: the normal is the proper. The opposite of "normal" in this sense is "inappropriate," "bad," "disgraceful." Social notions of stigma and shame typically link the two rather closely together: whoever does not do what most people do is treated as disgraceful or bad. The puzzle is why people should ever have drawn this peculiar connection. For obviously enough, what is typical may or may not be very good. Bad backs, bad eyes, and bad judgment are all very typical, and Roman Hruska's claim that intellectual mediocrity should be represented on the U.S. Supreme Court met the widespread mockery it deserved. As J. S. Mill observed, much progress in human affairs comes from people who are unusual and who live lives that the majority does not live or even like. So why, in more or less all societies, has the notion of the normal as the usual also served a normative function, setting the different up for stigmatizing treatment?

The puzzle becomes more complex when we recall Goffman's observation about the normal in the sense of the usual: that, as a composite picture of a person, it is actually a fictional construct. Almost nobody is, in every aspect, the "normal man." Even if with regard to each single attribute that attribute is widespread, when we combine the whole list of such attributes, there is almost nobody who has them all. Protestants, people under fifty, and heterosexuals may all be "usual" categories, but when you begin to combine them the intersection is smaller, of course; and by the time we go all the way down Goffman's list we get a person who is rare indeed, and highly temporary, given that we all move all too rapidly into the stigmatized category of the aging. So why should a category this elusive and in a sense contradictory have such power to mar human lives?

I believe that the use of the category "normal" to stigmatize deviant behavior should be understood as the outgrowth of the primitive shame that to some degree affects us all. Because we are all aware that there are many ways in which we fail to measure up to the exorbitant demand of infancy for complete control over the sources of good, because we retain our nostalgic longing for the bliss of infantile oneness with the womb or the breast, we need a surrogate kind of safety or completeness. And those who call themselves "normals" find this safety in the idea of a group that is both widespread, surrounding them on all sides, and good, lacking in nothing. By defining a certain sort of person as complete and good, and by surrounding themselves with such people, normals gain comfort and the illusion of safety. The idea of normalcy is like a surrogate womb, blotting out intrusive stimuli from the world of difference.

But of course this stratagem requires stigmatizing some other group of persons. Normals know that their bodies are frail and vulnerable; but when they can stigmatize the physically disabled they feel a lot better about their own human weaknesses. They feel really all right, almost immortal. Normals know that their intellects are flawed in many ways; all human beings have many deficiencies in knowledge, judgment, and understanding. But with the mentally disabled around them, stigmatized as "morons," "idiots," "Mongoloid idiots," or "crazy people," normals feel positively sage and brilliant. Normals know, again, that their relations with other people are vulnerable and that loss and betrayal may affect anyone; but when they stigmatize another group as morally depraved, they feel positively virtuous. In sexual relations all human beings feel deeply exposed, and sex is a particular site of both physical and emotional vulnerability; but if normals can brand a certain group as sexually deviant, this helps them avoid the shame that they are prone to feel. In short, by casting shame outwards, by branding the faces and the bodies of others, normals achieve a type of surrogate bliss, they satisfy their infantile wish for control and invulnerability. Goffman revealingly refers to the stigmatized person, therefore, as "the person he [the normal] is normal against."[35]

In short, I am suggesting that the stigmatizing behavior in which all societies engage is an aggressive reaction to infantile narcissism and to the shame born of our own incompleteness. Even if in many respects many human beings overcome infantile narcissism, learning to form relationships of mutual interdependence with other people and to recognize their separate reality, there is an instability to that recognition, given that people still don't want to be mortal and weak; in consequence there is a powerful tendency to revert to self-protective aggression when weakness makes itself felt. We might even say that the presence of disabled people functioning in our midst reminds normals too much of their own weakness, so that they feel an urge to reject from their sight those who wear their weakness on their face.

This analysis does not mean that when society holds out certain norms and asks people to live up to them, shaming them when they do not, those norms are never valuable and good. I have already said that shame can serve a valuable moral function in connection with good ideals. But thinking about the infantile roots of shame does inform us that society's shaming behavior is not to be easily trusted, nor taken at face value. Behind the parade of moralism and high ideals, there is often likely to be something much more primitive going on, something to which the precise content of the ideals in question, and their normative value, is basically irrelevant. Such reflections should make us more skeptical about even the moralizing type of shaming, more determined to sift and analyze the ideals in question, to see if they have more going for them than their sheer ubiquity.

Central to the operation of stigma is a dehumanization of the victim. The urge to brand the face keeps on recurring in the history of this topic, not only because the face is visible, as hands and calves may not be, but precisely because it does, as Constantine says, bear the mark of our humanity and individuality. Recall that one remarkable reflex of B's shame was the inability to recognize individual people or to call them by their Christian names. In his desire to control and to shut off sources of need, he saw other people only as vague looming threats to his projects; their qualitative distinctness could not be seen, and their separateness could not be acknowledged. So too with the narcissistic aggression that underlies much social stigmatizing: its urge is to efface the human individuality of the other, whether by a literal brand or simply by classifying the person as a member of a shamed class rather than as an individual person. By classifying a person as "a cripple," "a mongoloid idiot," "a homosexual," we deny both the humanity we share with the person and the person's individuality: as Goffman says, "He is thus reduced in our minds from a whole and usual person to a tainted, discounted one. . . . By definition, of course, we believe the person with a stigma is not quite human. On this assumption we exercise varieties of discrimination."[36]

An advantage of our approach to public policy issues through issues of infant development is that it alerts us to the dynamics frequently involved in shaming, and gives us reason to suppose that its dehumanizing tendency is no accident, nothing we might easily remove while keeping shame's expressive and deterrent potential. It is part of the logic of infantile narcissism itself.

5. SHAME AND THE "FACILITATING ENVIRONMENT"

Winnicott and W. R. D. Fairbairn describe a norm of human health, which is said to be the condition in which emotional development culminates in a person who has not suffered some unusually disturbing blow. Fairbairn revealingly uses the term "mature dependence," rather than "independence," and contrasts this with the young child's "infantile dependence."[37] In infantile dependence the child perceives itself as terribly needy and helpless, and its desire is to control and incorporate the sources of good. In mature dependence, by contrast, which from now on I shall call "mature interdependence," the child is able to accept the fact that those whom it loves and continues to need are separate from her and not mere instruments of her will. She allows herself to depend upon them in some ways, but she does not insist on omnipotence; and as she allows them, in return, to depend in certain ways upon her, she commits herself to being responsible for them in certain ways.

Although this acceptance is never achieved without anger, jealousy, and envy, the story of maturity is that at a certain point the child will be able to renounce envy and jealousy along with other attempts to control, and will be able to use the resources of gratitude and generosity that she has by now developed—in part on account of her guilt and sorrow—to establish the relationship on a footing of equality and mutuality. She acknowledges that she will always continue to need love and security, but sees that this can be pursued without a jealous attempt to possess and control. It is only at this point, Fairbairn stresses, that adult love is achieved, since love requires not only the recognition of its object's separateness, but also the wish that this separateness be protected.

But this state of health is a precarious achievement, highly prone to be destabilized by forces both personal and social. Behind the increasing competence and maturity—and, indeed, the mature and generous love—of such an adult lurk immature wishes that are never altogether displaced: seething jealousy, a demand to be the center of the world, a longing for bliss and comfort, a consequent desire to surround oneself with "normals" and to stigmatize vulnerable people and groups. The form these demands take will be influenced by each individual's familial and personal history; but it will also be influenced by the surrounding society, which can create to varying degrees what Winnicott calls a "facilitating environment"—to use Winnicott's phrase—for the emotional health of its citizens.

What, then, should these issues of stigma, shame, and narcissism mean for public policy? If the only issue we had to deal with were the emotional health of those who stigmatize others, some liberals might insist that law and public policy have no business promoting emotional health by moderating the influence of stigmatizing and branding in citizens' lives. If those "normals" are acting out an infantile type of shame, and failing to form relationships of mature interdependency, so much the worse for them, such a liberal might say, but that is part of their choice of a way of life, and the law has no business intervening. I think that even such a liberal might be answered, because surely the capacities for emotional health, for self-respect, and for mutually respectful relationships with other citizens are "primary goods" that it seems reasonable to think any liberal society should make available to its citizens. It is clear, however, that the stigmatizers and their mental health are not our only concern. The stigmatized suffer tremendous damage from the stigmatizing behavior of others. Sometimes they suffer legal and civil disabilities through no fault of their own —as when a minority religion or a minority lifestyle that does no harm to nonconsenting third parties is discriminated against under law. Still more frequently, they suffer from pervasive discrimination in housing, employment, and other social functions, with no legal recourse—as has long been the situation of gays and lesbians in most modern societies, along with the short, the fat, the HIV positive, and many others. Almost always, too, individual members of stigmatized groups suffer pain from mockery, taunting, and the assault on their human dignity and individuality that is so intrinsic a part of shaming.

This being the case, a liberal society, by which we typically mean one built on norms of mutual respect and reciprocity, has very strong reasons to consider how the harmful impact of stigma can be minimized. There are many directions in which a discussion of this topic might go: the laws of libel and slander, general antidiscrimination laws, and laws and policies against sexual harassment are all pertinent to thinking about how a liberal society protects its members from shame. I shall have time to look at only two salient issues: the revival of interest in shame penalties, and current efforts to inhibit stigma directed against the mentally and physically handicapped.

6. Shaming Penalties: Dignity and Narcissistic Rage

Shame penalties have recently attracted a great deal of interest. In part, this interest stems from a more general conservative desire to revive the blush of shame: the claim is that modern people have lost inhibitions and that social disorder and decay have been the result. We can best promote social order and give support to important values connected with family and social life if we stigmatize people who behave in a deviant way: single mothers, people living on welfare, and so on. Kahan and other proponents of shame penalties in the law are in part motivated by something like this general idea.

For Kahan, the basic purpose of punishment is expressive: by punishing certain sorts of offenders, society expresses its most basic values.[38] This being the case, he argues, shame penalties have a particular power. Humiliating someone in public makes a definite statement. The person cannot hide: his offense is exposed to the gaze of others. By contrast, even imprisonment, humiliating though it is, is too anonymous: the person is shut away behind closed doors, rather than being hung up for public viewing. And Kahan commends shaming particularly strongly as an alternative to other "alternative sanctions," that is, sanctions not involving imprisonment. Paying a fine is just not humiliating; thus fining really does not involve a statement by society that a given form of conduct is disgraceful. We think nothing much about paying a parking or even a speeding ticket; we think we have got off, and we don't feel disgraced. And the alternative of community service, Kahan argues, is even worse, because it rewards a person for disgraceful conduct. Instead of being humiliated, the person is given something good to do, something about which he can feel good himself, and something that will make others think well of him.

In addition, one could add, shame is likely to have a very power-ful deterrent effect.[39] People who pick up prostitutes will be far less likely to do so if they know that part of their penalty will be un-pleasant publicity in the newspapers. A driver will think twice about driving intoxicated if he knows he may have to drive around for a year with a license plate saying DUI. And those New York businessmen who went to Hoboken to eat lunch and then peed in the street would probably have thought twice about it had they known that the penalty would be not a quiet hidden fine but the public act of scrubbing the streets with a toothbrush. These are plausible claims. Shame does have powerful expressive and deter-rent effects. So I need to have more to say against it than simply the fact that I find it unpleasant. Let us, then, grant to Kahan that one thing punishments do is to express social values. If all shame penalties did was to express valuable, specific social norms and to give people (both the offenders and the general public) very strong incentives to live up to those norms, then there would be a case to be made for them.

Political liberals would still ask whether the norms being en-forced in this way are truly norms that the law should enforce. Are they central to the political conception of a liberal democracy, or are they the sort of thing about which citizens reasonably disagree, and whose enforcement is therefore, according to the political lib-eral, not the business of law? Such a liberal, while not strictly com-mitted to accepting Mill's harm principle as a necessary condition of the legal regulation of conduct, is likely to be quite sympathetic to that principle. Thus, the political liberal will still object to many shaming penalties on the grounds that they are penalties for of-fenses that really should not be offenses, because they involve "self-regarding" conduct, conduct that does no harm to nonconsenting third parties. Many laws dealing with drugs and sexual behavior, for example, fall in this category.

This objection, however, is not an objection to shaming penal-ties as such: it is an objection to all forms of punishment for of-fenses that fall in the category of the "self-regarding." And it is clear that one objection we often have to certain shaming penal-ties—for example, to newspaper publication of the names of men who solicit prostitutes—is that we are uneasy with the criminaliza-tion of prostitution and soliciting, and mind it even more when they are dealt with harshly. We need to separate that objection from the reasons we might have for objecting to shaming penalties as such. So from now on let us consider only offenses that meet Mill's test: they involve harm to others. Kahan's failure to separate these two categories of offense seems to me unfortunate, but we need not follow him. Let us, then, consider offenses such as drunken driving, theft, fraud, harmful sexual conduct (e.g., child molestation), and other related offenses.[40] These are really bad things that deserve to be punished.

Three arguments against shaming penalties have been advanced in the recent literature. I shall now argue that each of them receives a deeper rationale by being connected to the account of shame and stigma I have advanced above. Thus, we might oppose shaming penalties without endorsing that account; but the account gives more power and flesh to the arguments, and thus gives us new reasons to accept them.

The first argument that has been advanced is that shame penalties humiliate, and thus constitute an offense against human dignity.[41] This argument, rightly understood, does not require us to hold that people who receive these punishments actually *feel* humiliated; thus, it is not undermined by the phenomenon (known in the ancient Roman world as well as in subcultures today)[42] that groups targeted for shaming may come to feel pride in the marks inflicted upon them. Rightly understood, the argument focuses on what the penalty itself expresses: it expresses the intent to degrade and humiliate, and thus is incompatible with a political commitment to giving all citizens the social conditions of self-respect, even if, for some contingent reason, the person happens not to feel humiliation.

Why is shaming supposed to be an offense against human dignity in a way that fines and imprisonment are not? The claim is that those punishments are meted out for acts; they do not constitute a humiliation or degradation of the whole person (though they may come to have such features, as I shall discuss at the end of this section). Thus, they track guilt, and indeed are predicated on a finding of guilt. Shame targets not a single deed but the entire person. It is the person who must wear a sign, sit in the pillory, wear a tattoo for life, and so on. Shame brands this person as having, in Goffman's sense, a "spoiled identity," a degraded status.

And the argument is that this is incompatible with the proper public regard for the equal dignity of all citizens.

A variant of this argument, which does deal with the offender's actual feelings, has been recently advanced by Julia Annas.[43] Using evidence from literature and history, she argues that shame, because it targets the whole person, is particularly likely to be linked to "a broken spirit"—a long-term inability to recover self-respect and a sense of one's own worth. These psychological claims, which are plausible, would give additional impetus to the contention that shaming penalties rob people of a central "primary good."

Let us consider the dignity argument in the light of the account of shaming that I have presented. As I have suggested, one thing that shaming of subgroups typically expresses is a denigration of the very humanity of the people being shamed. They are somehow, in Goffman's terms, subhuman, not distinct human beings with individuality and dignity. More generally, in shaming people as deviant, the shamers set themselves up as a "normal" class above the shamed, and thus divide society into ranks and hierarchies. Such statements do have expressive power: they give voice to something many people deeply feel. But nonetheless there is surely something intolerable about the idea that a liberal society, one built upon ideas of human dignity and equality, and respect for the individual, would express that particular meaning through its public system of law. The basic attitude animating Kahan's policy is one that divides people into two groups, the frail and the above-it-all, and that scoffs at those disgraceful wretches down below us. (When Kahan first presented his ideas in a workshop at the University of Chicago Law School, and brought out, as a prime example, the case of the Hoboken toothbrush clean-up, one older colleague remarked, "But maybe they had prostate trouble." This possibility just hadn't dawned on Kahan, and that is significant: the attitude of the shamer is one that does not try to gain a sympathetic understanding of human weakness. It confidently sets up the shamer above the shamed, as if the shamer could not possibly do anything so disgraceful.)

So far I have relied only on my analysis of stigma and what it expresses, not on the underlying causal thesis about "primitive shame." And we could stop here. We have said enough to make the dignity argument a powerful one. But if we believe something like the causal story I have given, we have further reasons to accept it. For on that account, people who inflict shame are, very often, not expressing virtuous motives or high ideals, but rather a shrinking from their own human weakness and a rage against the very limits of human life. Their anger is not really, or at least not only, anger at immorality and vice. Behind the moralism is something much more primitive, something that cannot easily be defended by the sort of moral argument Kahan has presented. So if we have even a suspicion that this causal story, or something like it, is correct, we should at least be more skeptical of some likely retorts to the dignity argument. The social conditions of self-respect for all citizens do appear incompatible with the widespread use of punishments based upon shame.

Guilt, and punishments predicated upon guilt, do not suffer from a similar problem. For guilt contains within itself a separation between the person and the person's act, and is thus fully compatible with respect for the dignity of the person. Punishments may treat the act very harshly, while still expressing the sense that the person is worthy of regard, and of ultimate reintegration into society. By both holding people responsible for their crimes and then offering them ways through which to make reparation and to reintegrate themselves into society, we strengthen the reparative capacities, in the process treating the offender as someone from whom good things may come. Community service, for certain crimes, would be one way of promoting reparation and reintegration.

Let us now turn to a second argument against shaming penalties, an argument advanced by James Whitman.[44] Whitman argues that shaming penalties typically involve a type of mob justice, and are problematic for that reason alone. In shaming, the state does not simply mete out punishment through its own established institutions. It invites the public to punish the offender. This is not only an unreliable way to punish, but one that is intrinsically problematic, for it invites the "mob" to tyrannize over whoever they happen not to like. Justice by the mob is not the impartial, deliberative, neutral justice that a liberal/democratic society typically prizes.[45]

This argument, like the dignity argument, can be strengthened by linking it to an account of the group dynamics of stigmatization. If fears of inadequacy typically lead people to form groups and to define themselves as "normals" over against some less powerful group, and if the infliction of stigma and shame is typically connected with this process of group formation, as Goffman has powerfully argued, then we can see more clearly just what is likely to prove objectionable about it. These mechanisms of group self-protection look very different from the type of balanced and impartial administration of justice we rightly demand from a system of law.

Adding to Goffman's account of stigma the causal account of "primitive shame," we can go still further: often, the reasons why people form such groups and target others is a kind of deeply irrational fear of defect that is part of a more general shrinking from something troubling about human life, a search for an impossible type of hardness, safety, and self-sufficiency. This sense of the irrational roots of the desire to shame makes us see even more clearly why a system of law ought not to built its institutions on this motive. The claim is not that all emotions are unreliable as a basis for legal rules. The claim is a specific claim about the etiology and operations of this particular emotion.

A third argument, distinct from Whitman's though closely related to it, is Eric Posner's argument that shame penalties are simply unreliable.[46] History shows that they very often end up targeting the wrong people, and/or calibrating inaccurately the magnitude of the penalty. They therefore fail to fulfill well the deterrent function of punishment: they may deter behavior that is not bad, but simply unpopular, and fail to deter other far worse behavior. To the ample evidence from Europe presented by Posner (and also Whitman), I can add the ancient Roman evidence, which shows the same thing very clearly. Although shaming penalties in late antiquity were introduced with a clear class of real offenses in view (theft, fraud, etc.), they very quickly ended up being used to stigmatize whatever group happened to be unpopular at the time—sexual minorities, Christians, and, in the era of Christian domination, heretics.

Once again, the historical evidence by itself makes a very strong case for Posner's point. But history is slippery. Our data are always going to remain incomplete, and it is always hard to know how representative recorded cases are. It would be good to have a causal hypothesis, in addition, showing us some reasons why shaming can be expected to be unreliable and uneasily tethered to the nature and magnitude of actual offenses. My story about shame and stigma provides such a causal hypothesis. It is no accident that shame shifts rather rapidly from real offense to mere dissident identity, because shame is not about a bad act in the first place. It is addressed in the first place to a person or group of persons, and to a person seen as embodying some deviant characteristic against which a dominant group seeks to define, and thus protect, itself. When we add that the mechanism behind the protection is a search for invulnerability and narcissistic triumph, we can see that the people who are likely to be targets of the shamer's rage are not particularly likely to be real malefactors—but, instead, anyone who reminds the "normal" of his weakness, anyone who can become, as it were, the scapegoat of these weaknesses, carrying them out of the community. Narcissistic rage is inherently irrational (in the normative sense) and unbalanced, so it is no surprise that it goes after Christians as well as thieves, disabled people as well as forgers.

We have, then, three arguments against shaming penalties. All of them have independent force, and any one of them might be sufficient to convince us that these penalties are a bad idea. I have argued that we get additional support for these arguments from the account of shame I have presented, and a much deeper understanding of why shaming penalties should be thought to threaten key values of a liberal society.

Defenders of shame penalties frequently reply by insisting that these penalties serve well four primary purposes of punishment: retribution, deterrence, expression, and reform or reintegration. I have already argued that, though shame penalties are powerfully expressive, what they express is deeply problematic in a society based on ideas of dignity and equal worth. Their deterrent potential has also been called into question by Posner's convincing argument. But we need to consider further the claims about retribution and reform.

James Whitman has written that shame penalties are "beautifully retributive."[47] And of course there is something quite striking about punishments like the Hoboken toothbrush cleanup—they have a Dantesque flavor, and seem exquisitely tailored to the crime. Similarly Dantesque is the Kahan example of a slumlord who was sentenced to live for a period of time in one of his own rat-infested tenements. Some of these examples appear not to be about shame at all. The slumlord's punishment was not apt on account of the way it shamed him in front of others. In fact, we have no reason to suppose that he was watched by others, nor was he humiliated with respect to his entire person, as in the cases where people wear special signs or marks. This punishment seems like a perfectly ordinary guilt punishment: in retribution for his bad act, he is being assigned a penalty that seems more nearly apposite and proportional than simply going to prison.

If we consider the core group of shame penalties, however, it is not clear that they really do serve the purpose of retribution, as that notion is best understood. In an excellent recent article, Dan Markel has argued that the best way to make sense of retributivism in the theory of punishment is to think of it as a view about free riding and equal liberty.[48] We believe that all citizens are equal and should enjoy an equal liberty of action. The criminal offends against this basic social understanding, claiming for himself an unequal terrain of liberty. He implicitly says, I will steal and you will continue to obey the law; I will rape and nobody will rape me. As Kant argued, people who in this way make an exception of themselves are treating humanity as a mere means, rather than respecting it as an end. (This is the best way of connecting the Formula of Universal Law with the Formula of Humanity: the way we can tell whether we are using other people as a means is to test our conduct by seeing whether it could be made into a Universal Law of Nature.)[49] Retributive punishment brings the offender to book for that claim of unequal liberty: it says, no, you are not entitled to an unequal liberty, you will have to accept the limits that are compatible with a like liberty for others.[50] It is thus very different from revenge, which is typically based on personal motives and has little concern with general social equality.

If we understand retributivism in this way, we see, as Markel argues, that shame penalties are not at all retributive. They do not express a sense of the equal worth of persons and their liberty, but something very different, something connected to hierarchy and degradation. Returning to my account, we see this very clearly: for defining a top group against deviant groups is what shaming penalties seem to be all about. They certainly may and often do express the desire for revenge—and as I have argued there is often a powerful connection between primitive shame and vindictive rage. But they are not "beautifully retributive" in anything like Kant's sense, the sense in which retributivism is a defensible and powerful theory of punishment for a liberal democratic society.

What about reform? John Braithwaite has argued influentially that shaming penalties serve very well the purpose of confronting the offender with his offense and the toll it has taken on others, and, ultimately, of reintegrating the offender into the society.[51] He practices a type of "reintegrative conferencing" between victims and offenders that promotes these goals.[52] Such efforts are becoming increasingly common in a variety of liberal democracies.

Braithwaite's argument on behalf of shaming is a communitarian argument. He describes himself as a communitarian, and understands this to entail a strong concern to promote social homogeneity. In this respect he is close to Kahan and Etzioni. But his conception of shaming is very different. First of all, he makes it clear that he considers shaming appropriate only for a crime that involves harm to a victim: "predatory crime" is his characteristic phrase. Thus, he operates from the start within the limits of Mill's principle. Second, he draws a very strong distinction between shaming that stigmatizes and shaming that promotes reintegration. He is critical of the former (although at times he suggests that it might be better than no shaming at all), and supportive of the latter.

There are a number of difficulties with Braithwaite's analysis. His account of his own communitarian position is vague, using a contrast between "communitarianism" and "individualism" that is never fully defined or clarified. If "individualism" means egoism, there is of course no reason to suppose that liberal noncommunitarians are any more likely to be guilty of this vice than communitarians. If, by contrast, it means a commitment to certain core liberties and rights of individuals, then it does not stand opposed to liberalism in any simple way, since an attachment to such rights can be among the core shared values of a political culture. Nor does he ever make the crucial distinction between values that lie in the core of a shared political conception and values that belong to the religious and other comprehensive doctrines of citizens: so we cannot really tell whether he wishes to promote homogeneity of values across the board, or only in the political core. So it remains utterly unclear whether he really is a communitarian in any sense in which that is at odds with liberalism. His inordinate admiration for Japan surely strikes an ominous note: for Japanese public culture surely is very far from what Mill would favor, promoting homogeneity of values in public education and elsewhere, in ways that surely do lead to the stigmatization and marginalization of unpopular types of individuals (the disabled being one especially notorious case). But nothing in his theoretical argument commits him to a type of communitarianism that is at odds with liberalism, because he focuses on crimes that do harm and violate the rights of individuals.

But the central problem with Braithwaite's account, from the point of view of my argument here, is his failure to make any clear distinction between shame and guilt. He favors punishments that focus on the act rather than the person, and that ask the person to make atonement for an act as a prelude to being forgiven and reintegrated into the community. He insists that these punishments must be meted out without stigmatization, and in an atmosphere of mutual respect for humanity. All of this is very appealing, and I am inclined to have much sympathy with the proposals he advances. What is totally unclear is whether this has anything at all to do with shame. He insists on the fact that malefactors are not to be humiliated, and that we are to separate the act from the person. All this is characteristic of guilt rather than shame. Similarly, notions of forgiveness and atonement are at home in the world of guilt rather than shame. In fact, there would appear to be no important difference between Dan Markel's *Confrontational Conception of Retributivism*,[53] which focuses on expressing to the wrongdoer the badness of an act that claims an unequal liberty and violates the rights of others, as a prelude to atonement and forgiveness, and Braithwaite's so-called shaming penalties. But Markel, it seems to me correctly, situates his conception in the Kantian world of respect, guilt for an act, and subsequent apology and atonement. (Kant is not enamored of forgiveness, but that is a feature of Kant, not of the type of conception he advances.) So I conclude, tentatively, that Braithwaite's ideas are not only very far removed from those of Kahan and Etzioni—as he himself stresses —but also quite unconnected to traditional notions of shaming punishment, and part of the universe of guilt punishments.

Several residual questions remain. Julia Annas and Deborah Rhode suggest that shaming penalties might be appropriate for organizations that do harm, where they are inappropriate as applied to individuals.[54] Annas argues that organizations cannot suffer the deep harms that individuals suffer, and that they have, as such, no dignity to protect: thus, it may be appropriate to humiliate them by bad publicity. Rhode, thinking particularly of violations of norms of professional conduct, suggests that bad publicity for offending firms, for example, would not be objectionable in the way that shaming would be outside this institutional context. I have no clear view about this. They certainly make a strong argument with respect to issues of dignity; nor is bad publicity among one's peers the type of mob justice about which Whitman is most concerned. Whether Posner's worries about uneven deterrence apply here remains unclear. It seems to me that deterrence is likely to be most appropriate if the focus is on the acts of which the organization has been guilty, rather than on a simple shaming of the whole organization. To that extent, the punishment would be on the borderline between shame and guilt.

Etzioni raises another interesting question: Should shame penalties be used for acts that it makes no sense to render illegal? He focuses on failures to aid, arguing that "bad Samaritan" laws are probably not workable and that a much more feasible way of punishing people who do not intervene to help someone who is being assaulted, for example, is to give them bad publicity, thus promoting norms that encourage people to take risks for others. He recognizes that liberals will say: Why not focus on good publicity for people who do help? His answer is that people, as he sees it, are more likely to be motivated by fear of bad publicity than by desire for good publicity. Etzioni's psychological claim is speculative, and he offers no evidence for it. It also avoids the key question: Who does the publicizing? Obviously there can be no objection to citizens getting together to disseminate information of this sort, or to journalists making a practice of reporting on such failures. But that, of course, is not a shaming punishment. If, however, the state is really going to get involved, then what will be the basis for this involvement? If there is no bad-Samaritan law, what is the state saying, exactly, when it metes out a shame punishment for these bad acts? We are punishing you for something that is not illegal, and which we have no intention of rendering illegal? This would be a rather absurd proposal. Etzioni is so unclear about what he is actually proposing that we really do not yet have a position to assess.

Admittedly, there are numerous crimes for which community service and other types of restorative justice are not appropriate alternatives. Usually for these crimes shame sanctions are not appropriate, either, and prison is chosen. Nonetheless, defenders of shame sanctions point to the humiliating character of imprisonment, in order to convict the opponent of inconsistency: either reject prisons, the Kahan argument goes, or accept signs and placards and other types of public shaming.

We should admit that as they operate in many societies, and certainly in the United States, prisons are profoundly humiliating. The question is whether this must of necessity be so. James Whitman's extensive comparative study of punishment in the United States, France, and Germany establishes that the trend in Europe has been toward mildness in punishments and toward an acute concern with respect for human dignity.[55] Maria Archimandritou's new book *The Open Prison*,[56] a study of penal practices in the Nordic countries, Germany, and several others parts of Europe, comes to a similar conclusion, and finds that there has been a related trend toward extending to prisoners all the basic rights of citizens, including rights to health care. The United States is the outlier, and we should not allow the deplorable state of our prisons to make us believe humiliation and prison must always go together. Even in the United States, defenders of the rights of prisoners have long waged a campaign to establish in the courts and in the public mind the fact that prisoners are not just animals, that they have certain rights of privacy and rights to personal property.[57]

It seems to me that there is no reason to think that the whole institution of imprisonment is incompatible with basic human dignity and respect. The very fact of limiting a person's freedom for a period of time does not express the view that this person is not fully human. The right direction to go in order to respond to

Kahan is to pursue the humanization of prisons and the protection of certain basic rights of inmates—including, I would say, rethinking the grotesque U.S. policy that denies convicted felons the right to vote for life, a policy that surely does shame and stigmatize for life. Most European nations have never endorsed such an idea; indeed, in the nations where voting is compulsory, prisoners are required to vote like everyone else. Rethinking imprisonment along European lines (if the public will to do so could be created) would establish that prison is not a form of lifelong stigmatization but, rather, a basically respectful form of deterrence and/or retribution.

7. SHAME AND THE DISABLED

No group in society has been so painfully stigmatized as the physically and mentally handicapped. Moreover, many people who would whole-heartedly oppose all stigmatization based on race or sex or sexual orientation feel that some sort of differential treatment is appropriate for those who are disabled and different "by nature." Mrs. Dover is not atypical in feeling that she had better not emerge into society—for if she does she will be treated as a nonperson. People don't want to look at someone with half a nose. Far less, often, are they willing to look at a child with Down syndrome. Such children used to be summarily tossed into institutions and treated as "mongoloid idiots," without individual personality, without individual names, without genuine humanity. As Goffman says, the entire interaction with such a person is articulated in terms of the stigmatized trait,[58] which means that the person's full humanity cannot come into focus.

The first point to be made in confronting this issue is a familiar one—and yet it evidently needs repeating, since one hears so many arguments that ignore it. This is, that a handicap does not exist simply "by nature," if that means independently of human action. We might say that a disability in some area or areas of human functioning exists by nature, but it only becomes a handicap when society treats it in certain ways. Human beings are in general disabled: mortal, weak-eyed, weak-kneed, with terrible backs and necks, short memories, and so forth. But when a majority (or, the most powerful group) has such disabilities, society will adjust itself to cater for them. Thus, we do not find staircases built with step levels so high that only the giants of Brobdingnag can climb them, nor do we find our orchestras playing instruments at frequencies inaudible to the human ear and audible only to dog ears. The problem of many people in our society is that their disabilities have not been catered for, because they are thought to be flawed in an unusual way.

Put it that way, and it does not sound very nice: Why should mere atypicality give one a life of hardship? Typically, however, "normals" think of themselves as perfect without flaw, and of the unusually disabled as the only ones with flaws: they are the bad apples in the lot, the spoiled food amid the healthy food. What does one do with spoiled food? Throw it out, lest it contaminate the good. And the peculiar reluctance of most modern societies to tolerate the presence of the handicapped—especially the mentally handicapped—in schools and public places betrays this same uneasy sense that their very presence will spoil the lives of others. The fact that our own lives are also frail and disabled lives is thus the more effectively screened from view.[59]

The screening out of the disabled is aided and abetted, I now want to argue, by a pervasive myth about citizenship that has dominated the history of modern European political theory. The myth, deeply enshrined in classical social contract doctrine, is that the citizen is a competent independent adult. The parties to the social contract are assumed by Locke to be "free, equal, and independent."[60] Contemporary contractarians explicitly adopt such a hypothesis. For David Gauthier, people of unusual need are "not party to the moral relationships grounded by a contractarian theory."[61] Similarly, the citizens in John Rawls's Well-Ordered Society are "fully cooperating members of society over a complete life."[62] And since the partnership envisaged is for the mutual advantage of the contracting parties, provisions for people who aren't part of the bargain will be an afterthought—not part of the basic institutional structure to which they agree.[63]

Most forms of social contract doctrine do, of course, make provision for "normal" human needs; but they do screen from view all the times of asymmetrical or unusual dependency, even those that result from childhood or old age, stages of life through which all citizens pass. In that way, as Goffman observes, there is a public fiction that a sharp line divides the "normal" from the stigmatized; in reality, the normal and the stigmatized are a part of one another.

Any productive approach to the social situation of the atypically disabled must begin, then, by recognizing that we are all disabled, and that life includes not only "normal" needs but also periods, more or less prolonged, of unusual and asymmetrical dependency, during which the situation of the "normal" approximates to that of the unusually disabled, in one or more respects. This means that if we are to give even "normals" the social conditions of self-respect, we must at the same time think about the self-respect of the life-long disabled, and try to devise ways to recognize and support their full humanity and individuality. Thinking about them is thinking about us. But then, good thought about both requires revising the idea of the citizen as independent bargainer, and replacing it with a more complex image of a being both capable and needy, a being who moves from helplessness to "mutual interdependence," and, unfortunately, so often back to helplessness again.

There is a great deal to say about where these ideas might take us in thinking about public policy toward the disabled. I have tried to say some of this in a recent review piece in the *New York Review of Books*.[64] For now, let me conclude the topic by thinking about just one law, the Individuals with Disabilities Education Act (IDEA).

Our treatment of unusually disabled children has had many inequities. Often, such children do not get the medical care and the therapy they need. But the most egregious gap has been, perhaps, in the area of education. Stigmatized as either uneducable or not worth the expense, mentally disabled children, and many whose disabilities are physical, have been denied access to suitable education. In 1975, the Education for All Handicapped Children Act made some strides in giving such children enforceable rights to suitable education; but, despite some promising court cases, its provisions were insufficiently enforced, and it was believed that a new law, with more specific guidelines, would be necessary to rectify the situation. IDEA, passed in 1997, was the result.

IDEA begins from a simple yet profound idea: that of human individuality. Rather than regarding the various types of disabled persons as faceless classes of persons, the act assumes that they are in fact individuals, with varying needs, and that therefore all prescription for groups of them would be inappropriate. The guiding idea of the Act is thus that of the Individualized Education Program (IEP), "a written statement for each child with a disability that is developed, reviewed, and revised." In general, the act urges "mainstreaming" of these children—a practice defended by advocates for the disabled on ground of the benefit both to the disabled child and to other children, who learn about humanity and its diversity by being in a classroom with a child who has unusual disabilities. But the underlying recognition of individuality is paramount: thus, when a child seems to profit more from special education than from mainstreaming—as is the case with my nephew Arthur, whose life with Asperger's syndrome I described in a *New York Review of Books* piece, the state will be required to support such special education, even when, as in Arthur's case, paying tuition at a private school is the only appropriate option.

Such a law goes a long way to undermine stigma: for it tells society that mentally and physically disabled children have rights and are individuals; and that their rights include access to the same classroom as "normals." Teachers and parents have to play their part as well, but it is by now clear that the very fact of state recognition and attention, together with pressure applied to schools and teachers, has greatly changed the climate for stigmatized children. In his eloquent account of the life of his son Jamie, born with Down syndrome, Michael Bérubé writes about the achievement of raising a child who sees himself and is seen by others as Jamie, a particular child with particular tastes and a quirky sense of humor —not a member of some faceless class of "idiots." This is an achievement of which our society should be proud. But it is under threat now, in a time when many modern societies, in both Europe and America, increasingly push the fiction of competent adulthood and deplore the expense of caring for those who do not, as the saying goes, "pay their own way."

Perhaps the greatest insight of the liberal tradition is the insight that each human individual is profoundly valuable, spacious and deep, capable of separate life and imagination, capable of being more than just the creation of a tradition or a family style. This insight has been inconstantly and imperfectly implemented in liberal societies, insofar as they permit infantile narcissism to exercise political power, stigmatizing those who have weaknesses that make "normals" uncomfortable. But liberal societies can inhibit infantile narcissism and create "facilitating environments" in which people differently disabled can live lives of "subtle interplay." Liberalism is frightening. As B says in the paragraph quoted above: "The alarming thing about equality is that we are then both children, and the question is, where is father? We know where we are if one of us is the father." Similarly, we know where we are if one of us is normal, the independent productive citizen, and the other has his eyes downcast in shame. What liberalism requires of us is, however, something more chancy and fearful, some combination of adulthood and childhood, and aspiration without the fiction of perfection.

Nine months after the conclusion of the analysis, B wrote a letter to Winnicott. In his letter we see none of the rigidity, and also none of the shame, that characterized him earlier. Instead, he is willing to admit to uncertainty:

Dear Dr Winnicott,

. . . I am not at all sure what I will be doing after that. It is not yet possible for me to plan that far ahead. I am tempted at times to abandon analysis as I now feel so well. On the other hand, I do realise that the process is incomplete and I may then decide either to resume with you, or should that no longer be possible, to start with someone else. It seems to me to be a great step forward that I can accept that idea fairly easily.

Should we not resume later, I would like to use this opportunity to express my gratitude for all that you have done.

Yours sincerely,

That frank admission of incompleteness and uncertainty is a good place to begin, perhaps, as varyingly disabled people work together to create a liberal society.

NOTES

1. Erving Goffman, *Stigma: Notes on the Management of Spoiled Identity* (New York: Simon and Schuster, 1963), 128.
2. Ibid., 129 and 135.

3. I borrow this succinct characterization of Christopher Lasch's position from Toni Massaro, "The Meanings of Shame: Implications for Legal Reform," *Psychology, Public Policy and Law* 3 (1997): 645–680. See notes 2–3 of Massaro's article for references to conservative journalism in praise of shame.

4. Dan Kahan, "What Do Alternative Sanctions Mean?" *University of Chicago Law Review* 63 (1996): 591–653.

5. This account is an abbreviated version of the account of shame developed in chapter 4 of my *Upheavals of Thought: The Intelligence of Emotions* (Cambridge and New York: Cambridge University Press, 2001). Many of Winnicott's most important papers are published as *The Maturational Process and the Facilitating Environment* (New York: International Universities Press, 1965).

6. Lucretius 5.222–7.

7. Ibid., 229–230.

8. Christopher Bollas, *The Shadow of the Object* (London: Free Association Books, 1987), 13–29.

9. See Seneca, *Medea*, 329–330.

10. I choose these odd locutions—making the subject the infant's experience-world rather than the infant—to remind the reader that the infant does not yet, in the first eight weeks of life, begin to experience itself as a definite subject. Compare Daniel Stern, *Diary of a Baby* (New York: Basic Books, 1990), chap. 3.

11. See also Bollas, *The Shadow of the Object*, 29. Here, Bollas writes: "Transformation does not mean gratification. Growth is only partially promoted by gratification, and one of the mother's transformative functions must be to frustrate the infant."

12. Plato, *Symposium*, 190B.

13. Ibid.

14. Ibid., 191A.

15. Donald W. Winnicott, *Holding and Interpretation: Fragment of an Analysis* (New York: Grove Press, 1986), with a piece of the early part of the analysis, published as an article in 1972, appended to the text. The patient was nineteen at the time of the beginning of his first analysis; he was referred by his mother, herself in analysis with Winnicott. He made a good recovery. Eight years later, Winnicott wrote to the mother to inquire about B's progress; he interviewed her, and she described the pathologies in her own maternal care that she had by now discovered in her own analysis. Some time later the young man, now a medical intern, had had a breakdown and was hospitalized. Winnicott looked him up, and the patient began analysis a week later. During the last six months of the analysis, Winnicott wrote down his extensive notes after five crucial sessions, stat-

ing that, though difficult, it was not impossible to remember what had transpired. Fourteen years after the completion of the second analysis, Winnicott wrote to B to ask how he was doing; he had done well in both life and work.

16. Winnicott, *Holding,* 10. The patient's symptom was a fear of annihilation as a result of satisfaction itself, as if, once he finished feeding, he had no way of knowing that the good things would ever come again. The interpretation of B's early life that was developing in the analysis was confirmed by Winnicott's interview with his mother, during which she told Winnicott about material she had discovered in analysis with another analyst. As she reported to Winnicott during their interview, she became aware of a rigid demand for perfection in her maternal role and of a refusal to tolerate the separate life of the child: she understood perfection as a kind of death of the child, in which he would have nothing more to demand.

17. The mother emerges as an anxious but by no means passive figure: one gets the impression that she is flamboyant. In his last letter to B, responding to the news of the mother's death, Winnicott writes, "She was indeed a personality."

18. Winnicott, *Holding,* 96.

19. Ibid., 172. See also p. 163, where he writes: "The difficulty is the fear of the anger."

20. Ibid., 123.

21. See p. 96, where he writes: "I do not know if I could describe her. I have tended to assume you are not interested in her as a woman. Also I always have a difficulty in describing people. I never can describe a personality, the colour of people's hair, and all that sort of thing. . . . I am always reluctant to use Christian names."

22. For fundamental discussions of shame, see Andrew Morrison, *Shame: The Underside of Narcissism* (Hillsdale, NJ: Analytic Press, 1989); Leon Wurmser, *The Mask of Shame* (Baltimore: Johns Hopkins University Press, 1981); G. Piers and M. B. Singer, *Shame and Guilt: A Psychoanalytic and a Cultural Study* (Springfield, IL: Charles C. Thomas, 1953).

23. See the perceptive discussion in John Deigh, *The Sources of Moral Agency: Essays on Moral Psychology* (Cambridge: Cambridge University Press, 1996), 226–247.

24. Winnicott, *Holding,* 97.

25. See p. 97, where he describes wanting women to look at him as a perfect lover, and giving up in despair when he realizes that he is seen as human.

26. Ibid., 95.

27. Compare p. 147, where the patient gets angry at Winnicott and

says he is like "the ogre of childhood play." Winnicott expresses pleasure: "So you have been able to reach play with me, and in the playing I am an ogre."

28. Ibid., 166. Compare the experimental data in F. G. Lopez and K. A. Brennan, "Dynamic Processes Underlying Adult Attachment Organization," *Journal of Counseling Psychology* 47 (2000): 283–300, concerning the relationship between early attachment problems and inability to tolerate ambiguity and uncertainty, particularly in romantic life.

29. See also *The Maturational Process* for more extensive treatment of these themes.

30. Nancy Chodorow, *The Reproduction of Mothering: Psychoanalysis and the Sociology of Gender* (Berkeley and Los Angeles: University of California Press, 1978).

31. Winnicott, *Holding*, 165.

32. Ibid., 29.

33. On shame and guilt, see, more generally, Gabriele Taylor, *Pride, Shame, and Guilt* (Oxford: Clarendon Press, 1985); Piers and Singer, *Shame and Guilt;* Herbert Morris, *Guilt and Shame* (Belmont, CA: Wadsworth Publishing, 1971).

34. See also the excellent discussion in Michael Warner, *The Trouble with Normal: Sex, Politics, and the Ethics of Queer Life* (New York: Free Press, 1999).

35. Goffman, *Stigma*, 6.

36. Ibid., 3 and 5.

37. W. R. D. Fairbairn, *Psychoanalytic Studies of the Personality* (London and New York: Tavistock/Routledge, 1952). Compare Winnicott's use of the terms "absolute" and "relative" dependence.

38. Kahan, "What Do Alternative Sanctions Mean?" 591–653.

39. This is central to the case for shaming penalties in Amitai Etzioni, *The Monochrome Society* (Princeton, NJ: Princeton University Press, 2001).

40. For examples of shaming penalties actually in use for each of these, see Kahan, "What Do Alternative Sanctions Mean?" 631–634.

41. See Toni Massaro, "Shame, Culture, and American Criminal Law," *Michigan Law Review* 89 (1991): 1880–1942, and "The Meanings of Shame."

42. See Mark Gustafson, "*Inscripta in fronte*: Penal Tattooing in Late Antiquity," *Classical Antiquity* 16 (1997): 79–105, on the way in which Christians used the tattoos they received as a positive symbol, and even voluntarily tattooed themselves.

43. See Julia Annas, "Shame and Shaming Punishments," paper presented to the Workshop on Law and Social Control, University of Minnesota, November 2000.

44. See James Whitman, "What Is Wrong with Inflicting Shame Sanctions?" *Yale Law Journal* 107 (1998): 1055ff.

45. See also Dan Markel, "Are Shaming Punishments Beautifully Retributive? Retributivism and the Implications for the Alternative Sanctions Debate," *Vanderbilt Law Review* (2001), who argues that it is important for reasons of impartiality that punishments be administered by the state.

46. Eric A. Posner, *Law and Social Norms* (Cambridge, MA: Harvard University Press, 2000).

47. Whitman, "What Is Wrong with Inflicting Shame Sanctions?"

48. See Markel, "Are Shaming Punishments Beautifully Retributive?"

49. This parenthesis is me talking, not Markel; he is not responsible for my interpretation of the *Groundwork*.

50. Markel's analysis is a lot more detailed than this; I have presented only a crude summary.

51. See John Braithwaite, *Crime, Shame, and Reintegration* (Cambridge and New York: Cambridge University Press, 1989).

52. See John Braithwaite, "Restorative Justice: Assessing Optimistic and Pessimistic Accounts," *Crime and Justice* 25 (1999): 1–127.

53. See Markel, *Confrontational Conception of Retributivism.*

54. See Annas, "Shame and Shaming Punishments." See also Rhode, in a comment on this chapter at Stanford, June 4, 2001.

55. See James Whitman, *Harsh Justice: Criminal Punishment and the Widening Divide between America and Europe* (New York and Oxford: Oxford University Press, 2003).

56. Archimandritou (2000), written in modern Greek. My knowledge of the argument derives from conversation with the author.

57. See my discussion of *Hudson v. Palmer* in my *Poetic Justice: The Literary Imagination and Public Life* (Boston: Beacon Press, 1995). See also Richard Posner's very interesting (dissenting) opinion in *Johnson v. Phelan*, a case involving the privacy rights of prisoners.

58. Goffman, *Stigma,* 19.

59. See David Wasserman, "Distributive Justice," in *Disability, Difference, Discrimination: Perspectives on Justice in Bioethics and Public Policy,* ed. A. Silvers, D. Wasserman, and M. Mahowald (Lanham, MD: Rowman and Littlefield, 1998), 147–208. He suggests, following Anita Silvers, that a good question to pose oneself is how the world would be if the unusual disability were in fact usual. If, for example, most people used wheelchairs, would we continue to build staircases rather than ramps?

60. John Locke, *Second Treatise on Government,* chap. 8.

61. David Gauthier, *Morals by Agreement* (New York: Oxford University Press, 1986), 18, speaking of "all persons who decrease th[e] average level" of well-being in a society.

62. John Rawls, *Political Liberalism* (New York: Columbia University Press, expanded paper edition 1996), 183 and elsewhere.

63. See Goffman, *Stigma*, 17, for a moving first-person account of the stigmatizing of the unemployed: "How hard and humiliating it is to bear the name of an unemployed man. When I go out, I cast down my eyes because I feel myself wholly inferior. When I go along the street, it seems to me that I can't be compared with an average citizen, that everybody is pointing at me with his finger."

64. January 11, 2001, 34–37.

13

THE DURATION OF SHAME: "TIME SERVED" OR "LIFETIME"?

SANFORD LEVINSON

"Shame," Martha Nussbaum writes, "targets not a single deed but the entire person. It is the person who must wear a sign, sit in the pillory, wear a tattoo for life, and so on. Shame brands this person as having, in Goffman's sense, a 'spoiled identity,' a degraded status" (this volume, p. 262). As she immediately notes, it is difficult to distinguish this from ordinary, guilt-based punishment, which, after all, incarcerates the "entire person" by way of sanctioning the "single deed." Perhaps one way to grasp the difference is by focusing on postpunishment treatment of the relevant persons. Do we, for example, view serving time (or paying a fine, for that matter) as indeed "paying one's debt to society for the specific misdeeds that justify the punishment," after which, as with those who take advantage of legal bankruptcy laws, one is given a "fresh start"? Or, on the contrary, is the operative rule (something like) "once a felon, always a felon," so that one is indeed branded with that identity, the equivalent of wearing a scarlet F?

As an empirical matter it is hard to believe that we—that is, contemporary Americans—genuinely view serving time as all that is required to provide a clean slate and a fresh start in life. For example, Nussbaum mentions the fact that many American states deny convicted felons the right to vote for the rest of their lives, even as she condemns this as a "grotesque policy." As Alex Keyssar writes, the approximately four million felons and ex-felons "constitute the largest single group of American citizens [other than children] who are barred by law from participating in elections."[1] To be sure, the Supreme Court in 1974 almost perfunctorily upheld the right of states to deny convicted felons the right to vote on the basis of a singularly wooden textual analysis of Section 2 of the Fourteenth Amendment. Even if one accepts the Court's ruling as definitive in terms of constitutional meaning, though, this obviously is irrelevant with regard to the equities of the issue. This could, after all, like the death penalty or the electoral college, be simply one more substantive injustice that is in fact tolerated by a highly imperfect Constitution.

So how should philosophical liberals—or political progressives —sympathetic to Nussbaum's general argument treat persons after their release from prison? One clue might be provided by how we refer to these persons. Are they "released felons" or, instead, "*former* felons," having been cleansed, as it were, by their time in prison? Perhaps the nub of the issue is precisely whether we use what might be termed the present-tense or past-tense modalities of speech when referring to the person in question. Nussbaum's analysis would predict that Kahan and other "shamers," including proponents of disenfranchisement, would omit the word "former," whereas devotees of her form of liberalism might insist on its use.

This is, obviously, far too simple, certainly as a matter of practice and as a matter of theory as well. As to the former, consider only that a significant post–September 11 debate revolved around the possibility that convicted criminals might be hired to inspect airline baggage and participate in other activities involving aviation security. The presupposition of almost all discussion of which I am aware is that it quite literally goes without saying that no one with a criminal record should be available for such positions. The problem, of course, might be in overgeneralizing from the term "criminal record," since this could cover a remarkable range of offenses, especially in the modern state that criminalizes many offenses that scarcely fit the classic definition of *malum in se*.

So consider the response if one suggested that paroled sex offenders—or offenders released after serving their full terms—should be legitimate candidates for a position within a school. Perhaps they have paid their debt to society, but does this fact really lead most of us to wipe their slates clean, treating their past behavior as irrelevant? Or consider a story in the December 27, 2001, *New York Times* detailing the efforts of a convicted murderer who, following his parole, attended the Arizona State Law School and who now has applied for admission to the Arizona state bar. Were I on the committee examining his (present) "character and fitness" to join the bar, I would have little hesitation to grant him membership, but I suspect that I am in a minority, except, perhaps, among legal academics who do not think all that highly of the "character and fitness" of many contemporary denizens of the bar. The *Times* had no trouble finding a number of lawyers who believe that it is almost literally unthinkable that a (former?) murderer should be welcomed into the ranks of those charged with special duties to uphold the law. Even in my own case, I confess that my willingness to admit the murderer is derived from the belief that relatively few murderers are likely to do it again. (Were this particular murderer, say, a professional hit man rather than someone who as a relatively young man exploded in fury, I would be less forgiving.) I would have greater trouble supporting admission to the bar of a convicted embezzler or con artist, since so much of lawyering involves placing great trust in a basically unmonitored lawyer.

What, if anything, justifies such cordoning off of at least some convicted criminals from the polity (as with the right to vote) and much of the economy (as with disabilities with regard to eligibility for many jobs)? Is it not (something like) a belief that their misbehavior reflects some character flaw, some disposition that is, as a matter of empirical fact, sufficiently unlikely to be removed by the process of punishment that we can offer a completely fresh start? Of course, to the extent one believes this, it is hard to explain why the penalty for *any* serious crime is not life imprisonment, since, by definition, any shorter time runs a significant risk of releasing back into the general population someone with a proved disposition toward antisocial conduct.

An intermediate position is to say that serving time (or paying a fine) can in fact be an effective means of personality re-formation, but, at the least, one would like to see some evidence of this—say, five years of impeccable conduct. It is interesting, for example, that Nussbaum emphasizes the grotesquerie of taking from convicted felons the suffrage "for life." I heartily agree with her, but would it be acceptable if the deprivation were only for five or even ten years? Similarly, even if one finds equally grotesque a lifetime ban from the job of providing security for air travelers, would one really support eligibility for such jobs of those released from prison, say, only a year or two ago?

Indeed, at the end of the day, it would be interesting to know how much Nussbaum and Kahan would actually agree or disagree with regard to such specific examples. It is hard to believe that Kahan, for all of his "communitarian" insistence on the importance of essentially Durkheimian reinforcement through shaming mechanisms of some of our basic social norms, would defend the present allocation of the suffrage or the extent of the displacement from the economy of convicted felons, just as it is equally difficult to imagine Nussbaum's adopting what I am terming the "clean-slate" view that would simply ignore a person's past misconduct after he or she has paid the Holmesian price for that act in question.

Nussbaum's most effective arguments involve conduct that most of us, at least those within the contemporary American academy (and likely to read books such as this one) believe ought not be treated as criminal (or even morally wrong) in the first place, including much sexual experimentation. There is good reason to distinguish between acts that are *malum in se* and *malum prohibitum,* though it is hardly the case that one should treat with indifference a refusal to obey all (or even many) laws in the latter category, that is, the strongest arguments for disobeying them is that they are in fact immoral, not merely that they are inconvenient or stupid, even if that be true. A morally based disobedience obviously reveals one to be a serious (and potentially admirable) individual, which makes it especially wrong to treat legal wrongdoing as such as dispositive. It is hard to make such arguments, though, if the basis of the illegal conduct is not morally based.

Indeed, Nussbaum clearly does not grant free license to sexual conduct that is indeed coercive, not to mention many other violations of the criminal code that she would no doubt condemn. So the question remains for all of us what we "do" with the convicted felon and whether, as a practical matter, our stance toward him or her—and it would be interesting in addition to test the extent to which our responses are linked to the gender of the person in question—varies by whether we identify ourselves as "liberal" or "communitarian" (or, for that matter, "conservative"), "guilt" or "shame oriented."

I also want to emphasize that what we are discussing is the more general issue of the extent to which *information* about one's past deeds should become available to others, to be used as the basis for assessment. One of the most dramatic aspects of the arguments made by proponents of "shaming" sanctions, after all, is precisely that the victims of these sanctions should be forced to abase themselves before an on-looking public. Consider, for example, the punishment discussed by Nussbaum (and defended by Kahan) of forcing some businessmen who had engaged in the crime of public urination in Hoboken to clean the streets with toothbrushes. I presume that this humiliating punishment was to be carried out at a time and place that would be observable by the general community, just as persons were once placed in stocks during the day rather than in the middle of the night. This is, of course, an example of what Michel Foucault taught all of us to refer to as the decidedly unwanted "gaze" inflicted by society on those labeled as antisocial. It is no coincidence that Jeffrey Rosen titled his recent book *The Unwanted Gaze: The Destruction of Privacy in America.*[2] Most often, we think of these gazes as involving "real-time" behavior, the observation of sexual activity, the reading of one's email, and the like.

As Foucault (among many others) also taught us, though, the ability of the state to amass information about one's past behavior also provides the material for gazing and, obviously, for inference about present possibilities. Richard Posner argued many years ago that protection of "privacy" often serves to deprive consumers of entirely relevant information. So, for example, Posner argued that someone who wishes to hire an employee should be able to gather whatever information they (rationally) believe useful to their decision making. This could well include, for example, information

about past encounters with the criminal justice system. I hypothe-
size that Kahan would be (relatively) sympathetic with Posner's
perspective and Nussbaum concomitantly unsympathetic.

Let me conclude these brief remarks by returning to the issue
of whom we welcome into the electorate (and the rest of our
society), this time focusing on those who are noncitizens. This is
particularly appropriate, I think, for a symposium whose general
theme is the inclusion or exclusion of persons from political life.
Again, one does not have to move beyond the front pages of contemporary newspapers in order to grasp the importance assigned
to one's juridical status. To what extent does the denial of voting
rights (or even, as with airport security, employment rights) to the
millions of long-term resident aliens rest on an ideology of shame?

Begin with the fact that whether a long-term resident is a citizen
or an alien is entirely a function of his or her choice. It is not analogous, for example, to the possession of a genetic predisposition
toward cancer, possession of which might be viewed as "shameful"
for the same reasons that Nussbaum outlines with regard, say, to
the "shame" inflicted on the overtly disabled or bodily deformed,
though presumably everyone in this audience, at least, agrees with
her that the infliction of such shaming in this context is indefensible. To what extent, though, is the reason our assumption that the
condition is not the person's "fault"? Given the element of agency
with regard to naturalization, do we wish to stigmatize resident
aliens and make their refusal to "join us" quite literally "shameful"?

Nussbaum is famously cosmopolitan, and I presume that she
would (properly) have trouble defending the proposition that
there is good reason to prefer an American citizen to a long-term
resident alien when hiring persons to inspect baggage or, for that
matter, when serving on juries or electing political leaders. Indeed, I think that *any* political liberal should feel hesitation in defending such practices. Again, though, I am generally uncertain
whether a critic of liberalism such as Kahan *would* offer a defense.
This ultimately is to repeat the most basic question generated
by reading both Nussbaum and Kahan, though, which is whether
declaring one's abstract commitment or opposition to a highly
generalized term like "shaming" necessarily generates particular
conclusions when one turns to the practicalities of constructing
policies adequate to the complex world within which we live.

NOTES

1. Alex Keyssar, *The Right to Vote: The Contested History of Democracy in the United States* (New York: Basic Books, 2000), 308.

2. (New York: Random House, 2000).

PART IV

SEXUAL DOMINANCE

14

GENOCIDE'S SEXUALITY

CATHARINE A. MACKINNON

. . . nor do those who commit genocide forget that to destroy a people, one must destroy the women.

—Andrea Dworkin[1]

I do not fear the shells and bombs that may fall on my house. They do not ask for my name. I fear the foot soldiers who come into my house and kill and wound in a very personal way and commit atrocities in front of my children.

—Bosnian Muslim woman[2]

To destroy a people, mass slaughter should be enough. Actual genocides testify to the contrary. Extermination destroys peoples, but peoples are also destroyed by certain acts short of killing. Sexual atrocities in particular first became highly visible as genocidal in Croatia and Bosnia-Herzegovina from 1991 to 1994. There, along with mass slaughter, Serbs aiming to eject and destroy non-Serbs as peoples sexually attacked women and some men on a mass scale.[3] Looking back from this pivotal Bosnian moment to the Holocaust of World War II, and then forward to Rwanda, where Hutus committed mass sexual atrocities against Tutsi in the 1994 genocide, focuses the question: What is the sex *doing* in the genocide? Sexuality in various forms can express, mobilize, and deploy destructive group animus with particular potency, observation of its role in these three genocidal situations suggests. But what makes sexual forms of abuse available for specifically genocidal ends? What genocidal functions does it serve? In other words, why can sexuality become an instrumentality of genocide, and how does it help destroy a people as a people?

The present tentative analysis presumes that when an attack is sexual, that fact is relevant information, on the view that social behavior is not random and that its regularities are evidence. By illustration, when batterers rape rather than beat, a specific tool of domination is selected, a distinctive message and meaning conveyed, a particular social pattern reinforced, a specific form of power drawn upon, a distinctive group dynamic expressed and enacted. When men rape and do not kill, or rape then kill, or kill then rape, the same is true in genocide. Presumably as well, tools of domination that impose social hierarchies are selected in part for their efficacy: if they did not work, or were not thought to work, they would not be used. Under precepts of diagnostic economy, the specific weapon selected may even do something that cannot be done in any other way.

To be genocidal under law, specified acts must be undertaken with intent to destroy a racial, ethnic, religious, or national group "as such."[4] For purposes of social analysis, however, individual perpetrators down the chain of command need not necessarily know why sexual means of destruction are deployed and are destructive (although often they do) in order for them to inflict such attacks and for the attacks to promote genocidal ends. The purpose of this essay is not to establish situations as genocidal through showing that certain acts for specific motives took place. It does not suggest that some sexual assaults are more serious or worse than others. It investigates and analyzes sexual atrocities that have been largely ignored within known genocidal settings. On these assumptions and observations, and for this purpose, the recurrent use of specifically sexual atrocities to destroy peoples has sources, meanings, and implications. This essay inquires into them through the Bosnian lens.

I

Sexual atrocities exploded in the Bosnian genocide; certainly awareness of them did. In the spring of 1992, Serbian men who lived next door to Muslim women for years put on flak jackets and raped their neighbors in the name of Greater Serbia, the neo-equivalent of *Lebensraum*. When Serbian military forces, regular and irregular, massed and took over town after town, Muslim and

Croat women were first raped and then slaughtered the way animals are slaughtered, their throats slit with knives, on hillsides, in yards, in their own fields. Adolescent girls torn from their families, young Muslim wives abducted with their children, were locked into former cafés or roadside hotels or shacks for animals that were recast as brothels and violated serially by soldiers for months until they escaped or died. As all non-Serbian peoples were murdered or impounded or ejected, non-Serbian women were rounded up by Serbian forces and interned in houses or former public buildings to be called out, night after night, and raped. Violently anti-Muslim and anti-Catholic epithets, slurs, and insults routinely accompanied these rapes.

Some women were held captive and repeatedly used for sex in concentration camps that were mainly for men, where the women also cooked and cleaned up after the torture of male captives. Some were impregnated, held for several months, refused abortions, and released in prisoner exchanges after abortion was unsafe. In some of the rape/death camps, men were also sexually tortured in lynchinglike atrocities, including through public attacks on their genitals. Serbian forces raped ethnic Muslim and Croat women, they said, to create what they imagined would be Serbian babies, using sex reproductively on an ethnic basis with the aim of producing a dominant ethnicity. Integral to the Serbian policy of "ethnic cleansing" (these perpetrators' euphemism for this genocide),[5] these coordinated sexual assaults were mounted for the purpose of destroying peoples of non-Serbian ethnicity in order to create an ethnically homogeneous Serbian state.[6] Hundreds of thousands of people were killed and tens of thousands of women and girls were raped.[7]

Rape and other sexual assault were also employed as genocidal spectacle in the Bosnian conflagration. Public rape served as ritual degradation of Muslim women. Serbian guards forced men to sexually assault family members and forced other family members to watch, for example.[8] Serbs filmed non-Serbian women being raped by Serbian soldiers; these films are out there, somewhere.[9] Sexuality was also enlisted to serve a more conventional propaganda function. Prior to the outbreak of violent hostilities, pornography sexualized abuse of non-Serbs, eroticizing ethnicity to denigrate the targets, desensitizing users to violence against them, priming the perpetrator group sexually for the enactment of sexual violence.[10]

In an unprecedented development, women sexually violated on the combined sex and ethnic/religious/national basis spoke out in public about what was being done to women while the genocide was still ongoing. In Bosnia, sexual atrocities were exposed after a historical period in which rape had been publicly reframed as a political outrage to women, supporting disclosure. One could say that the world came to comprehend that the Serbian campaign was genocidal (as opposed to a civil war) through understanding that the rapes in it were real and were being systematically directed against non-Serbian women. Most distinctively, in the Bosnian onslaught, sexuality, including forced sex and forced pregnancy, became conscious, organized weapons of a genocidal policy.[11] Or at least, observers distinctively became aware that it was serving this purpose, and thus collected and connected the evidence.

After Bosnia, looking back at the Holocaust, the paradigmatic genocide, can reconfigure aspects of its history that had previously formed no clear pattern. Unlike in the Bosnian setting, sexual atrocities have not been prominently visible in the Holocaust. When the Genocide Convention, written soon after, listed as part of the definition of genocide what the Nazis specifically did to try to destroy the Jews as a people, sexual atrocities were not explicitly listed. This was not, however, because no sexual atrocities had occurred, and it was not because the Holocaust had no salient sexual dimensions.[12] Rather, with survivors reticent and the rest of the world content to be relatively oblivious and complacent, sexual attacks could be minimized both in numbers and significance, the integral function of sexual violation in genocidal destruction overlooked.[13]

As Dagmar Herzog notes, "The Nazis . . . used sexuality to consolidate their appeal."[14] Hostility to Jews was sexualized in Nazi hate propaganda, a record that survives in the material itself. Julius Streicher's well-known propaganda engine, *Der Stürmer*, presents eroticized pictures and words of intense hostility toward Jews. The sexualized drawings and text convey, among other things, that the Jews should be destroyed because Jewish men take over "Aryan" women when they have sex with them. If barely sexually explicit by today's desensitized standards, *Der Stürmer,* described as "often lewd and disgusting" by the Nuremberg court,[15] is virulently anti-Semitic. Its sexualized denigration of being Jewish harnessed sexual excitement in the service of genocidal animus.[16] Yet the Third Reich is widely portrayed as antisex, George Mosse going so far as to assert that Nazism is hostile to "all printed material that . . . could produce an erotic effect."[17] In fact, precisely that was deployed by the Nazis for genocidal purposes.

The Nazis used law to control sexual activity, both wanted and unwanted, of women and men, along the lines of their genocide. Under the Third Reich, heterosexual intercourse between the group the genocide principally sought to destroy, Jews, and those it sought to establish as racially supreme, so-called Aryans, was prohibited by the Law for the Protection of German Blood and Honor enacted in 1935.[18] Its crime of so-called *Rassenschande,*[19] or racial defilement, literally race-shaming or race-rape, was directed primarily against wanted intergroup sexual intercourse on an antimiscegenation rationale. Just as antimiscegenation laws in the United States were written to protect only so-called white people from marrying people of African heritage, doing nothing for Black women who were raped by white men (which was routine and routinely permitted), *Rassenschande* was not made a crime to protect Jewish women from being raped by German men; a huge banner at a Nazi mass rally "Women and girls! The Jews are your seducers!"[20] patently referred to German women and girls. It was to keep German women for German men, to create a pretext for prosecuting Jewish men, and to stigmatize the sexuality of Jewish women and men to further dehumanize the group. The blood-and-honor law was variously enforced and ignored, making Jewish people vulnerable to capricious denunciations while successfully stigmatizing Jewish women and men sexually.[21]

Ensuring the triumph of the master race called for not only preventing "blood"-mixing with "undesirables" but for supporting the propagation of racially desirable children. Sexuality was thus impressed into affirmative reproductive service under the Third Reich. The aim of Himmler's *Lebensborn* project was for German men to reproduce with women of "Aryan" racial stock.[22] About 20,000 children were estimated to have been born in *Lebensborn* homes in Germany and Nazi-occupied Norway; there were more in France, Belgium, and Luxembourg.[23] Whether the *Lebensborn* program per se initiated pregnancies or only welcomed already pregnant women is disputed. Indeed, whether women voluntarily had sex with Nazis and were then warmly received or lucked onto or were dragooned into the *Lebensborn* maternity homes after illegitimate conception; whether the women were impregnated consensually or forcibly, abducted or romanced; the degree to which even physically unforced participation (including of German women) was manipulated or pressured under the official program; and whether the resulting children were stolen or abandoned or exterminated by the Germans—all this remains fairly murky. Some evidence exists for each description.[24] *Lebensborn* clearly intended to stimulate propagation of a master race through reproductive means. Whether or not the program encompassed sexual intercourse, that had to happen for it to proceed. But neither the Nuremberg prosecutors, who investigated the project quite extensively, nor contemporary historians, concerned to avoid the titillating,[25] have investigated the sexual conditions of the impregnations involved.

Lebensborn baby-catching certainly converged with large-scale impregnation of non-German women by German soldiers. Thousands of French women conceived with German military occupiers, attracting the racial scrutiny of the Nazis, who impounded them and the children if deemed desirable, or exterminated them if not.[26] Yet whether any of these women were raped seems not to have been asked then or since. Nordic women who conceived with German soldiers were often brutally stigmatized as traitors in their own communities, the resulting children spirited away to foster parents in Germany or exterminated—again depending on Nazi judgments of their racial value. Although it is widely conceded that the German occupation of Nordic countries relied on terror and violent repression of the population, and some claims are being brought at long last on behalf of the forsaken *Lebensborn* children,[27] no actual information has yet emerged on whether the sexual relations the Nordic and other women had with German soldiers leading to these births was forced or free. Most sources coyly assume the latter.[28]

The Nuremberg prosecutors' accounts of Nazi eugenic practices that amounted to forced abortions of non-German women

who worked as slaves, by contrast, are factually detailed, straight-
forward, and conceptually fairly subtle on the same questions:

> The Nazis paid lip service to the idea that all abortions were volun-
> tary but this was obviously not the case. These unfortunate women
> working as slaves under terrible conditions in a hostile country
> found themselves subjected to all manner of pressure, both direct
> and indirect. They lived and labored under conditions which would
> not permit them to take care of their children. Moreover, every
> pregnancy had to be reported to the dreaded Gestapo. The sugges-
> tions of an abortion by that organization did not invite argument
> from Polish and Russian women. . . . [Abortion] was nothing more
> than another technique in furtherance of the basic crime of geno-
> cide and Germanization.[29]

Women under occupation also lived under conditions of severe
constraint—conditions under which they are widely supposed to
have been having a fling.

To this day, the absence of interest in the sexual conditions
under which women conceived with German soldiers during military occupation is matched by a lack of inquiry into how the enslaved women who had the forced abortions became pregnant.
It is not known whether they were pregnant only with men of
their own nationalities or whether the sex preceding the unwanted
pregnancy was wanted. One recent study based on contemporane-
ous documents and interviews with witnesses and survivors sub-
stantiates the fact of forced abortions and killings of newborns of
Polish forced laborers in Germany, but as to the sex that produced
the pregnancies, this is all that is said: "Many of the children had
been fathered by local men who took sexual advantage of these
young foreign girls who had neither rights nor advocates."[30] When
it comes to having sex, though, the "terrible conditions in a hostile
country" under which the enslaved women were "subjected to all
manner of pressure, both direct and indirect" are not even mentioned. If women could not care for any children they might conceive and had to report their pregnancies to the dreaded Gestapo,
can the meaningfulness of their initiative or control over the
sexual interactions in which they became pregnant, even with men
of their own group, be presumed? What of those pregnancies
caused by German men? If abortion under these circumstances

was Germanization, and "nothing more than another technique in furtherance of the basic crime of genocide," what was the sex that preceded it?

Moreover, to assume that there was no forced sex between Jewish women and German men because all sex between them was illegal, while doubtless a deterrent in some instances, is not only to misunderstand the primary point of the *Rassenschande* law, which was to prohibit mutually desired sexual contact between Jewish people and "Aryans." It is also to conflate wanted and unwanted sex, to minimize the extent to which sexuality was harnessed for genocide by the Third Reich, and to substitute presumption for evidence. Reports of Jewish women being raped by German men during the Holocaust are scant; analysts who stress their exceptionality are plentiful. For Jews who survived and for their successor communities, identification of facts *of* sexual assault—even if their shame rightly belongs to the perpetrators—seems to entail identification *with* those facts, making their relative obscurity unsurprising. Underreporting of sexual assault even under better circumstances together with the utter absence of responsive authorities to whom to report, combined with overwhelming starvation and mass murder demanding priority, suggest that such evidence as does exist may be the tip of an iceberg.

Sexual contact across the group lines that marked the Shoah was a crime when wanted but appears likely to have been ignored when forced by members of the dominating group, particularly by its military men, on the subordinated one. Actually, reports of forced sex during the Holocaust seem more prominent in accounts of the period than they have been since. One book published in 1943, with supporting first-person affidavits from Warsaw in 1940, stated simply:

> The racist principles of the Nuremberg Laws were not always strictly applied by the Germans to the Jews of Poland. This was especially true of the primary racist tenet which forbids the mixing of Aryan with Jewish blood. Nazis forced their way into Jewish houses and raped Jewish women, and even young girls. Their brutality in such cases reached extreme proportions.[31]

Single girls and young women were reported raped prior to being murdered in *Einsatzgruppen* actions.[32] A well-documented early report recounts a Warsaw ghetto *Judenrat* was ordered by the Nazi health department to set up a brothel of fifty Jewish women for the use of German soldiers: "Don't let the race-laws bother you," a Nazi official reportedly said. "War is war, and in such a situation all theories die out."[33] In 1942, the *New York Times* printed extracts of a translated letter from a Jewish schoolgirl from Krakow describing the intended suicide by poison of herself and ninety-two of her fellow students rather than submit to the prostitution imminently to be forced upon them by German soldiers.[34] Hilberg notes an archival document of 1943 reporting that "German private army managers kept Jewish women as sexual slaves" in the Galician area of Poland.[35] Without being able to know for certain in hindsight if the acts were freely willed or forced, Birgit Beck interprets wartime documents estimating that between 50 and 80 percent of the SS and police forces stationed in Eastern Europe fell afoul of the standards of the racial laws through acts in which coerced intercourse played a role.[36] Some Jewish women said they were raped by Gentiles when in hiding,[37] but "the Anne Franks who survived rape don't write their stories."[38]

Concentration camp settings provide further accounts. One survivor reported her uncle said he witnessed mass raping of Jewish girls who were then buried alive in mass graves they had been forced to dig.[39] One survivor was told by a mother that, in a forced labor camp, "she was forced to undress her daughter and to look on while the girl was violated by dogs whom the Nazis had specially trained for this sport" and that "[t]hat happened to other girls."[40] One survivor, after describing Jewish girls taken out of her block to be raped, said: "Rape of Jewish girls was allowed. That was no *Rassenschande*."[41] And the direct: "I was raped in Auschwitz."[42] One consequence of these actions being legally forbidden appears to have been that the women were frequently killed afterward.[43] Since so many of these women were killed anyway, their sexual injuries were submerged in the tide of murder.

Historians who pronounce rape rare under the Third Reich plainly are not thinking of the brothels in these terms.[44] Under the Nazis after 1939, prostitution was legal, institutionalized, and officially run throughout the Reich.[45] The Nazis seem to have thought that using women sexually served to motivate men to fight and work harder.[46] State- and police-run brothels were organized in communities for civilians, military brothels were set up for the *Wehrmacht,* foreign women were impressed into brothels for the foreign slave laborers, and prisoners were used in brothels in the concentration and extermination camps by the captives and staff of those camps. These brothels were organized along genocidal lines in two ways. People at the bottom of the Nazi social hierarchy, who could only use and be used by their own group in the brothels, were sexually constrained by the racial laws. The SS elite ignored those laws (as did the *Wehrmacht* generally at least until 1942),[47] making the brothels just one more way that Jewish women could be destroyed.

At Himmler's determined instigation, there were at least nine brothels in the concentration camp system by the end of the war, Christa Paul estimates.[48] Many women imprisoned in Ravensbrück were forced or recruited into them, as well as into the army and the SS brothels.[49] Before the Nazis embraced prostitution, tens of thousands of prostitutes had been sent to concentration camps as "asocial"; some of them, along with women impounded for *Rassenschande,* were then forced to work in the brothels, sexually exploited twice over.[50] Women who "volunteered" were told they would be fed, would not have to work, and would be released after six months of "service to clients."[51] "SS men were known to occasionally 'try out' a volunteer before rendering a decision on her qualifications."[52] Some of the brothel women were German, Polish, Chechen, Russian, and Hungarian; women in the brothels for foreign workers were of the same nationalities as the slave laborers. However, ten women recruits arriving at Flossenburg for the brothel were described by one surviving prisoner as "almost all Jews and Gypsies."[53] In the slave labor camps, where brothel visits were rewards for exceptional productivity at work, records were kept of visits, and payment was made through labor coupons.[54] For food to stay alive, to keep better jobs, and for protection from other sexual aggression, many young men in the concentration camps became "dolly-boys" of Kapos and other privileged inmates, who used them sexually nightly.[55] The men who used the camp brothel women were mainly Jewish,[56] but block seniors and Kapos (far fewer in number and often not Jewish) used them as well.

Jewish women were imprisoned in special brothels in some places for use by the elite SS guards.[57] One report from a woman survivor who was used in this way recounts that attractive women at the first selection at Auschwitz were "ordered out of the line" and subsequently "used for the most licentious purposes, kept alive solely to satisfy the base instincts of several sadistic and bestial Nazis."[58] A document at the time confirms that the women for the brothels "would be selected by the doctor and the commander, went on the transport, the best for the SS and officers, the worse quality for the prisoners."[59] One survivor recalls, "Despite the Nazi theories on racial pollution, we heard that a number of attractive internees were drafted for these brothels."[60] Christa Paul concludes, "No doubt remains that, despite the prohibition on intercourse with Jews, Jewish women were taken away to military brothels. . . . The women had to sexually serve the soldiers under threat of death."[61] Thus did the Nazis institutionalize the violation of their own sexual racial laws. The women in the camp and army brothels were forced to exchange sex for survival and freedom;[62] as often happens in prostitution, the exchange largely failed them. Most were exterminated. (This did not prevent the later insinuation that any woman survivor had whored.)[63] Although the realities varied by time and place, these brothels, where serial rape was organized in the form of prostitution, functioned integrally to the genocide.

Survivor chronicles of the period provide a wider context in which everyday life for the women of the genocidally targeted group both in and outside camps contains features of prostitution. The extreme vulnerability of Jews under genocidal conditions, starving and desperate, facing death at every turn, meant that sex could be, and therefore often was, exacted to make life possible. Survivor accounts of the time, in and outside camps, provide windows into lives lived on prostitution's terms: rape for survival. "Women were prepared to sell their bodies for food."[64] With starvation, "food was the coin that paid for sexual privileges."[65] Perhaps better: sex was the coin that paid for the privilege of staying alive. One woman raised orthodox in Chelm described being taken aback when her mother told her to "do anything anybody asks you to do, just so you save your life." Months later, she remembered this when "faced with a situation in which I had to make a snap decision about bestowing a sexual favor in exchange for a temporary rescue from the German authorities."[66] In such a situation, intimate access becomes at once a currency of exchange and a tool for dehumanization. Any glimmer of humanity involved looms larger in fiction than in recorded historical reality; presumably, where humanity was found, survival did not come at a sexual price. In the Holocaust, a corrupted sexual economy of force targeted Jewish women for prostitution in all its forms, integrally to the genocidal destruction of the Jewish people.

Sexual aggression in the KZ setting that took advantage of genocidal vulnerabilities and furthered genocidal aims was hardly limited to heterosexual intercourse. On admission to the camps, women were made to strip, stand genitally exposed on two stools where they were internally searched and genitally shaved while being sexually ridiculed. In one account, women were reported forced to lie on their sides naked while being poked in their private parts as SS officers gawked and jeered.[67] A member of the Sonderkommando reported that one SS officer "had the custom of standing at the doorway . . . and feeling the private parts of the young women entering the gas bunker. There were also instances of SS men of all ranks pushing their fingers into the sexual organs of pretty young women."[68] After Jewish women were gassed, they were then "also searched to see if they had not hidden jewelry in the intimate parts of their bodies."[69] As Myrna Goldenberg observed, "[N]ot only were they violated in life, but they were violated in death as well."[70]

Jews were live pornography for Nazis when the SS leader at Auschwitz "had holes drilled in the brothel rooms for himself and his SS underlings, so that they would get a good look at the 'love life' of their prisoners,"[71] and when Jewish men nearly dead in the freezing experiments were put into bed with naked women to see if "animal heat" would revive them.[72] The sexual use of Jewish women in camps was organized as public sexual spectacle when they were made to exercise naked so German guards could watch, or, just before being killed in gas chambers, to run naked to be filmed by guards. The films remain.[73] How they were used at the time is not yet publicly known. The dehumanization and humiliation of these Jewish women was clearly sexual, its link with their murders at once enhancing the sexual potency of the films and underlining their place in the genocide. Finally, the most explicit instances of sexual sadism were not *Rassenschande;* the torture that

was also sex was allowed and sexual precisely because it was inflicted by Germans as supposed superiors on Jews as supposed
inferiors.

If a pattern of the use of sex to destroy a people can be dis-
cerned in hindsight under the Third Reich, it takes no reconstruction to discern it in the Rwandan genocide of April to July 1994.[74]
There, integral to the organized slaughter of half a million to a
million people in under four months, Hutus raped and otherwise
sexually violated Tutsi women en masse as part of the attempted
destruction of that ethnic group as such.[75] In some cases, the leaders, such as Laurent Semanza, ordered these killings. A credible
witness claims he said the following: "Are you sure you're not
killing Tutsi women and girls before sleeping with them. . . . You
should do that and even if they have some illness, you should do it
with sticks."[76] Interahamwe men went through Tutsi women like
scythes through wheat fields. Some observers say that not a single
Tutsi woman or girl who remains alive from the conflagration was
not sexually assaulted.[77] "[R]ape was the rule and its absence the
exception."[78] Vicious sexualization and denigrating sexual stereo-
typing of Tutsi women was a staple on the radio and in newspapers
preceding and throughout the atrocities.[79] Many sexual attacks
as public spectacle were also reported.[80] Anti-Tutsi slogans made
their genocidal animus and objective vivid.[81] Rape and other sexual violence were often accompanied by "humiliating utterances,
which clearly indicated that the intention underlying each specific
act was to destroy the tutsi group as a whole . . . [for example,]
'The pride of the Tutsis will end today.'"[82] Each genocide is
unique, but perhaps Bosnia provided or exposed a new model of
the mass instrumentalization of sexuality for genocidal purposes.
It certainly advanced awareness of sexual atrocities in genocides by
outsiders.

II

What accounts for the presence of sexual atrocities in genocide?
The ubiquity of rape and other sexual abuse in social life does not
fully explain its particular escalation and chosen deployment for
specifically genocidal ends. Nor does the violence of genocides or
violence in general fully explain the specifically sexual forms that

violence takes, when it does. Given the ubiquity of male dominance and the place of rape in it, no doubt men rape in part
because and when they can, so that anything that increases opportunity, access, and impunity increases sexual assaults. But neither
chaos hypotheses nor opportunism completely accounts for the
decision and policy and planned campaign of sexual forms of
abuse—including rape both executed under orders and perva-
sively permitted, live sexual spectacles, and pornography—for the
purpose of destroying groups on a racial, ethnic, national, or religious basis that is in evidence in genocidal settings. Perhaps the
reasons sexual abuse is functional are specific to each genocide.
But the increasingly prominent, perhaps increasing, role of mass
sexual atrocities in the genocides that marked the late twentieth
century frames the more general question: How and why do sexual
attacks destroy a people?

While the genocidal utility of rape seems obvious to those who
do it, its genocidal role has been long denied or elided, continuing to elude some observers who enter after the fact.[83] As legal
interpretation (approached here as statutory construction), the
conceptual fit of sexual assault in genocide is not difficult, however. Under the Genocide Convention (1949), genocide occurs
when any of a list of acts is "committed with intent to destroy, in
whole or in part, a national, ethnical, racial or religious group, as
such."[84] The covered acts include killing group members, causing
them serious bodily or mental harm, deliberately inflicting on
them conditions of life calculated to physically destroy the group,
and imposing measures intended to prevent births within the
group. As a matter of usage, the term *genocide* is not considered
legally applicable unless large numbers of people are so treated,
and many are killed on purpose.

In this framework, once intent and group ground are established, obviously many acts short of extermination contribute to
the destruction of peoples as such, hence are genocidal.[85] Although it has always been a legal (as well as real) fact that not only
killing is genocidal, the recognition of this has grown in part due
to the visibility of rape in genocides since the Bosnian one.[86] Sexual atrocities readily fit into the definition's subcategories. Some
victims are raped to death or otherwise lethally assaulted sexually
(such as vaginally penetrated with machetes and other objects).

Rape necessarily inflicts serious bodily and mental harm.[87] Systematic rape over time, imposed as a condition of life, is physically destructive. Perhaps the least numerically significant of sexuality's roles in genocide seems most easily grasped by many: every woman pregnant with the child of an attacking group is prevented from conceiving a child of other biological heritage. Each act of sexual abuse committed with intent to destroy the (usually) women of a group defined by its nationality, ethnicity, religion, and/or race is therefore legally an act of genocide. Rapes undertaken as part of a genocide in fact are thus genocidal in law,[88] as the Rwanda Tribunal recognized in *Akayesu*.[89]

On many levels, rape is rape. Yet genocidal rape can be distinguished, for example, from rape in war in a number of respects. Even though many civilians are often killed in wars because of who they are, and genocides can be carried out in part through war, war is not always genocidal. Rape is pervasive in wars and often has an ethnic component, such as in the "Rape of Nanking" during which Japanese military forces mass raped Chinese women,[90] or the rape of German women by the invading Russian forces at the end of World War II. In neither situation were the rapes genocidal because neither situation was a genocide: there was no intent to destroy the peoples as such on the proscribed grounds. Similarly, rape on an ethnic or national basis can be officially organized in war, as with the so-called comfort women—the Japanese government's organized use of women of various ethnicities (prominently Korean) as sexual slaves to service Japanese military men during World War II. This forced prostitution was officially organized ethnic rape, but if it lacked intent to destroy their ethnic groups as such, it was not genocidal. As a weapon or tool of war, rape in war aims to further the war effort, whether that is taking over land, government, or people, or pacifying and motivating soldiers. As a by-product of war, rape in war also merges with male violence in war and generally. Rape in war is a war crime. It is not genocidal until it is part of an aim to destroy a people as such on one of the listed grounds. The rapes of Jewish women during World War II are commonly misinterpreted as a side effect of the war, although they were as genocidal as the Holocaust to which they were integral.

Genocide is a war against peoples, which legally speaking is not a war at all.[91] The line between genocide and war is not always a fine one in practice, as conflicts like that in Guatemala, with its combined political war and genocidal attacks on Mayan peasants that included sexual atrocities, illustrate. But the line is there. War by definition takes place between combatants, whether regulars or irregulars, usually for territory or state rule. The target of genocides is groups in civil society; the goal is their destruction as such, not simply their rule. Genocides are often carried out with only one side armed, as under the Third Reich and in Bosnia-Herzegovina, with the victims having no army of their own. War has combatants on at least two sides; rape in war is also typically bilateral in being inflicted on women on both sides of the conflict. Genocide is relentlessly one-sided. So is rape in genocide, even when the genocide is carried out in part through war, and some war-related rape occurs on both sides, as it usually does (and did in Germany and in Bosnia-Herzegovina). If the targets of a genocide eventually manage to fight back, its victims do not simply become the civilian casualties of war, making the question of the role of rape in genocide one version of its role in war. The victims of some war rapes do not even know which soldiers or side raped them.[92] Genocidal rapes do not happen this way. In genocides, the perpetrators and the victims know who they are in terms of group identification. None of the participants are under any illusions: their social group membership is why the rape is happening.

Descriptively, rape in war (the role of which is also doubtless incompletely understood) aims to terrorize and degrade, hence demoralize, the vanquished, to symbolically and sexually reward and revenge the victors, and/or to interrupt reproductive continuity.[93] It has been used as a ritual of degradation of the other side, a way of instilling terror, a tactic of demoralization, a plundering of booty, and a humiliation rite for the men on the other side who cannot (in masculinity's terms) protect "their" women. Many of these acts make women's bodies into a medium of men's expression, the means through which one group of men says what it wants to say to another. Apart from affirming manhood, which rape always does, rape in war thus serves as specific psychological warfare and method of communication, providing symbolic as well as actual reward and symbolic as well as actual revenge. It means supremacy: we are better than you. And possession: we own you.

Rapes in genocide often have the same or similar effects and often work in the same or similar ways. But only when the purpose, the victory, is the destruction of the peoples of which the raped is a member, only when the message as well as the means is the destruction of peoples as such, is the rape genocidal. For that, it need not take place in a war.

What further marks rape in war, which generally happens through cadre initiative, is its mostly out-of-control quality. It is what armed men do in groups when there is nothing to stop them. Rape in genocide is anything but rape out of control. It is rape under control. Men do it in groups usually because they are told or encouraged or systematically permitted or ordered to, knowing they are doing it as members of their race, ethnicity, religion, or nationality. It happens on purpose, not just with the function of harming people, or of having sex, or of planting a flag, but to destroy peoples as such on the designated group bases. The destruction of peoples on the group basis is not a by-product of the rape. It is its point.

Genocide goes beyond war. It can, and does, take place in civil society and among noncombatants, outside any armed conflict proper. Its specific purpose to end the existence of a people marks the sexual atrocities that take place in it. Genocide is actually more continuous with discrimination than with war: it is a violent practice of discrimination. It is extreme inequality, effectuated through systematic violence—violence that is sometimes spearheaded through a state and sometimes more loosely deployed through cadres or unofficial military forces. Even if sexual atrocities do in genocides some things that they do in wars, and even if genocides are carried out in part through wars, genocides, and the genocidal work performed in them by sexual assault, remain distinct phenomena.[94]

III

Genocide, both in reality and by conventional definition, is defined by the intent to destroy "groups as such." If all members of a group are killed, the group is presumably destroyed as such. But genocide is defined by aim, not success, and acts that aim at destroying a group as such "in part" are also genocidal. Destruction, in other words, is more than killing. The core of what makes acts genocidal is the meaning of "as" in relation to the groups whose grounds are prohibited as a basis for destruction. What does it mean to be killed or raped *as* a member of one's group—as a Jewish woman or as a Tutsi woman—and how is that combined group dimension to be known, evidenced, identified? The same question arises in discrimination law—for example, in asking whether a sexually harassed woman is harassed because she is a woman, that is, whether her sexual abuse is "based on sex," or harassed "based on race and sex."

In the law of genocide, the term "group as such," although key to distinguishing genocides from other mass atrocities, has to date been given little clear meaning on its own. Most crimes, including international ones, are traditionally conceived as acts of individuals against individuals. This seems to make the collective quality of some crimes—those not merely mass in numbers but inherently group based in nature—difficult for law to grasp and articulate. Authorities accordingly tend to collapse the "group as such" element into the *mens rea* of "willful destruction" or to treat it as an appendage to the numerical calculus of "in whole or in part."[95] In *Eichmann,* the term was part of the scale or overarchingness of the crime—"the all-embracing total form which this crime is liable to take."[96] Even when not wrong, clarifying language often tends to restate what is to be clarified, as when the Ad Hoc Committee on Genocide (1948) said that "as such" means "qua group,"[97] or when the International Tribunal for the Former Yugoslavia (ICTY) said that "the significance of the phrase 'as such'" is that the evidence must establish that "the group had been targeted, and not merely specific individuals within that group."[98] Although arguably crucial in distinguishing genocide from other crimes, the "as such" element has often functioned as a makeweight, adding little or nothing unique. But it is more than a highlighter or backstop for other terms.

Coming close to the heart of the matter, the International Law Commission explained that, under the Genocide Convention, "the intention must be to destroy the group 'as such,' meaning as a separate and distinct entity, and not merely some individuals because of their membership in a particular group."[99] Homing in more precisely, the Commission of Experts on war crimes in the former Yugoslavia explained that "as such" indicated that "the crimes against a number of individuals must be directed against them in their collectivity or at them in their collective character or capacity."[100] The Rwanda Tribunal in its *Akayesu* opinion advanced furthest: "The victim of the act is therefore a member of a group, chosen as such, which, hence, means that the victim of the crime of genocide is the group itself and not only the individual."[101] As this insight was later formulated in *Rutuganda*, "as such" means "the victim of the crime of genocide is the group itself and not the individual alone."[102] To attempt to destroy a group "as such" is thus to attack, through attacking group members because they are group members, that aspect of the group whole that is more than the sum of its individual parts, that quality of collectivity and identifications that make up the substance and glue of community that lives on when individual members die. In some real sense, to destroy a group, especially to end it forever, is to destroy the idea and meaning of it within and between those whose relationships comprise it.

Now notice that what is done in genocides to destroy women of racially, ethnically, nationally, or religiously designated groups is routinely done to women everywhere every day on the basis of their sex. All the sexual atrocities that become genocidal in genocides are inflicted on women every day under conditions of sex inequality. Arguably, they are inflicted on them as women.[103] Rape, prostitution, forced pregnancy, forced and precluded abortion, violating sexual spectacles, pornography—all of these are inflicted on women not only within wars and genocides but outside them, because they are women, often because they are women of a specific race, ethnicity, religion, nationality. In this light, examination of genocidal sexual atrocities, as one potent form of group destruction short of physical extermination, may illuminate the crucial but shadowy legal element of destruction "as such."[104] Why sexuality can be made to work genocidal destruction and what the term "as such" means may thus have simultaneous answers close at hand.

Consider that sexual atrocities, acts in which men dominate women on the basis of sex, destroy women as such, both as individuals and as a group.[105] Sexual atrocities on this analysis are inherently collective crimes, directed against the group through violating its members, meaningless without the social meaning of being a woman that they destroy (and in destroying, in part create). This well-traveled road then becomes one avenue to destruction of groups on the basis of ethnicity, race, religion, and nationality, when the women of those groups are destroyed in that same way. Every day, the existence of the group—women—is not sought to be ended in the precisely genocidal sense of extermination, but it is precluded as human. Many women are killed for misogynistic reasons;[106] sexual atrocities might be said to seek the destruction of the group women as such in the sense of debasing their human status or creating them in the image of a socially destroyed self. Just as an ethnic group can be destroyed without killing all its members, perhaps the group women illustrates how a group can be destroyed while leaving its members alive and seeming intact, subordinated as lesser humans, with sexual atrocities distinctively performing this function. If this is right, rape in genocide—gender combined with ethnicity, nationality, or religion in genocidal rape—does to women and men on a combined sex and racial, ethnic, national, and religious basis what rape does to women outside genocides on a sex and gender basis every day.

Suppose further that this same behavior of sexual subordination, outside war and genocide, also contributes to creating women as a subordinated group under conditions of sex inequality by defining them as a group, hence individually, on the basis of their social availability for sexual use and abuse.[107] Perhaps women are destroyed as a people as such by this—so destroyed as such as never to have been thought of as a "people" at all. Women are thus created as a destroyed group in part through sexual abuse. In this light, sexual assault destroys women as women, including their capacity to cohere as such, just as genocidal rape destroys or seeks to destroy Muslims and Croats and Tutsis and Jews, defining, and in so doing in part constituting, the groups as subordinated peoples. Pioneered and practiced on women as such with stunning effectiveness on a daily basis, rape can just as effectively destroy peoples as such on racial, ethnic, national, and religious grounds. Thus, men do to women (and some men) through sexual abuse outside of genocides what some men do in genocides when they sexually abuse women (and some men, especially sexually defined groups of men such as gay men) on the basis of their ethnicity, religion, nationality, or race.

Much sexual attack outside genocides is ethnic and racially inflected and grounded much of the time, of course, even as much racist violence is sexual.[108] This confluence points up the continuity between rape in and out of genocide without making each instance of ethnic rape genocidal, the relation between discrimination and genocide being one of degree.[109] Enslaved women of African descent in the United States, for example, were raped as chattel for both sexual and reproductive purposes, including to increase the slave labor force. Since slavery, African American women have been raped by white men to subordinate them based on their ethnicity and sex combined, fusing racism with sexism. This process, needless to say, has been extremely destructive of African peoples in America even though the presence of an intent to destroy them as such in the sense of the legal definition of genocide may be questionable.[110] In a reality that highlights the artificiality of the intent requirement in the genocide definition, these rapes in particular, however destructive they were to the women and the communities, were not arguably for the purpose of destroying a people, but for enslaving a people, and to use, denigrate, and subordinate African American women as women.

But *why* does sexual assault destroy groups? In genocidal rape, ethnic or racial or religious identity, combined with sex, is the basis for intimate violation. Socially, sexuality means intimacy; forced sex violates a person in a way that, as intimate, is seen and experienced as especially violating. As sex is relational, sexual atrocities destroy relationships. Perhaps in part because it is seen and felt to destroy one's humanity and relational place in community indelibly and irreparably, in a way the victim never lives without, rape is sometimes termed "worse than death."[111] A Rwandan witness testified that a woman "who was left for dead by those who raped her, had indeed been killed in a way."[112] People identify closely with their sexual selves; sexuality is socially central to gender identity, both to oneself and to others. When that is seen as having been violated, one's self is often experienced as spoiled, stolen, ruined. Sexuality socially means possession; forced sex means that the raped belongs to the rapist, instead of to herself or to the people with whom she identifies herself and to whom she gives herself intimately. It is the identity and identification that are destroyed when this particular form that humanity takes when embodied in group identity is violated, destroyed. This may go some way to explain why rape destroys women as such: it violates the female-identified part of a woman, a deeply and closely held aspect of self-conception that intrinsically involves identification with, and identification by others with,[113] one's group. It is an inherently relational and collective element of identity. When women are raped because they are Muslim women or Jewish women or Tutsi women, it works on the combined grounds in the same way.

Genocidal rape parallels rape outside genocidal contexts in its combination of systematicity and randomness. Women every day are raped, systematically, as women, and are randomly selected as individuals within that group, sometimes systematically on an ethnic or other group basis. The way genocide works is similar: people are selected systematically for domination as peoples by randomly, within the group, picking out certain ones for certain atrocities, sometimes systematically on sex or other group basis. The atrocities against each individual function to destroy the solidarity of—terrorize and control and subject, that is, work the destruction of—the group. Genocidal rape is thus doubly effective. Being relatively random within the group while systematic to the group as such, rape works the same way in male dominance generally that genocidal rape works in genocide: it creates dominance of the men of one ethnic group over the men and women of another by destroying the group's definition as one of dignity, security, and self-determination, and replacing it with fear, self-revulsion, and degraded identity.

Functionally, what sexual assault does on the basis of race, ethnicity, religion, and nationality is what it does on the basis of sex: create a cowed, submissive, controllable, terrorized, dissociated group of people who know this could be done to them at any time, who feel shame at being who they are, who want to leave the place that happened and never come back, who may hate themselves and despise others who are identified with them by their common ability to be subjected to this form of abuse at any time, who are often socially regarded as a lower form of life because this is something that can be and has been done to them, who may identify with and even idealize their violators even as they, and often because they, fear them. People who are seen as, and see themselves as, stained and stigmatized by having been used and being usable sexually will do a lot to avoid being a person who is treated this way. If and when these effects do not happen, it is because resistance has succeeded. But just because the Holocaust did not succeed in destroying the Jews as such does not mean it was not genocidal.

Attempting to avoid rape, meaning, under these circumstances, avoiding being much of who one is, to oneself and others, can be a form of resistance but can also create a captive, compliant population with an urgent desire to please its captors and to display its compliance. For lack of a better descriptive vocabulary, all the signs of mass posttraumatic stress, including denial, fear, disidentification, and sometimes identification with the aggressor[114] characterize large numbers of women. So, classically, do dispossessed survivor groups subjected to genocidal attacks, at least for a time. Literal disassociation may operate on an interpersonal and social level as powerfully as it does on an individual psychological one. Rape is thus an excellent means of social control and domination, as the evidence of the group women—many of whom have been raped at least once by conventional definition,[115] many of whom have been sexually assaulted many times over—eloquently testifies. It should be no surprise that sexual abuse works in controlling and dominating ethnically, racially, and religiously defined populations as well.

In other words, if what effectively destroys women as such (with or without intent to do so) is done to an ethnic group as part of a genocide, not only will the women of that group be destroyed on the basis of their sex and ethnicity combined; the acts in so doing will work to destroy the ethnic group as such. Women are a subordinated group throughout the world; sexuality is used both to create the sex women as such and to destroy them as such; sexual assault both subordinates them as women one at a time and keeps them a subordinated group. What creates and defines women as a subordinated group—vulnerability and subjection to sexual assault—engenders disidentification with women as a people, destroying women as a people. Identification with the identity sought to be appropriated and defiled can reclaim and restore part of what the rape destroyed: the particularity of one's humanity and the particular meaning of collective identity. This partly explains why understanding that one was raped as a woman, not as an individual—identification with women in that sense—can be experienced as affirming and healing. It can go some distance to restore the specific part of one's humanity that sexual violation took away.

Sexual atrocities thus give a distinctive content to the term "as such" in genocide's definition. Just as women very often want to leave where they were raped and never return, making rape a useful weapon for forcing deportation, sexual atrocities can reasonably produce revulsion to the identity that marked the person for the intimate violation, making the raped want to abandon who they are forever. When the shared identity for which one is raped is ruined, shattered in oneself and relationally between oneself and others, the group quality of the group so defined is destroyed. In this respect, as others, rape functions much like torture can when inflicted on a group basis. When Jewish women were sexually used in brothels in concentration camps during the Holocaust, they were used as Jewish women "as such," no matter who else was used with them.[116]

Sexual atrocities shatter community, the ability to relate and cohere through a common identification, to identify with one another. As in life outside genocide, this result can be aggravated or mitigated depending on whether the men and women of the targeted communities reject or support those who are sexually violated. It is common for victims to be rejected. As one survivor of genocidal rape in Rwanda put it, "[A]fter rape, you don't have value in the community."[117] Whatever the response, the destructive power of sexual assault—robust across cultures, if with variations —seems to lie in what rape means: the (usually) women have been intimately violated, subjugated, claimed for the other, used, defiled, ruined, lowered. Just as women often do not want to identify with one another, members of communities subjected to genocidal attack through sexual atrocities often disidentify as well. Rape is human code for domination, for being made less, for subjugation per se; it means violation itself, inferiority as such. Even if members are left alive, their cohesion, their identification with one another, the identification of others with them, can be destroyed. In this light, what rape does in genocide is what it does the rest of the time: ruins identity, marks who you are as less, hence devastates community, the glue of group. It destroys the willingness to identify with the group designation on the basis of which the rape took place, hence works to destroy the group as such. Who wants to be one of them?

The term "symbolic" is sometimes used for such a function or consequence. However intangible, it is highly material: it is what makes a group be a group that is destroyed. To destroy a group "as such" is to attack the groupness of the group, its meaning to its members and others. Sexual atrocities despoil and rupture the meaning of the group identity through making it an object of violation, ultimately (as is the case for women) through making the group name mean violation itself. To be sexually attacked on the basis of being a woman or a Muslim woman or a Tutsi woman, to be raped by men who "ask for my name,"[118] thereafter indelibly stains the group name as it becomes part of defining what being a member of that group means.

Women not being considered a people, there is as yet no international law against destroying the group women as such. "Sex" is not on the list of legal grounds on the basis of which destruction of peoples as such is prohibited. For women as such, there is no legal equivalent to genocide—the destruction of women as such that Andrea Dworkin proposed calling gynocide[119]—presumably because it is commonplace, built into the relative status of the sexes in everyday life. That the destruction of the group women may often not be intentional in the way the conventional definition of genocide requires serves to underscore the fact that no law has been shaped to the realities of the destruction of the group women, as it has for some destruction of groups defined on other grounds. Because much sexual force is built into existing social standards for how sexuality is supposed to work, the destructive functions of sexual atrocities are more visible when directed against groups on the basis of ethnicity, race, nationality, or religion as well as sex than when they are directed on the basis of sex alone. Andrea Dworkin observed, "It has been easiest to see rape as hostile and hating when the rape is nationalistic or racist or colonial."[120] On the same group grounds, it has been easier to see rape as destructive to groups as such.

One judicial opinion identified specific evidence going to

"group as such" that could also describe the role of sexual atrocities in genocides. In *Krstic*, a prosecution for the mass murders of Bosnian Muslims at Srebrenica, the ICTY said:

> [T]here is a strong indication of the intent to destroy the group as such in the concealment of the bodies in mass graves, which were later dug up, the bodies mutilated and reburied in other mass graves located in even more remote areas, thereby preventing any decent burial in accord with religious and ethnic customs and causing terrible distress to the mourning survivors, many of whom have been unable to come to a closure until the death of their men is finally verified.[121]

Defilement, desecration, distress at indignity of violation give concrete meaning to the intent to destroy a group "as such." If digging up and moving dead bodies does, so does rape, not to mention rape of dead bodies, which produces similar effects on members of groups who share the identification on which the atrocities were based with the violated. Such survivors are "unable to come to a closure" because in a sense the injury never ends. When children are conceived in such rapes, this becomes even more true. Destroying a people in these ways short of killing them all gives new dimension to the old view that rape is a fate worse than death.

Public sexual spectacles are particularly effective for destruction purposes. In the Rwandan genocide, a Tutsi woman was vaginally penetrated with a sharp pointed stick after she was dead, her corpse left with the stick protruding by a public road for three days.[122] In Gujarat, much as in the Holocaust, "groups of [Muslim] women were stripped naked and then made to run for miles, before being gang-raped and burnt alive. In some cases religious symbols were carved onto their bodies."[123] Sexually destroying the women of these groups in these ways destroys the group. When the women are murdered in such instances, the genocidal point lies less in what such acts do to the violated women who are sacrificed to make it, and more in what the atrocities say and do to the surviving group members. In such spectacles, sexual abuse performs, and in so doing enacts, the destruction of the target peoples.

Bosnian Muslim and Croat women subjected to sexual atrocities often said that in that genocide, Bosnia-Herzegovina was being feminized. In light of the analysis proposed here, this was not metaphor. The destruction of women through sexual assault, common outside genocidal settings, was enlisted there against both women and men by the Serbian fascists on an ethnic, religious, and national basis. Men dominated men and women of non-Serbian ethnic groups the way men dominate women under male dominance. Male dominance was thus made to serve genocidal ends. Genocidal rape did to race, ethnicity, religion, and nationality what rape outside genocides does to sex. When and to the degree that it works, rape destroys national and ethnic groups in genocides as it destroys women as a group under sex inequality.

In actualizing and expressing dominion, sexual abuse does in genocide what it does in misogyny; indeed, it deploys misogyny against ethnic groups. Whatever group it is leveled against, the fact that this particular act means violation and subjugation constitutes its distinctive injury to the group. As expressive action, what it does and what it says are inseparable. That men occupy the status over women of being the people who can do this, and are therefore socially supreme, is widely taken for granted, making rape on the basis of sex widely regarded as inevitable and common. When an ethnic, racial, religious, or national group—a group that includes men—loses its sovereignty this way, the group and ground may make the atrocities noticed. That sexual atrocities would first be seen as destructively group based in international law in situations in which they are used for racial, ethnic, or religious domination is thus far from coincidence.[124]

In the Holocaust, in particular, the genocidal role of sexual atrocities has been largely denied, women being as relatively invisible as their sexual abuse has been. Holocaust survivors understandably do not want to be pornography. Although it is not simple, sexual atrocities can be exposed and analyzed without fueling them. Atrocities can be sexual without discussing them being sexually explicit. That they are sexual does not mean they should not be investigated. Suppressing sexual abuse fuels it more than criticizing it openly does. Arguably, covering up the realities of sexual abuse in genocide has enhanced its eroticization partly by supporting the illusion that Holocaust pornography is fantasy, not fascism. Plausibly, public exposure of sexual abuse as integral to mass extermination could go some distance to counter its present mass exploitation in pornography and allure in other fiction.

Once the sexual abuse in genocide is brought more fully into the open, its function faced, the legal definition of genocide—including its group grounds (should sex be added?), its subparts (should sexual atrocities be made express?), its intent element (should it be there at all? should it reflect how misogyny actually works?)—as well as the advisability of a separate gynocide protocol or convention can be revisited in a more realistic factual and theoretical context. Elizabeth Heineman urges analyzing "the ways that sex enables people to commit genocide."[125] For those who come after, this is a missing piece of the genocidal paradigm. Sexual abuse, in reality, is a perfect genocidal tool. It does to ethnic, racial, religious, and national groups as such what has been done to women as such from time immemorial in one of the most effective systems of domination-to-destruction in history. The perpetrators have not failed to notice.[126]

NOTES

1. Andrea Dworkin, "The Unremembered: Searching for Women at the Holocaust Memorial Museum," 5:3 *Ms.* 48, 54 (Nov. 1994).

2. *Prosecutor v. Kupreskic et al.*, No. IT-95-16-T, Judgment (transcript of oral opinion of Judge Cassese, ICTY, January 14, 2000) (quoting words of Muslim woman from Bosnia-Herzegovina testified to by witness at trial). Judge Cassese uses this quotation to illustrate persecution, not genocide, in that the aim of the acts was expulsion, not destruction. In my view, forced expulsion can be genocidal and the acts described can be genocidal. On this point, see *Case Concerning Application of the Convention on the Prevention and Punishment of the Crime of Genocide (Bosnia and Herzegovina v. Yugoslavia (Serbia and Montenegro))*, 1993 I.C.J., available at 1993 WL 589842, para. 69 of separate opinion of Judge Lauterpacht (Sept. 13, 1993) (hereinafter "Bosnia and Herzegovina v. Yugoslavia").

3. See generally United Nations, Commission of Experts on the Former Yugoslavia, *Final Report of the Commission of Experts Established Pursuant to Security Council Resolution 780* (1992) and Annexes, Prepared by Professor M. Cherif Bassiouni and the Staff of the DePaul University College of Law and its International Human Rights Law Institute (IHRLI) in Chicago (hereinafter "Bassiouni Report").

4. Convention on the Prevention and Punishment of the Crime of

Genocide, Dec. 9, 1949, 78 U.N.T.S. 277 (hereinafter "Genocide Convention") (Art. 2 defines genocide as "any of the following acts committed with intent to destroy, in whole or in part, a national, ethnical, racial or religious group, as such: (a) Killing members of the group; (b) causing serious bodily or mental harm to members of the group; (c) deliberately inflicting on the group conditions of life calculated to bring about its physical destruction in whole or in part; (d) imposing measures intended to prevent births within the group; (e) forcibly transferring children of the group to another group."

5. As stated by Judge Lauterpacht of the ICJ, acts of "'ethnic cleansing'...[are] difficult to regard as other than acts of genocide." *Bosnia and Herzegovina v. Yugoslavia,* para. 69.

6. The sources for the account in the above paragraphs are my clients in *Kadic v. Karadzic,* 70 F.3d 232 (2d Cir. 1996). Other first-person accounts are provided by Seada Vranic, *Breaking the Wall of Silence: The Voices of Raped Bosnia* (Zagreb: Izdanja Antibarbarus, 1996); Alexandra Stiglmayer, *Massenvergewaltigung: Krieg gegen die Frauen* (Freiberg i Breisgau: Kore, 1993). Some of the facts mentioned above were prosecuted successfully by the ICTY, prominently the Foça case. See generally *Prosecutor v. Kunarac,* No. IT-96-23 and IT-96-23/1, Judgment (Feb. 22, 2001), misconceiving those rapes as slavery when they were genocidal.

7. See Bassiouni Report, supra. For statistics on killings, see Annex V sec. I and V; Annex VI, sec. I C and I D; and Annex X, II A. For a summary of statistics on sexual assaults, see Annex IX sec. I A ("1. There are approximately 1,100 reported cases of rape and sexual assault; 2. About 800 victims are named, or the submitting source appears to know the identity of the victim, but does not disclose it; 3. About 1,800 victims are specifically referred to but are not named or identified sufficiently by the witness reporting the incident; 4. Witness reports also refer to additional numbers of victims through approximations. These reports suggest there may be about 10,000 additional victims the reports could eventually lead to; 5. About 550 of the reported cases refer to victims of rape and sexual assault but are unspecific and do not give any identifying information. . . . This statistical information may not represent the true extent of what has occurred in the former Yugoslavia").

8. See Mladen Lonçar, "Sexual Torture of Men in the War," in Libby Tata Arcel, ed., *War Violence, Trauma and the Coping Process: Armed Conflict in Europe and the Survivor Response* 212 (Zagreb: Nakladnistvo Lumin, 1998). A man's testicles were bitten off as public torture in the Omarska camp. See *Prosecutor v. Tadic,* No. IT-94-1, Opinion & Judgment, para. 206 (ICTY, May 7, 1997).

9. See Catharine A. MacKinnon, "Turning Rape into Pornography: Postmodern Genocide," *Ms.*, 24–30 (July/Aug. 1993) (documenting the making of a film of a rape of a Muslim woman by Serbian forces).

10. Ibid.

11. See *Kadic v. Karadzic,* supra; *Prosecutor v. Milosevic,* No. IT-01-51-I, Indictment, para. 32 (Nov. 22, 2001). On the larger context of the Bosnian genocide, see Norman Cigar, *Genocide in Bosnia: The Policy of Ethnic Cleansing* (College Station: Texas A&M University Press, 1995); Philip Cohen, *Serbia's Secret War: Propaganda and the Deceit of History* (College Station: Texas A&M University Press, 1996).

12. For a stunning psychoanalytic study of the Freikorps, a private army in Germany between the wars, connecting the rise of fascism with sexual misogyny, see Klaus Theweleit, *Male Fantasies* (Minneapolis: University of Minnesota Press, 1987).

13. Joan Ringelheim perceptively observed that, in her interviews with Jewish women Holocaust survivors, "although there are many stories of sexual abuse, they are not easy to come by. Some think it inappropriate to talk about these matters; discussions about sexuality desecrate the memories of the dead, or the living, or the Holocaust itself. For others, it is simply too difficult and painful. Still others think it may be a trivial issue. One survivor told me that she had been sexually abused by a number of Gentile men while she was in hiding, when she was about eleven years old. Her comment about this was that it 'was not important . . . except to me.' She meant that it had no significance within the larger picture of the Holocaust." Joan Ringelheim, "Women and the Holocaust: A Reconsideration of Research," 10 *Signs: Journal of Women in Culture and Society* 741, 745 (Summer 1985). As to the social meaning of the sexual, it is worth pondering that people who can describe thousands of people being killed on a single day in front of them find it a desecration of the memory to talk about brothels, or those who can tell of their families falling on top of them when shot in a pit find it too painful to discuss having been raped. Ringelheim reports that at a conference that presented panels on myriad details of the Holocaust, when she questioned the lack of a single mention of women or gender, the organizers at the Holocaust Memorial Museum said, "We forgot." Joan Ringelheim, "The Split between Gender and the Holocaust," in Lenore J. Weitzman and Dalia Ofer, eds., *Women in the Holocaust,* 340, 346 (New Haven: Yale University Press, 1998).

14. Dagmar Herzog, "Hubris and Hypocrisy, Incitement and Disavowal: Sexuality and German Fascism," 11:1/2 *Journal of the History of Sexuality* 6, 6 (Jan./Apr. 2002).

15. *Trial of the Major War Criminals,* Vol. XXII, at 547 (1948) (Nuremberg, 1947–49) (reading the conclusions of the court at sentencing).

16. Streicher, for publishing, was convicted for incitement to murder and extermination, a form of persecution on political and racial grounds, a crime against humanity, and executed. *Trial of the Major War Criminals, supra,* at Vol. XXII, 549 (finding Streicher guilty on one count); and Vol. I, 365 (sentencing him to death).

17. George Mosse, *The Image of Man: The Creation of Modern Masculinity,* 175 (New York and Oxford: Oxford University Press, 1996).

18. Gesetz zum Schutze des Deutschen Blutes und der Deutschen Ehre, 1935 Reichsgesetzblatt, Teil 1, 1146. This provision forbids "marriages between Jews and German nationals of German or related blood" (art. 1) and "sexual intercourse (except in marriage) between Jews and German nationals of German or related blood" (art. 2). For an illuminating historical discussion of the Nazi concept of "blood," see Allyson D. Polsky, "Blood, Race, and National Identity: Scientific and Popular Discourses," 23:3/4 *Journal of Medical Humanities* 171, 174–178. Only men violating the prohibition on extramarital intergroup sexual intercourse were to be punished with imprisonment or hard labor (art. 5, sec. 2). Jews were also forbidden to employ German women under forty-five years of age in their households (art. 3).

19. For early documentation, see Hensley Henson, *The Yellow Spot: The Outlawing of Half a Million Human Beings,* 216–234 (London: Victor Gollancz, 1936).

20. Photograph in Deborah Dwork, ed., *Voices & Views: A History of the Holocaust,* 142 (2002) (photograph of August 15, 1935).

21. See Patricia Szobar, "Telling Sexual Stories in the Nazi Courts of Law: Race Defilement in Germany, 1933 to 1945," 11 *Journal of the History of Sexuality* 131 (Jan./Apr. 2002). See also Alexandra Przyrembel, "'Race Defilement' in Court" (unpublished paper from Workshop, Yad Vashem, Jerusalem, Nov. 20–23, 2001) (reporting research on over five hundred prosecutions for *Rassenschande* in Nazi courts).

22. An overview of the project is provided by the indictment of its operatives under Control Council Law No. 10 in *Trial of the Major War Criminals,* Vol. IV, at 608 (Nuremberg, 1947–49), especially indictments of Sollmann, Ebner, Tesch, and Viermetz. The judgments can be found in Vol. V at 162–164.

23. See Joshua Hammer, "Hitler's Children," *Newsweek International,* March 20, 2000; Georg Lilienthal, *Der 'Lebensborn e.V.': ein Instrument nationalsozialistischer Rassenpolitik* (Mainz: Akademie der Wissenschaften und der Literatur, 1985). The best article in English is Larry V. Thompson, "Lebensborn and the Eugenics Policy of the Reichsführer-SS," 4:1 *Central European History,* 54–77 (Mar. 1971).

24. Clay and Leapman carefully canvass the evidence on the question

of whether *Lebensborn* homes were stud farms, including Himmler's reported remark that "I have made it known privately that any unmarried woman who is alone and longs for a child can turn to lebensborn with perfect confidence . . . [W]e recommend only racially faultless men as 'conception assistants.'" Felix Kersten, *The Kersten Memoirs*, 1940–45, Hutchinson, 1956, quoted in Catrine Clay and Michael Leapman, *Master Race: the Lebensborn Experiment in Nazi Germany* 71 (London: Hodder & Stoughton, 1995). German carrots and sticks are reported. Ibid. at 53–69. It is also noted that the suspicion that *Lebensborn* homes provided for arranged liaisons between suitable potential racial stock and SS men was widespread at the time, id. at 69, but asserted that the real disapproval of such arrangements was on grounds that they encouraged conception outside marriage. Marc Hillel and Clarissa Henry, *Lebensborn e.V.: Im Namen der Rasse* (Wein: Paul Szolnay Verlag 1975), discusses all aspects of the project in detail but never focuses on how the women, whether German women or those of occupied countries, became pregnant. One source that purports to provide contemporary evidence that *Lebensborn* included reproductive brothels, *Freiwillige Erzeugen* (voluntary breeding) establishments, is Peter Neumann's account as an officer on leave of his experience with a young German woman. See Peter Neumann, *Other Men's Graves*, 74–85, trans. Constantine Fitz Gibbon (London: Weidenfeld and Nicolson, 1958). Dialogue includes: "[Her:] Don't you think it's pretty horrible this business of selling one's body as an instrument of procreation?" [Him:] "You aren't selling your body. You're giving it to Germany, which is a very different matter." Id. at 83. Many people who have studied the subject in depth seem certain that the homes were maternity homes set up to further racist eugenics rather than breeding farms. See also Jacques Delarue, *The Gestapo: A History of Horror*, 70–71, trans. Mervyn Savill (New York: William Morrow, 1964). Evans comments on "the attempts by the Nazis to mobilize women voluntarily by means of a massive propaganda campaign" for reproduction of Germans. Richard J. Evans, "German Women and the Triumph of Hitler," *Journal of Modern History*, Vol. 48, Issue 1, On-Demand Supplement (Mar. 1976), 123–175, on p. 149. Manfred Wolfson's "Constraint and Choice in the SS leadership," *Western Political Quarterly*, Vol. 18, Issue 3 (Sep. 1965), 551, 557, describes *Lebensborn* as "providing secret confinements in special lying-in homes for the unwed companions of SS men." Annette Timm, "Sex with a Purpose: Prostitution, Venereal Disease, and Militarized Masculinity in the Third Reich," 11:1/2 *Journal of the History of Sexuality* 223, 246–247 (Jan./Apr. 2002), takes the same view, but also references Bluel's account of a "policy of providing soldiers on leave with pleasant female company with a view both to increasing the men's support for the party and to creating social situations that might in the end have positive population political outcomes," id. at 247, which is precisely what Neumann describes. The Nazis destroyed as many of the *Lebensborn* files as they could during the last days of World War II, although some have since been recovered. See "Hitler Race Project Records Revealed," AP Berlin (November 23, 1999).

25. Timm, for example, comments: "Sex in the Third Reich was for too long a virtual terra incognita for historians of Germany. There was an understandable desire to avoid providing titillating details about so murderous a regime." "Sex with a Purpose," supra, at 223. Why accounts of sexual atrocities would necessarily be titillating is not explained and the possible role of sexuality in making the regime murderous is evaded.

26. See Thompson, supra, at 71–72 and Lilienthal, supra.

27. On the Norwegian *Lebensborn* homes and children generally, see Clay and Leapman, supra, at 131–149. Attorney Randi Hagen Spydevold sued the Norwegian government for compensation for *Lebensborn* children in early 2001, alleging Norwegian official cooperation in the maltreatment of an estimated 12,000 children born to Norwegian women by Germans under the *Lebensborn* program. One article on this lawsuit noted that "[a]cross occupied Europe, German soldiers fathered more than 200,000 children." Carl Honore, "Children of Nazis Seeking Peace with Their Past, Norwegian Lawsuit: Many endured 'systematic torture' in mental asylums after Germany's defeat," *National Post,* September 11, 2000. Three hundred thousand *Wehrmacht* soldiers were stationed in Norway, which was governed by the infamous collaborator Quisling. Can it be that none of these children were conceived through rape?

28. Usually, commentaries use language that presumes that women, whether German women or women of occupied countries, giving birth out of wedlock to children of the Nazi SS had sex with them voluntarily. Larry V. Thompson speaks of several thousand French women impregnated by occupying soldiers in terms of "the inevitable fraternization between the troops and the natives." "Lebensborn and the Eugenics Policy of the Reichsfuhrer-SS," *Central European History,* 4:1 (Mar. 1971), 71. Catrine Clay and Michael Leapman, *Master Race: The Lebensborn Experiment in Nazi Germany* (London: Hodder & Stoughton, 1995), emphasize sexual freedom: "Although the whole concept of selective racial breeding is disgusting, the suggestion of random and wholesale loveless coupling is not wholly appropriate. While some of the pregnancies may well have been motivated by a woman's strong sense of duty to the state, or in some cases have been brought about by coercion, the scant available evidence suggests genuine affection between many of the mothers and their SS lovers. They were, after all, healthy young women with normal emotional needs." Anette Warring, *Tyskerpiger—under besoettelse og retsopgor,* states, "During the

occupation tens of thousands of Danish women *had affairs* with Werhmacht soldiers resulting in more than five thousand war children" (emphasis added). Tony Paterson and Allan Hall, "Norwegian Government Sued over Children Nazis Left Behind," *The Telegraph* [London], Issue 2102, Sunday, February 25, 2001. The article notes that Himmler's policy "actively promoted sexual relations between German troops and women classed as true Aryans—such as the Norwegians," but also that "an estimated 50,000 Norwegian women were thought to have *had affairs* with Germans during the occupation." Again, were none of these women raped?

29. Opening statement of the prosecution, the Rusha Case, Prosecutor McHaney, *Trials of War Criminals before the Nuernberg Military Tribunals,* Vol. IV, (Buffalo, NY: W. S. Hein, 1997), at 687.

30. Anna Rosmus, "Involuntary Abortions for Polish Forced Laborers," in Elizabeth R. Baer and Myrna Goldenberg, eds., *Experience and Expression: Women, the Nazis, and the Holocaust,* 76, 78 (Detroit: Wayne State University Press, 2003).

31. Jacob Apenslak et al., eds., *The Black Book of Polish Jewry: An Account of the Martyrdom of Polish Jewry under the Nazi Occupation,* 25 (Bodenheim: Syndikat Buchgesellschaft, 1995) (1943).

32. Yaffa Eliach, "Women and the Holocaust: Historical Background," in *Women of Valor: Partisans and Resistance Fighters,* originally published in 6:4 *Journal of the Center for Holocaust Studies* 8, 8 (Spring 1990).

33. Apenslak, supra, at 27. The Jewish community leaders reportedly adamantly refused.

34. See the *New York Times,* Jan. 8, 1942 (letter of Chaya Feldman), reprinted in Zev Garber, *Shoah: The Paradigmatic Genocide,* 98 (Lanham, MD: University Press of America, 1994) (discussing authenticity of letter).

35. Raul Hilberg, *Perpetrators, Victims, Bystanders: The Jewish Catastrophe 1933–1945,* 213 (New York: Aaron Asher Books, 1992) (quoting report by the Security Service in Galicia, Kommandeur of Security Police/III-A-4, to Obersturmbannführer Willi Seibert in Berlin and to Standartenführer [Colonel] Heim in Krakow, July 2, 1943, National Archives of the United States Record Group 242, T175, Roll 575).

36. Birgit Beck, "Vergewaltigung von Frauen als Kriegsstrategie im Zweiten Weltkrieg?" in Andreas Gestrich Ausübung, *Erfahrung und Verweigerung von Gewalt in Kriegen des 20. Jahrhunderts,* 34, 43–44 (Münster and Hamburg: Lit, 1996). See also Doris Bergen, *War and Genocide: A Concise History of the Holocaust* 107, 110 (Lanham, MD: Rowman and Littlefield, 2003).

37. Supra, note 13.

38. Judith M. Isaacson, *Seed of Sarah: Memoirs of a Survivor* 144–145

(Urbana and Chicago: University of Illinois Press, 1990). For an analysis that gives further depth to Anne Frank herself, see Catherine A. Bernard, "Anne Frank: The Cultivation of the Inspirational Victim," in Baer and Goldenberg, supra, at 201.

39. Isaacson, supra, at 53.

40. Olga Lengyel, *Five Chimneys: The Story of Auschwitz*, 185 (Chicago and New York: Ziff Davis, 1947).

41. Ruth Elias, *Die Hoffnung erheilt mich am Leben: Mein Weg von Theresienstadt und Auschwitz nach Israel*, 149 (Munich, 1988) ("Vergewaltigung der jüdischen Mädchen war erlaubt. Das war doch keine Rassenschande").

42. Survivor quoted by Joan Ringelheim, "The Split Between" in Weitzman & Ofer, eds., supra, at 341.

43. See, e.g., the account of Stanley Rustin, "Camps," in Esther Katz and Joan M. Ringelheim, eds., *Proceedings of the Conference of Women Surviving the Holocaust*, 165 (New York: Institute for Research in History, 1983) (on Skarzysko).

44. They are legion. See Helen Fein, "Genocide and Gender: The Uses of Women and Group Destiny," 1 *Journal of Genocide Research* 43, 53 (1999) ("What is striking about the Holocaust . . . is the lack of a pattern of gender discrimination and sanctioned rape"); Myrna Goldenberg, "Memoirs of Auschwitz Survivors: The Burden of Gender," in Weitzman and Ofer, supra, at 336; Jack G. Morrison, *Ravensbrück: Everyday Life in a Women's Concentration Camp, 1939–45*, 177–178 (Princeton: Markus Wiener, 2000); Melissa Raphael, *The Female Face of God in Auschwitz: A Jewish Feminist Theology of the Holocaust*, 183 n. 48 (2003).

45. See Julia Roos, "Backlash against Prostitutes' Rights: Origins and Dynamics of Nazi Prostitution Policies," 11:1/2 *Journal of the History of Sexuality* 67, 69 (Jan./Apr. 2002); Christa Paul, *Zwangsprostitution: Staatlich Errichtete Bordelle im Nationalsozialismus* (Berlin: Edition Hentrich, 1994).

46. See Timm, supra, at 227.

47. Jewish women were apparently no longer officially permitted to be used in Wehrmacht brothels after March 1942. Helke Sander and Barbara John, eds., *Befrier und Befreite: Krieg, Vergewaltigungen, Kinder* (Munich: Kunstmann, 1992).

48. Paul, supra.

49. Morrison collects sources describing these recruitments in detail with no mention of religion, race, or ethnicity. See Morrison, supra, at 201–204.

50. See Nanda Herbermann, *The Blessed Abyss: Inmate #6582 in Ravensbrück Concentration Camp for Women*, 132, trans. Hester Baer (Detroit: Wayne State University Press, 2000) (account by a German Catholic resistance

member inmate from 1941 to 1943 who was block elder at Ravensbrück for four hundred prostitutes). See also Timm, supra, at 224.

51. Heinz Heger, *The Men with the Pink Triangle: The True Life-and-Death Story of Homosexuals in the Nazi Death Camps*, 96, trans. David Fernbach (London: Gay Men's Press, 1980), and Morrison, supra, at 202, both report this.

52. Christa Schulz, "Weibliche Haftlinge aus Ravensbrück in Bordellen der Männerkonzentrationslager," in Claus Fullberg-Stolberg, Martina Jung, Renate Reibe, and Martina Scheitenberger, eds., *Frauen in Konzentrationslagern, Bergen-Belsen, Ravensbrück*, 135, 139 (Bremen: Edition Temmen, 1994).

53. Heger, supra, at 96.

54. See Enno Georg, *Die Wirtschlaftlichen Unternehmungen der SS*, 116 and n. 471 (1963); "Instructions Concerning the Granting of Special Favors to Prisoners," trans. of Document No. NC-400, Office of Chief of Counsel for War Crimes; Reinhild Kassig and Christa Paul, "Haftlings-Bordelle in deutschen KZs," *EMMA*, 32–37, Mar. 1992.

55. Heger, supra, at 61. No focused attention appears to have been paid to the ethnicity or nationality of these young men, although Heger's report focuses on Poles. Heger, who was Austrian, was used in this way. The literature, frustratingly, tends to omit racial, ethnic, or religious specifications once a person is sexually defined, for example, as a prostitute or homosexual.

56. As a further factor in nonreporting, it should be noted that, through these arrangements, Jewish men had the possible shame of using women in captive settings as rewards from exterminators for forced labor contributing to their own demise, on top of whatever shame might otherwise come from men using captive or prostituted women. There are also reports that Jewish men used Jewish women for sex for survival outside the brothels, and raped them; under genocidal conditions, women are under even more pressures not to report intracommunity sexual assaults than otherwise. Jewish women also had the possible shame of being used in this way as well as, for those who lived, the shame of having survived possibly for that reason. Perhaps the evocative description of the shaming effects of the *Rassenschande* context also applies in the context of sexual abuse: "They were ashamed of their black hair, their Semitic nose, their defenselessness. . . . They were ashamed of their shame." Joel König, *Den Netzen entronnen*, 155 (Göttingen, 1967), here cited as Kweit/Eschwege, Selbstbehauptung.

57. See Eugen Kogon, *Der SS-Staat: Das System der deutschen Konzentrationslager*, 215 (Munich: Wilhelm Heyne Verlag, 1994) (1947); Ka-Tzetnik 135633, *House of Dolls*, trans. Moshe M. Kohn (London: Shakespeare

Head Press, 1956). This book was written by Karol Cetynski, also named Yehiel Dinur, based on the diary of Daniella Preleshnik, a fourteen-year-old (in 1939) Polish Jew who was forced into prostitution in Auschwitz's "House of Dolls" brothel. She is identified in some editions as his sister. Christa Paul found that, while Ravensbrück was used to supply the brothels in most of the camps, women at Auschwitz were forced into prostitution there for its three brothels and at its satellites. See Paul, supra, at 26.

58. Jehoshua Eibeshitz and Anna Eibeshitz, eds. and trans., *Women in the Holocaust: A Collection of Testimonies,* viii (New York: Remember, 1992); Jehoshua Eibeshitz, in *Remember! A Collection of Testimonies,* trans. Anna Eilenberg-Eibeshitz, ed. Esther Sarah Eilenberg, 12–13 (Haifa: Institute for Holocaust Studies, 1992) (story of "Miriam").

59. See Paul, supra, at 106 (quoting it).

60. Olga Lengyel, supra, at 181.

61. Paul, supra, at 104. The literature contains much denial of this fact, concluding to the contrary with varying degrees of insistence and vehemence, based primarily on lack of evidence and the view that since it was illegal, the Nazis could not have done it. Typical instances are Morrison, supra, at 73, 202. For further discussion, see Janet Anschutz, Kerstin Meier, and Sanja Obajdin, "'Dieses leere Gefuhl, und die Blicke der anderen . . .': Sexuelle Gewalt gegen Frauen," in *Frauen in Konzentrationslagern,* supra, at 130–131; Christa Schultz, "Weibliche Haftlinge aus Ravensbrück in Bordellen der Mannerkonzentrationslager," id. at 135. Until Paul's book, there was not a lot of evidence, but what did exist was firsthand. That the Nazis were law abiding, particularly in the camps and where forced sex was concerned, seems an odd article of faith.

62. Elizabeth Heineman comments: "Research into Nazi-era brothels challenges our use of the model of 'prostitution' (which forefronts exchange) to describe acts that might better be described as 'rape' (which forefronts violence)." 11:1/2 *Journal of the History of Sexuality* 22, 66 (Jan./Apr. 2002). She understands that brothel sex was rape, but this understanding could illuminate prostitution in general rather than challenge the usage of the term in this setting. Her analysis misses both the exchange of sex for survival in the camps and the forms of coercion involved in that same exchange in most instances of prostitution outside of camps. By contrast, Magnus Hirschfeld, Andreas Gaspar, and F. Aquila, eds., in *Sittengeschichte des Zweiten Weltkrieges,* 341 (Hanau: Müller und Kiepenheuer, 1968), observe: "The term prostitution should not be narrowly defined when speaking of prostitution in war. It not only includes brothels but almost always includes relationships between occupying forces and local women who hope to manage an advantage through love affairs. Often there is also forced prostitution which is equivalent to rape."

63. See Andrea Dworkin, *Scapegoat: The Jews, Israel, and Women's Liberation*, 33 (New York: Free Press, 2000).

64. Elie A. Cohen, *Human Behaviour in the Concentration Camp*, 135 (London: Free Association Books, 1988). See also Edith Bruck, *Who Loves You Like This*, 31, 44, 57, 113–115 (Philadelphia: Paul Dry Books, 2001).

65. Lengyel, supra, at 182.

66. Felicia Berland Hyatt, *Close Calls: Memoirs of a Survivor*, 76–77 (New York: Holocaust Library, 1991).

67. Cecile Klein, *Sentenced to Live*, 73 (New York: Holocaust Library, 1988). For further reports, see Rose Meth, *Women of Valor: Partisans and Resistance Fighters* [online]. Judy Cohen, *Women and the Holocaust*, 2001 (visited August 10, 2003), http://www.columbia.edu/acis/.bartleby/jewett. Sarah Nomberg-Pryztyk, Eli Pfefferkorn, and David H. Hersch, eds., *Auschwitz: True Tales from a Grotesque Land*, 14, trans. Roslyn Hirsch (Chapel Hill and London: University of North Carolina Press, 1985); Raphael, supra, at 183, n. 48.

68. Leib Langfuss, "The Horrors of Murder," in Ber Mark, ed., *The Scrolls of Auschwitz*, 209 (Tel Aviv: Am Oved, 1985).

69. Jeremy Noakes and Geoffrey Pridham, eds., Vol. 2, *Nazism, 1919–1945: A History in Documents and Eyewitness Accounts*, 1180 (New York: Schocken Books, 1983).

70. Myrna Goldenberg, quoted by Judy Cohen, "Women's Holocaust Narratives: Violence and Sexuality as a Theme in Memoirs by Women Survivors," 2001; http://www.interlog.com/~mighty/essays/lessons2.htm (visited 12 August 2003). I was originally referred to the sources referenced in notes 40 and 64–70 by Judy Cohen's excellent Web site.

71. Heger, supra, at 97.

72. This aspect of the freezing experiments is described in *Trial of the Major War Criminals*, supra, Vol. II, 525 ("Himmler personally ordered that rewarming by the warmth of human bodies also be attempted" which was done "by placing the chilled victim between two naked [Gypsy] women" from Ravensbrück).

73. They can be seen at Yad Vashem and the Holocaust Memorial Museum.

74. See *Prosecutor v. Akayesu*, No. ICTR-96-4-T, Judgment, 45 (Sept. 2, 1998), paras. 112–129.

75. See generally Binaifer Nowrojee, *Shattered Lives: Sexual Violence during the Rwandan Genocide and Its Aftermath* (New York: Human Rights Watch, 1996). The perpetrators were Hutu and all the targets were Tutsi and some moderate and intermarried Hutu. See Human Rights Watch, *Slaughter among Neighbors: The Political Origins of Communal Violence*, 24 (New Haven: Yale University Press, 1995).

76. *Prosecutor v. Laurent Semanza,* Case No. ICTR-97-20-T, para. 253 (May 15, 2003). The court clarified at idem that the witness explained that "the Accused used the Kinyarwaanda word *kurongora,* which means 'to marry' as well as 'to to make love.'"

77. Catherine Bonnet, "Le viol des femmes survivants de genocide du Rwanda," in Raymond Verdier, Emmanuel Ecaux, and Jean-Pierre Chretien, eds., *Rwanda: Un genocide du XXe siecle,* 18 (Paris: Editions L'Harmattan, 1995).

78. United Nations, *Report on the Situation of Human Rights in Rwanda submitted by Mr. Rene Degni-Segui, Special Rapporteur of the Commission on Human Rights,* under paragraph 20 of the Resolution S-3/1 of May 25, 1994, E/CN.4/1996/68, January 29, 1996, at 7 (estimating from at least 250,000 pregnancies to at the most 500,000 cases of rape in Rwandan genocide). One typical account is: "The soldiers told the Interahamwe to go to work, and they killed people and also singled out some girls and put them aside. According to the witness they 'had their way' with these girls and then killed them. Most of the women killed were stripped of their clothing, 'so that Tutsi women could be seen naked.' The Interahamwe continued to 'have their way' until they left satisfied at around 11 P.M." *Prosecutor v. Rutuganda,* No. ICTR-96-3-T, Judgment and Sentence, Trial Chamber, para. 271 (December 6, 1999).

79. See Nowrojee, supra, at 15–19; *Prosecutor v. Nahimana,* Case No. ICTR-99-52-T, Judgment and Sentence, paras. 114, 139, 117–180, 182, 188, 210, 245, 935, 964, 1079 (December 3, 2003).

80. See, e.g., *Prosecutor v. Akayesu,* supra, para. 449.

81. See, e.g., *Prosecutor v. Musema,* No. ICTR-96-5-D, Judgment and Sentence, para. 932 (January 27, 2000).

82. *Musema,* supra, para. 933.

83. See, e.g., Rhonda Copelon, "Surfacing Gender: Reconceptualizing Crimes against Women in Time of War," in Rebecca Cook, ed., *Women's Rights, Human Rights: International Feminist Perspectives,* 199 (Toronto: Faculty of Law, University of Toronto, 1996); contrast Nowrojee, supra, at 34–36.

84. Genocide Convention, supra n. 5.

85. "Contrary to popular belief, the crime of genocide does not imply the actual extermination of [a] group in its entirety, but is understood as such once any one of the acts mentioned in Article 2(2) through 2(2)(e) is committed with the specific intent to destroy 'in whole or in part' a national, ethnical, racial or religious group." *Akayesu,* supra, para. 497.

86. See, e.g., Comision para el Esclarecimiento Historico (CEH), *Guatemala: Memoria del Silencio,* Vol. 3, para. 2249 (CEH, 1999) ("when sexual violence [rape], that form of violence directed specifically against

women, is utilized in a massive and public manner it is an indication of the intention to exterminate a group"). See also United States Commission on International Religious Freedom, *Hearing on Communal Violence in Gujarat, India, and the U.S. Response,* June 10, 2002, Washington, D.C.; Ruth Baldwin, "Gujarat's Gendered Violence," in Betsy Reed, ed., *Nothing Sacred: Women Respond to Religious Fundamentalism and Terror,* 185 (New York: Thunder's Mouth Press/Nation Books, 2002).

87. The Supreme Court of Canada instructively so found in *R. v. McCraw* (1991), 3 S.C.R. 72, 83–84.

88. *Kadic v. Karadzic,* supra, established this conceptualization under international law in the United States under the Alien Tort Act in the Second Circuit.

89. *Akayesu,* supra, paras. 731–734. Why the Yugoslav Tribunal did not prosecute genocidal rape until its Milosevic indictment (see *Milosevic,* supra, para. 32), until then charging rape as anything but genocide and as genocide all violent acts but rape, remains difficult to explain.

90. See, e.g., James Yin and Shi Young, *The Rape of Nanking: An Undeniable History in Photographs* (Chicago: Innovative Publishing Group, 1996).

91. That the Nazi genocide killed and transported Jews *to* Germany for liquidation and the Bosnian genocide killed and deported or ejected all non-Serbs *from* Bosnia-Herzegovina only defines the perpetrators' respective territorial ambitions and levels of organization; it does not make one a genocide, the other not.

92. This is at least reported in Joanne Csete, *The War within the War: Sexual Violence against Women and Girls in Eastern Congo,* 25 (New York: Human Rights Watch, 2002).

93. Helpful work on this topic is Roger Smith, "Genocide and the Politics of Rape," paper presented at the conference of the Association of Genocide Scholars, College of William and Mary, Williamsburg, VA, June 14–16 (1995); Hsu-Ming Teo, "The Continuum of Sexual Violence in Occupied Germany, 1945–49," 5:2 *Women's History Review* 191, 1996.

94. I did not say that it is worse, here or anywhere, and I do not think so. It apparently bears repeating that nothing here implies, suggests, or presupposes any hierarchy of harm, value, or seriousness between rape in war, rape in genocide, rape in slavery, and rape in other settings. For example, to say that genocide goes beyond war is simply an empirical observation that genocide is not confined to wartime settings. Nor is the purpose here to create a typology or to produce criteria on the basis of which rapes can be classified one way or another. Nor is this analysis a moral discussion.

95. *Prosecutor v. Jelisic,* No. IT-95-10-T, Judgment, paras. 78–83 (ICTY Trial Chamber, Dec. 14, 1999); Case Concerning Legality of Use of Force

(*Yugoslavia v. Belgium*), 1999 I.C.J., available at 1999 WL 1693067, para. 35 (June 2, 1999); see also *Prosecutor v. Bagilishema*, No. ICTR-95-1A-T, para. 64 (opinion of Judge Gunawardana, June 7, 2001); *Prosecutor v. Kayishema and Obed Ruzindana*, No. ICTR-95-1-T, Judgment, paras. 95–97 (May 21, 1999) ("'in part' requires the intention to destroy a considerable number of individuals who are part of the group. Individuals must be targeted due to their membership in the group to satisfy this definition"). Of interest also is the ICJ's opinion in the Kosova bombing case, finding that the NATO bombings, although intensive and sustained, including of populated areas of Yugoslavia, was not genocidal in part because it did not entail destructive intent "towards a group as such." Case Concerning Legality of Use of Force (*Yugoslavia v. Belgium*), supra, para. 40.

96. *A-G Israel v. Eichmann*, (1968) 36 ILR 18 (District Court, Jerusalem), para. 190.

97. Ad Hoc Committee on Genocide, 3 GAOR, Part I, Sixth Committee Summary Records (1948), 124–125 (76th mtg.), as cited in 11 *Human Rights Quarterly*, 110, n. 101; Kayishema and Ruzindana, supra, para. 99: "'Destroying' has to be directed at the group *as such*, that is, *qua group*."

98. *Prosecutor v. Sikirica et al.*, No. IT-95-8-T, Judgment on Defence Motion to Acquit, para. 89 (ICTY, Sept. 3, 2001).

99. Report of the International Law Commission on the Work of Its Fourth–Eighth Session, May 6–July 30, 1996, UN Doc. A/51/10, 88.

100. Bassiouni Report, supra, at sec. II H I 3.

101. *Akayesu*, supra, para. 521; also *Rutuganda*: "because they belonged to the Tutsi group and for the very fact that they belonged to the said group," supra, at para. 399.

102. *Rutuganda*, supra, at para. 60.

103. See Catharine A. MacKinnon, "A Sex Equality Approach to Sexual Assault," 989 *Ann. N.Y. Acad. Sci.* 1 (2003), in R. Prentky, E. Janus, and M. Seto, eds., *Sexual Coercion: Understanding and Management* 265 (2003), for further elaboration.

104. The history of the addition of "as such" to the language of the convention is no guide. Venezuela, offering a compromise between those who wanted to delete motive and those who wanted to retain or even strengthen it, proposed adding "as such"; the idea was that motives would be included but not enumerated. See Nehemiah Robinson, *The Genocide Convention: A Commentary*, 60–61 (New York: Institute of Jewish Affairs, World Jewish Congress, 1960); William A. Schabas, *Genocide in International Law: The Crimes of Crimes*, 245–253 (Cambridge and New York: Cambridge University Press, 2000). Whether the term added a motive element that was otherwise not there, or removed one that might have been stronger, remains cloudy.

105. This analysis is presented in Catharine A. MacKinnon, *Toward a Feminist Theory of the State* (Cambridge, MA: Harvard University Press, 1989).

106. See Jill Radford and Diana E. H. Russell, eds., *Femicide: The Politics of Woman Killing*, 10–11 (New York: Twayne, 1992).

107. This is argued in *Toward a Feminist Theory of the State*, supra.

108. For a stunning study in the latter, see Lisa Cardyn, "Sexualized Racism/Gendered Violence: Trauma and the Body Politic in the Reconstruction South," Ph.D. dissertation, Yale University, May 2003.

109. Sometimes resistance succeeds. In the case of African Americans, for example, rape had a shattering effect without entirely destroying community cohesion. The long-term effects of systematic rape by white men in particular on that community could doubtless use further study. The fact that rape is racist does not alone make it genocidal, which is not to say that it is not destructive. The distinctions lie in other aspects of the genocide definition, specifically with intent.

110. Indeed, from slavery forward, the perpetrators of the rapes have been arguably obsessed with preserving African Americans as a distinct group, while destroying their family structure and serving to obliterate the distinctiveness of each culture from which they came. The point was to exploit them for labor and keep the new group, African Americans, socially distinct to maintain white supremacy. If this group was destroyed qua group, against whom would whites define themselves as superior by distinction? Who would do the hard and unpleasant and low-paid work? However murderous, racism against African Americans has had a stake in preserving rather than destroying the group as such. That American racism, including the rape under slavery, included crimes against humanity is incontestable. The ICTY's opinion in the Foça case, in conceiving some rapes in the Bosnian situation as "slavery" (see *Prosecutor v. Kunarac*, supra) was thus able to bring out many functions of sexual subordination through this parallel; but putting them in the slavery framework at the same time failed to contextualize the acts within the genocide of which they were a part.

111. See *Musema*, supra, at para. 933 ("Accordingly, the Chamber notes that on the basis of the evidence presented, it emerges that acts of serious bodily and mental harm, including rape and other forms of sexual violence were often accompanied by humiliating utterances, which clearly indicated that the intention underlying each specific act was to destroy the Tutsi group as a whole. The Chamber notes, for example, that during the rape of Nyiramusugi, Musema declared: 'The pride of the Tutsis will end today.' In this context, the acts of rape and sexual violence were an integral part of the plan conceived to destroy the Tutsi group. Such acts tar-

geted Tutsi women, in particular, and specifically contributed to their destruction and therefore that of the Tutsi group as such. Witness N testified before the Chamber that Nyiramusugi, who was left for dead by those who raped her, had indeed been killed in a way. Indeed, the Witness specified that 'what they did to her is worse than death'").

112. Id.

113. Group itself, for purposes of genocidal intent, includes being "identified as such by others, including perpetrators of the crimes." *Kayeshima and Ruzindana*, supra, at para. 98. See also *Bagilishema*, supra, at para. 65; *Rutuganda*, supra, at para. 56; *Musema*, supra, at para. 161. Given that identity is a social fact, comprised in substantial part of identification by others, this is appropriate.

114. For general information, see Bessel A. van der Kolk, Alexander C. McFarlane, and Lars Weisaeth, eds., *Traumatic Stress: The Effects of Overwhelming Experience on Mind, Body, and Society* (New York: Guilford Press, 1996).

115. See Diana E. H. Russell and Rebecca M. Bolen, *The Epidemic of Rape and Child Sexual Abuse in the United States* (London: Sage Publications, 2000). For summaries of and references to data, see Catharine A. MacKinnon, *Sex Equality*, 776–778 (New York: Foundation Press, 2001).

116. A powerful example of being tortured as a Jew (in Argentina) is provided by Jacobo Timerman, *Prisoner without a Name, Cell without a Number*, trans. Toby Talbot (New York: Alfred A. Knopf, 1981).

117. Quoted in Nowrojee, supra, at 25. There was much talk during the Bosnian conflagration about Muslim men rejecting raped Bosnian Muslim women. Our experience was that the rejection was no greater and in many cases less than what is standard for men in the United States relative to women in their families who are raped.

118. Quoted in *Kupreskic*, supra, at id.

119. See Andrea Dworkin, "Remembering the Witches," in *Our Blood: Prophesies and Discourses on Sexual Politics*, 16 ("Gynocide is the word that designates the relentless violence perpetrated by the gender class men against the gender class women"). See also Mary Daly with Jane Caputi, *Webster's First New Intergalactic Wickedary of the English Language*, 77 (Boston: Beacon Press (1987). For a discussion of femicide, see Diana E. H. Russell and Roberta A. Harmes, eds., *Femicide in Global Perspective*, 20–23 (New York: Teacher's College Press, 2001).

120. Andrea Dworkin, *Scapegoat: The Jews, Israel, and Women's Liberation*, 48 (New York: Free Press, 2000).

121. *Prosecutor v. Krstic*, No. IT-98-33-T, Judgment, para. 596 (Aug. 2, 2001).

122. *Prosecutor v. Niyitegeka*, No. ICTR-96-14-T, Judgment and Sentence,

para. 463 (May 16, 2003) (finding accused guilty of sexual violence to the body of a dead woman as an inhumane act, a crime against humanity) ("The Accused ordered Interahamwe to undress the body of a Tutsi woman who had just been shot dead, and to sharpen a piece of wood, which he then instructed them to insert into her genitalia. The body of the woman with the piece of wood protruding from it was left on the roadside for some three days thereafter"). Although the defendant was also found guilty of genocide, this particular act was not included in those findings.

123. Shabnam Hashmi, quoted in Ruth Baldwin, "Gujarat's Gendered Violence," in Reed, supra, at 185. See also Concerned Citizens Tribunal, *Crime against Humanity: An Inquiry into the Carnage in Gujarat* (Siddhi Off-set Pvt. Ltd, 2002); Citizens Committee for Extraordinary Report on Gujarat, India, *Submissions to the Cedaw Committee for Seeking Intervention on Gender Based Crimes and the Gendered Impact of the Gujarat Carnage* (May 2003).

124. In addition to being genocidal when they occur in genocides as conventionally defined, sexual atrocities in some circumstances outside genocides may well be "crimes against humanity" under existing international humanitarian law, which does not require a showing of intent, and now prohibits widespread and systematic attacks on the basis of sex as well as other grounds. See Rome Statute of the International Criminal Court, 1998, U.N. Doc. A/CONF.183/9 (1998), reprinted in 37 I.L.M. 999 (1998) (Art. 7.1 defines "crime against humanity" as any of the following acts when committed as part of a widespread or systematic attack directed against any civilian population, with knowledge of the attack: . . . (g) Rape, sexual slavery, enforced prostitution, or any other form of sexual violence of comparable gravity. (h) Persecution against any identifiable group or collectivity on political, racial, national, ethnic, cultural, religious, gender as defined in paragraph 3, or other grounds that are universally recognized as impermissible under international law, in connection with any act referred to in this paragraph or any crime within the jurisdiction of the Court. "Gender" refers to "the two sexes, male and female, within the context of society").

125. Heineman, supra, at 55.

126. This essay was originally delivered on April 11, 2002, as the 2002 Otto Mainzer Lecture at New York University. Its generous sponsors were memorable models of support, interest, and graciousness. The helpful comments of Kent Harvey, Melissa Williams, Lisa Cardyn, Daniel Rothenberg, Jose Alvarez, Ryan Goodman, and Jessica Neuwirth, and the research and technical assistance of Ron Levy, Hillary Cameron, Lisa Cardyn, John Stoltenberg, Leila Masson, and the University of Michigan Law Library are gratefully acknowledged. Translations are mine.

INDEX

Adams, John. *See* Arendt, Hannah
African Americans, 9–10, 29, 34, 51,
  69n. 32, 77, 83, 170; Arendt on, 33–
  35; freedom of, 61; and invisibility,
  77–79; moral equality of, 18; and
  rape, 354n. 109, 354n. 110; and sacrifice, 9, 35–40, 43, 58–59, 85;
  NAACP, 33–34, 40–43. *See also* "Battle at Little Rock"; Ellison, Ralph;
  Slavery/slaves
Agonism: and democracy, 17–18, 19,
  195, 208–209, 230–232, 236, 242,
  251–252; and liberalism, 230–242.
  See also Contest (contestation, contestability); Deliberative democracy;
  Democratic deliberation; Disagreement
Anderson, Benedict, 75n. 97
Annas, Julia, 284, 291
Anti-semitism, 233, 236. *See also* Holocaust; Jews
Archimanditrou, Maria, 292
Arendt, Hannah, 7–10; on John Adams,
  52–53; and "Battle at Little Rock,"
  32–61; critique of NAACP, 33–34,
  43; on democratic citizenship, 34–
  35; on disagreement, 44–46; and Ellison, 7–9, 32–63; on friendship, 47–
  48, 49; on fraternity, 49, 54; on heroism, 33–35, 170; *The Human Condition*, 34, 48, 53; on invisibility, 8, 9,
  32, 51–55, 77; *Men in Dark Times*, 8,
  44–45, 47, 48, 52; on "no-rule," 131,
  153n. 7; positive account of justice

in, 32, 44, 48; "Reflections on Little
  Rock," 33, 54, 55; republican approach of, 169–170; on republican
  thought, 119, 131; on revolution,
  147–148; *On Revolution*, 52; on rule
  of law, 119; on segregation, 32, 33–
  44, 55. *See also* Citizenship
Aristophanes, 266–267
Aristotle, 4, 73n. 64, 180
Assimilation: as form of domination,
  191–217; "domestication" as, 215–
  216; to dominant identities, 216. *See
  also* Exclusion

"Battle at Little Rock," 7–8, 32, 33–36,
  38, 39, 40–44, 61, 62–63; and demo-
  cratic citizenship, 33–44; Eckford,
  Elizabeth, 28, 33, 36, 39–43, 59, 62–
  63, 68n. 20; involvement of children
  in, 41–43; the Little Rock Nine, 36;
  Massery, Hazel Bryan, 33, 36, 62;
  NAACP and, 40–43. *See also* Arendt,
  Hannah; Ellison, Ralph
Benjamin, Jessica, 46
Bérubé, Michael, 296
Bollas, Christopher, 264–265
Bosnia, 23; genocide and mass sexual
  atrocities in, 313, 314–316, 338–
  339, 354n. 10
Boy Scouts, 5
Braithewaite, John, 289–291
Brecher, Jeremy, 210–211
Buchanan, James, 185
Butler, Richard, 233–235

the contractualist sense, 113–114;
Machiavelli on, 134–135; as master-
concept, 12; as measurable ideal,
114; as moral principle, 172, 174;
and "no-rule," 12–13, 119–120,
130–131, 138–140, 213; and political order, 134; promotion of, 96. *See
also* Domination; Exclusion; Freedom; Political ideals; State
Non-interference, 10–11, 12, 108, 120,
122–124, 138, 185, 186–187, 213;
ideal of, 95–96; as negative liberty,
13. *See also* Freedom; Political ideals
Normality. *See* Shame and shaming
No-rule. *See* Non-domination; Rule of
law
North American Free Trade Agreement
(NAFTA), 248–249
Nozick, Robert, 90

Oakeshott, Michael, 127, 150
Oppression. *See* Domination

Patterson, Orlando, 3
Pettit, Philip, on "democratic contestability," 121, 130, 132–133
Phelps, Fred (Rev.), 233–235
Plato: *Apology*, 208; *Gorgias*, 4; *Symposium*, 266–267
Pluralism, 172. *See also* Monism
Political ideals, 10–12, 87–115; complaint and, 11–12, 88–92, 99, 171–
172; constraints upon, 11–12, 88,
90–92, 100–107, 171–172; ideal of
community, 110–112; ideal of equality, 108–110; ideal of functioning capability, 112; ideal of justice in the
contractualist sense, 113–114; ideal
of liberty, 107–108; ideal of nondomination, 11, 87, 95, 97, 106, 125,
144, 172–173; ideal of non-interference, 95–96; and master-concepts,
164, 166–170; as measurable, 114;
and monism, 171–174; and moral
principles, 172; and political philos-

ophy, 125; republican, 10–12, 87,
92, 97, 125; and roof-concepts, 167–
168, 175n. 8
Political philosophy/theory: as activity
of citizenship, 16–17; and citizenship, 19; and constitutional democracy, 191, 196, 206, 207–211; and
democratic deliberation, 207–210,
245; "dialogical turn" in, 19, 207–
210; and Enlightenment, 207–208;
and evaluation of institutions, 173–
75, 183; and law, 128–129; liberal
political philosophy, 17–20, 232,
236–242, 244–246; and master-concepts, 164–175, 183; and metaphor,
179–180; and monism, 164–175;
and normative claims and propositions, 17–18; Rawls and, 184; and
search for unifying values, 183–185;
and the social sciences, 183; task of,
14–20, 183–185; and theories of justice, 17, 170–174, 177n. 19; theory
versus practice in, 207–211, 240–
242, 253; and universal norms or
principles, 16–18, 183
Popular sovereignty. *See* Democratic
principle (principle of democracy)
Posner, Eric, 286–287
Posner, Richard, 307–308
Power: as constituent/constituted, 13,
131–132, 146, 148–149, 151–152;
corporate, 18; extra-legal, 13; of the
people, 13, 131–132, 148–150. *See
also* Revolution
Prestige research, 176n. 14
Punishment, 21–22; and disenfranchisement, 303–306, 308; incarceration, 292–293; liberalism and, 282–
284, 303–308; mob justice, 285; and
reform, 289–291; and retribution,
287–289; and shame, 21–22, 261–
263, 281–293. *See also* Shame and
shaming
Prostitution. *See* Genocide; Rape; Sexual domination